Y0-AAM-199

Multimedia Multimedia Multimedia Multimedia Multimedia Design with HyperCard

Stephen Wilson

San Francisco State University

PRENTICE HALL, Englewood Cliffs, New Jersey 07632

Library of Congress Cataloging-in-Publication Data

Wilson, Stephen
    Multimedia design with HyperCard / Stephen Wilson.
        p. cm.
    ISBN 0-13-488891-X
    1. Macintosh (Computer)—Programming.   2. HyperCard (Computer
program)   3. Computer graphics.   I. Title.
    QA76.8.M3W58   1991
    005.6'765—dc20   90-48102
                                                                CIP

Editorial/production supervision: *Mark Tobey*
Cover design: *Ray Lundgren Graphics, LTD.*
Prepress buyer: *Herb Klein*
Manufacturing buyer: *Dave Dickey*

 © 1991 by Stephen Wilson

All rights reserved. No part of this book may be
reproduced, in any form or by any means,
without permission in writing from Stephen Wilson.

Printed in the United States of America

10 9 8 7 6 5 4 3 2 1

ISBN   0-13-488891-X

Prentice-Hall International (UK) Limited, *London*
Prentice-Hall of Australia Pty. Limited, *Sydney*
Prentice-Hall Canada Inc., *Toronto*
Prentice-Hall Hispanoamericana, S.A., *Mexico*
Prentice-Hall of India Private Limited, *New Delhi*
Prentice-Hall of Japan, Inc., *Tokyo*
Simon & Schuster Asia Pte. Ltd., *Singapore*
Editora Prentice-Hall do Brasil, Ltda., *Rio de Janeiro*

CONTENTS

Chapter 8
Scripts That Control Graphics   79

Chapter 9
Using Loops and Variables in Graphics Programming 91

Chapter 10
Cards, Backgrounds, Visual Effect Transitions,
Navigation through Stacks, and Animation   111

Chapter 11
Transformations of Images: The Paint Menu   129

Chapter 12
Backgrounds and HyperCard Object Layers   141

Chapter 13
Scripts to Use Text   151

Chapter 14
Data Structures and Randomness   159

Chapter 15
Interactivity   173

Chapter 16
Self-running Stacks and Animation   191

Chapter 17
Sound Programming   211

Chapter 18
Time-based Art   247

Chapter 23
New Opportunities and Challenges for the Arts   **389**

Appendix
An Annotated Guide and Index to HyperCard
Features, Commands, Functions, Messages,
and Properties   **398**

PREFACE

We are at the beginning of a cultural revolution that may be even more profound than the one begun by the invention of the printing press. Microcomputer technology allows the creation of unprecedented kinds of artifacts that can mimic sophisticated human intellectual and sensory capabilities and that promote extraordinary forms of communication.

This book is aimed at helping readers to participate in this revolution by becoming competent in multimedia design—extending communication beyond text to embrace all kinds of visual and sound material—and interactive programming—creating events which dynamically adapt to the user's desires and needs. It assumes no technical background, is filled with concrete annotated examples, and is based on 10 years of classroom-tested experience in demystifying programming for those who come from disciplines outside of computer science.

The book focuses on HyperCard™, which is one the new generation of programming environments optimized for easy scrpting by non–specialists and simultaneous work with text, image, and sound. It differs than other HyperCard books because of its attention to broader issues of art and design, its exploration of the cultural implications and future possibilities of interactive multimedia, and its use of a highly visual method of teaching.

It is aimed at a wide range of readers stretching from specialists experimenting with computer based art, design, and media to professionals in fields such as education, business, advertising, and science who want to enhance the sophistication of their use of the multimedia capabilities of their computers, to all those users of Macintosh computers who are searching for an easy and interesting way to learn about the capabilities of HyperCard.

Teaching and learning are like a mirror-dance in which the location of the dancer and the reflection are constantly changing. My thanks go to all those students who have been my partners in this dance of inquiry.

For this book thanks go to Wendy Layne, Janet Taggart, and Margaret Williams for letting me know about the problems in the text that would confuse and madden future readers; to Lewis Siegel for fractal assistance; to Ann Lindner for an accelerated tutorial on the joys and woes of desktop publishing; to Bruce Emmer, Gary Croyts, Mark Tobey for the battle against typos and other text demons; to the artists, who graciously agreed to share their experiments with readers; and to the hackers and visionaries who have treated the microcomputer as more than merely a business. Thanks to my editor, Bud Therien, for the vision to help the arts embrace the twentieth century. Finally, special thanks go to Catherine Witzling for editing and critical commentary and, even more, for help in keeping one foot on the ground as I search these new places.

Apple, Macintosh, HyperCard, and HyperTalk are trademarks of Apple Computer, Inc. Screen shots used with permission of Apple Computer, Inc.

Multimedia
Multimedia
Multimedia
Multimedia
Multimedia
Design
with HyperCard

Chapter 1
Programming Interactive Multimedia Events

Multimedia

Artists historically defy boundaries. In their quest for discovery and expression, they push beyond traditional definitions of what the culture expects. In the twentieth century, they have especially challenged the shibboleth of *medium*. Following the imperatives of their ideas, emotions, and spiritual impulses wherever they lead, they have combined media and invented new ones. For example, painters have incorporated sculpture; sculptors have employed text and sound; performance artists have used film and video; and poets have incorporated visual design. *Multimedia* is a term often applied to this work across media.

Contemporary computer technology powerfully enables this cross-boundary creative enterprise. Philosophers note that computers are universal machines. They can be adaptively programmed to symbolically manipulate information, which can be input or output in a great variety of forms — textual, visual, sonic, or spatial. Practically, this means that artists are invited by the computer's flexibility to create events that incorporate text, graphic image, video, music, speech, and the control of kinetic devices. Ironically, at the same time that computers make multimedia work easier, they complicate the design process. Artists and designers who would work across media must master the sensitivities and skills of many disciplines. Even more, they must confront the new design challenges of making information in different sensual modes work together. *Introduction to Multimedia Design* prepares the reader to use computers to concieve and create multimedia works. HyperCard will be used as the concrete environment in which to begin to learn these skills.

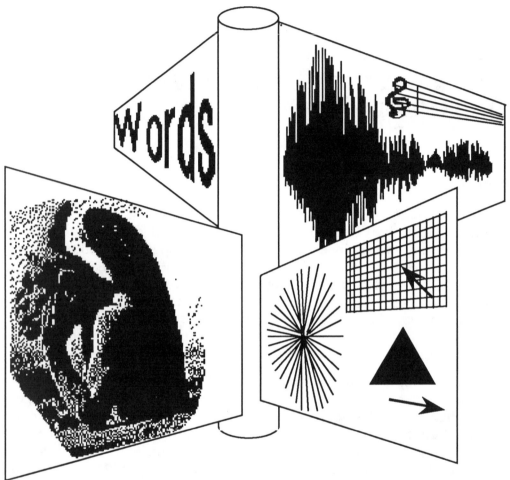

Figure 1.1   Artists Are Able to Integrate Multiple Media with New Computer Tools

These challenges of working across media will not be limited to artists and designers alone. The ubiquity of computers, combined with their multimedia potentials, means that the expectations for communication in everyday life are increasing. For example, normal business communications are already expected to incorporate a sophistication in graphics and typography that was unheard of in the days of typewriters. Thus, many people who don't think of themselves as aritists and designers will find themselves requiring these skills and sensitivities as they compose multimedia communications in their personal and occupational life, in which the flow of image, sound, and text is to be clear and appealing.

Interactivity and Hypermedia

Computers are bringing more revolutionary changes than just allowing work with several media simultaneously. Programmability means that the creator of multimedia works can easily design them so that the audience can make choices that affect the flow of text, image, and sound. Each work is actually a family of events that can be customized in accordance with the receiver's desires or needs.

Hypermedia is a term sometimes used to describe this new way of thinking about the storage and retrieval of information. The *hyper* part of the term refers to nonlinear methods of moving through a body of information. One idea or image gives rise to many associated ideas and images, which in turn give rise to others, rather than moving in a linear fashion, as in a traditional novel. Some analysts characterize normal human thinking by its associationism. There is rarely one invariant path through a subject that all people's minds will follow. The *media* part of the term refers to the fact that contemporary information is available in a variety of formats in addition to text, as described previously — e.g., graphics, audio, video, and animated graphics.

In this kind of system, a person looking at a computer display could at any time access material on related topics by simply clicking a mouse pointer on words or images that would serve as gateways to the related information. The browser would not have to worry about which books each part of the information was stored in. Someone reading an article on Gaugin could click on the word *Tahiti* for more detailed information, then again on *tropical plants* for more related information, and so on. The computer would keep track of where information was and facilitate the flow of inquiry.

This tendency toward interactivity is parallel to a growing interest in interactive art. Artists are questioning the idea of the passive audience. Indeed, our culture seems to be questioning passivity, perhaps inspired by the development of new two-way technologies. Increasingly, education, entertainment, and commercial settings are highlighting interactive systems. This movement is an extremely important antidote to the dangers of centralization that could result from the expansion of new technologies.

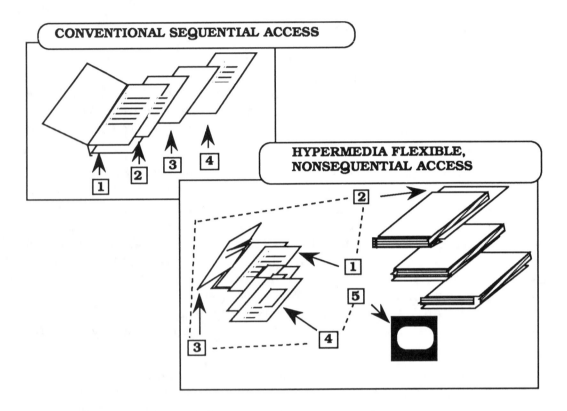

Figure 1.2   Hypermedia Nonsequential Access

HyperCard and the Importance of Programming to Artists and Designers

Currently, several computer languages are being developed that are optimized for the creation of highly interactive multimedia programs. These programs assume that someone viewing the work will continually want to make decisions about the course of events. HyperCard is the best known of the first generation of these languages supporting creation of multiple-branching, free-search environments. It has commands that allow easy linkage of text, image, and sound stored anywhere in the computer system. Many built-in commands and structures allow the program to monitor the user's actions with mouse and keyboard in order for the program to respond. For example, in HyperCard it is very easy to know if a user has pushed the mouse button and where on the screen the mouse is pointing.

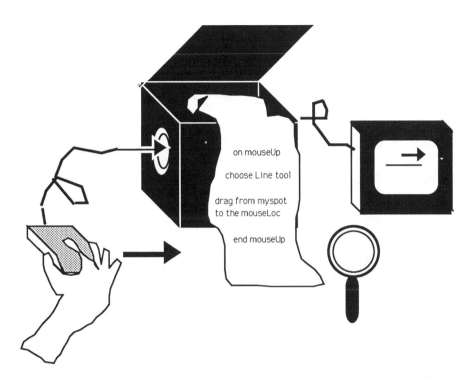

on mouseUp

choose Line tool

drag from myspot
to the mouseLoc

end mouseUp

*1.3   The Black Box Can Be Opened : The Computer's Ability to Draw a Line
Need Be No Mystery*

To create highly interactive multimedia works, the artist or designer must learn to program the computer. Actually, programming is a much easier skill to learn than many believe — especially in HyperCard.

Artists work with technology in order to have it help them manipulate image, sound, and text. Each technology demands that the user follow a series of steps to accomplish what he or she wants. For example, use of a photographic enlarger requires a systematic approach of getting materials ready, adjusting exposures, and developing the prints to test settings. Throwing clay pots requires procedures to work the clay, glaze it, and fire it. Eventually these processes become so ingrained that the user loses conscious awareness of the steps.

As a form of technology, computers can seem to be effortless. Some computers apparently react to a user without being taught a series of steps. For example, in MacPaint or similar programs, anyone can step up and start moving a mouse device around and see corresponding responses on the computer screen. They can automatically proceed through a series of steps to generate images, sound, and text.

In fact, the computer is "taught" these steps through a process that is called programming. Someone else has written a complex set of instructions, called an application program, that gives the computer its appearance of effortless, intrinsic intelligence. This set of instructions includes processes by which the computer constantly monitors the keyboard or movements of a mouse.

These application programs provide a wonderful, easy way for artists and designers to work with computers. Almost instantly, artists can start creating work. Indeed, HyperCard itself allows this kind of easy user engagement.

In the future, however, artists may find that merely using existing applications is too limiting for the following reasons.

- They may want to do things that are impossible within the application.
- They may want to create multimedia events that transcend the limits of particular applications.
- They may become wary of being dependent on a technology that they don't understand.
- In their roles as cultural commentators, they may want to know as much as possible about the technologies that are shaping the world.

This book is aimed at those artists and others who want to learn how to program computers to create graphic and sound events. HyperCard (and its programming language, HyperTalk) is one of the new unified multimedia systems designed to create integrated image, sound, and text events. Conceptually, the language encourages the creation of highly visual display screens. Many systems are moving toward visual interfaces based on the analysis that the human visual channel allows for high-density information exchange and intuitive, comfortable interactions between humans and machines.

HyperCard (in this book, references to HyperCard will also encompass the programming language HyperTalk) is easy to use because it responds to instructions that are close to regular English. Also, it makes use of metaphors that link its language elements with objects that are in everyday common use, such as buttons and cards. Indeed, HyperCard has been called a "software erector set" because of its ease of use, its organization into basic components that can be fitted together with infinite malleability, and its stimulation of experimentation.

HyperCard is constructed along the model of object-oriented computer languages as opposed to procedural computer languages. Although an extended discussion of this distinction is out of place here, some differences can be noted. Procedural languages such as the much used BASIC, Pascal, and C have been the most common until recently. They are organized into one set of instructions that describe an invariant flow of the action. Object-oriented languages, by contrast, are built out of self-contained modules that can be flexibly assembled into various orders and can be reused in other programs. Because of their flexibility, object-oriented languages are extremely useful to artists and designers whose professions focus on experimentation. In addition, many visual or sound objects can be associated with a functional programmed capability. This linking makes for a conceptual mapping between image and program.

Examples of Artists Working With HyperCard

Artists are beginning to explore the possibilities of HyperCard–like environments. They are creating works that make unique use of Hyper-Card's features. Some of the works weave sound, image, and text into new multimedia tapestries. Some create media environments by using Hyper-Card's ability to interactively control external devices such as videodiscs, MIDI sound synthesizers, and kinetic environments. Some focus on the interactive hypermedia aspects to require viewers to act as cocreators in navigating an art information space.

The following sections present very brief introductions to some of these works. Clearly, exciting new areas of artistic inquiry lie ahead.

"We Make Memories" — Abbe Don.   Artist Abbe Don used HyperCard in her interactive videodisc work "We Make Memories." Viewers can wander around a visual interface that resembles an array of photos from a family photo album. Building on an analysis of the nonlinear structure of oral history, the artist allowed viewers to use the mouse to move chronologically and among points of view in the family history. Clicking on images activates relevant sections of a videodisc record of people telling family stories. The interface and the structure of the information themselves become aesthetic elements. This is a copy of the artist's statement about the work:

> As my great-grandmother told stories, she weaved in and out of the past and present, the old country and America, English and Yiddish, business and family, changing voice from first person to direct address to third person. Each detail was part of the narrative continuum and potentially linked to several other stories or digressions, some of them new, some which I had heard before. However, both content and meaning were affected by the context: the presence of other visitors, whether we were baking together, looking at

Figure 1.4   Interface Screen from "We Make Memories" © Abbe Don, 1989

photos in her scrapbook, or if I interrupted the flow of the story to ask for more details. It was as if she had a chronological, topical and associative matrix that enabled her to generate stories in which content, structure, and context were interdependent.

I have used my great-grandmother's storytelling style as a model of interactivity to reveal how our family history has been constructed and passed down matrilinearly. A pictorial timeline of family photographs that date from 1890 to the present enables viewers to move through time on the Macintosh screen. By clicking on one of the headshots, viewers hear stories from my great-grandmother, my grandmother, my mother and me that weave in and out of the past and present, the old country and America, English and Yiddish, business and family.

"Hyperpoems" — William Dickey.   William Dickey is an award-winning poet who has published in traditional print formats for many years. He has become interested in hypermedia as an extension of his poetic ideas about the reintegration of image and text and about the possibilities of poems that can be read in any order. The following is a statement describing some of this work.

For several years I have been working on multi-media poems, including text, original and collaged clip art graphics, and sound resources, using HyperCard as my vehicle. In Spring 1989 I offered a graduate creative writing workshop in this subject, and found students in it whose efforts outdistanced mine in sophistication, particularly in their use of animation.

The first important element of these experimental poems is, to me, their effort to avoid the traditional separation of text and illustration, a separation that has governed Western printing since the days of mediaeval manuscripts—I hope we may find a way to think of text and illustration as one continuous field, as it is in the Book of Kells.

The second vital element is the avoidance of hierarchical linear organization. Ideally, any hyperpoem can be read in as many different ways as the number of its cards permits. Up to now I have programmed alternative paths through HyperCard stacks that contain the poems; in the future I expect to replace some of this programming with random sequences.

While it is possible to print out the Hyperpoems, and even to make small Hyperbooks of them, the real nature of the form requires that the poems be viewed on a computer (or that the books containing them be cut apart and the individual cards shuffled and dealt for each subsequent reading).

Figure 1.5   Screens from the hyperpoem "HERESY" © William Dickey, 1988. (Clip art is taken from MacCalligraphy files and from Dragons, copyright 1986 and 1987 by Enzan-Hoshigumi Co., and button icons from Icon Factory libraries, copyright 1988 by Hyperpress Publishing Corp. The typefaces used in the poem are Bookman and Broadway.)

"Eat" — Michael Naimark and San Francisco Art Institute Performance/Video Class.   These artists created an installation that explored the idea of menus and virtual restaurants. HyperCard was used to present a videodisc "meal" that each visitor could order. The following statement describes the installation

> "EAT" is an installation about consumption. "EAT" is a short single-user experience, where the participant is seated alone at a formal dining arrangement and orders food from a live waiter with a menu. The waiter then lifts up the plate cover, revealing the requested "food" projected on the dinner plate. Also on the table, a large red button labelled "EAT" may be pressed, creating various actions within the projection. After dining, the participant is given a personalized "guest check" and thanked for dining at "EAT."

Figure 1.6   *Restaurant Installation Tabletop with Interactive Videodisc Dinner Plate. Michael Naimark and San Francisco Art Institute Performance/Video Class, 1989.*

The Manhole — Robyn and Rand Miller.   The Manhole is an
interactive HyperCard-based fantasy image-and-sound world that users
can explore by clicking on objects and characters. For example, clicking on
a manhole on the screen causes a beanstalk to grow. The user can then
climb up the beanstalk or go down the manhole. In this art/game event,
there are no puzzles to solve, aliens to kill, or points to win; exploration and
discovery are their own rewards. The enormous memory capacities of CD-
ROM offer the explorer complex images and sounds to investigate.

Figure 1.7   *The Manhole, by Robyn and Rand Miller.*
           Mediagenic (© 1988, Cyan).

" Deep Contact" — Lynn Hershman and Sara Roberts.   Artists Lynn Hershman and Sara Roberts created a virtual garden of mystery through which the viewer can wander. The viewer can navigate the garden through HyperCard, which presents videodisc images of the places and persons.

Guided by individual desires, participants design segmented fantasy vignettes in which they follow Marion, our heroine, down alternating paths in a Japanese Tea Garden, meeting a Demon or Zen Master along the way. Each character invites the viewer to learn more about contact, perception or responsiveness. Intimacy requires involvement through text, sound and (most especially) touch.

The video is designed towards transgressing the screen (or distanced observer) inviting deep contact with not only characters being watched, but including as well the player/participant's memories, and ambitions. Viewers' surrogate decisions open new windows to such issues as alienation and contact in contemporary mediated society. Participants become active collaborators in the system, inverting the distancing caused not only by modern communications systems, but between individuals and machines and more, individuals and each other!

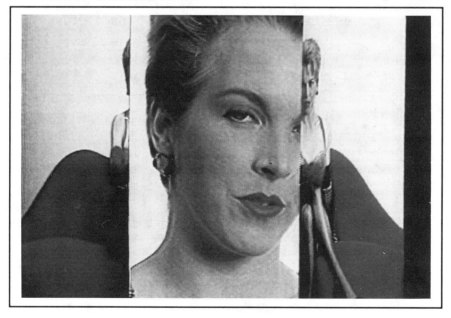

Figure 1.8   "Making Contact" Video Display Screen from Interactive Videodisc "Deep Contact," by Lynn Hershman and Sara Roberts, 1989.

"XHERONE1.3, An Interactive Video/Music Installation" — Joel Slayton, Kelvin Chan, and Jurgen Brauiger. Artists Joel Slayton, Kelvin Chan, and Jurgen Brauiger created an installation using HyperCard in which each viewer could idiosyncratically sequence image and sound. The installation experimented with an instructionless interface in which visual icons stood for videodisc and sound. Following is the artists' statement that accompanied the installation.

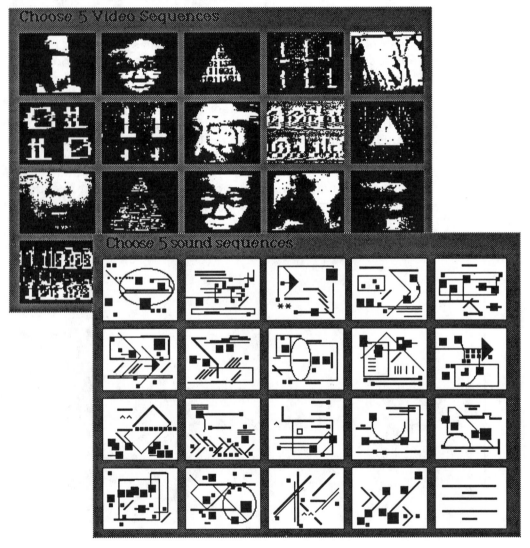

Figure 1.9   *Image Selection and Sound Selection Interfaces from* <u>*XHERONE1.3*</u> *by Joel Slayton (Art Director), Kelvin Chan (System Engineer), and Jurgen Brauiger (Music Scorer).*

It seems obvious that interactive multi-media should avail itself to idiosyncratic participation. Viewer-controlled systems should include the viewer as a conceptual assistant and collaborator.

XHERONE1.3 is a viewer-controlled interactive video disc installation that explores computer-assisted sequencing of computer graphics, image processed video and digital-acoustic compositions. XHERONE1.3 is best described as computer driven video-music juke box offering over 2 billion playback scenarios.

An instructionless computer interface stimulates viewer selection and sequencing of digitally created graphic and sound events. Custom software then examines the acoustic selections and assigns a complimentary graphics editing scenario. Image and acoustic aspects are automatically integrated for playback events unique to each individual user/viewer. Linear continuity of playback is preserved by controlling frame access to 23,400 images, display rates, forward/reverse playback, and random access editing.

"Father Why: Excursions in Emotional Hyperspace"— Stephen Wilson. I created an installation in which HyperCard was used as the control center to orchestrate speech, music, and kinetic light events. Viewer physical exploration became a gateway to exploration of concepts and feelings. The following statement explains the installation.

Interactive computer technology is used to create a physical space that is a metaphor for the web of emotions surrounding the imminent death of a loved one. Physical locations become the homes of emotions such as sadness, anger, longing, and forgetfulness. Viewers can explore the emotional space by moving about the physical space. The computer senses human presence and generates digitized music and speech in response out of the speaker in that physical location. For example, the "Place of Anger" explores the anger associated with someone dying — anger toward the self, the person, and the Cosmos.

Viewers can "direct" the evolving discourse by their presence. Continuing presence in one location causes the computerized dialog to explore increasing depths and nuances of the emotions which that location is home to. Walking away and into another place causes the reflections on the first emotion to stop and reflections on a new emotion to start. Multiple viewers in different locations can create a textured sound space in which each location is generating sound related to the emotion it knows.

Occasionally the computer will stop to invite a viewer in one of the locations to speak a phrase related to that emotion. It then digitizes and stores those words. For the remaining days of the installation, these phrases become part of the sound repertoire — a kind of chorus — that is associated with that particular emotional and physical place.

Figure 1.10   Visitors Interact with the "Place of Forgetfulness" and the "Place of Longing" in the "Father Why" Installation by Stephen Wilson, 1989.

This brief tour demonstrates early generations of artisitic exploration with the new interactive multimedia tools. Artists and their audiences will have a new relationship. Future works promise even more provocative explorations of interactivity as an aesthetic element.

CHAPTER 2
THE BASIC STRUCTURE OF HYPERCARD AND HYPERTALK

Computer Languages as Vocabularies and Grammars

Despite the mystification associated with computer languages, they are in fact similar to human language. Every computer language has its own semantics (vocabulary) and syntax (grammar rules). That is, each has a set of words it knows and needs its words arranged in a certain order.

Computer languages are much more limited than human languages both in the words they can understand and in their tolerance for variations in order. In addition, they are to some degree arbitrary systems. That is, software designers have dreamed up the specific vocabulary and grammar rules that the computer will understand. Different languages have different vocabularies and structures.

The computer can be made to understand different computer languages by loading in special metaprograms called *compilers*. At its most fundamental level, each computer can understand only one primitive language determined by the particular electronic microprocessor chip at its heart. All higher-level languages — for example, HyperTalk, BASIC, Pascal — are special programs that someone has written to translate English-like statements and word orders into the primitive language the chips can understand. For more details, see my book, *Using Computers to Create Art* (Prentice Hall, 1986).

Learning to program a computer in a particular language is fundamentally a matter of learning the language's structure, vocabulary, and grammar. The more difficult and interesting part of the process is learning how to translate a set of ideas into a form that computers can understand. For example, getting the computer to create a certain animated graphic given the limited vocabulary and grammar rules of a particular language is a challenge.

Just as with learning another human language, comfort with the basic structure allows one to become extremely expressive. Remember that the whole body of literature produced in English was built out of only 26 letters and a limited set of grammar rules. The focus of this book is on becoming fluent and expressive in programming languages.

Organizational Structure of HyperCard: Objects and Messages

HyperCard is organized around a hierarchical structure of object categories . Each of these objects can be given a certain intelligence to react to messages. That means that programming in HyperTalk is a matter of writing a series of statements telling each object what to do when it gets a certain message. The messages come from other objects and from actions by users. The only limit is that these statements must be written out of the vocabulary and grammar rules that HyperCard understands. These are actually the program. In HyperCard and some other similar languages, they are called message handlers. Message handlers are programs that can be written that allow HyperCard objects to respond to various messages.

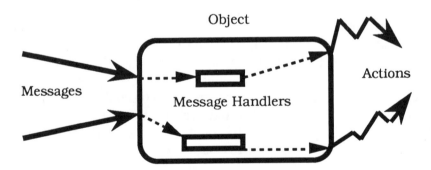

Figure 2.1   Message Handlers Are Written To Allow Objects
to Respond to Messages

For example, the designers of HyperCard included a structure that allows one to create button objects that are sensitive to some user actions such as pointing the mouse at the button and clicking on the mouse button. Using HyperCard-allowed words, one can then create a series of statements that are attached to that button and tell it what to do — for example, beep five times if someone clicks. In this example, a click on a mouse button is the message to which the screen button object responds. In HyperCard, objects often have some visual manifestation in addition to their procedural intelligence. Often a button looks like a push button.

The structure is hierarchical. The lowest objects in the hierarchy try to handle the message first. If they do not have the set of statements attached to handle the message (a message handler), they pass the message up to the next level. In some ways it is quite like a bureaucracy such as a university. Consider some question a student might have about university requirements. The student asks the professor. If the professor doesn't know, the student is then sent to the department chair. This process continues up the bureaucracy through the dean, the provost, the president and so on. If the question doesn't get answered, we could say that none of those bureaucratic objects had the appropriate message handler.

The advantage of this kind of system in a computer language is that one message handler high in the hierarchy can take care of many different objects. Objects lower in the hierarchy can inherit the message-handling capabilities of higher objects.

Cards, Backgrounds, Stacks, and Home Stacks

For the sake of learning HyperCard, cards will arbitrarily be considered as the central object. In this introduction, the details of creation and manipulation of these objects will be postponed until after the basic structure of HyperCard's object hierarchy has been described. Each card can be given a unique visual appearance. In addition, one can add capabilities so that the card can perform visual, audio, text, and computational activities. These capabilities can be added by writing message handlers for the card or by adding to the card lower-level objects that each have their own capabilities.

Further up in the hierarchy are other objects called backgrounds. Several cards can share a common background. Again, this background object can have both visual and procedural characteristics. These characteristics are active for all cards sharing that background. For example, the beep button, put in the background, would appear on every card that shared that same background if the designer wanted this. It would also

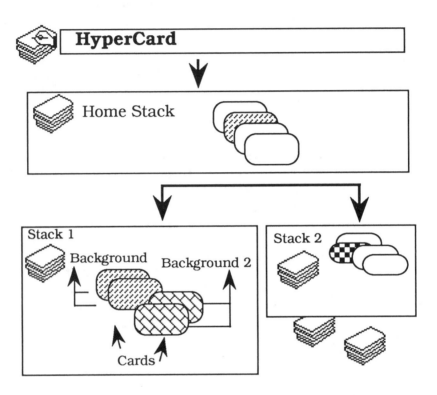

*Figure 2.2   Object Hierarchies: Cards > Backgrounds > Stacks > Home
            Stack > Hypercard*

respond to mouse clicks on any of those cards. One would need to create
its appearance and message handler only once.

Stacks are sequential accumulations of cards and backgrounds. The
number of cards that can be put into a stack is limited only by memory
storage. Message handlers can be written to govern activities on all the
cards in one stack.

The structure of cards, backgrounds, and stacks allows one to
organize materials into related categories. For example, one could have one
stack of cards with the names, addresses, and telephone numbers of
friends. Another stack could have cards containing notes about art works
seen and studied. The conceptual details of how information should be

organized into stacks and cards varies according to the user. Indeed, different people might have very different approaches to organizing even the same body of information, and these differences could be reflected in the way HyperCard stacks are organized. Stacks designed for artistic purposes might have similarly expressive conceptual structures.

As one gets more advanced in HyperCard, decisions about the conceptual structure used to organize work into cards, backgrounds, and stacks will become critical. It is important to remember that there is no single right way.

Further up the hierarchy is a special stack called the home stack. This is the first place HyperCard goes after it is started. HyperCard demands that there be a home stack even if there is only one empty card in it. Home stacks can be used in various ways. They can serve as the main index for all the other stacks. For example, there can be buttons on the home stack card that take the user to other available stacks. The home stack that comes with HyperCard is like this. The home stack can also be used to start a particular stack automatically, to store scripts and message handlers that will be used by other stacks, and to set parameters that affect the behavior of HyperCard such as the user level (to be described shortly).

The highest level is HyperCard itself. Messages that have no handlers in lower levels are finally sent up to HyperCard. It is the fundamental language environment, with the vocabulary of command words that define the language. The commands can be thought of as messages. If a message or a command gets here and it doesn't understand, it will send back a message in a dialog box saying that it doesn't understand whatever was sent. A later chapter on external commands will show that even here, additional command words can be added, provided that one knows computer languages such as C or Pascal.

Buttons and Fields

Each card or background can have accumulations of lower-level objects. In HyperCard, these are called buttons and fields. Within limits, these can be given unique visual appearances, and message handlers can be written to enable them to respond to certain kinds of messages.

Buttons have intrinsic capabilities to respond to actions by the user with the mouse — for example, moving the pointer to point inside the visual button on the screen and clicking the mouse button. Fields are optimized for responding to keyboard text actions. Words can be stored in them and easily manipulated. For example, message handlers can be written to search through the fields for particular words or names. Chapter 12 will offer more details on working with buttons and fields.

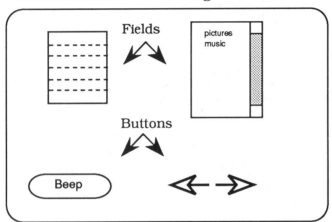

Figure 2.3   *Buttons and Text Fields*

User Levels

Most people work with HyperCard as users rather than program creators. HyperCard allows the original program creator to set the amount of control a user may have. For example, a creator of a stack might want to allow viewers to type information into fields but not to change the field's appearance or the nature of its response. This limitation on the depth of control allowed is called the user level. The level can be set in a message handler that automatically activates wherever anyone opens that stack. Generally, a user can change the level via the message box feature that will be described.

HyperCard allows five levels of control:

1. Browsing — user can look at cards and click buttons.
2. Typing — user can type into fields.
3. Painting — user can change the visual display.
4. Authoring — user can make buttons link to cards and stacks.
5. Scripting — user has full control over creating objects and scripts.

Scripting

This book focuses on preparing the user to work at the highest level, scripting. HyperCard is innovative in that it provides for people to create interactive events even without understanding the internal workings of computer languages. This book assumes, however, that artists and designers, who will want to use the computer at its fullest potential, will want and need to know the system at its most unrestricted use level.

A *script* is the HyperCard term for a sequence of instructions that tells objects how to respond. In other languages, scripts are called programs. One writes scripts that function as message handlers for the objects that exist in the system. Every script must be attached to some object.

The set of commands is similar to a recipe or assembly instructions. Sometimes the scripts are straightforward statements of sequences of actions the computer must do to realize an idea. The instructions are much like those one would tell a friend over the phone. As mentioned earlier, the expression of some complex ideas requires some experience with the unique vocabulary and grammar of the computer language before ideas can be translated. This book is designed to get readers to that point of comfort.

Chapter 3
Creation of Scripts

Message Box

HyperCard includes a special feature called the Message box that allows one to communicate directly with it. The Message box is a special kind of object with message handlers that interpret and attempt to act on any typed sentence. Thus, it lets one try out commands.

To do so, type a line of text into the Message box and then press the return key. The message can be to objects or to HyperCard. It is a good place to start learning how to script in HyperCard.

The preceding exercise shows one how to open the message box and type commands into it. HyperCard understands the word *beep* because it is part of its special vocabulary. HyperCard also understands the convention of numbers with a plus sign (+) between them. Other words that were not part of the limited vocabulary would not work. Also there are some kinds of HyperCard commands that will not work in the direct mode of typing them in the Message box even though they will work in scripts.

In addition, the Message box can help the user to debug scripts — that is, to find out why a script or program didn't do what was intended. The word *debug* comes from an apochryphal story about an early computer that was malfunctioning. Engineers spent days searching for what was wrong by checking their circuits and rewriting their programs. Eventually someone discovered the problem was caused by an insect in the tubes.

The Details of Creating a Stack

The basic environment for working with HyperCard is the stack. HyperCard positions a user in the home stack when it is first started up. The original HyperCard disks that come with the Macintosh display a special

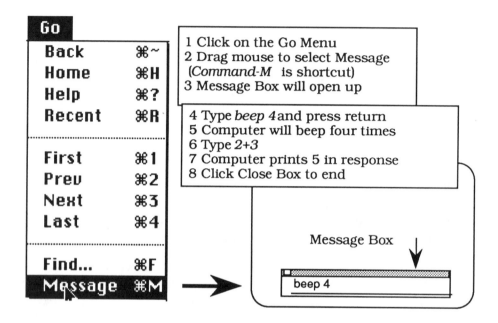

Figure 3.1   Use of the Message Box to Test Commands Directly

home stack screen with many icons representing stacks one could inspect. They are accessed by clicking on the icon buttons.

To learn the HyperTalk programming language, the user will want to create personal stacks. To accomplish this, first tell HyperCard to create a new stack. If the computer indicates that this command is not available, then it is necessary to reset the user level. HyperCard will not let a user create new stacks if the home stack has set the user level to something below level 5. One can reset the user level to level 5 by opening the Message box as described earlier and typing *set the userLevel to 5* and then pressing the return key.

To create a new stack, click on File in the Menu bar. Then drag the mouse down to New Stack. It will highlight (turn inverse). When the mouse button is released, HyperCard will display a New Stack Information Box with questions. At this time one can type a name for the new stack. *Copy current background* will have an *x* marked in the box. This allows the user to copy the background of the stack currently being displayed into the new stack. For now, click in that box to toggle off that option.

This new stack dialog box also allows choices about the location of the new stack. It uses the standard Macintosh conventions of naming the target volume above the eject button. One should make sure it is putting the stack on the desired disk. Clicking on the new button will confirm the process, and the screen display will change to show the first and only card in the new stack.

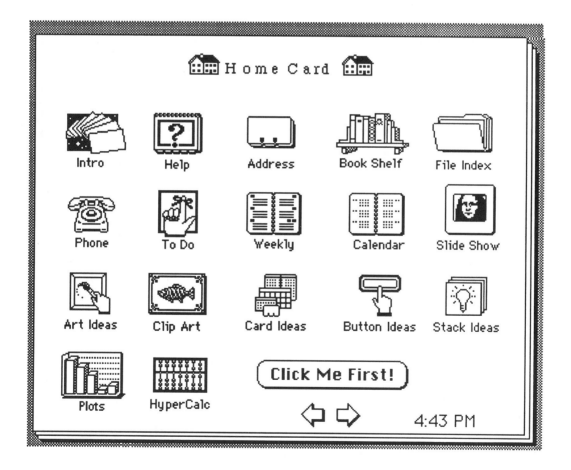

Figure 3.2   Apple Computer's Home Stack Index Card

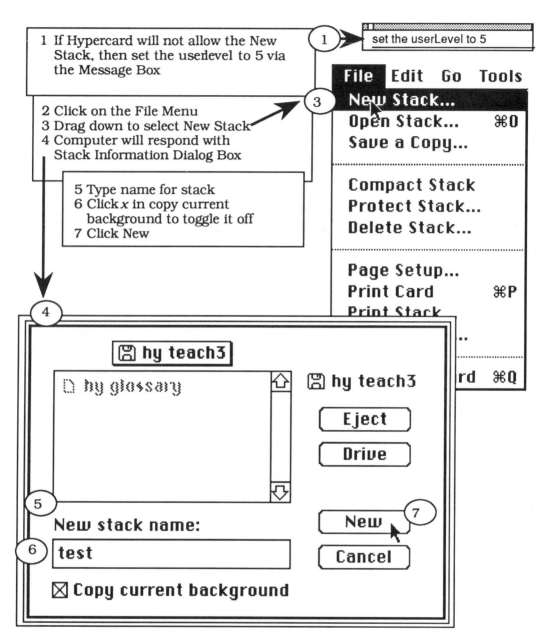

1 If Hypercard will not allow the New Stack, then set the userlevel to 5 via the Message Box

set the userLevel to 5

2 Click on the File Menu
3 Drag down to select New Stack
4 Computer will respond with Stack Information Dialog Box

5 Type name for stack
6 Click *x* in copy current background to toggle it off
7 Click New

File   Edit   Go   Tools
New Stack...
Open Stack...   ⌘O
Save a Copy...

Compact Stack
Protect Stack...
Delete Stack...

Page Setup...
Print Card   ⌘P
Print Stack

rd   ⌘Q

🖫 hy teach3

◻ hy glossary

🖫 hy teach3

Eject

Drive

New stack name:

test

New

Cancel

☒ Copy current background

Figure 3.3   Process for Creating a New Stack

To teach scripting, this book will first demonstrate how to create button objects with their associated scripts. The instructions being written will tell the button what to do when someone clicks a mouse on them. The lines written will be the message handler for the message *mouseclick*. Remember that these instructions must follow the limited vocabulary and grammar rules that HyperCard can understand. The following instructions assume that the screen is displaying a blank white space that occurred when a new stack was created. Actually, the screen is displaying the first card of the stack just created. The computer is waiting for the user to add objects, such as buttons, to this card.

Use the Objects Menu to create new buttons and fields and their associated message handlers. A click on the Objects item in the Menu bar opens up a series of options. Eventually, each of these options will be explained. The exercise focuses on the New Button option.

The process consists of naming the button and then proceeding to the script window for that button. Remember that *script* is the name HyperCard gives to the set of instructions. The list of instructions is called a program in other computer languages.

For buttons, a script window opens up with the beginning and ending lines of a script already inserted to handle a button click. HyperCard uses the phrase *on* followed by the name of the message to start a script. In this situation it is *on mouseUp*. *MouseUp* refers to the action of someone pushing down and then letting go of the button on the mouse device. It ends scripts with the word *end* followed by the name of the same message. In this situation it is *end mouseUp*. Eventually one will be able to write scripts to respond to other kinds of messages. HyperCard assumes these phrases as the defaults because button scripts often respond to *mouseUp* messages. Once in the script window, one can enter text much as one does in word processors or other Macintosh text editing.

In figure 3.1, *beep* is a valid command in HyperTalk to cause the computer to beep. HyperTalk also accepts the grammatical rule that a number after the command *beep* will cause the computer to beep that many times.

This process has created a button object that is sitting on a card object. The button has both a visual appearance and the intelligence to respond to a *mouseUp* message. Later chapters will show how to change the visual appearance of buttons.

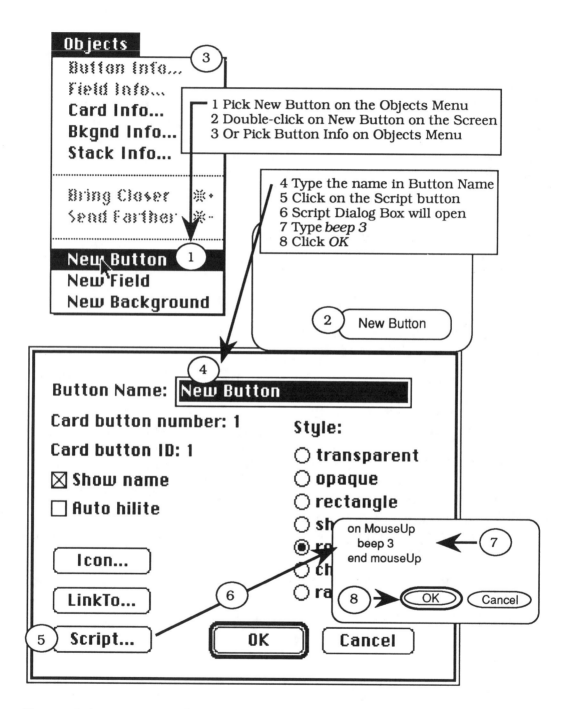

Objects

Button Info...
Field Info...
Card Info...
Bkgnd Info...
Stack Info...

Bring Closer   ⌘+
Send Farther   ⌘-

New Button ①
New Field
New Background

③

1 Pick New Button on the Objects Menu
2 Double-click on New Button on the Screen
3 Or Pick Button Info on Objects Menu

4 Type the name in Button Name
5 Click on the Script button
6 Script Dialog Box will open
7 Type *beep 3*
8 Click *OK*

②   New Button

④

Button Name: New Button

Card button number: 1

Card button ID: 1

☒ Show name

☐ Auto hilite

Style:
○ transparent
○ opaque
○ rectangle
○ sh
● ro
○ ch
○ ra

on MouseUp
beep 3
end mouseUp

⑦

Icon...

LinkTo...

⑥

⑤ Script...

OK   Cancel

⑧ ➤ OK   Cancel

Figure 3.4   *Process of Creating New Button and Message Handler*

Scripts are not fixed for all time. Indeed, much of the programming and visual design processes is characterized by continual refinement. For example, assume that one wanted the button to do something other than to beep three times. One would then need to change the script that handled the *mouseUp* action.

To accomplish this, choose the Button Info item from the Objects Menu. Click twice on the button in question in order to open the Button Information Box. To display the Script Box, click on the Script button. The script could then be edited — for example, to beep seven times instead of three. Clicking OK will confirm the change. One then must click on the hand icon in the Tools Menu to get out of button mode. Clicking on the button will then cause it to beep seven times.

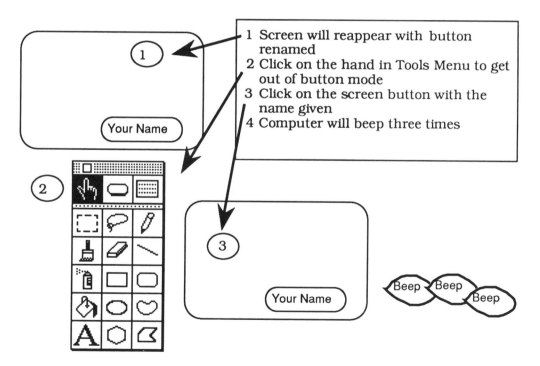

Figure 3.5   Activation of Button After Writing Script

CHAPTER 4
GRAPHICS AND THE
COORDINATE SYSTEM

Pixels, Lines, and the Cartesian Coordinate System

Many designers and artists focus on the computer's ability to generate visual graphics. Indeed, the Macintosh's ascendancy in many fields is based on its graphics abilities. These graphics can be produced either on video display monitors or on paper. This introduction to computer graphics programming focuses on the graphics that can be produced on the computer monitor, although many of the principles are the same regardless of what form of output is produced.

Most contemporary computer languages have graphics commands in their list of vocabulary. HyperCard is especially rich in its graphics features. The challenge in computer graphics programming is to translate visual ideas into the specific commands and grammar that the particular computer language can understand. This book will specifically introduce the HyperCard commands related to graphics, although it will also highlight basic principles that apply to graphics programs in general.

Imagine telling someone over the phone how to draw a particular picture on a sheet of paper. One would have to describe the kinds of lines wanted and where they should be. If it were important that an exact duplicate be produced, one would have to find a way to specify precisely how the other person would have to proceed. One must do the same for a computer. Because the computer is dumber than people in some ways, it needs very precise instructions.

All monitor-based computer graphics are based on the primitive component of the pixel. A pixel is the smallest addressable graphic unit on the screen. On a black and white system, a pixel can be on or off. On a color system, a pixel can be any of the colors that are electronically possible on a particular system. All complex images — lines, shapes, digitized images — are built up from the pixels. For example, a line is a series of pixels arranged right next to each other along the path of the shortest distance between the start and finish. Ultimately, computer graphics programming is a matter of telling the computer which pixels should be on or off. For more details on the way computers electronically produce graphic displays, see my book USING COMPUTERS TO CREATE ART (Prentice Hall, 1986). Many computer languages have alleviated some of the drudgery of controlling individual pixels by providing commands that affect the appropriate set of pixels to create what we call lines, shapes, and the like.

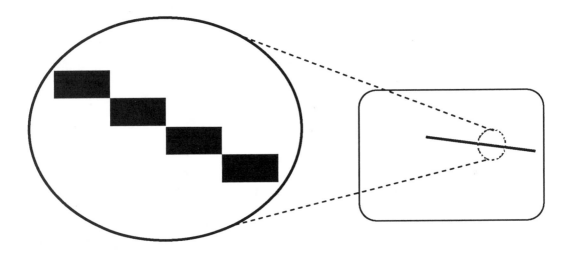

Figure 4.1   The Pixels That Make Up a Line

How can one tell the computer precisely what pixels to turn on or off? Luckily, mathematicians developed a system for describing spatial relationships long before the advent of computers. The French philosopher and mathematician René Descartes developed what is now called the Cartesian coordinate system. Given certain assumptions, this system allows one to specify particular points in space exactly. Every point has a unique address that identifies it.

A coordinate system can be created by the following steps:

1. Assume some point that will be the origin or point from which all others will be measured.
2. Assume a horizontal line drawn through this point that extends infinitely to the right and the left. This line is called the horizontal axis.

3. Assume a vertical line, perpendicular to the line through the origin, that extends infinitely up and down. This line is called the vertical axis.
4. Assume some standard measuring unit that will be used in the system. It could be anything — for example, inches, millimeters, miles.
5. Assume that each axis is marked off with equal units of this measurement starting from the origin. The origin is assumed to have measure 0 in both the horizontal and vertical directions. Units to the right are positive, and units to the left are negative. Units verti-

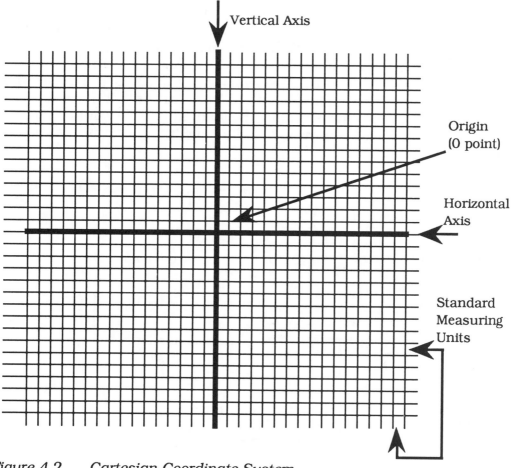

Figure 4.2   Cartesian Coordinate System

cally up are positive and units vertically down are negative.

6. After the axes have been marked, assume that horizontal lines parallel to the first horizontal axis are drawn at each marker on the vertical axis.

7. Assume that vertical lines parallel to the first vertical axis are drawn at each marker on the horizontal axis.

8. This is a Cartesian coordinate grid.

Any point on this grid can be identified by giving its coordinates: the distance in the standard measuring units horizontally and vertically from the origin point. Convention requires that the horizontal position be given first, followed by the vertical position. For example, the origin has the address (0,0). A point 3 units over and 5 units up would be given the address (3,5). A point 4 units to the left of the origin and 3 units up would have the coordinates (-4,3). A point 2 units down right on the vertical axis would have the address (0,-2). Convention assigns negative addresses to points to the left or down from the origin. Points in between the grid lines are given decimal coordinates — for example, the point at (2.5, 3) would be halfway between the grid lines going through units 2 and 3 on the horizontal axis and

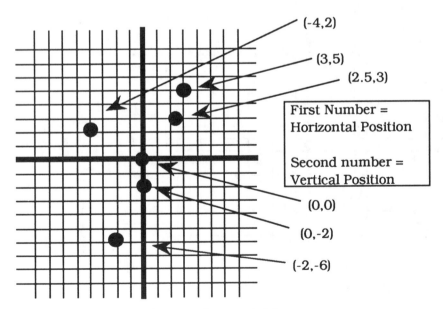

Figure 4.3   Sample Coordinate Addresses

6 units up from the horizontal axis. Beginners most often make the mistake of reversing the horizontal and vertical addresses.

This simple system allows precise computations about spatial relationships and descriptions of objects. Line distances, areas, and transformations of shapes such as scaling, translations, and rotations are easily calculable.

Much of Western science and the Western world view is based on deep assumptions inherent in this coordinate system — for example, that space is uniform in all directions, physical laws apply the same everywhere, units of measurement do not change, and there can be a single origin point. Tremendous progress has been made by mapping physical realities such as the movement of physical bodies onto this analytical system. Other systems of belief — for example, the Hindu — adopt other assumptions. Artists also have begun to explore other symbolic approaches to space — for example, grids that change unit size in accordance with emotional valence. Readers are encouraged to keep these deeper philosophical questions in mind even as they exploit the usefulness of the Cartesian coordinate system.

Those working with computer graphics have adopted the Cartesian coordinate system as a clear method of communicating with computer graphics systems. Every pixel can be given a precise address. Furthermore, the centuries of mathematical work to develop the implications of spatial relationships can be implemented to make computer graphics processing more efficient.

The coordinate system used in computer graphics systems is usually modified from the standard Cartesian coordinate system. To simplify measurements, designers often place the origin or (0,0) point at the left upper corner of the screen. Also, the system is set up so that positive values go down the screen rather than up. These arrangements ensure that all the coordinate addresses of pixels will be positive. Since pixels are the smallest addressable units, no decimal coordinates are allowed. The pixels fill all the space. Note that some systems put the 0,0 point at the bottom left.

The size of the pixels and the number of them available horizontally and vertically are fixed by the electronics of the computer graphics display system and the computer graphics software. These numbers describe the resolution of a system. Conventionally, the horizontal number is given first. For example, the HyperCard display has a resolution of 512 by 342. This means there are 512 horizontal pixel position and 342 vertical positions.

Often the horizontal axis is called the *x* axis and the vertical axis is called the *y* axis.

Thus, a pixel approximately halfway across the screen at the top would have the coordinates (256,0). 256 is half of the 512 total possible horizontally. The lower left corner (from the viewer's perspective) of the screen would have the coordinates (512,342). The lower right corner would have coordinates (0,342)

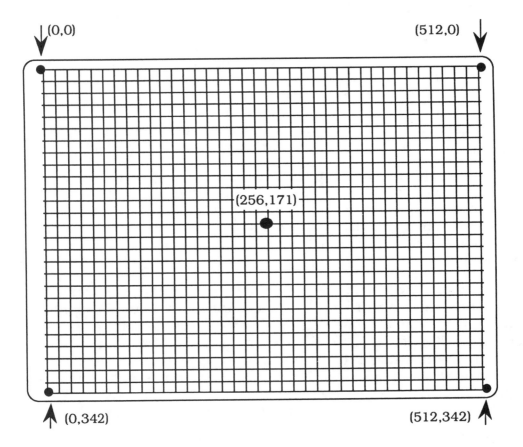

Figure 4.4   Coordinates of the HyperCard Screen (not to scale)

Other languages and displays would offer other resolutions. For example, a Macintosh II standard Apple video display has a resolution of 640 by 480. Some of the full-page displays have resolutions of 1280 by 760.

The creation of computer graphics via paint programs do not seem to require this same kind of measurement precision of the user. The person doing the drawing merely moves the mouse pointer around the screen and sees corresponding lines drawn on the screen by the paint application program. But remember that an application is a complex program that someone else has written to make these operations invisible for the user. That program must ultimately translate the mouse movements into the co-ordinate system described.

Programming Graphics in HyperCard

The coordinate system simplifies the task of programming computer graphics. Instructions must tell the computer exactly where things are. An investigation of HyperCard's graphic commands and capabilities will make this system clearer. The line is a primitive component in most computer graphics languages. Complex images are built out of lines. The vocabulary and syntax vary but the basic concept is the same. Tell the computer where the start and finish are by specifying their coordinates, and most systems will figure out which pixels they need to turn on to give the best approxima-tion of a straight line it can, given the limitations of pixel size. Sometimes diagonal and curved lines look jagged. These jaggies are a consequence mostly of the resolution of the system. Since pixels are discrete units, a computer graphics display cannot draw a smooth line made of all the small changes that make up a line. It does the best it can. On systems with big pixels, the eyes can see the staircase.

The commands in HyperCard to create a line are *choose line tool* followed by instructions to drag from one point indicated by its coordinates to another point indicated by its coordinate. These commands will be illustrated by the creation of another button object that will draw lines. This example will assume that one is still at the same place as when the beep button was created. If not, the reader should follow those steps to get to that point of being on a new card in a new stack. This example will create a button called Lines that will draw lines in the form of a triangle.

Try the button out. To do so, one must get out of the button creation mode. This is accomplished by clicking on the hand icon in the Tool Menu in order to go into tool mode. For more, see the discussion at the beginning of Chapter 5.

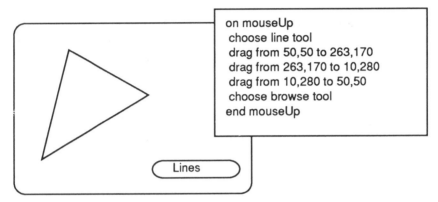

```
on mouseUp
  choose line tool
  drag from 50,50 to 263,170
  drag from 263,170 to 10,280
  drag from 10,280 to 50,50
  choose browse tool
end mouseUp
```

Lines

Figure 4.5   A Line-drawing Button Script

When one clicks the button, it should draw a triangle by drawing three lines to attach the coordinates specified. Note that the lines could have been drawn in any order. The end result would have been the same. Sometimes the order will not matter because one is interested only in the final result. Sometimes the sequence in which images get drawn will be important. This sequence could be thought of as simple animation. Animations are discussed later in Chapter 9.

Chapter 5 discusses the different tool modes available in HyperCard preparatory to creating more complex graphics.

Chapter 5
Hypercard Tools: Browse, Buttons, Fields, and Paint

HyperCard offers different tools for various kinds of activities. The default tool setting is the browse mode, which allows moving through cards, clicking on buttons, and writing in fields, depending on the user level allowed in the current stack. In HyperCard, particular tools must be activated in order to create buttons, fields, and visual displays. These tools can be accessed by clicking on the word *tools* and opening up the Tools Menu, which is a grid of visual icons. The top three represent the browse, button, and field tool modes.

The hand icon represents the browse tool mode. This is the default mode for HyperCard when starting up. One must be in this mode to click buttons, write in fields, and move around and through various stacks and cards.

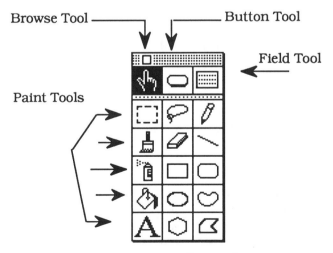

Figure 5.1   Hypercard's Tools Menu

The next rounded rectangle icon represents the button tool mode. This mode allows the creation and change of buttons. For example, one can give them names, choose and change their visual representation, resize them, place them anywhere on the screen, and assign icons to them.

The next lined-rectangle icon represents the field tool. This allows the creation and change of fields. The user can name fields, choose and change their visual representation, resize them, place them anywhere on the screen, and choose how they will respond to text.

One can occasionally get to these tools by other means. For example, picking New Button or New Field automatically switches HyperCard into the appropriate tool mode.

Below the top line is a grid of 12 icons. These represent HyperCard's painting tools. They allow one to create images on the cards in HyperCard. The line tool used in the button example is one of these painting tools. These tools will be explored in great detail in the chapters that follow. Note also that the script of the line-drawing button had a last line: *choose browse tool.* Without that, it would not have been able to try the button out by clicking since clicking is possible only in the browse mode. The button and field tool modes will be explained in more detail in this chapter; the paint tools will be explained in several following chapters.

Button Tool

HyperCard presents many choices about the appearance of buttons. Choice of New Button from the Objects Menu produces the Button Dialog Box.

The button name field allows naming of the button. It is usually advisable to give the button a name related to its function. The scripts one writes will often refer to the button by name.

The card button number is automatically given in sequence as one creates buttons for each card. Scripts can also refer to these numbers. The card button ID is also given automatically. The card button number can change if one uses some advanced modes of rearranging buttons such as the *move closer* and *send further* commands. The button ID will stay the same for the life of the stack.

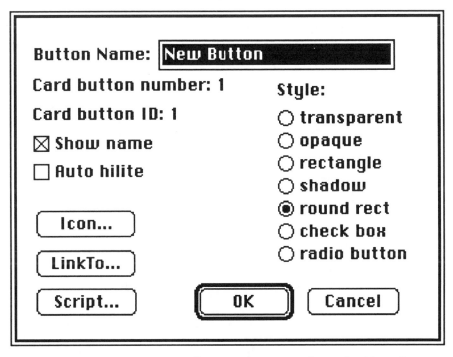

Figure 5.2   *New Button Dialog Box (accessed via the New Button item on the Options Menu)*

The Show Name Check Box tells HyperCard whether to display the name of the button when it shows the card. It is a toggle, which means that one can turn it off and on by clicking in the same box. It will become important to be able to control the appearance of this name text as one begins to attend to the graphic design of the cards.

The *Auto hilite* feature determines whether or not a button will turn negative when someone clicks on it. Good interactive design usually requires some kind of feedback for the user. HyperCard provides this automatic feature.

The set of circular radio buttons control buttons' visual appearance. Each button can have only one style. The different styles are illustrated in Figure 5.3. The Transparent option gives the flexibility to create custom graphics to overlay the button.

The icon button in the dialog box allows the user to link particular visual icons to the buttons. HyperCard comes with several such images–the arrows, house symbol, telephones and the like. HyperCard opens up the Icon Dialog Box (Figure 5.4), which allows choice of a visual image. The active area is always the rectangle surrounding the image.

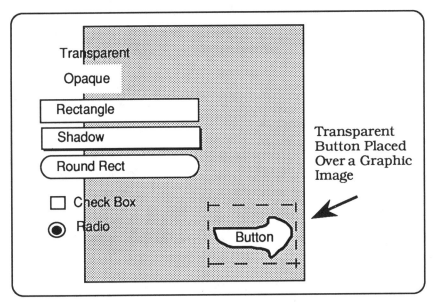

Figure 5.3   Button Styles

One can also buy stacks of button icons from companies that advertise in computer magazines and from user groups. These icons allow visual customization of stacks. Visually they also indicate the interactive actions possible on a button — for example, the house icon usually means that clicking will take one back to the home stack. Clicking on the icon button allows one to see options and assign them to buttons created. Many new stack creators go button crazy and assign icons to buttons just because they can. The best-looking stacks, however, have well-considered use of button icons. Icon should be used for specific conceptual or visual reasons.

Some programs, such as IconMaker (dicussed in Chapter 20), allow the creation of custom icons. Also, the Transparent button option essentially lets one attach any visual graphic to buttons, including digitized photos. This approach will be described in Chapter 12. The icons are easier to work with, however, because HyperCard moves them with the associated

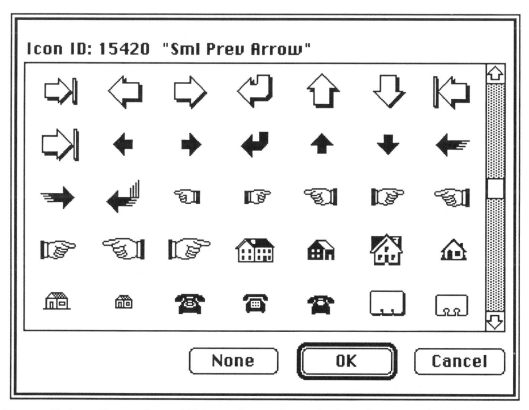

Figure 5.4   Examples of Button Icons Provided with HyperCard

button.   The Transparent button and an underlying graphic are not automatically so linked.

The Script button on the dialog box takes HyperCard into the script window, where one can create program scripts to tell the button how to behave.

The LinkTo button on the dialog box allows people who do not know scripting to have a button lead to another card. HyperCard automatically writes the script. Clicking on the LinkTo button leads to a dialog box that allows one to pick a particular card. HyperCard then creates a script for that button that will jump to the designated card whenever anyone clicks just as though the user had written such a script. People who know scripting, however, can have much more expanded control over the behavior of their buttons.

The OK and Cancel buttons allow confirmation of decisions. They are not fixed until one clicks the OK button. Clicking Cancel will cause the settings to revert to whatever they were originally.

If a button has already been created, access to this dialog information box can be gained in another way. Click on the button tool icon in the Tools Menu; the screen will display outlines around all the existing buttons. Double-clicking on any button will cause its information box to appear. Changes can then be made.

Text Field Tool

The text field tool allows creation of special text objects that are designed for the manipulation of text. Users can easily type text into them or edit text that is already there. Editing is done by the standard MacIntosh conventions as available in word processors. Clicking on the New Field item

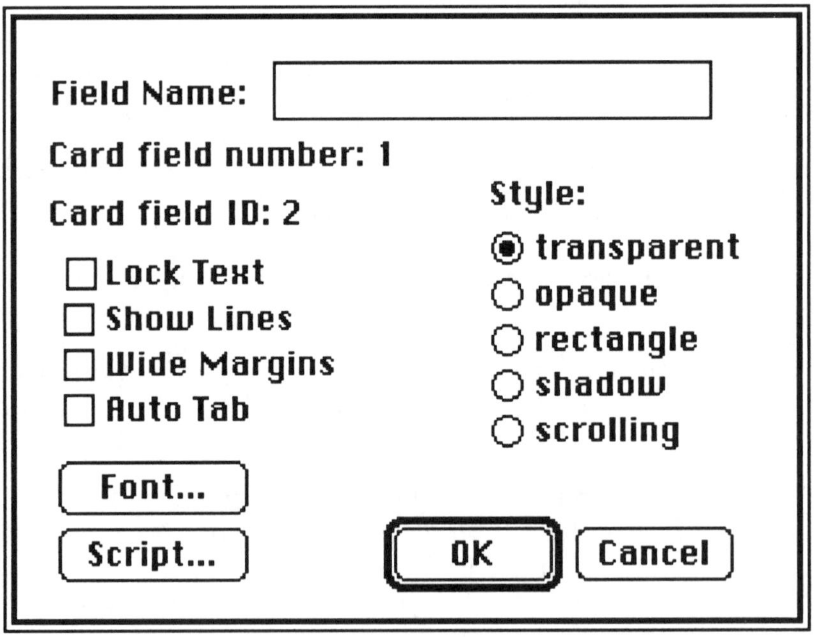

```
┌──────────────────────────────────────────────────┐
│                                                    │
│  Field Name: ┌──────────────────────────────┐     │
│              └──────────────────────────────┘     │
│  Card field number: 1                              │
│                                   Style:           │
│  Card field ID: 2                                  │
│                                 ⦿ transparent      │
│   ☐ Lock Text                   ○ opaque           │
│   ☐ Show Lines                  ○ rectangle        │
│   ☐ Wide Margins                ○ shadow           │
│   ☐ Auto Tab                    ○ scrolling        │
│                                                    │
│   ┌─────────┐                                      │
│   │ Font... │                                      │
│   └─────────┘         ┌────────┐  ┌────────┐       │
│   ┌─────────┐         │   OK   │  │ Cancel │       │
│   │ Script... │       └────────┘  └────────┘       │
│   └─────────┘                                      │
└──────────────────────────────────────────────────┘
```

Figure 5.5   New Field Dialog Box (accessed via the New Field item in the Objects Menu)

in the option opens the Text Field Dialog Box.

HyperCard automatically provides a card field number and a card field ID number, as it does with s button. Fields can be named, though, unlike buttons, the name will not show.

As illustrated in Figure 5.6, many different styles for fields are possible. The scrolling style allows one to create fields that can store much more information than they can display at one time.

The Lock Text toggle box allows creation of a field that shows text that cannot be modified. Show Lines shows the lines in the text field, and Wide Margins inserts white space between the text and the borders of the text field.

The Script, OK, and Cancel buttons work just as they do with the Button Dialog Box. The Font button leads to a special Font Dialog Box that lets one determine the font, style, and size of text that will appear in the

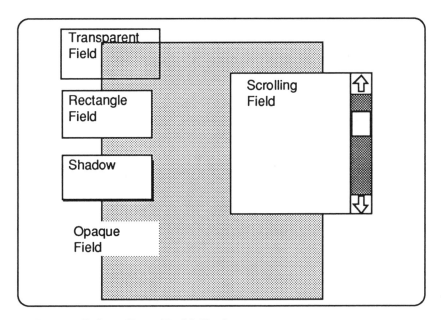

Figure 5.6   Text Field Styles

field. Since this set of visual choices is so important, it is treated separately in Chapter 13.

      If a field has already been created, access to this Text Field Dialog Box can be gained by clicking on the lined rectangle field tool in the Tools Menu. The screen will then display outlines around all existing fields. Double-clicking on any field will cause its dialog box to appear. Changes can then be made.

CHAPTER 6
GRAPHICS PAINT TOOLS

Because of the focus on multimedia modes of information, Hyper-Card's designers endowed it with an extremely rich set of visual graphics capabilities. The grid of 12 icons below the top line of the Tools Menu represents HyperCard's paint tools. Clicking on any of these 12 puts a user into the paint tool mode. Notice that a click on these also opens up new Menu bar items related to visual work. The Objects Menu goes away and is replaced by the Paint, Options, and Patterns Menus. In addition, some of the choices available on the File Menu change to introduce new options related to importing and exporting pictures to and from other graphics programs. These new options will be explained in more detail later.

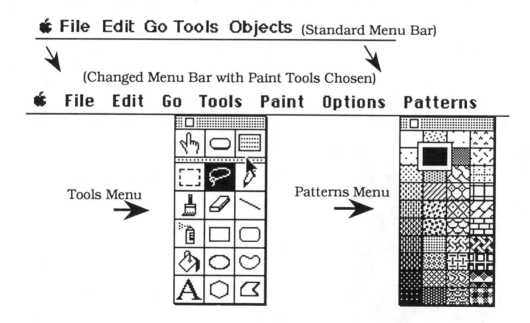

Figure 6.1   Standard Menu bar, Tools Menu, and Patterns Menu

Each of the icons in the grid represents a particular graphics capability. The user can experiment with them all by clicking on the icon and then moving the mouse about. One can think of this as a paint application program similar to MacPaint or SuperPaint that exists as part of HyperCard. Many of these capabilities are standard with just about all computer paint programs.

However, HyperCard's paint tools differ from these applications in one crucial way. Almost all of these features can be activated by script programs. One can create programs in which the computer can be instructed to do automatically just about anything that one can do by hand in interactive paint mode. In fact, the best way to plan what a program should do is first to do it by hand, noting exactly what steps are involved. In addition, many of these capabilities have special modes that are activated by pressing the option, shift, or command key as one moves the mouse. The reader is urged to explore what these tools can do in immediate interactive mode as a stimulus to thinking about what will be possible in programming mode. This chapter will describe the basic and enhanced capabilities of the paint tools. Later chapters will demonstrate how scripts can automatically accomplish the same actions.

Pencil

The pencil tool allows one to draw freehand on the screen. Click on the pencil icon and then let go. Next, click anywhere on the screen and move

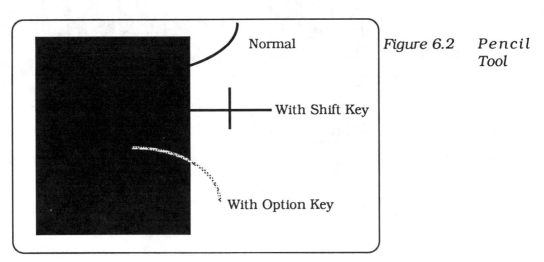

Figure 6.2   Pencil Tool

the mouse around as the button is held down. A freehand line one pixel in size corresponding to the hand movements will appear on the screen. Starting in a white area results in a black line. Starting in a black area results in a white line. Holding down on the shift key as one drags the mouse constrains the line to vertical or horizontal directions.

Undo Command

What if one makes a mistake? Following sections will describe the eraser and select tools, which allow for correction of mistakes. Computer graphics programs often offer a unique method of correction called the *undo* function. Undoubtedly, most readers have had the experience of trying out some graphic addition to a work and wishing they could return it to its state before that action. The *undo* function does exactly that; it allows the return to the visual appearance immediately before the last action.

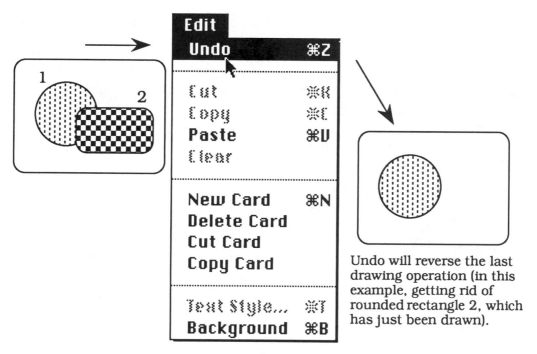

Undo will reverse the last drawing operation (in this example, getting rid of rounded rectangle 2, which has just been drawn).

Figure 6.3   Undo Command and Its Results

Consider the following example. Someone drawing with the pencil tool has a good composition under way built out of several pencil lines. On the next drag of the mouse, the hand slips and ruins the composition. The *undo* function will allow return to the appearance immediately before the bad slip *provided that there has been no other action since.* Beginners are often frustrated that *undo* won't work to correct a mistake. Usually they have done some insignificant action such as clicking the mouse button. HyperCard cannot go back more than one step. Some advanced computer graphic programs have the ability to go back up to 100 steps, but not HyperCard.

One activates the *undo* function via the Edit Menu. To activate, click on the Edit listing on the Menu bar, and drag the mouse pointer down to *Undo* while holding the mouse button. Let go, and the screen will return to its previous state. Realize that there are a few graphics actions that the *undo* function will not remedy.

Brush Tool and Spray(can) Tool

The brush tool allows the creation of thicker, freehand lines. It will also create patterned lines if the pattern is changed via the Patterns Menu. The process is exactly the same as with the pencil. Click on the brush icon, let go, and then click again when pointing at the start point and drag the mouse around. The spray icon creates lines that look like they were created with a paint sprayer — that is, a small area of random dots. As with real sprayers, the length of time the mouse stays in one place affects the density of the mark. For example, a quickly moving mouse will leave a spraycan line with lots of spaces between the dots.

In both brush and spray mode, holding the shift key down while moving the mouse constrains the movement to strictly horizontal and vertical lines even if the mouse is moved unevenly. In the spray mode, holding the option key down causes spray to come out in the form of the current pattern. In brush mode, holding the command key results in the paintbrush erasing as it moves. If a pattern is selected, it will erase only in accordance with that pattern. A user can select a variety of shapes for the brush via the Brush Shape item in the Options Menu. There are 32 different shapes made of squares, circles, lines, and dotted forms. These shapes are illustrated in Chapter 8. Experimentation will show that each of these

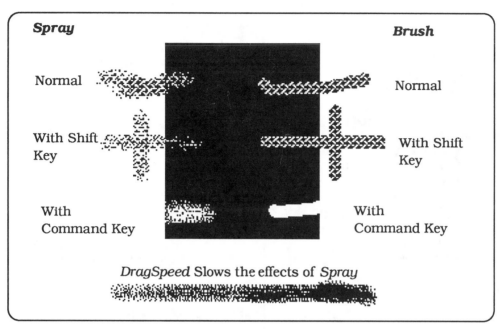

Figure 6.4   Brush and Spray Tools

brush shapes has a slightly different look, sometimes approaching the feel of an ink brush.   Shortcut access to this item can be achieved by double-clicking on the mouse button while in *brush* mode.

Line Tool

The line tool allows easy drawing of straight lines. Click on the line icon and let go. Click anywhere on the screen to identify one of the endpoints of the line, and then drag the mouse while holding the button down. HyperCard draws tentative lines from the original point to wherever one has moved the mouse. When the mouse button is released, the line becomes confirmed.

Holding the shift key while in line mode limits the lines to change in increments of exactly 15-degree angles as the mouse is moved around the original point. Holding the option key while in line mode results in straight lines drawn in the currently selected pattern. The patterns interact with the angles of the lines to produce sometimes unexpected results.

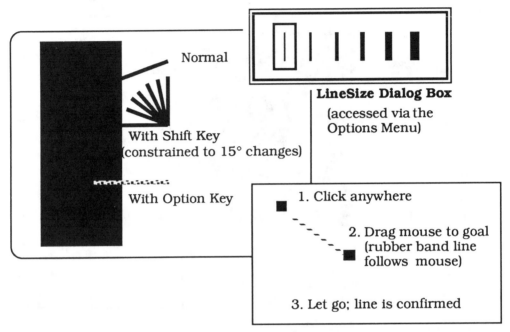

Figure 6.5　　*Line Tool and Line Size Dialog Boxes*

Lines can be drawn in different thicknesses. Six thicknesses can be chosen via the Line Size item on the Options Menu, discussed in Chapter 7. Shortcut access to this item can be achieved by double-clicking the mouse button when in line tool mode.

Rectangle, Rounded Rectangle, Oval, and Regular Polygon Tools

The rectangle tool makes shapes that look like squares and rectangles. The rounded rectangle allows drawing of squares and rectangles with rounded corners. The oval tool draws circles and ovals. The regular polygon tool draws a polygon with equal-length sides. To use these tools, click on the icon in the Tools Menu and let go. Then move the mouse pointer to the upper left or lower right corner of the desired shape; click the mouse button and hold it down while dragging to the opposite corner. Letting go then confirms the shape. The polygon is slightly different in that the first click establishes the center, not the corner.

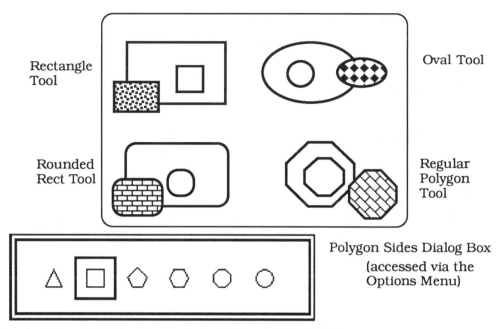

Rectangle Tool

Oval Tool

Rounded Rect Tool

Regular Polygon Tool

Polygon Sides Dialog Box
(accessed via the Options Menu)

Figure 6.6　　*Rectangle, Rounded Rectangle, Oval,*
　　　　　　　and Regular Polygon Tools

Holding the shift key while dragging causes the two *rectangle* tools to draw squares and the *oval* tool to draw circles. It allows one to rotate the regular polygon in 15 degree angles. Holding the option key while dragging allows these tools to draw in whatever the active pattern is. The default pattern is black.

Additional options available in the Options Menu can affect the actions of these tools. The pattern can be chosen in the Patterns Menu. The Draw Filled item causes all drawing to be solid patterned shapes instead of frame outlines. Double-clicking on the tool icon automatically sets the draw filled attribute as though one had clicked on this menu item. The Draw Centered item causes the first click in a drawing action to determine the center and not the corner and the subsequent drag to cause a symmetrical expansion about that center. The Line Size item affects the thickness of the lines that frame the shapes. The Polygon Sides item determines the number of sides for the polygon. A dialog box opens to allow selection of the number of sides. Double-clicking on this icon provides shortcut access to this feature.

Curve and Irregular Polygon Tools

These tools allow drawing of free-form shapes. The curve tool creates a closed shape outlined by a freehand drawn line. The irregular polygon tool allows drawing of a polygon with any number of sides drawn enclosed in straight lines of any given length and angles.

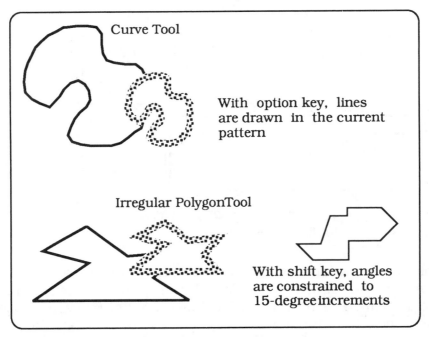

Figure 6.7   Curve and Irregular Polygon Tools

The curve, like all others, is activated by clicking on the icon and letting go. The shape is then created by clicking on a starting point and holding the mouse button down as the mouse is dragged about the screen much like the procedure with the pencil tool. Release of the mouse button at the end confirms the shape. HyperCard draws a line from that ending point back to the starting point.

The irregular polygon works slightly differently. After selection of the tool, one clicks on a starting point and then lets go of the mouse button. HyperCard creates a rubber band line that stretches from the first point to wherever the mouse is pointing. This allows experimentation with place-ment. The line is confirmed by clicking the button when the rubber band line is satisfactory. HyperCard then draws this first side of the polygon. Again, rubber band lines will follow the movements of the mouse as the second straight line side of the polygon is positioned. Clicking again confirms this line. This process can go on for any number of sides. The polygon is finished by clicking on the starting point or double-clicking the mouse button. HyperCard will then draw a line from that point back to the starting point.

Holding the option key as one draws causes the frame outlines to appear in the current pattern, instead of the default black. Holding the shift key with the irregular polygon tool constrains the angles of the straight line sides to change in 15-degree jumps in spite of uneven hand movements. Double-clicking on the tool icon automatically turns on the Draw Filled option from the Options Menu so that the shapes will be filled with the current pattern instead of empty outlines.

Eraser Tool

The eraser tool allows the erasing of black pixels on the screen. Clicking on the eraser icon activates a white box on the screen that erases any pixels it goes over. Holding the shift key while moving the eraser constrains it to horizontal and vertical motion. Holding the command key while moving it causes it to turn black pixels into white as it moves along.

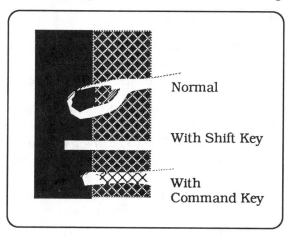

Normal

With Shift Key

With Command Key

Figure 6.8   Eraser Tool

Double-clicking on the eraser icon erases the entire picture layer on the screen.

Be aware that HyperCard actually has two picture layers — one on the card and one on the background. Erasure of card-level images does not erase background images; thus, erasing might serve to reveal the background images underneath. For more on layers, see Chapter 12.

Bucket Tool

The bucket tool allows the user to fill enclosed areas with the current pattern. By pointing at any area solidly bounded by black and clicking the mouse button, digital "paint" pours out. The active spot in the icon is the tip of the paint pouring out, so it must be aimed carefully. The tool will find all the nooks and crannies up to the nearest continuous black border. Note that the bucket tool is dangerous in that if even one pixel in the border is white, it will leak out and fill everything up to the next border it can find. Beginners are often shocked to see beautiful compositions completely filled over. Luckily, the Undo command described earlier allows one to go back before the mistake. Often the continuity of the border is unclear in a normal display. The Fat Bits item in the Options Menu allows a detailed pixel-by-pixel inspection of the border. Double-clicking on the bucket icon provides shortcut access to the Patterns Menu.

Bit-mapped and Object-oriented Graphics

Care is required in HyperCard graphic composition and modification because of the nature of the graphics created. Sometimes erasing and cutting objects does not result in what the user would intuitively expect.

Computer graphics systems offer two radically different ways of working with shapes. Bit-mapped graphics function much like paint. Painting on top of a surface makes it almost impossible to recover what was underneath. In a computer system, the pixels are changed forever when one shape is put on top of another (unless one makes immediate use of the *Undo* function). If one cut out the shape on top, a blank space would remain below as illustrated in Figure 6.10. The new top graphics replace everything underneath. Cutting them away does not reveal the original graphics.

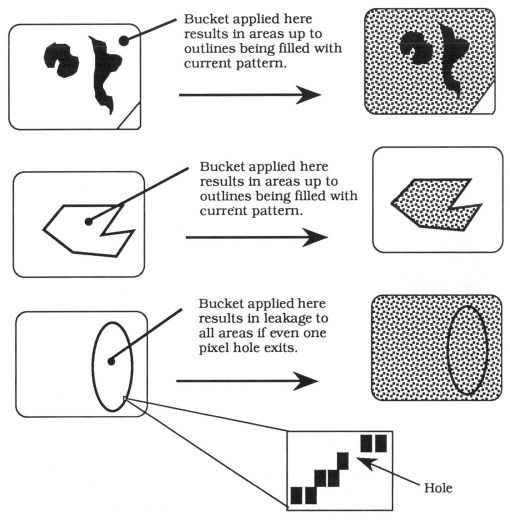

Bucket applied here results in areas up to outlines being filled with current pattern.

Bucket applied here results in areas up to outlines being filled with current pattern.

Bucket applied here results in leakage to all areas if even one pixel hole exits.

Hole

Figure 6.9   Bucket Tool and Dangers of Leakage

Object-oriented graphics store the instructions for drawing each shape individually. One can move shapes around without destroying the shapes underneath because the system can reconstruct shapes from its stored record of each shape. Thus, moving a shape sitting on top of another reveals the other one underneath. This process is more like a paste-up board that uses temporary cement than like paint. Graphics form a modifiable collage of independent objects rather than replacing what they are put on top of.

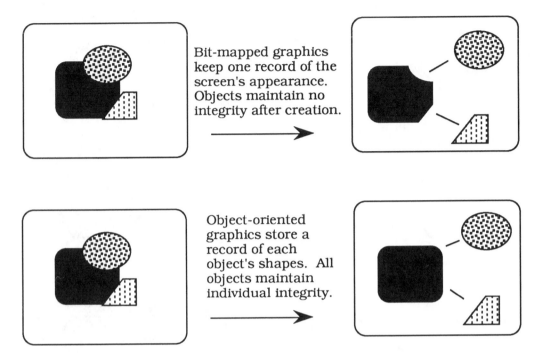

Figure 6.10   Bit-mapped and Object-oiented Graphics

Select and Lasso Tool

The select and lasso tools are unique to computer graphics. They allow one to copy, delete, move, scale, store, and otherwise manipulate portions of a picture. The select tool is activated by clicking on the dotted rectangle in the tool grid. The lasso tool is activated by the lasso icon.

With the select tool, one can indicate a rectangular shape one wants to work with. Clicking on the screen with the mouse button establishes a starting point. Dragging the mouse while holding down the mouse button continually selects possible opposite corners of the rectangle. A rubber-band-lined rectangle with moving dots shows the changing rectangle. Letting go of the mouse button confirms the rectangle in its current size. Everything inside the rectangle is selected, including the white space.

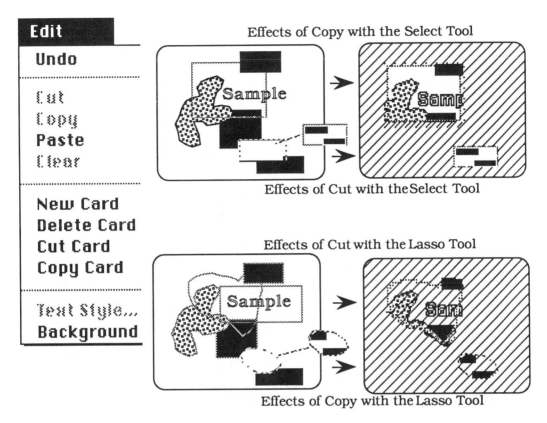

Figure 6.11 Select and Lasso Tools

Once an area is selected, there are many possibilities, many of which are reflected in the items in the Edit Menu. Cut will remove the rectangular area, leaving a blank white space. It will temporarily be stored in the clipboard area of memory, from which it can be pasted back as long as nothing else is subsequently put in the clipboard. Copy will make a copy of the selected area on the screen and store in the clipboard without removing the original. Clear will permanently erase whatever was in the area. The delete key will accomplish the same result when some area is selected.

Once something has been put in the clipboard, Paste becomes available. Notice that Paste in the menu is dimmed unless something previously has been cut or copied. The selected area can be pasted back on the same card or on any other cards. The rectangle will come back exactly in the same

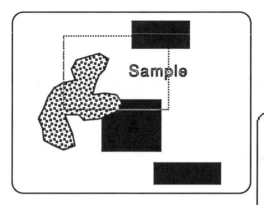

Once copied to the clipboard, the scale of the image can be changed by rescaling the select rectangle in a new position before pasting back.

Figure 6.12   Rescaling a Copied Image by Adjusting the Select Rectangle

relative rectangle if no intervening actions are made. The item can be scaled or put back in other positions by first using the selection tool to frame a new select rectangle before pasting (Figure 6.12). For example, the pasted image can be fitted into a larger rectangle or one of different dimensions.   The scaling operation often distorts the original images and can emphasize the blockiness of the pixels, so it is necessary to experiment. The original item stays in the clipboard until a new selection is put into it by a cut or copy action or the computer is turned off.

The *Select* Tool with Command Key

Will collapse to find the smallest rectangle possible if the command key is pressed as the mouse is dragged to form the selection rectangle.

The *Select* Tool with Option Key

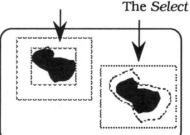

Will collapse to hug the image and converts into the lasso tool.

Figure 6.13   Effects of Using the Select Tool With the Command or Option Key Pressed

Clicking and dragging with the command key depressed while in select tool mode causes the selection rectangle to surround an item with the smallest rectangle possible (Figure 6.13). This method will not work when items overlap or have broken lines because the process tries to find the rectangle surrounding the best continuous line of black pixels it can. Holding the option key while dragging causes the select tool to turn into a lasso that hugs the item without a rectangle (see next section). Double-clicking on the select icon selects the whole picture on the screen. The following lasso describes the effects of the option and shift keys while in this mode.

Lasso Tool

The lasso tool functions much like the select tool except that it does not create a rectangle. Once in the lasso mode, the user traces a freehand line around the material to be selected while holding the mouse button down. When the button is released, everything inside is selected and is then available for cutting, copying, clearing, and pasting. If the mouse button is let go before dragging back to the starting point, HyperCard will complete the shape with an automatic straight line back to the starting point. This feature is useful for selecting items very close to each other for which a hand drag might be imprecise. The lasso differs from the selection tool in that white spaces inside the area selected are transparent rather than white.

Clicking here in lasso mode will hug the object perfectly. Nothing else will be selected.

Clicking here in lasso mode will not hug the object. HyperCard will trace all the contiguous black pixels it can find and will include parts of the other objects.

Figure 6.14   Effects of Using the Lasso Tool with the Command Key Pressed

The command key and lasso combination allows a special kind of selection. Once in lasso mode, clicking inside an item with the command key depressed causes HyperCard to expand from that click to select the nearest continuous black pixels. Simple shapes can thus be selected from the inside out as illustrated in Figure 6.14. Use of this technique with overlapping images produces unusual effects. Double-clicking on the lasso icon selects the whole screen.

Items selected with either the select rectangle or the lasso can be moved by clicking inside the object and holding the mouse button down as it is dragged. The selected area becomes affixed to the moving mouse pointer and will follow the mouse, leaving a white space behind. Dragging with the shift key depressed constrains the motion to horizontal or vertical directions. The same process undertaken with the option key depressed (Figure 6.15) causes a copy of the selected material to be made on the spot. This copy then follows the mouse pointer while leaving the original intact.

Selected areas can be manipulated in many additional ways using enhancement keys. The table on the facing page lists possible effects.

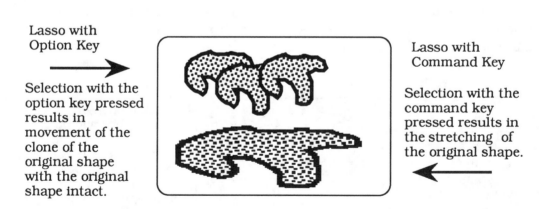

Lasso with
Option Key

Selection with the option key pressed results in movement of the clone of the original shape with the original shape intact.

Lasso with
Command Key

Selection with the command key pressed results in the stretching of the original shape.

Figure 6.15   Effects of the Lasso Tool with the Option or Command Key Pressed

Tool/Key	Shift	Option	Command	Double Click
select	constrained	clone	negative	select screen
lasso	constrained	clone	+hug inside	select screen
pencil	constrained	—	fat bits	fat bits
brush	constrained	—	pattern erase	brush shapes
eraser	constrained	—	neg pixels	whole screen
line	constrain 15°	pattern	—	line size
spray	constrained	—	erase	—
rectangle	square	pattern	—	filled
round rect.	square	pattern	—	filled
oval	circle	pattern	—	filled
polygon	constrain 15°	pattern	—	filled
curve	—	pattern	—	filled
irreg. poly.	constrain 15°	pattern	—	filled
bucket	—	—	—	patterns
text	<> sizes	—	w/shift <> fonts	text style

Text Tool

The text tool allows the creation of text as graphics. One can enter text anywhere on the screen as part of the screen picture. These text elements can be combined with the other graphics and manipulated in the same ways — for example, with the lasso tool. HyperCard promotes the use of graphic text as a design element. This tool is activated by clicking on the text icon, letting go, and then clicking anywhere on the screen. Typing on

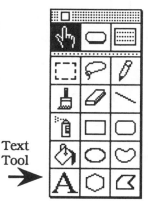

Text
Tool

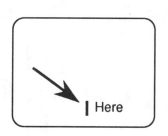

Here

Keyboard text will appear
wherever the I-beam
cursor is positioned.

Figure 6.16   Text Tool

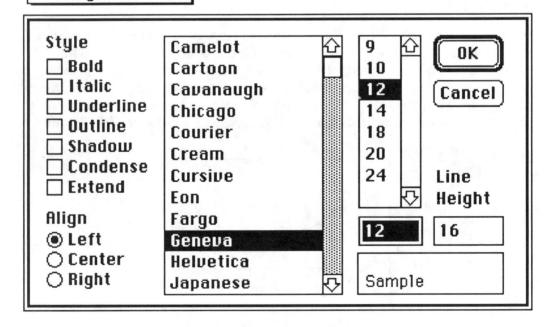

Figure 6.17 Text Style Item on the Edit Menu and the Text Dialog Box

the keyboard will produce text beside the I-beam pointer.

The Macintosh is well known for its text variety. One has a choice of size, style, font, and alignment. These choices are accessed via the Text Style item on the Edit Menu. Shortcut access to these choices can be achieved by double-clicking on the text icon in the Tools Menu.

A special dialog box opens up, showing the choices for text. The choices are the same as those available in other word processors and paint programs. The box offers one line of choices for style, another for alignment, size, and font. Styles can be combined, but alignment, font, and size demand a single choice.

Fonts are families of text referring to the specific design parameters of letters. The word *font* comes from the metal or wood pieces of type that printers used to form the printed page. Decisions about the angles, curves, components, thicknesses, flourishes, and relationships of the strokes that make up letters are codified into fonts. Different fonts have very different feels and can have significant expressive impact. The particular fonts available depend on what fonts happen to be installed in the system file of the system folder with which the computer was booted. Some of the standard fonts that come with the systems provided by Apple are Chicago,

Font \ Style	Bold	Outline	Italics
Chicago	**ChicagoBold**	Chicago Outline	*Chicago Italics*
Geneva	**GenevaBold**	Geneva Outline	*Geneva Italics*
Helvetica	**HelveticaBold**	Helvetica Outline	*Helvetica Italics*
Monaco	**MonacoBold**	Monaco Outline	*Monaco Italics*
New York	**NewYorkBold**	NewYork Outline	*NewYork Italics*
Times	**Times Bold**	Times Outline	*Times Italics*

Figure 6.18   Font Families and Font Styles

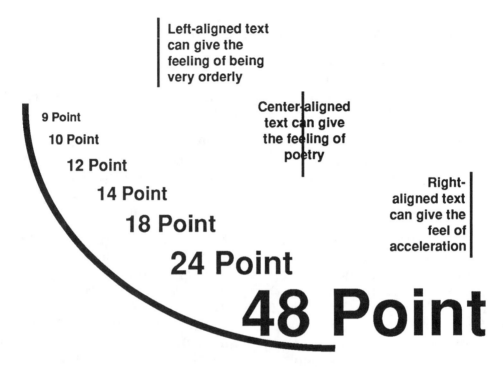

Figure 6.19   Text Point Sizes and Text Alignments

Geneva, New York, and Times. In addition, many other fascinating fonts may be bought or obtained from user groups. Fonts must be installed in the system folder using the special Font/DA mover program that is provided with the basic system disks. The number of fonts installed may have to be limited on floppy disk–based systems because of memory limitations. The Font/DA mover and resources for fonts are described in Chapter 20.

Sizes are expressed in points, a printer's term. There are 72 points to the inch. Again, the specific sizes available depend on what is installed in the system file. Styles allow the creation of bold, outline, shadow, italic, condensed, and extended text. Text can be aligned so that all lines of text align at the left or right margins or with the centers of lines. Only one style, font, and size can be used during one I-beam entry session. Of course, by clicking elsewhere, it is possible to create other kinds of text that can be

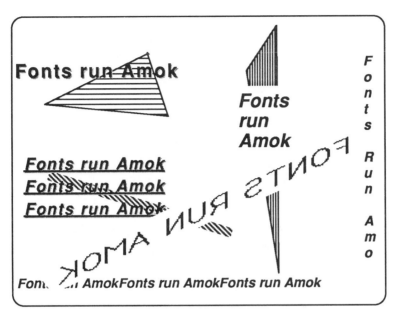

Figure 6.20   Fonts Run Amok

selected and moved next to the first.

Shortcut access to changing font sizes can be gained by holding the command key down and hitting the < or > key. < moves to lower sizes, and > moves to higher. Holding the shift and command key down and pressing the < or > key allows fonts to be changed.

The text created with the text tool behaves in a manner different from text that is entered into text fields. The text in a text field acts like the object-oriented graphics entities: It maintains its independence. It can be edited and have its attributes changed at any time. The field text can be moved around freely without affecting what is below it. It appears to float above the screen picture, much like buttons do. Text tool text acts like the other graphics. Once the mouse is clicked elsewhere, it is fixed. The only way to change it is to erase or select and cut it.

Beginners tend to go font-crazy with the text options. Be aware that text font and style are powerful design elements. Too many in one display conflict and dilute the power of the fonts. Readers are urged to use font differences carefully.

CHAPTER 7
OPTIONS AND PATTERNS MENUS

Many of the items on the Options Menu have already been discussed in relation to enhancements to the tools described previously. For example, Line Size affects all the line drawing tools. Brush Shape affects the shape of the brush. Polygon Sides affects the number of sides in the regular polygon. Draw Filled determines whether shapes will be drawn filled or in outline form. Draw Centered determines whether shapes will be drawn by dragging from corner to corner or symmetrically by dragging from the center out to the perimeter. This chapter discusses the use of the remaining options.

Options

Grid
FatBits
Power Keys

Line Size...
Brush Shape...
Edit Pattern...
Polygon Sides...

Draw Filled
Draw Centered
Draw Multiple

Figure 7.1   Options Menu

Draw Multiple

The Draw Multiple item creates multiple versions of the shape selected as the mouse is dragged. It can achieve stunning effects. It can work in combination with any of the regular shape tools — oval, rectangle, or regular polygon. The number of pixels in the interval between copies can be determined by pressing the option key and any number between 1 and 9. The Draw Multiple item is a toggle so, clicking it changes its status from on to off or off to on. It can be combined with the Draw Centered and Draw Filled items to accomplish unusual effects. Also, the movement of the mouse drag path affects the resulting image.

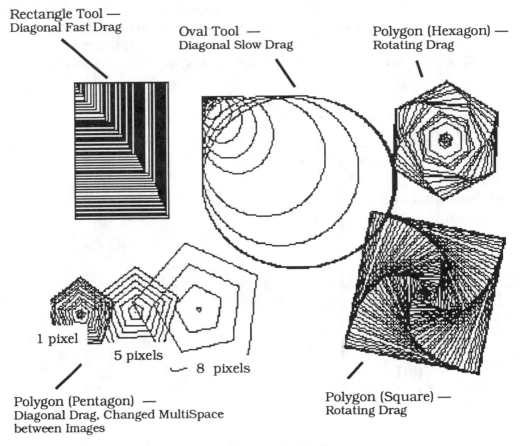

Figure 7.2   Examples of the Draw Multiple Option

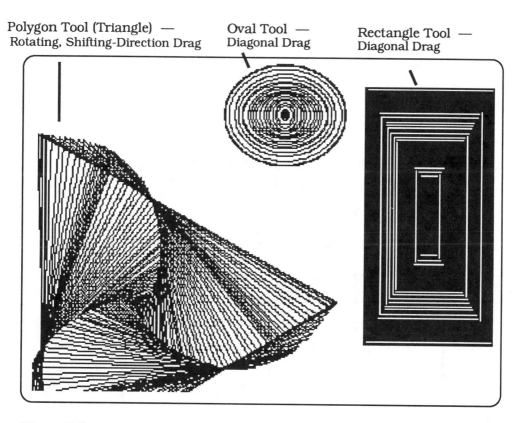

Polygon Tool (Triangle) —
Rotating, Shifting-Direction Drag

Oval Tool —
Diagonal Drag

Rectangle Tool —
Diagonal Drag

Figure7.3   *More Examples of the Draw Multiple Option*

The Grid

Often it is difficult to line objects up precisely. The grid tool creates an invisible grid of horizontal and vertical lines 8 pixels apart. If it is toggled on, all lines will line up on the nearest grid line. Moving items with the selection tool will similarly move in 8 pixel jumps.

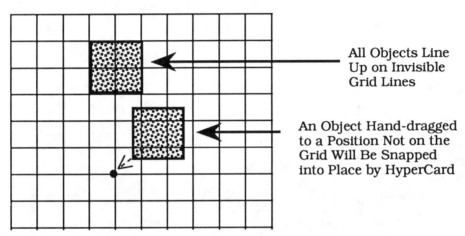

All Objects Line
Up on Invisible
Grid Lines

An Object Hand-dragged
to a Position Not on the
Grid Will Be Snapped
into Place by HyperCard

Figure 7.4   Grid Option Locks Objects onto an Invisible Grid

FatBits

With experience, great control can be achieved over the composition of computer images. Fat Bits is a snapshot into the basic pixel nature of all computer graphics. It was described earlier in regard to finding the pixel gaps before using the bucket tool. FatBits creates a blowup of the screen to allow detail work. Each pixel is magnified into big black squares. Only a small section of the screen can be presented, with a small inset showing the appearance of that section in normal size. To scroll around, press the option key. The icon turns into a hand. Moving the mouse with the mouse button down will move different sections of the screen into the magnified presentation. FatBits can also be accessed by double-clicking on the pencil tool. FatBits can be exited by toggling the FatBits item, double-clicking on the pencil icon, or clicking inside the inset window.

All the normal tools work while in FatBits mode. However, drawing in FatBits requires some experimentation because the effects of one's actions can be difficult to anticipate.

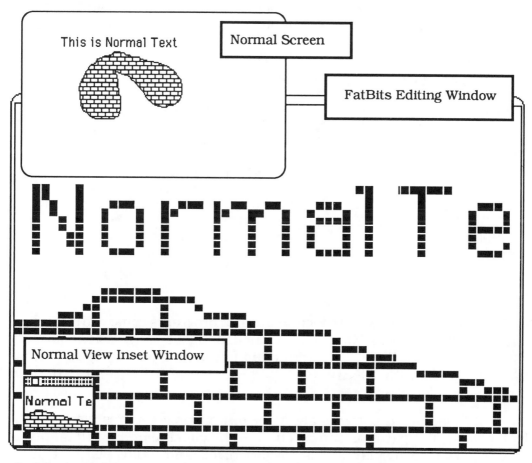

1 Selection of FatBits in the Options Menu opens a special enlarged view for detatiled editing.
2 Movement of the FatBits window can be achieved by pressing the option key, which converts the normal cursor into a hand.
3 Return to normal display can be achieved by clicking the mouse in the normal view inset window or toggling the FatBits item on the menu.

Figure 7.5   FatBits Option Allows Detailed Editing

Power Keys

The Power Keys option gives one access to keyboard shortcuts to call up particular tools and processes. Some of these refer to Paint Menu options that will be described in a later chapter. The list is presented below.

A	Select All	S	Select
B	Black Pattern	T	Transparent
C	Toggle Centered	V	Flip Vertical
D	Darker	W	White Pattern
E	Trace Edges	1	Set line 1 pixel thick
F	Fill with Current Pattern	2	Set line 2 pixels thick
G	Toggle Grid	3	Set line 3 pixels thick
H	Flip Horizontal	4	Set line 4 pixels thick
I	Invert	6	Set line 6 pixels thick
L	Lighter	8	Set line 8 pixels thick
M	Toggle Multiple	[	Rotate left
O	Opaque	]	Rotate right
P	Pick Up	Backspace	Clear current
R	Revert		

Edit Pattern

HyperCard and most Macintosh paint programs come with standard patterns. The Patterns Menu is illustrated in Figure 7.6. Custom patterns can be created via the Edit Pattern option. Clicking on this option brings up a dialog box with a FatBits-like presentation of the current pattern in normal and blown-up size.

All Macintosh patterns are made out of basic squares measuring 8 by 8 pixels. The patterns can be changed by clicking on individual pixels in the blown-up display. This toggles black and white pixels to their opposites. An amazing array of patterns can be created in this way. The normal size pattern is reflected in the opposite box. Changes are confirmed with the OK button.

Sometimes beginners go pattern-crazy, overusing patterns. Many of the standard Macintosh patterns have even become clichés. Readers are urged to create custom patterns that relate conceptually and visually to their compositions rather than merely accepting the standard provided patterns.

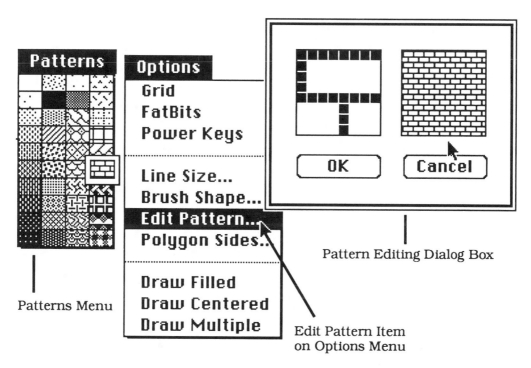

Figure 7.6   *Patterns Menu, Options Menu, and Pattern Editing Dialog Box*

The Patterns Menu

The Patterns Menu presents 40 patterns. The currently active pattern is indicated by an outline rectangle; it can be changed by clicking in a new pattern. The current pattern affects all tools that use patterns, including the Draw Filled option, the brush, bucket, and spray tools, and the option key enhancements to all the line drawing tools.

The Paint Menu also allows many special effects; these will be discussed in Chapter 11.

CHAPTER 8
SCRIPTS THAT CONTROL GRAPHICS

Problem Solving, Algorithms, Flowcharts, and Heuristics

We have shown how to use HyperCard as a paint program. Images can be created, as in MacPaint and other paint programs, merely by selecting menu items and then dragging the mouse in desired directions. The reader is urged to become familiar with conventional use of the paint

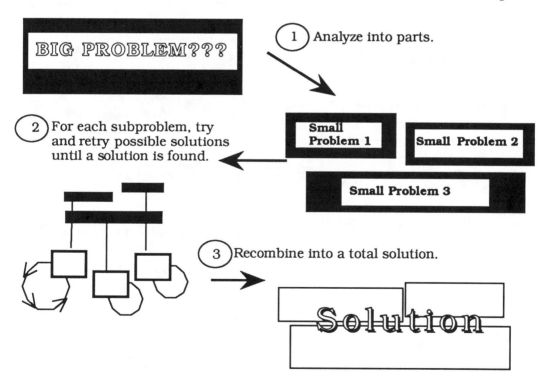

Figure 8.1   Algorithmic Problem-solving Process

tools because that knowledge is a prerequisite to programming graphics. One needs to know what is possible before one can devise a program. Almost all HyperCard paint sequences accomplishable by hand can be translated into computer program scripts.

People unfamiliar with computers often make the mistake of underestimating the step of human analysis that must precede design of programs — for example, having a clear visual goal in mind. Most current computer programs are unable to create interesting images by themselves. After this planning, the computer can be helpful in realizing those designs. Also, as is true with hand processes, the program's mistakes can make serendipitous contributions to future ideas. Human design and analysis is the crucial first step in all programming.

Programmers typically use a structured process of systems analysis

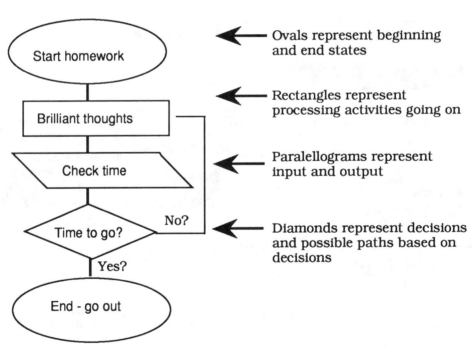

Figure 8.2   Flowchart of a Typical Life Event

to design their programs. The basic idea is to analyze carefully the desired end state, describe it, analyze the steps necessary to get there, and refine until a foolproof scheme is devised. In doing so, each goal is broken down into progressively smaller subgoals. Each subprocess is cyclically tried out, evaluated, revised, and retried until it works flawlessly. The subprocesses are reassembled and tried out again.

The basic idea is appealing. The guaranteed series of steps to accomplish some goal is called an algorithm. This approach has made significant accomplishments in engineering and some kinds of computer programming. It has also met some significant limits, as in the fields of artificial intelligence, simulation of human thinking, and social analysis.

Diagrams of the process, called flowcharts, are drawn to make the relationships clear. In the flowchart, visual icons represent particular kinds of processes — for example, inputs, outputs, and decisions. The visual chart can be a powerful aid to understanding complex systems and planning actions in those systems. These processes of flowcharting and systems analysis are now being applied in many areas outside computer work such as business and government. Unrecognized aspects of processes are often made manifest through the process.

Although this approach is appealing to those who like certainty, it is occasionally seen as alien to the arts. Artists often do not know exactly where they are going before they start. They discover the end through the processes of exploration and serendipity. Intuition is often valued in addition to analysis. The judgment of a best way to a goal is often difficult to make because of competing values. Artists seek to synthesize rather than analyze. New fields of computer science have realized the value of these approaches and seek to develop heuristics (workable ways to move toward goals), instead of seeking foolproof algorithms.

This book is based on the premise that artists can benefit from learning to use both kinds of processes. One needs both intuition and systematic analysis to work successfully with computer graphics and sound. The examples in this book focus on the specific vocabulary and grammar of HyperCard. The processes of thinking about graphics and programming, however, will be applicable in any computer language.

Translations from Hand Drawing into Programmed Graphics in HyperCard

This section shows the process of creating scripts to produce graphics. It uses the technique of creating button objects, as introduced in earlier chapters. Buttons will be given message handlers that cause them to respond to mouse clicks by creating graphics. Button creation is a convenient modular approach to learning graphics programming commands. Later chapters will demonstrate the process of making the button objects self activating so that they will not need someone to click on them.

As with all programming, one needs to start with an idea about the desired goal. In these examples, one should plan the appearance of the final visual outcome; to do so, one can use graph paper or can sketch in paint mode. If the order in which the images appear is important, one should time-design the sequence.

To start, one needs to get into button creation mode as described in Chapter 2. Select the New Button item from the Objects Menu. Double- click on the new button that appears on the screen. Once the Button Info Dialog Box appears, name the button to indicate what it does. Click the script button on the dialog box to get into the Script Creation Box. Type the desired command lines between the *on mouseUp* and *end mouseUp* lines. Click Ok to confirm. Click the hand icon in the Tools Menu to get back into browse mode in order to try out the button.

It is easy to reopen the script and change it if the button is unsatisfactory. In fact, one of the great strengths of computer graphics work is the ease of trial and error. Some critics believe that the process is too easy, and work may be discarded too readily without taking the time for reflection.

These beginning exercises will place all the buttons on the same card. Eventually they will be placeable anywhere. All of these scripts will be based on the hand processes used with the paint tools discussed in earlier chapters.

The *choose, drag,* and *click at* Commands

Consider the process of drawing an X by hand with the paint tools. One would click on the line tool, click at the starting point in one corner, drag

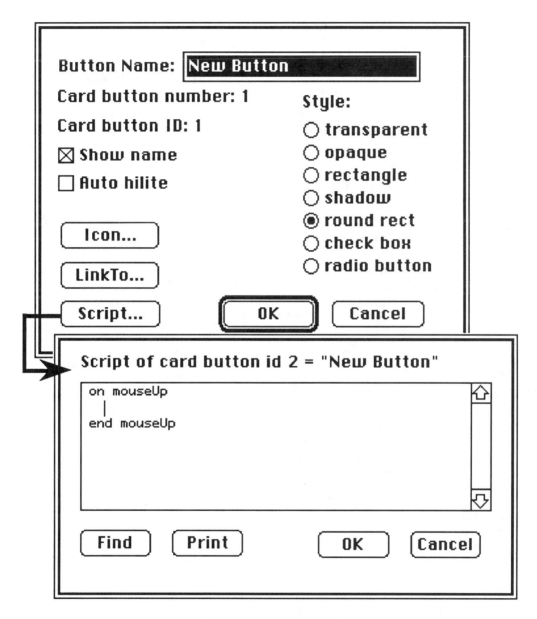

Figure 8.3   Button Information Dialog Box and Script Creation Dialog Box

to the opposite corner, let go, click at the other corner, drag to the opposite corner, and let go. A script to accomplish this would need command lines for each of these actions.

The first command line duplicates the act of clicking on the line tool. As described inChapter 4, this is accomplished with the command *choose line tool*. The word *line* could be replaced by the name of any of the other tools for other kinds of actions. The next command has to duplicate the act of clicking at one corner and dragging down to the other corner. Use the command line *drag from (coordinates of first point) to t (coordinates of second point)* — for example, *drag from 10,10 to 512,300*. The next command line needs another drag statement specifying the coordinates of the second line — for example, *drag from 512,10 to 10,300*. These sequences of commands can be placed in button scripts via the process described. Notice the importance of the analysis of what one would have done by hand to create the program. Figure 8.4 demonstrates button scripts to accomplish simple graphics using some of the paint tools.

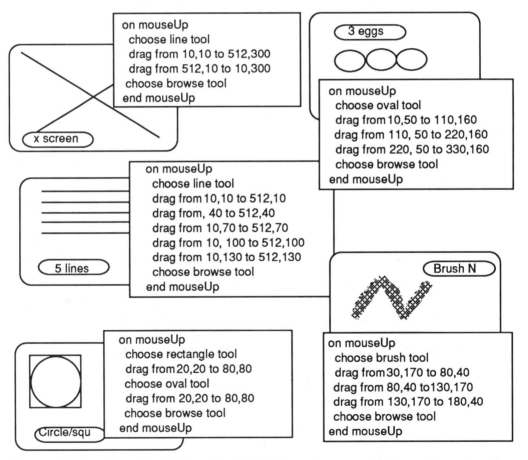

Figure 8.4   Sample Button Scripts Using choose and drag Commands

Click At Command

The *click at* command controls where the text tool will place text and where the bucket will start filling. The command can be easily used in scripts.

Shift, Option, and Command Key Enhancements

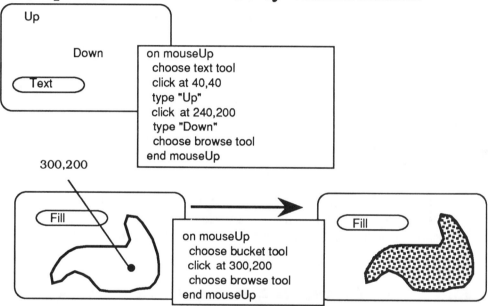

```
on mouseUp
  choose text tool
  click at 40,40
  type "Up"
  click  at 240,200
  type "Down"
  choose browse tool
end mouseUp
```

```
on mouseUp
  choose bucket tool
  click  at 300,200
  choose browse tool
end mouseUp
```

Figure 8.5   Examples of Button Scripts Using the Click at Command

Most of the shift, option, and command key enhancements that work with the paint tools are also available for inclusion in scripts. In hand actions, these enhancements are accomplished by holding these keys down while dragging the mouse. For example, the line tool draws with the current pattern instead of black when the option key is depressed. The shift key constrains motion to horizontal, vertical, or to 15-degree angles. The table in Chapter 6 summarizes these effects. Scripts simulate the action of dragging the mouse while holding a keyboard key down by adding the words *with optionkey* or *with commandkey* or *with shiftkey* at the end of the command line started with *drag*.

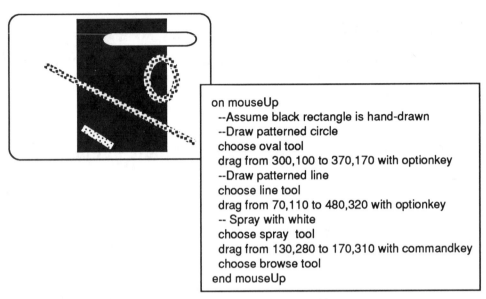

```
on mouseUp
  --Assume black rectangle is hand-drawn
  --Draw patterned circle
  choose oval tool
  drag from 300,100 to 370,170 with optionkey
  --Draw patterned line
  choose line tool
  drag from 70,110 to 480,320 with optionkey
  -- Spray with white
  choose spray  tool
  drag from 130,280 to 170,310 with commandkey
  choose browse tool
end mouseUp
```

*Figure 8.6   Examples of Button Scripts Using a
               "Drag with" Enhancement Key*

It does not really make sense to use the shift key constraints in these commands because careful selection of the coordinates in a command line can place motions precisely in a way that would be difficult by hand.

Options Menu Access: *set, doMenu, the filled, draw centered,* and *draw multiple*

The Options Menu can also affect the action of the paint tools for drawing shapes that can be filled, centered, or multiple. Line Size, Brush Shape, and Polygon Sides can all be changed. Working by hand, one would first select the desired paint tool, then open the Options Menu and select the item desired. For filled, centered, and multiple items, this would toggle the setting — changing it to the opposite of whatever it was previously. Selecting the Line Size, Polygon Sides, and Brush Shape items opens up additional dialog boxes in which decisions need to be made.

HyperCard offers easy script commands that simulate these actions. For example, assume that one wants to draw a filled rectangle. The *DoMenu* command simulates opening a menu and clicking an item. Its format requires the word *DoMenu* followed by the exact words that appear in the menu. Thus, the command *doMenu draw filled* would toggle the filled characteristic. The *doMenu* would work similarly for the *draw centered* and *draw multiple* commands.

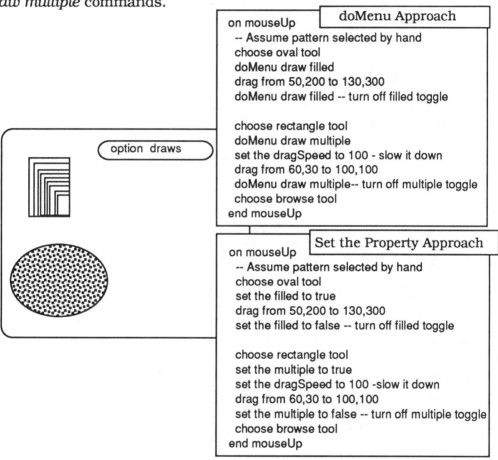

Figure 8.7   Button Scripts That Access the Options Menu Commands

The *DoMenu* command would not work so well for the other items in the Options Menu because the script has trouble indicating the next level of choices, which appear in a dialog box. HyperCard offers another, more flexible approach to setting these Options Menu items by using the *set* command to give a property a desired value. For example, *set the filled to true* would accomplish the same as the *doMenu* command illustrated in Figure 8.7.

To use the *set* command, one must know the name that HyperCard gives to each painting property and its possible values. For example, the characteristic that controls whether shapes are filled is called *the filled*. It can take two values — either false for outline shapes or true for filled shapes. The *draw centered* and *draw multiple* commands work in the same way.

Line Size, Brush Shape, and Polygon Sides Properties

These characteristics have more than two values. In interactive hand mode, one picks the desired value by clicking in the dialog box that appears after clicking in the Options Menu. To use the *set* command, one needs to know the official HyperCard name of the property and the number equivalents of the various possible choices.

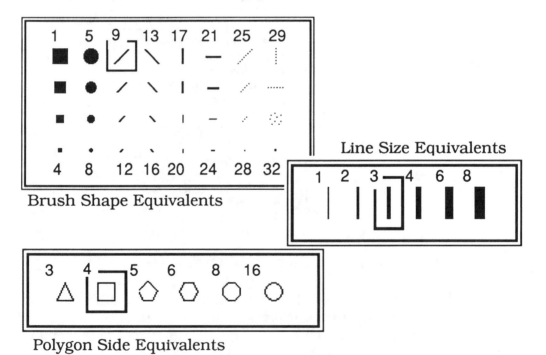

Brush Shape Equivalents

Line Size Equivalents

Polygon Side Equivalents

Figure 8.8   Number Equivalents of Options Menu Settings

The property controlling line size is called *the lineSize*. It can take any value from 1 to 9 pixels. The property controlling the number of polygon sides is called *the polySides*. It can take any value greater than 0. The brush shape is called *the brush* and can take any value form 1 to 42. In addition, the space between multiple images is called *the multiSpace* and can take values from 1 to 9, these representing the number of pixels between images. The correspondence between *the lineSize, polySides* and *brush* properties and their numbers is shown in Figure 8.8. Scripts to use each of these consist of command lines to set the property to a value followed by commands that use the properties.

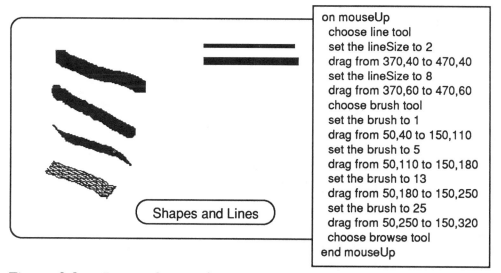

Figure 8.9   *Button Script That Sets the lineSize and brush Properties*

Patterns Menu

HyperCard offers 40 stock patterns that can be used with any command or tool that uses patterns including the bucket, spray, *draw filled*, and the line-drawing tools with option key enhancement. In the interactive hand mode, one clicks on the Patterns Menu in the Menubar and drags the mouse down to point at the desired pattern.

Again, the same effect can be accomplished by using the *set* command. The property is called *the pattern* and can take values from 1 to 40. White is 1 and black is 12. Figure 8.10 shows the numbers corresponding to patterns. A script command *set the pattern to 36* will cause all subsequent pattern drawing to use the brick pattern.

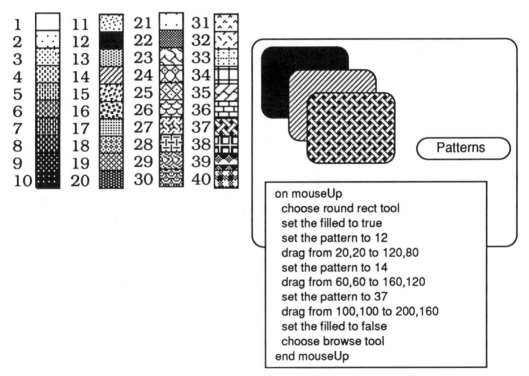

8.10 *Patterns Menu Equivalents and Sample Script*

Chapter 9
Using Loops and Variables in Graphics Programming

Loops and the Repeat Command: *repeat for*

In nature and in graphics, many beautiful images are composed of repeated forms. It should be clear by now that graphics scripts are easy to construct once one knows the structure and vocabulary of HyperTalk or any other language. Buttons that accomplish complex pictures can be built out of the simple scripts demonstrated in Chapter 8. However, complex images, such as those requiring repeated forms, would require many lines of code and would become tedious to program.

Most computer languages offer sophisticated control commands that can automate scripts. Repeated forms are ideal for computer work. Conceptually, most computer accomplishments are based on the notion of repeating simple actions with lightning speed — e.g., filling a screen by changing the value of every pixel. Multiplication in a computer is accomplished by controlled loops that add 1 over and over.

Just about every computer language offers a grammatical structure to accomplish loops. In HyperCard they are called repeat loops. One can build a script that repeats by using the appropriate command words. There are several kinds of repeat commands that can be inserted into message handlers. Figure 9.1 demonstrates a button containing a simple repeat loop to beep 13 times. The repeat loop opens with the command line *repeat for (some number)*, follows with the commands that are to be repeated, and ends with the command line *end repeat.* Note that the same effect could have been accomplished by using the command *beep 13.*

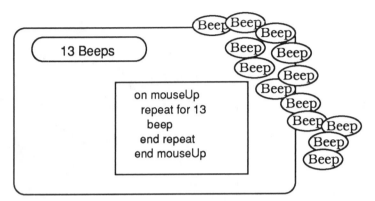

Figure 9.1   *Script Using Repeat for*

Variables

Some repeat commands have more intelligence: instead of repeating a fixed number of times, they will repeat until some condition is fulfilled. To accomplish this, they may need to make use of variables. A variable is a symbolic container in which changing values can be stored. It allows one to make statements that apply to whole classes of situations. After the values are given a symbolic name, one can refer to the value they hold by referring to the name. For example, any reference to q (assuming that one has created a variable called q) will yield the value q stands for rather than the letter q. In computer systems, variables are actual physical locations in memory that the computer allocates to store values. The values stored in a variable can be letters or numbers.

Variables are essential for work in science, which purports to develop theories describing whole classes of phenomena instead of just one particular event. To do so, principles must be stated in generic form. For example, the symbolic statement $a = gt^2$ describes the acceleration of an object pulled by gravity. It says that acceleration (a) is equal to the force of gravity (g) times the time (t) squared. The variables a, g, and t stand for the effects of gravity anywhere in the universe. If an apple is dropped anywhere on the moon or on earth, it is possible to calculate how fast it will be going at the end of a period of time. One only needs to put different values into the variable containers. Art makes extensive use of symbolic variables also, but they are usually represented with visual symbols.

Variables are also essential for work with computers because they allow programs and scripts to control families of actions instead of just one event. For example, *drag from 10,10 to 244,180* describes the movement of a mouse from coordinate 10,10 to coordinate 244,180. It will mean this for all time. The statement *drag from x,y to a,b* could represent the generic action of dragging a mouse from one point to another. One only needs to know the values of the variables *a, b, x,* and *y* and then one knows what specific line the statement represents this time.

In HyperCard, variables can be named anything as long as their name starts with a letter and they are not words reserved for the names of properties or commands. Variables are called containers in HyperCard. The syntax for putting something into a container is *put 5* (or whatever quantity is desired) *into name* (or whatever the container has been called). HyperCard is arranged so that it remembers the value of a variable only for the duration of the message handler in which it is used. This is called a local variable. Chapter 14 describes the process of creating global variables that are remembered until one exits HyperCard.

For example, suppose that a symbolic container arbitrarily named *a* has been given the value 5 and a symbolic container named *b* has been given the value 3. HyperCard allocates particular areas in its memory to store these values. Anytime these names are referred to, HyperCard will return the values stored in them.

The Message Box allows testing of the ways variables work. Open the Message Box by picking the Message item in the Edit Menu or typing *command-M.* Then type the command *put 5 into a* and press the return key. Next type *put 3 into b* and press return. Then type *a+b* and press return. It will print back 8 (Figure 9.2).

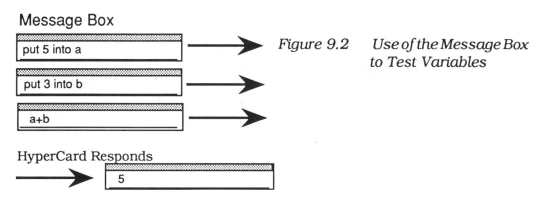

Message Box

put 5 into a

put 3 into b

a+b

Figure 9.2   *Use of the Message Box to Test Variables*

HyperCard Responds

5

Variables can also store letters. For example, *type put "happy" into emotion* and press return. Type *emotion* (the name of the container) into the Message Box. HyperCard tries to find the value of whatever is typed into the Message Box. It will thus retrieve the present value of the container called *emotion,* so it will return back *happy* into the Message Box. It will print *happy.*

If another symbolic name is typed into the Message Box that hasn't had a value assigned to it, HyperCard will have a problem. It will not find the symbolic name of the variable in memory and will return an error message to you: *can't understand (variable name).* Figure 9.3 shows the result of typing an unknown word.

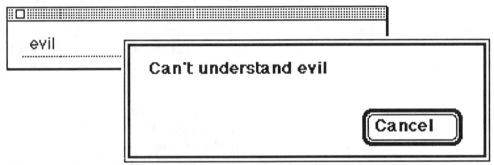

• Typing a word HyperCard does not understand results in the Can't Understand Dialog Box.
• Variables must have been assigned values with *put (value) into (variable name)* before being used. HyperCard thinks "evil" is a variable name that has not yet received a value.

9.3   "Can't Understand" Dialog Box

The *repeat with* Command

The great value of containers in creating graphics programs will become apparent with more work in programming. Several other forms of the repeat command exist besides *repeat for.* These can use information about which repeat cycle is currently active and can control the number of repeats by checking for test situations. That is, they keep doing it until some condition is fulfilled.

The *repeat with* command uses a counter variable to keep track of how many times it should do something. For example, *repeat with n = 1 to 9* means it will do something 9 times and add 1 to the value of a variable called *n* each time. The changing value of *n* in the loop can then be used to create other visual effects. For example, consider a graphics program that draws a series of lines. Without a repeat command, one would need to script separate command lines to draw each line. A repeat loop can automate this process. Figure 9.4 shows a button script to draw a fan. Remember that there are 512 horizontal positions across the screen.

In this script, a loop is created using the *repeat with* command. The *repeat with* starts with *x = 1* and counts up to the time when *x = 512*. The variable *x* keeps count. The first time through it is equal to 1; the second time, 2; and so on. The *repeat with* automatically takes care of adding 1 each time and checking whether the final number is reached yet. When *x* finally becomes equal to 512, the script goes on to the next command in the script, which is *end mouseUp.*

This script also uses the *x* variable to specify the starting point for each line. The basic action line inside the script is *drag from x,0 to 256,300.* The 256,300 coordinate was chosen because it is halfway across the screen and at the bottom. Visually, a series of lines drawn from every point on the top of the screen to this point would appear like a fan. Thus, the variable is doing double duty: It counts, and it also specifies the horizontal coordinate of the starting point.

The first time through the loop, HyperCard encounters the command *drag from x,0 to 256,340.* It interprets *x* as the name of a container variable and goes to its memory to see if it knows the value of *x*. The repeat loop has automatically given it the value 1. HyperCard substitutes the current value of *x* (which is 1) for *x* and drags from 1,0 to 262,340. Next time it substitutes the new current value for *x* (which is 2) and drags from 2,0 to 256,340. Eventually lines are drawn from all points along the top of the screen stretching from horizontal coordinate 1 to horizontal coordinate 512.

Figure 9.4 illustrates this fan repeat script and another slightly different script that draws 512 vertical lines filling the screen. The only difference in the second script is that the coordinates of the endpoint also use the variable — that is, *drag from x,0 to x,340.* The horizontal position of the second coordinate changes with the first one; both use the variable *x*.

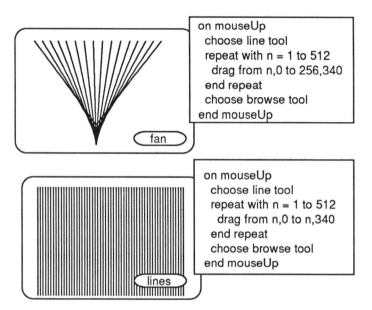

Figure 9.4   Use of the repeat with Command

Other variables can be used in a script in conjunction with the counter of the repeat loop, enabling the user to gain much more control. For example, assume that one wanted the parallel lines to be spaced apart from each other — say, every 5 pixels. First, one would need to figure out how many lines would be needed to fill the 512-pixel space. This fraction's value is 512/5 = 102 . Thus, one would need a repeat loop with 102 repeats in order to draw 102 lines spaced 5 pixels across. A script in this situation could use *repeat for* or *repeat with n = 1 to 102.*

Inside the loop, something is needed to adjust the starting position of the line. The counter of the loop won't work because it counts from 1 to 512 by ones. Something is needed to jump 5 each time. Another variable, called *horiz,* can be used to represent the horizontal starting position. The name given is arbitrary, but it is often useful to give variables names that relate to their actions. Each time through the loop, the script will change the value of *horiz.*

The script uses a command line *put horiz+5 into horiz*, an expression that may seem strange.   When HyperCard sees this line, it retrieves the current value of the container called *horiz*, adds 5 more to it, and stores the new value. Then it draws a new line starting at the new horizontal position. Visually adding 5 each time creates 5 white spaces between each line. The amount of white space can be altered easily by changing the amount the

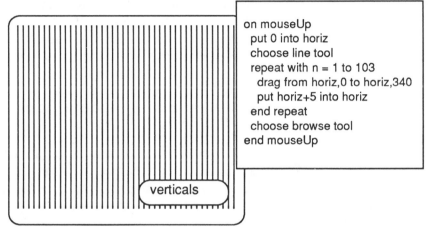

```
on mouseUp
  put 0 into horiz
  choose line tool
  repeat with n = 1 to 103
    drag from horiz,0 to horiz,340
    put horiz+5 into horiz
  end repeat
  choose browse tool
end mouseUp
```

verticals

*Figure 9.5   Script to Create Verticals Using a Variable to Control
                Horizontal Position*

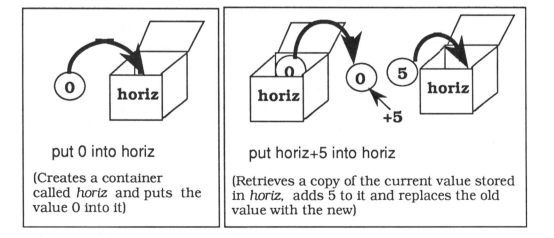

put 0 into horiz

(Creates a container called *horiz* and puts the value 0 into it)

put horiz+5 into horiz

(Retrieves a copy of the current value stored in *horiz*, adds 5 to it and replaces the old value with the new)

Figure 9.6   How Variables Work

script adds each time. *The command put horiz+10 into horiz* would result in a series of lines 10 spaces apart. Notice also that since straight vertical lines are desired, the changing horizontal coordinate called *horiz* must be the same in both the start and the finish coordinates.

The analysis performed to write this script produced a computer algorithm. First, there was an idea — parallel vertical lines 5 spaces apart. Next, a way was devised to accomplish the idea within the limitations of a particular programming language, since a computer requires instructions to be stated precisely, using the vocabulary it understands (semantics) in the exact order it understands (syntax). Other computer languages would require other words, but the fundamental approach would be the same. As it stands now, HyperCard uses more English-like commands than many computer languages. Eventually, computer systems may understand plain human languages.

This artificial intelligence goal, however, has turned out to be difficult to realize because everyday human discourse is more complex than it first appears. We use many elliptical shortcuts in speech and fill in the unstated with common sense. Endowing a computer system with that common sense has so far proved impossible*.

Later, it will become evident that there are many other approaches to creating parallel lines; This phenomenon is called equifinality in computer jargon, and it refers to the fact that many programs can produce the same end state. The wider philosophical implications of this notion are interesting. For example, a Zen master is reported to have said, "There are many paths to the top of the mountain, but the view is always the same."

To accomplish complex actions, it is almost always useful to break them down into simpler parts. In this situation, the complex outcome is a whole screen full of lines. The simplest component is just one line. A good rule of thumb for the development of computer algorithms is to figure out how to do one basic action and then build on that.

* For more details, see Stephen Wilson, *Fleshing Out Artificial Intelligence* (unpublished, 1989); Herbert Dreyfus, *What Computers Can't Do* (Free Press, 1982); Roger Schank, *Cognitive Computer* (Addison Wesley, 1987); and John Haugeland, Artificial Intelligence (MIT Press, 86).

The command to draw one vertical line in HyperCard is: *Drag from horiz, top to horiz, bottom.* This means to start at some horizontal position at the top and draw to the same horizontal position at the bottom. If one changed the horizontal position of the end relative to the beginning, one would end up with a line that was not strictly vertical. All of these symbolic names need values, but the names were used to make sure the core concepts were clear.

On the HyperCard screen, the coordinate of the top is 0. The coordinate of the bottom is 340. Because in this example we want vertical lines that always start at the top and end at the bottom, these values will stay the same throughout the loop. If we wanted lines that started in the middle of the screen instead of the top, we could substitute some other value — for example, 160 — for the 0.

In continuing to develop this algorithm, one would ask the next question derived from visual analysis of the desired result. If the horizontal position does not change each time the repeat loop operates, one would end up with only one line. The repeat loop would keep drawing the same line. The visual outcome desired is lines 5 spaces apart. Horizontally, the script must move the starting and ending point 5 units each time through the loop. In a coordinate system, one can accomplish that by adding 5 to the horizontal coordinate. In HyperCard, the words it understands to accomplish that is *put horiz+5 into horiz.* Note that the name *horiz* is arbitrary. One could call it anything as long as the script was consistent throughout.

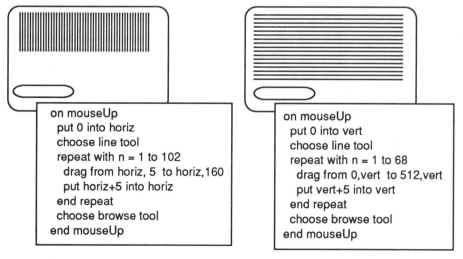

Figure 9.7   Scripts to Create Half-Screen Vertical and Horizontal Lines

Note that a loop algorithm to create parallel horizontal lines would be similar. The visual/conceptual analysis would require the same kind of thinking. What stays the same in a set of horizontal lines is the left and right ending points, not the top and bottom. In HyperCard, the left endpoint of the screen is coordinate 0 and the right endpoint is coordinate 512. The value that would change each time would be the vertical position, which could arbitrarily be called *vert*. The variable *vert* would be the one that had something added each time.

For this example, assume 5 spaces again. One would need to figure out how many horizontal lines 5 spaces apart would fit onto the screen. Since there are 340 pixels vertically, this would be 340/5 = 68. One could use the *repeat with* loop again.

The *repeat until* and *repeat while* Commands

The HyperCard commands *repeat until* and *repeat while* offer a way to avoid calculations. These commands do not repeat for a prespecified number of times as in the previous examples. Rather they repeat until some particular specified condition is met. For example, a script could tell the loop to keep generating horizontal lines until the vertical position was beyond the limits of the screen or to keep generating lines while the vertical position is less than that limit. Of course, one would need to translate these ideas into expressions that HyperCard can understand. Since the vertical coordinate at the bottom of the screen is 340, a repeat loop could check for that condition. HyperCard uses the standard mathematical symbols > (greater than) and < (less than). Thus, the loop should keep adding 5 *while vert < 341* or *until vert > 340*. These two statements are roughly equivalent. Figure 9.8 illustrates three almost equivalent scripts.

Multiple Loops: Sequential

Scripts can contain more than one loop. Combining these two loops for vertical lines and horizontal lines would result in a button that creates a grid (Figure 9.9).

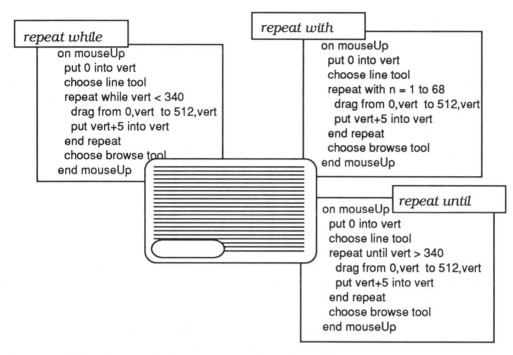

repeat while

```
on mouseUp
  put 0 into vert
  choose line tool
  repeat while vert < 340
    drag from 0,vert to 512,vert
    put vert+5 into vert
  end repeat
  choose browse tool
end mouseUp
```

repeat with

```
on mouseUp
  put 0 into vert
  choose line tool
  repeat with n = 1 to 68
    drag from 0,vert to 512,vert
    put vert+5 into vert
  end repeat
  choose browse tool
end mouseUp
```

repeat until

```
on mouseUp
  put 0 into vert
  choose line tool
  repeat until vert > 340
    drag from 0,vert to 512,vert
    put vert+5 into vert
  end repeat
  choose browse tool
end mouseUp
```

Figure 9.8   Three Almost Equivalent Scripts Using Different Repeat Commands to Draw Horizontal Lines

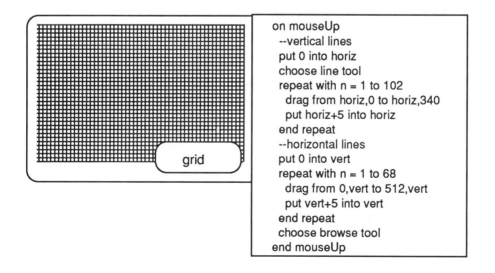

```
on mouseUp
  --vertical lines
  put 0 into horiz
  choose line tool
  repeat with n = 1 to 102
    drag from horiz,0 to horiz,340
    put horiz+5 into horiz
  end repeat
  --horizontal lines
  put 0 into vert
  repeat with n = 1 to 68
    drag from 0,vert to 512,vert
    put vert+5 into vert
  end repeat
  choose browse tool
end mouseUp
```

Figure 9.9   Script to Create a Grid Using Two Sequential Repeat Loops

Multiple Loops: Nested

Another set of examples will demonstrate the power of the repeat loop. If the goal is to create a set of six repeating ovals or rectangles, even though one could write a script with each command line creating one oval, a repeat loop allows an elegant automation of the process. Again, one would need to develop a programming approach by analyzing the goal idea visually, breaking it into simpler parts, and then translating those desires into commands that HyperCard can understand. Figure 9.11 illustrates these loops.

The commands to draw an oval require one to choose the oval tool and then drag from the upper left corner to the lower right corner. A repeat loop would need to do the oval action six times. The actions to draw one oval would be: *Chose oval tool, drag from upper left corner to lower right corner.* To translate for HyperCard, one would have to give it specific coordinates for the upper left corner and lower right corners, for example, *drag from 50,50 to 80,70* (Figure 9.10).

This works fine for one oval but would not work for a set of six ovals. Assuming that one visually wanted the ovals to be side by side horizontally, one would need to arrange to change the horizontal position each time the

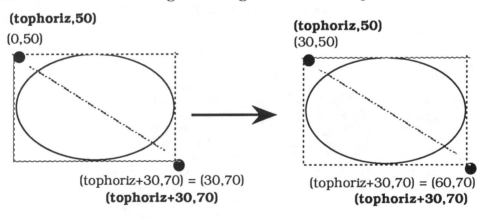

The command *put tophoriz+30 into tophoriz*
changes the starting point for the next oval.

*Figure 9.10   Use of a Variable to Describe a Generic Oval 30 Pixels Wide
and 20 Pixels High (starting at vertical position 50)*

loop repeated. Thus, the horizontal position of the upper left and lower right corners must be expressed as variables, i.e, values that can change. The vertical positions of both corners should stay constant if one wants all the ovals to line up — for this example, assume the tops at vertical coordinate 50 and the bottoms at vertical coordinate 70. The command to create one oval using variables for the horizontal positions could be expressed as *drag from tophoriz,50 to lowhoriz,70*. The names *tophoriz* and *lowhoriz* are fairly descriptive.

The horizontal position of the tops and bottoms are not really independent, however. Since all the ovals are to be the same size, the mouse will be dragged the same amount each time. In this example, the ovals are to extend 30 pixels in the horizontal direction. If one wanted all the ovals

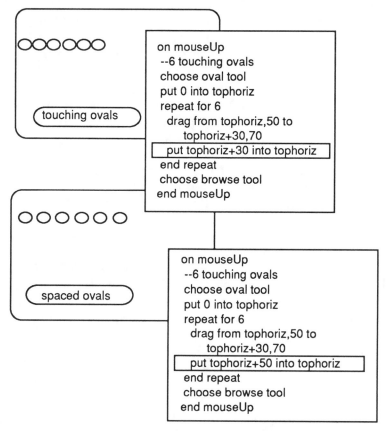

Figure 9.11   Scripts to Create Six Touching and Six Spaced Ovals

to fit on the screen, one would need to be sure that six ovals 30 pixels across could fit. One needs to calculate mentally to see if 6 times 30 will be less than the 512 pixels horizontal size of the screen. All the ovals should do the same. The bottom horizontal position is always going to be 30 more across than the top horizontal position. One needs to find a symbolic way to express that fact. The expression *tophoriz+30* captures that idea. The prototype oval drawing command could be written *drag from tophoriz,50 to tophoriz+30,70.*

Now this command is ready to be used in a loop. Since this example simply calls for six ovals, one could use a *repeat for 6* command. Again, the other repeat commands could be used as well if the script were arranged correctly. The script would need to initialize the variable *tophoriz* to indicate the starting position. In this example, a value of 0 is chosen. Then the *choose oval tool* command would tell HyperCard what the following actions are to be. A *repeat for* loop would be set up. Inside the loop the *drag* command would create an oval using the variables *tophoriz* and *tophoriz+30* to define the horizontal coordinates of the top and bottom. Then a *put tophoriz + 30 into tophoriz* command would need to move *tophoriz* for the next time through the loop. Note that selection of *+30* ensures that the ovals would just touch. Choice of movement less than 30 would make overlapping ovals and choice of movement more than 30 would leave space between.

The previous grid example in Figure 9.9 demonstrated the use of two consecutive loops. Placing one loop inside another can also serve useful purposes. This kind of structure is called nested loops. One could for example create three lines of the six ovals above to create a grid of 18 ovals.

Once more, the problem is solved by partialization. For example, the algorithm for six ovals was built on the commands for one oval. Similarly, this script can be built on this derived script. What would need to change in the example above to get the ovals to move vertically? The way it works now, the vertical position of each oval is fixed by the number coordinate values 50 and 70, which stay constant throughout the loop. Those ovals are never going to be able to move vertically if these are always fixed numbers.

Just as with the six oval example, one can prepare to allow something to change by substituting variable containers for fixed numbers (Figure 9.13). Here, the name *topvert* can be substituted for the 50. As before, a

totally different name could be substituted for the bottom vertical coordinate, but that would not represent the relationship of the bottom to the top.
In this example, the bottom coordinate is always 20 more than the top (e.g.
70-50). This is the nature of the ovals used in this example. That abstract

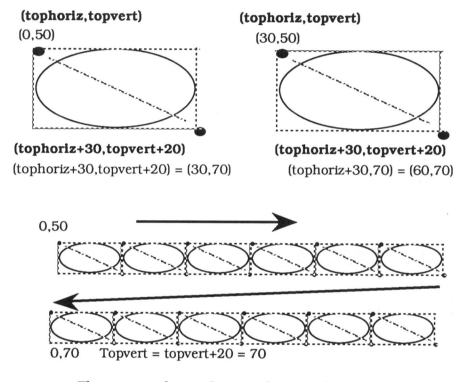

- The commands *put 0 into tophoriz* and *put 50 into
  topvert* initialize these values.

- The command *put tophoriz+30 into tophoriz*
  changes the starting point for the next oval. *Topvert*
  stays the same.

- The command *put topvert+20 into topvert*
  changes the vertical starting point for the new
  row. *Tophoriz* is set back to 0.

*Figure 9.12   Use of a Variable to Describe a Generic Oval 30 Pixels Wide
and 20 Pixels High in a Nested Loop*

relationship can be represented by giving the bottom coordinate a value based on the top — *tophoriz+20*. Thus, the prototypical command line to draw one oval that can move horizontally and vertically is *drag from tophoriz,topvert to tophoriz+30,topvert+20*.

Now this command can be put into nested loops to create the set of 18. Again, one needs to make a visual/conceptual decision before proceeding. Should the program draw three rows of horizontal ovals or six columns of vertical ovals? One needs to decide in order to proceed. Building on the earlier example, this example will assume three rows of horizontal ovals. Figure 9.13 demonstrates both.

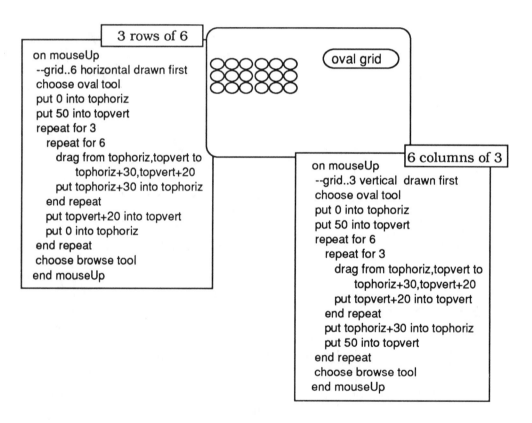

Figure 9.13   Scripts to Create Six by Three Grid of Ovals

Nested loops work by finishing inner loops entirely before proceeding to outer loops. In the first part of Figure 9.13, the *repeat for 6* is the inner loop. Figure 9.14 shows the scripts and the flowchart and the inner dialog that HyperCard might have as it proceeds through this script.

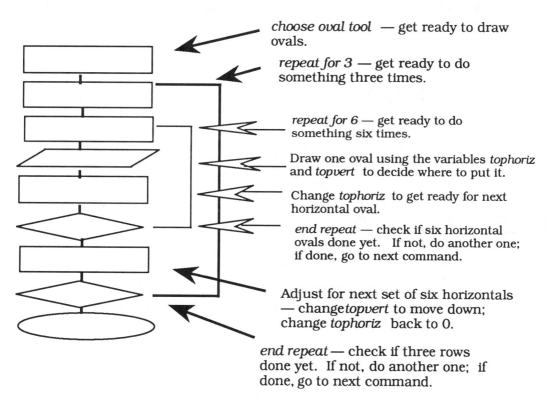

choose oval tool — get ready to draw ovals.

repeat for 3 — get ready to do something three times.

repeat for 6 — get ready to do something six times.

Draw one oval using the variables *tophoriz* and *topvert* to decide where to put it.

Change *tophoriz* to get ready for next horizontal oval.

end repeat — check if six horizontal ovals done yet. If not, do another one; if done, go to next command.

Adjust for next set of six horizontals — change *topvert* to move down; change *tophoriz* back to 0.

end repeat — check if three rows done yet. If not, do another one; if done, go to next command.

Figure 9.14   Flowchart Analysis of a Nested Loop to Draw Ovals

Loops to Change Properties

Generally, anything that has a value can be expressed in a variable and be changed in a loop. For example, the pattern used in drawing a filled image is set by the property called *the pattern*. Recall that it can take a value from 1 to 40. The following example demonstrates the drawing of six horizontal rectangles that each are filled with a different pattern. It is built on the previous examples.

This script differs from the original in three ways: It draws rectangles instead of ovals by choosing the rectangle tool, it arranges to draw filled rectangles by setting *the filled* property to *true*, and it changes *the pattern* property by changing a variable called *pat* to a different number each time.

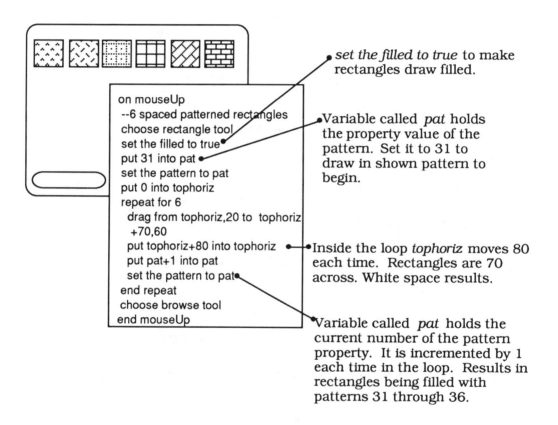

set *the filled to true* to make rectangles draw filled.

Variable called *pat* holds the property value of the pattern. Set it to 31 to draw in shown pattern to begin.

Inside the loop *tophoriz* moves 80 each time. Rectangles are 70 across. White space results.

Variable called *pat* holds the current number of the pattern property. It is incremented by 1 each time in the loop. Results in rectangles being filled with patterns 31 through 36.

```
on mouseUp
  --6 spaced patterned rectangles
  choose rectangle tool
  set the filled to true
  put 31 into pat
  set the pattern to pat
  put 0 into tophoriz
  repeat for 6
    drag from tophoriz,20 to  tophoriz
    +70,60
    put tophoriz+80 into tophoriz
    put pat+1 into pat
    set the pattern to pat
  end repeat
  choose browse tool
end mouseUp
```

Figure 9.15   Repeat Loop to Change the Pattern of a Rectangle

Loops to Do Simple Animation

Chapter 14 will discuss animation in more detail. Briefly, animation is the illusion of movement. Program scripts are ideal for the creation of animations because they execute over time. Every script example so far has created an image that grows over time — for example, the 18 ovals appearing in order.

This section offers a simple animation example to illustrate more uses for repeat loops — in this case, a line that appears to move across the screen. The core idea of horizontal movement of the line is very similar to the previous examples of drawing multiple shapes next to each other. Some variable must be used to change the horizontal coordinate.

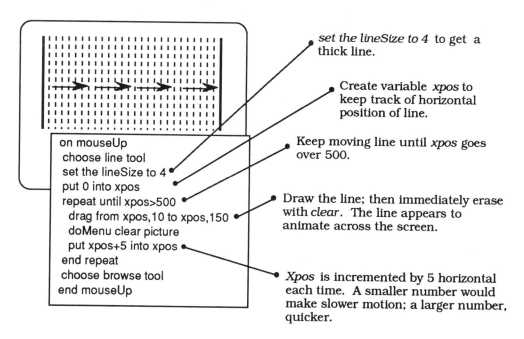

set the lineSize to 4 to get a thick line.

Create variable *xpos* to keep track of horizontal position of line.

Keep moving line until *xpos* goes over 500.

```
on mouseUp
  choose line tool
  set the lineSize to 4
  put 0 into xpos
  repeat until xpos>500
    drag from xpos,10 to xpos,150
    doMenu clear picture
    put xpos+5 into xpos
  end repeat
  choose browse tool
end mouseUp
```

Draw the line; then immediately erase with *clear*. The line appears to animate across the screen.

Xpos is incremented by 5 horizontal each time. A smaller number would make slower motion; a larger number, quicker.

Figure 9.16   Script for Simple Animation of a Line

The script must be different, however, in that one line must disappear before the next one appears in order to give the illusion of motion. The script in Figure 9.16 accomplishes that by arranging to draw a black line by setting the pattern to 12 (black), drawing the line, changing the pattern to white (pattern 0), and then drawing the line in the same position. Because the background is white, the line will seem to disappear. If this is done quickly enough, the line will appear to be moving. This script moves the line 5 pixels at a time; any other values could be chosen, depending on the animation desired. Also, this script uses a thick line by setting *the lineSize* to 4 so that the line can be seen better.

The repeat concept is very powerful in visual and audio work. The computer shows its unique power in repeating forms. Many visual and sound compositions are built out of repeating forms. Since computer loops do not have to repeat the exact forms mindlessly, planned variations can be introduced.

CHAPTER 10
CARDS, BACKGROUNDS, VISUAL EFFECT TRANSITIONS, NAVIGATION THROUGH STACKS, AND ANIMATION

Conceptual Structures for the Organization of Information

Many HyperCard users focus on creating cards (the basic information unit) and stacks (compilations of cards) rather than becoming involved with other programming activities. For them, interactivity is achieved by allowing users to move flexibly through a collection of cards. The broadest design potential, however, is achieved through the combination of programming and navigation. This chapter focuses on the creation, sequencing, and navigation through cards. Also, if the reader has built all the buttons described in earlier chapters on one card, that card is now very crowded. This chapter aims to make the reader comfortable with the structure of cards and the associated commands to move around them.

A stack is a collection of cards. HyperCard stores the cards sequentially, although one can arrange for users to access the cards in non-linear ways. For example, the first card on a stack could function like a book index. It could be full of buttons that each send the user to a card that elaborates on the theme represented by the button. Another organization might provide a linear multiple-branching structure in which the choices a user made on each card lead to different sequences. Hypermedia's unique strength lies in the way that it allows the stack creator to devise the most appropriate structure for containing a particular type of information. Artists can design structures that relate to their expressive goals.

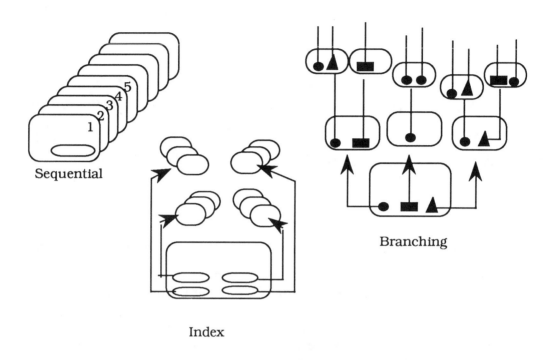

Figure 10.1   Sequential, Index, and Branching Stack Structures

Using the Card Commands in HyperCard: New Card, Cut Card, Copy Card, and Delete Card

The Edit Menu allows access to the commands related to card manipulation. New Card inserts a new card right after the one displayed on the screen and moves to display that new blank card. HyperCard numbers each card in the stack. Thus, if one were looking at card 2 of a four card stack and created a new card, that new card would become number 3, and old 3 would become 4, and the old 4 would become 5.

The command Delete Card gets rid of the currently displayed card and adjusts the numbers appropriately. The command Cut Card takes the currently displayed card away but puts it into the temporary memory clipboard, from which it can be retrieved to be pasted in the same or different

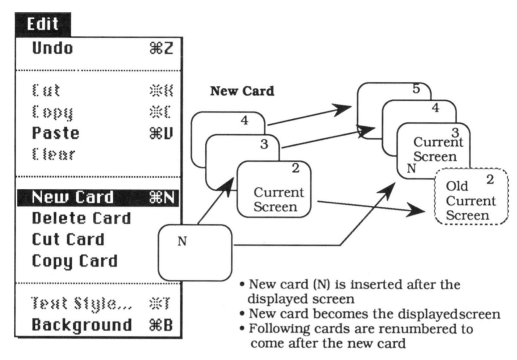

Figure 10.2   Process of Creating a New Card

stack. Again the sequence of cards is adjusted for the disappearance of the card. Copy Card puts a copy of the current card into the clipboard, but does not erase the presently displayed card.

Once a card has been cut or copied, the Paste Card command becomes active. Pasting a card will insert it immediately after the currently displayed card. These commands make it easy for the user to resequence and reuse cards. As mentioned previously, the object-oriented nature of HyperCard means that objects such as cards and buttons can be reused in many different situations.

To illustrate these and the following navigation commands, the reader is urged to create a series of cards with drawn numbers on them similar to the example. Choose the New Stack command from the Files Menu as described in Chapter 3. Using any of the paint tools, draw a 1 on that first card that appears. Choose the New Card item from the Edit Menu. Draw a 2 on that card. Do this until there are six cards in the stack.

Navigation through Stacks and Cards

All navigation features are available for scripts as well as for the interactive hand mode. For example, one can create buttons that allow users to make decisions on the fly about what information they want to see next.

First, Last, Previous, Next, and Back Commands

The Go Menu allows a user to move around flexibly within and between stacks. The First item causes the first card in a stack to be displayed. The Last item causes the last one to be displayed. The Next item causes the one immediately preceding the present one to be displayed. Prev (for previous) displays the card immediately before the present one in the stack sequence. If one is at the beginning or end, the Next and Prev commands will wrap around — that is, the first card in the stack will be the

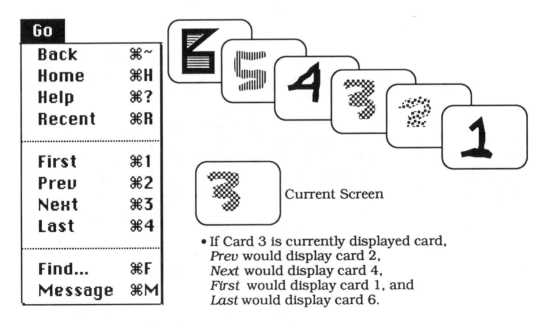

> • If Card 3 is currently displayed card,
>   *Prev* would display card 2,
>   *Next* would display card 4,
>   *First* would display card 1, and
>   *Last* would display card 6.

Figure 10.3   Go Menu: First, Prev, Next, Last

next one after the last card. Back displays the last card displayed even if it wasn't in the same stack.   Each of these have command key shortcuts. Also, the arrow keys on the keyboard allow movement forward and backward through the sequence.

Recent

The Recent item provides a quick visual summary of up to the last 42 cards that have been displayed. It presents miniaturized visual displays of cards aligned in rows of six by seven. A user can gain quick access to any of the cards merely by clicking on the small image of the desired card.

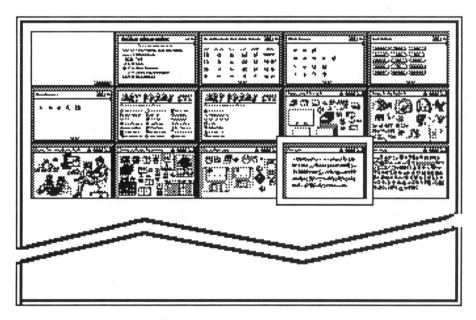

Figure 10.4   Hypercard's Recent Dialog Box Showing Miniaturized Versions of the Last Cards Displayed

HyperCard responds by moving to that card. As expansions in computer capability allow access to increasingly larger bodies of information (for example, through CD ROM and network linkages), development of visually strong and clear methods of navigation such as the Recent display will become increasingly important.

Help

The Help item gives immediate access to the special Help Stack that comes with HyperCard. This stack provides definitions and examples of HyperCard features and commands. Unfortunately, it takes up a lot of disk storage space. The Help item works only if the Help Stack is present. If a system has no hard disk storage, there is often not enough room for this stack. The Home item takes the user back to the original home card of the Home Stack with which HyperCard was started up.

HyperCard works best in a system with much internal and external memory. It makes assumptions about the user's environment: Its information model is based on the notion that users should be able to access any card in any stack instantaneously. It makes the details of stack location invisible if the creator of the environment desires. Indeed, some stacks are being distributed commercially that will not work without a hard disk. Unfortunately, many users are still working with systems that don't meet these memory requirements. This book takes that limitation into account, although readers should be aware that sometimes HyperCard might get lost looking for something that is not available such as the Help Stack. HyperCard comes back with a "Where Is" Dialog Box (Figure 10.5).

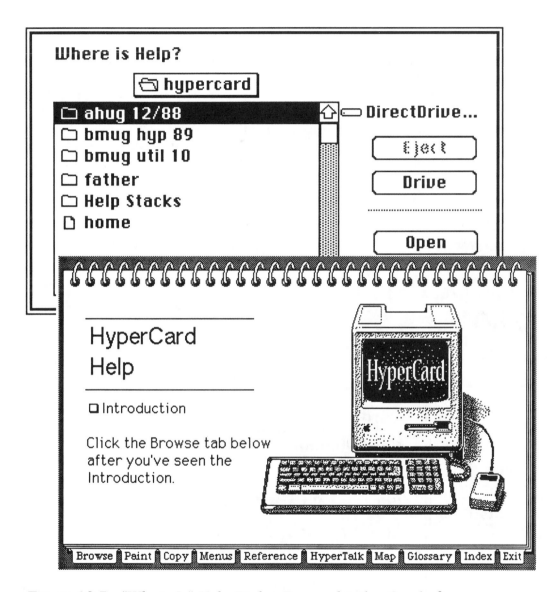

Figure 10.5   *"Where Is" Help Dialog Box and Index Card of*
                  Hypercard's Help Stack

Card Characteristics

To accomplish free-form navigation, there must be ways to identify specific stacks and cards. Each stack is given a name at its creation. Cards can be identified in several ways. Like buttons, each card is given a sequence number depending on where it stands in the stack. Each card is also given a unique Card ID number. Finally, each card can be given a name at any time via the Card Information Dialog Box (Figure 10.6). To get access to this box, select the Card Info item in the Objects Menu while a specific card is displayed.

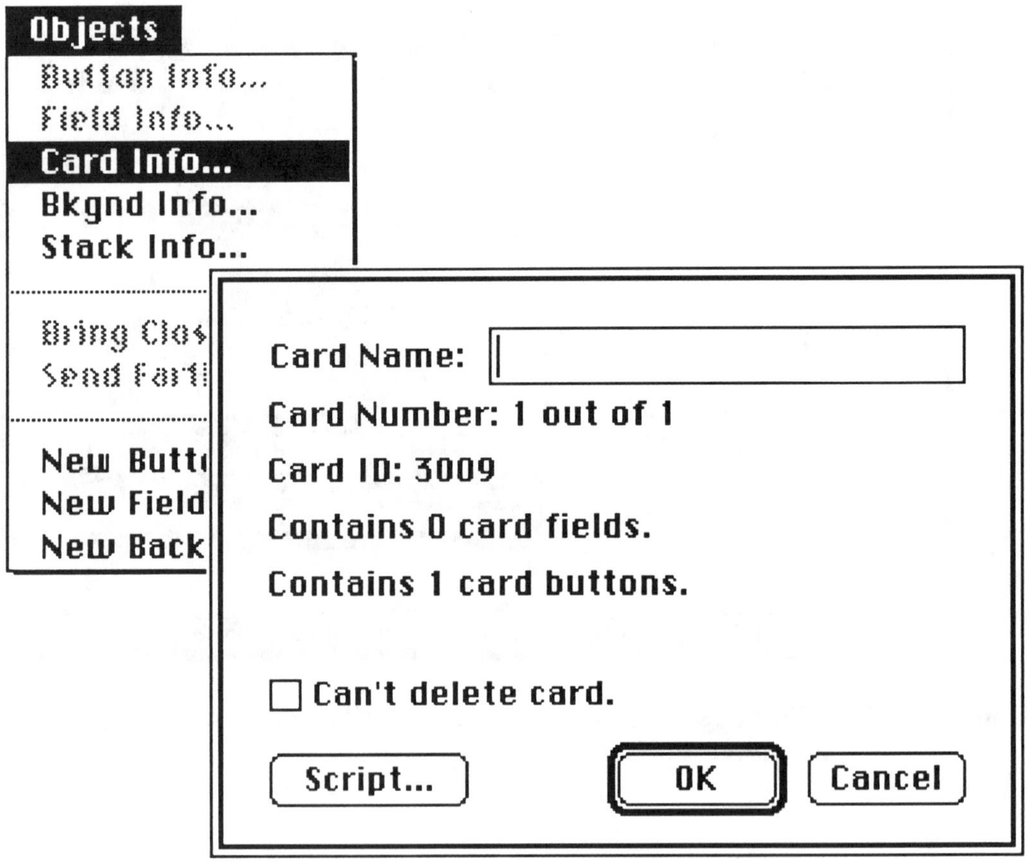

Objects

Button Info...
Field Info...
Card Info...
Bkgnd Info...
Stack Info...

Bring Clos
Send Far1

New Butt
New Field
New Back

Card Name: [   ]

Card Number: 1 out of 1

Card ID: 3009

Contains 0 card fields.

Contains 1 card buttons.

☐ Can't delete card.

(Script...)   ((OK))   (Cancel)

Figure 10.6   Objects Menu and Card Information Dialog Box

This dialog box allows typing of a name. It also shows the card sequence number, and the unique ID number. Further, it displays the number of buttons and fields that are contained on the card. One can also toggle the *can't delete* property. If that property is set, the card cannot be deleted by the Delete Card command without resetting the toggle. The dialog box also gives access to the Script Creation Box to attach message handlers to this card. One must click OK to confirm a change of name or *can't delete* property.

Scripts for Navigation Through Cards: The *go* Command

One can easily create buttons that facilitate easy navigation through the cards in stacks. The sample HyperCard stacks provided by Apple even adopt a series of conventions for navigation buttons (Figure 10.7). The arrow icons are attached to buttons with scripts to go to the next and previous card. The house icon takes the user back to the home stack.

Figure 10.7 shows simple scripts for navigation. The *go* command followed by a word telling where to go is the required syntax — for example, *go to next card, go to previous card, go to first card, go to last card.* On all of these, the words *to* and *card* can be dropped. In addition, *go back, go home, go help,* and *go recent* all do the same as the corresponding menu items.

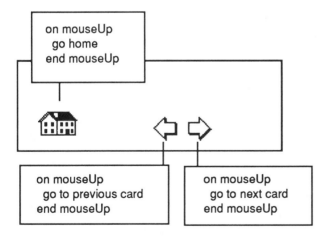

```
on mouseUp
  go home
end mouseUp
```

```
on mouseUp
  go to previous card
end mouseUp
```

```
on mouseUp
  go to next card
end mouseUp
```

Figure 10.7   Standard HyperCard Buttons and Their Scripts

Often one needs to control navigation to cards other than the first and the last. The *go* command can specify the target by the sequential number, the unique ID number, or the card name. The *go* command can use ordinal words also such as *first, second, third,* and so on up to *tenth.* It can also use the words *last, any,* and *middle. Any* picks a random card. Chapter 5 discussed the automatic *LinkTo* feature of buttons, which uses the unique ID. A *go* command must list the name of the stack also if the card is in a different stack than the currently displayed card. The following are valid *go* commands:

> *go card 4*   *go card ID 13243*
> *go card "Circles"*   *go third card*
> *go last card*   *go middle card*
> *go any card*
> *go card 5 of stack "examples"*

Generally, it is recommended that script writers develop their own unique naming scheme for cards in order to have precise control. The sequential numbers and ordinal names can change as cards are added and deleted from a stack, and the unique ID number does not give someone reading a script as much information as a name.

Figure 10.8 illustrates how buttons might work in a simple script. Assume a stack of cards that do simple animations of geometric forms. The stack starts with an index card. Each of the cards gives users a further choice about what to see next. The cards are arbitrarily named. The index card has buttons that lead to each of the other cards. Each of those cards has a button to return to the index.

Animation

The section on repeat loops introduced a simple kind of animation. This section continues that discussion. Animation depends on a characteristic of human sight called persistence of vision. The retina holds a virtual image of what the eye has seen for a fraction of a second after the original object is gone. Thus, a series of discrete images presented will appear to produce continuous motion if the images are presented fast enough. If they are presented too slowly, the eye will perceive a flicker. Animation is an optical illusion.

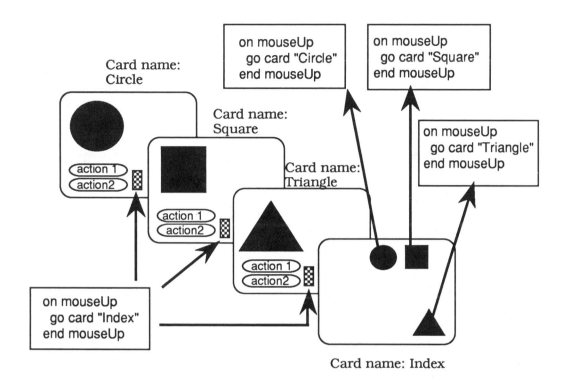

Figure 10.8   Sample Stack with Buttons for Navigation

Cinema normally presents images at the rate of 24 frames a second. Inspection of movie film clearly shows the discrete images that make up the illusion.   Standard broadcast TV presents images at the rate of 30 per second. These rates are fast enough to create convincing illusions.

Film animation, such as that in cartoons, is created by photographing a series of images one at a time on a copy stand. Conventionally, these have been drawn on clear film. They are then projected at normal speed to produce the illusion of motion. The individual drawings are called cels and the process is called cel animation. One can see simple examples of these effects in children's flip books and rotoscopes.

The sophisticated computer graphics animations of commercial films are produced in a similar way. Instead of being drawn, each frame is rendered on a computer. Each complex, textured 3-D image can take an half hour or more to compose. Once the image is rendered, an animation

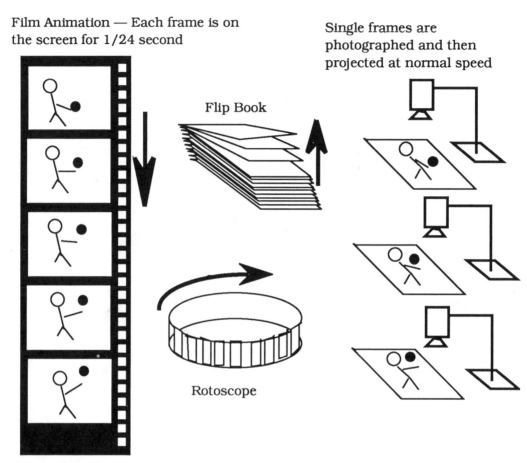

Film Animation — Each frame is on the screen for 1/24 second

Single frames are photographed and then projected at normal speed

Flip Book

Rotoscope

Figure 10.9   Traditional Techniques of Animation

camera automatically takes a picture of the one frame and the process starts again. Since a one-minute commercial is composed of 1440 frames (24 frames each second times 60 seconds), this process can take a long time — 1440 half hours or thirty 24-hour days. For more on this process see my book, *Using Computers to Create Art*.

Careful analysis of the desired motion is an essential preliminary step to creating animations. One needs to decide how much change is appropriate in each frame transition in order to create convincing motion. Indeed, Edward Muybridge's experimental photographic analysis of motion in the nineteenth century was a major impetus to the film and animation industry.

Animation in HyperCard

A computer graphics system such as HyperCard offers several options for creating animations. As mentioned previously, a graphics-oriented script is intrinsically animation of sorts because the image unfolds over time as each command does its work. More explicit animation can be created by alternating drawing and erasing motions to create the appearance of motion. For simple shapes, HyperCard is quick enough to do this process within the limits of human persistence of vision. Complex images will flicker, however.

This kind of animation is called real-time animation. Many people working in computer graphics await the day when computers are fast enough to animate complex images in real time. For now, one must use specialized programs such as Videoworks™ (described in a later chapter), which are optimized for the accelerating drawing and redrawing process. There is even a special program that will allow use within HyperCard of animations created in Videoworks.

HyperCard offers another kind of animation that is close to that used in film. Here, one can prepare a sequence of cards in which each card represents the appearance of some moving image a fraction of a second later. A script can be written to cycle through the cards, creating the appearance of animation.

A simple example (Figure 10.10) of a man waving his arm will be used to illustrate card-based animation. Assume that there is a series of five cards, each with the hand in a slightly different position. A button on the first script will activate a series of *go* commands that will move from card to card.

Even this simple example illustrates important features of animation design. One needs to think carefully about what stays the same and what changes. Continual reuse of the part that stays the same as a template can save considerable drawing time. Film animators use a series of transparent cels that sit on top of each other. The part that stays the same remains on the bottom, and only the cel with the changing part is replaced for each frame's photograph. The computer graphics feature of cutting and pasting simplifies this procedure. The constant part can be cut to the clipboard and pasted on each card in the sequence. Then the changing part can be cut and pasted to the next card and modified to reflect the change that occurred during the fraction of a second.

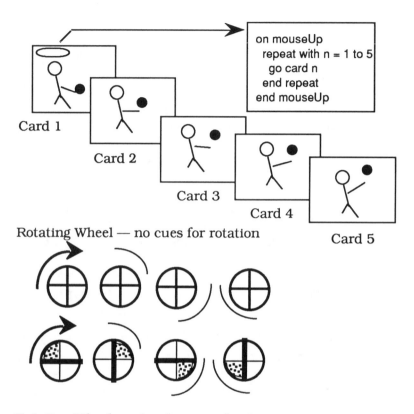

```
on mouseUp
  repeat with n = 1 to 5
    go card n
  end repeat
end mouseUp
```

Card 1

Card 2

Card 3

Card 4

Card 5

Rotating Wheel — no cues for rotation

Rotating Wheel — visual cues indicate movement

Figure 10.10   Animation Using Card Sequences —
Visual Cues for Animation

One needs to simplify the designs to highlight motion. Components must be designed to give cues about their motion. For example, a circle will not necesarily look like a rotating wheel. Making the wheel an irregular shape or putting in varied spokes will give the required cues.

Visual Effects Transitions

In silent movies, scene changes were often indicated via visual conventions of transitions. For example, the scene with the heroine tied to the train track would be ended with an iris closing in. The next scene would be started with an iris opening out, to reveal the hero searching for the heroine. Other conventions such as wipes indicated time passing.

HyperCard offers an automatic set of these visual effects that can be used as programs move from card to card. That is, instead of having the screen display one card and then pop-display another, one can chose the way the visual display moves from one to another. These effects add an animation effect even to simple transitions. The effects available in Hyper-Card are the following:

wipe up/wipe down   *scroll up/scroll down*
wipe left/wipe right   *scroll left/scroll right*
zoom open/zoom in   *zoom close/zoom open*
iris open/iris close   *dissolve*
checkerboard   *venetian blinds*
barn door open/ barn door close

These effects are activated by using the command line before the next *go* command. They do not need to be used immediately before the *go* command; HyperCard will remember and use the effect with the next *go* command it encounters. Good scripting practice would suggest that the effect command be put close to the *go* command it will effect if possible. Note that these commands will not have any visual effect if a computer's monitor settings (in the control panel) are set to anything except two-color black and white. The illustration gives some idea of what these effects are like. The syntax for the command is as follows:

visual (effect) effect name (speed) (to transition color)
go card "wave3" (substitute your card names for example)

All of the words in parentheses are optional. All that is strictly needed is the command word *visual* followed by the name of the effect. The word *effect* can be used or not. The speed specification controlling the apparent speed of the effect is optional. HyperCard assumes normal speed unless something else is indicated. Also, the transition color controlling the color of the intervening screen between transitions is optional.

The speed options available are *very slow*, *slow*, and *fast*. Color options are *to black*, *to white*, *to gray*, or *to inverse*. The following give examples of valid effects commands:

> *visual effect zoom open slow to gray*
> *visual dissolve*
> *visual barn door close to black*
> *visual effect scroll up fast*

The visual effects are a fascinating tool. Of course, as with many of HyperCard's visual capabilities, these transitions can be overused and depowered. Designers of stacks should use them only when there are visual or conceptual reasons — the transitions should interact with the content of the cards that are part of the transition. Also, stack creators can consider transitions that are symmetrical, if the content warrants. For example, buttons on an index card that zoom open to cards that give more detail may have counterpart buttons on those cards that zoom closed to go back to the index card.

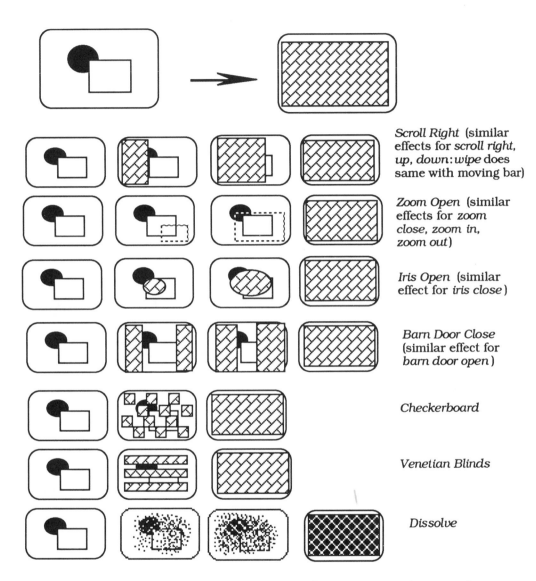

Scroll Right (similar effects for *scroll right, up, down: wipe* does same with moving bar)

Zoom Open (similar effects for *zoom close, zoom in, zoom out*)

Iris Open (similar effect for *iris close*)

Barn Door Close (similar effect for *barn door open*)

Checkerboard

Venetian Blinds

Dissolve

Figure 10.11 Visual Effects Transitions from One Card to Another

Chapter 11
Transformations of Images: The Paint Menu

Some visual transformations are especially easy to implement on computer graphics systems because of the way computers store graphics information. For example, inversion of images is easy because of the ways in which pixel color relates to values stored in memory. In a black-and-white system, digital ones in memory often represent black pixels and digital zeros represent white pixels. Inversion of an image requires a swap of ones for zeros. The screen is really a snapshot of values stored in a computer's electronic random-access memory (RAM).

Many transformations have become standard attributes of almost all computer paint programs. Artists working with computers have begun to explore the unique aesthetic potential of these transformations. HyperCard allows easy access to them via its Paint Menu.

The operation of most options requires that a user first select something that is to be transformed. That is, invert cannot operate unless the computer knows what to invert. Selection can be accomplished via use of the select rectangle and lasso on the Tools Menu (described in Chapter 6). It also can be accomplished via the Select and Select All items on the Paint Menu. As with most HyperCard menus, these features are available both in interactive hand mode and through the use of automatic scripts.

Use of the Paint Menu Options in Interactive Hand Mode: Select and Select All

The Select All command selects the entire screen. It is the same as dragging the select rectangle tool from the upper left to the lower right corner. After use of this command, any Paint Menu operation will apply to the whole screen.

Paint

| Select | ⌘S |
| Select All | ⌘A |

Fill
Invert
Pickup
Darken
Lighten
Trace Edges
Rotate Left
Rotate Right
Flip Vertical
Flip Horizontal

Opaque
Transparent

Keep
Revert

Figure 11.1   Paint Menu

The Select command works on the last item drawn on the screen. For example, if one had drawn an oval and then chose the Select item, the oval would be surrounded as though by the lasso (Figure 11.2).

Fill and Invert

The Fill command will fill the currently selected area with the current pattern. The Invert command will invert everything in the current selection — turning white pixels black and black pixels white (Figure 11.3).

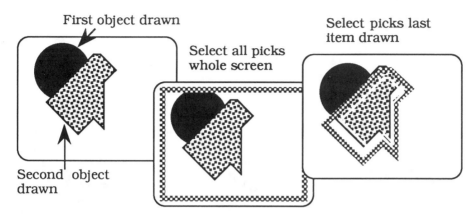

Figure 11.2   Select and Select All Commands

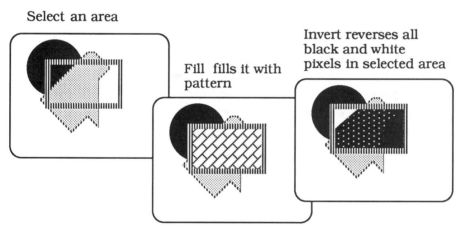

Figure 11.3   Fill and Invert Commands

Darken and Lighten

The Darken command introduces randomly spaced black dots in the selected area. The Lighten command introduces randomly spaced white dots (Figure 11.4). It takes many repeated applications of this item to turn an area totally black or white.

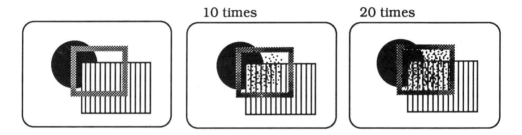

Figure 11.4   Darken Command

Rotate Left and Rotate Right

The Rotate Left and Rotate Right commands rotate the selected area in the indicated direction. Unfortunately, HyperCard is only capable of rotating in 90-degree shifts. Right moves clockwise and Left moves counter-clockwise. Because of the bit-mapped nature of HyperCard graphics, images can be rotated so that part will be cut off at the screen's edges (Figure 11.5).

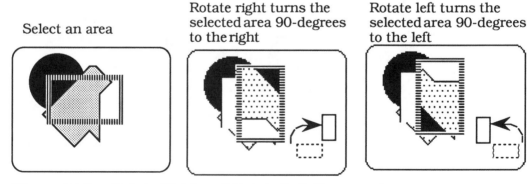

Figure 11.5   Rotate Right and Rotate Left Commands

Flip Horizontal and Flip Vertical

The Flip Horizontal command flips the selected area in the horizontal direction. The new image appears as a mirror image of the original or as the image would look if viewed from behind. Flip Vertical flips the selected area in the vertical direction (Figure 11.6).

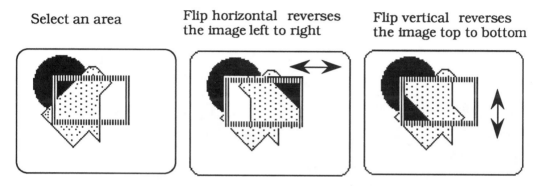

Figure 11.6   Flip Horizontal and Flip Vertical Commands

Pickup

The Pickup command will pick up a portion of an on-screen picture in any shape a user draws. That filled shape then becomes available for cutting, copying, moving, and scaling. The effect is the same as drawing a shape with the lasso tool. For example, one could draw a filled rectangle over other images and then choose Pickup. Everything under the rectangle would be selected (Figure 11.7).

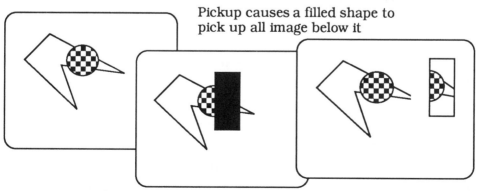

Figure 11.7   Pickup Command

Trace Edges

The Trace Edges command changes all black pixels to white and all the bordering pixels on either side to black. On simple shapes, this has the effect of creating an outline. On more complex images, its effects are more difficult to characterize. Repeated applications of this command can result

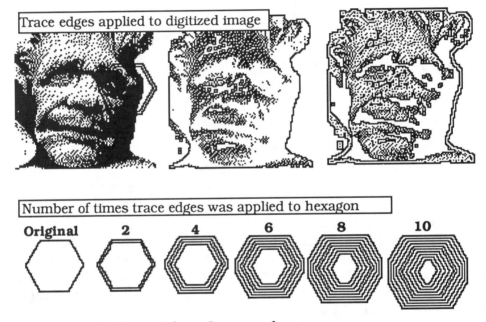

Figure 11.8   Trace Edges Command

in striking images. Sometimes they appear to be much like the photographic process of posterization (Figure 11.8).

Keep and Revert

On most operations, HyperCard automatically saves any changes to a card. With applications of paint tools, however, HyperCard does not save changes until one exits the paint tool mode or moves to another card. This feature was designed to give room for experimentation without changing the original graphic until desired. The Keep command forces HyperCard to save the present graphic to disk even while still in the paint mode. While in paint tool mode, the Revert command will restore the original graphic if the Keep command has not been used or will restore the last appearance when the Keep command was last used.

Some stack designers prefer to create several cards with different versions of a graphic instead of using these commands. That is, they create a base graphic, copy that graphic into the clipboard, create a new card, modify the graphic, create a new card, paste the original graphic, modify it in another way, and so on. One can then choose from this sketchbook full of choices rather than being forced to a decision during the process of experimentation.

Transparent and Opaque

The Transparent and Opaque commands allow control over the effect of white pixels on the screen. When in transparent mode, they allow the viewer to see the background underneath. In opaque mode, they block vision of what is beneath. The chapter on backgrounds and HyperCard's object layers will provide more details.

Scripts That Use the Paint Menu

All of the commands in the Paint Menu are available in scripts as well as interactive hand mode. Indeed, scripts are able to create effects that would be impossible by hand because they have the ability to apply certain functions repeatedly or to mix functions quickly. The following examples demonstrate some of the possibilities. Most of these make use of the *doMenu* command repeatedly applied, much as though a user had selected one of the Paint Menu items over and over.

Rotation Animation

A drawn shape or a selected area can be animated in a circular motion by repeated use of the *rotate* command. The shape must be designed carefully to clearly indicate rotation, given the limits of 90-degree rotation. In Figure 11.9 the script starts with selection of the object to be drawn via use of the *select* rectangle. The repeat loop then applies the *rotate right* command four times to give the appearance of rotation.

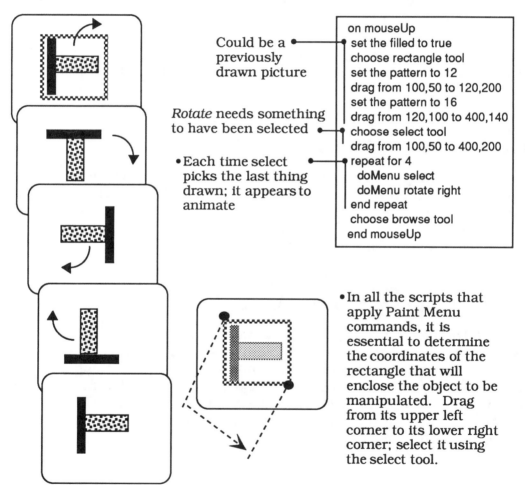

Could be a previously drawn picture

Rotate needs something to have been selected

- Each time select picks the last thing drawn; it appears to animate

```
on mouseUp
  set the filled to true
  choose rectangle tool
  set the pattern to 12
  drag from 100,50 to 120,200
  set the pattern to 16
  drag from 120,100 to 400,140
  choose select tool
  drag from 100,50 to 400,200
  repeat for 4
    doMenu select
    doMenu rotate right
  end repeat
  choose browse tool
end mouseUp
```

- In all the scripts that apply Paint Menu commands, it is essential to determine the coordinates of the rectangle that will enclose the object to be manipulated. Drag from its upper left corner to its lower right corner; select it using the select tool.

Fiigure 11.9 Script to Rotate a Selected Area

Trace Edges Animation

The *trace edges* function can bring about remarkable transformations. In hand mode, the continual need to choose the function interferes with the appearance. Figure 11.10 demonstrates an animation of the *trace edges* function within a repeat loop.

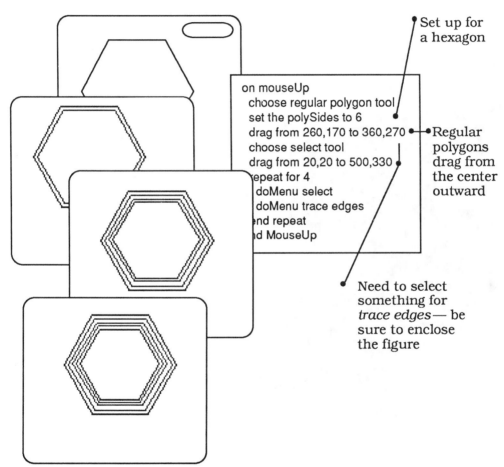

Set up for a hexagon

```
on mouseUp
  choose regular polygon tool
  set the polySides to 6
  drag from 260,170 to 360,270
  choose select tool
  drag from 20,20 to 500,330
  repeat for 4
    doMenu select
    doMenu trace edges
  end repeat
end MouseUp
```

Regular polygons drag from the center outward

Need to select something for *trace edges*— be sure to enclose the figure

Figure 11.10   Script to Animate trace edges

Darken Animation

The *darken* and *lighten* commands can cause images to appear to fade into the background. Figure 11.11 shows a script to fade an image into a black background.

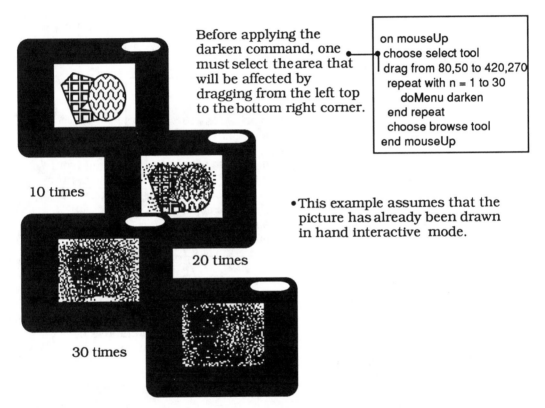

Before applying the darken command, one must select the area that will be affected by dragging from the left top to the bottom right corner.

```
on mouseUp
  choose select tool
  drag from 80,50 to 420,270
  repeat with n = 1 to 30
    doMenu darken
  end repeat
  choose browse tool
end mouseUp
```

10 times

20 times

30 times

• This example assumes that the picture has already been drawn in hand interactive mode.

Figure 11.11   Script to Animate the Darkening Process

Pickup Motion

The *pickup* command combined with *drag* commands can give the appearance of a section of the screen moving about (Figure 11.12).

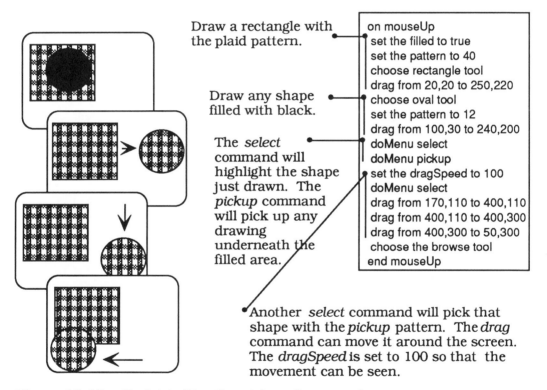

Draw a rectangle with the plaid pattern.

Draw any shape filled with black.

The *select* command will highlight the shape just drawn. The *pickup* command will pick up any drawing underneath the filled area.

```
on mouseUp
  set the filled to true
  set the pattern to 40
  choose rectangle tool
  drag from 20,20 to 250,220
  choose oval tool
  set the pattern to 12
  drag from 100,30 to 240,200
  doMenu select
  doMenu pickup
  set the dragSpeed to 100
  doMenu select
  drag from 170,110 to 400,110
  drag from 400,110 to 400,300
  drag from 400,300 to 50,300
  choose the browse tool
end mouseUp
```

Another *select* command will pick that shape with the *pickup* pattern. The *drag* command can move it around the screen. The *dragSpeed* is set to 100 so that the movement can be seen.

Figure 11.12   Script to Use the pickup Command

CHAPTER 12
BACKGROUNDS AND HYPERCARD OBJECT LAYERS

Object Layers: Buttons and Fields

For the sake of simplification, we have so far ignored certain complexities of the visual and conceptual structure of HyperCard. HyperCard keeps track of the sequential order in which objects such as buttons and fields are created. For example, the first button created on a card becomes card button 1, the second button becomes card button 2, and so on. Fields are created in the same way. Scripts can make use of this order if desired.

This hierarchical order also manifests visually and interactively. If objects overlap, the most recently created, highest-numbered object acts as though it sits on top of the others. Thus, the screen display will show non-transparent overlapping buttons in accordance with their order. Visually,

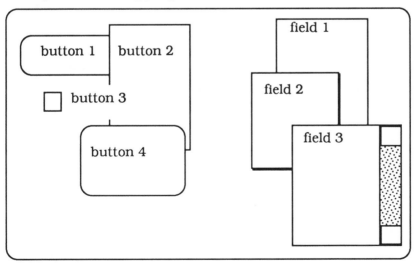

Figure 12.1   Buttons and Fields Visually Indicate Their Sequential Order

the latest buttons will seem to be sitting on top of the other buttons. This order also applies to interactive actions. A mouse click on a pile of buttons will be picked up and interpreted by the highest-numbered button.

Bring Closer and Send Further Commands

The Bring Closer and Send Further commands of the Objects Menu allow manipulation of sequential order when in button or field tool mode. Once in button or field mode, one can select a particular button or field by clicking on it. After it is selected, activation of the Bring Closer item will cause the button or field to move one up in the order. Every other button or field will adjust its sequential number. The change will be reflected both visually and interactively. For example, the newly numbered button will now overlap the button that used to be one closer. The order for buttons and for fields is maintained separately.

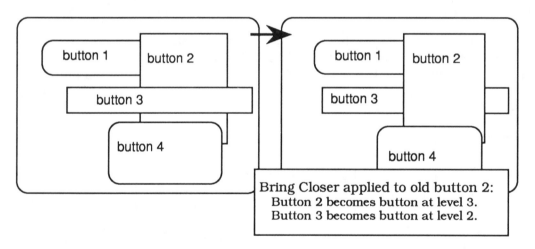

Figure 12.2   Bring Closer Command

Object Layers: Backgrounds

The fact that several cards can share a common background (briefly mentioned in Chapter 3) creates an efficient hierarchy by allowing one script handler, button, or field to service many cards. Backgrounds also introduce a level of visual complexity and potential that has not been discussed previously.

The screen display is actually a composite of two graphics — the card and the background. Since the card is displayed as being closer than the background, images and objects on the card will obscure objects on the background. Each layer can have its own collection of buttons, fields, and graphics. For example, a card button will obscure a background button sitting underneath it. Interactive actions such as a mouseclick are handled by the nearest object. Confusion is inevitable until a stack creator gets used to working with the two levels.

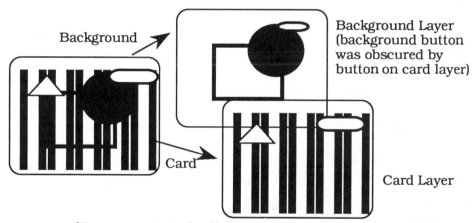

Background

Background Layer
(background button
was obscured by
button on card layer)

Card

Card Layer

(Transparent pixels allow the background to show. White pixels obscure the background. Buttons on the card layer obscure buttons and other objects on the background layer. Buttons and other objects seem to float above graphics.)

Figure 12.3   Graphics and Objects in the Background and Card Layers

Accessing the Background

HyperCard places a user into the card level by default. Special action must be taken to work on the background — for example, to create buttons or graphics. To gain access, choose the Background command from the Edit Menu or choose New Background from the Objects Menu, or press the command-B key combination. The screen display then puts a special crosshatching to indicate the background mode (Figure 12.4). Access to the card level requires reactivation of the Background command. If the user does not stay constantly aware of what level is active, actions can have unanticipated outcomes.

File   Edit   Go   Tools   Objects

Background layer indicated by crosshatching. Work on the background can only be accessed by the Background command on the Edit Menu or the New Background command on the Objects Menu.

Background Information Dialog Box. The New Card command automatically copies the background. The New Background command is the only way to create a new background.

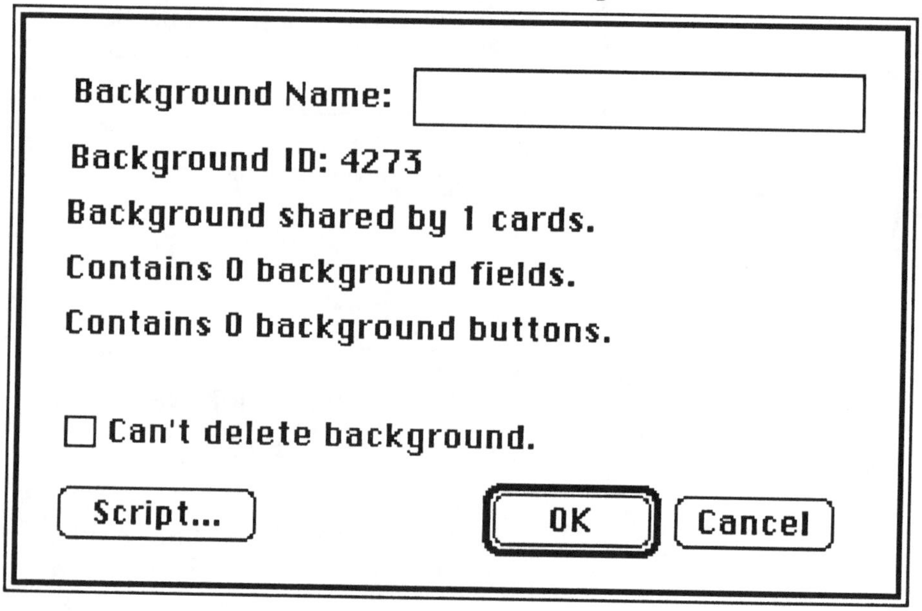

Background Name:

Background ID: 4273

Background shared by 1 cards.

Contains 0 background fields.

Contains 0 background buttons.

☐ **Can't delete background.**

[Script...]   [OK]   [Cancel]

Figure 12.4   Background Dialog Box and Crosshatch Indicator

New Background and Background Information Commands

The New Card command assumes that one wants the new card to have the same background as the previously displayed background. The only way to get a new background is through the New Background command on the Objects Menu. This item also brings up a new card to display because one can't have a new background without at least one card related to it.

As with cards, one can name the background whatever one wants and attach message handler scripts. These actions are accomplished by choosing the Background Information item on the Objects Menu. A dialog box is opened similar to the one available for card information.

Card Layer and Background Layer Graphics: Erasing

Both cards and backgrounds can have their own unique graphics. The graphics on the card layer obscure the graphics on the background layer unless the card pixels are transparent. This complexity can often be confusing when working with paint features such as erasing and patterns.

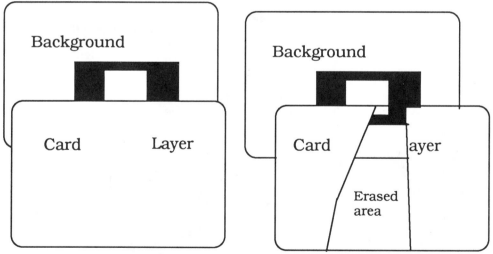

Erasing card-layer graphics erases both black and white pixels, revealing the background.

Figure 12.5   Effects of Erase Actions on a Graphics Display

HyperCard assumes that the card layer is transparent when starting. Any graphics added to the card layer will obscure the background graphics. One can change this by special actions. For example, erasing an image on the card layer does not take it back to white. It erases both black and white pixels so that anything on the background shows through unless one uses one of the special enhancement keys with the eraser or spray tools. Thus, erasing black pixels on the card level reveals what is beneath. The new display could result in black pixels showing if that is what is displayed below. One cannot tell by looking at a display screen whether the apparently white pixels are really white or are transparent and showing the white pixels of the background underneath.

Card Layer and Background Layer Graphics: Transparent and Opaque Commands

The Transparent and Opaque options on the Paint Menu also give control over the behavior of card-level pixels. Transparent will turn all card-level white pixels in a selected area into transparent pixels that show

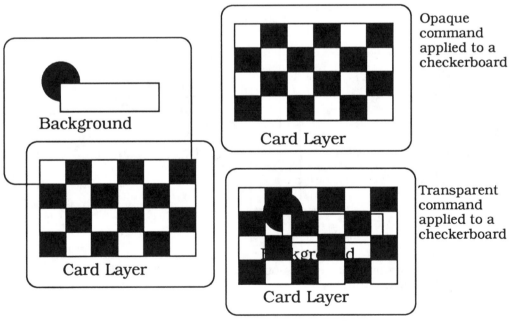

Figure 12.6   Opaque and Transparent Commands

background layer graphics. Opaque will do the opposite — turning all transparent pixels within the selected area into genuinely white card layer pixels (Figure 12.6).

Card Layer and Background Layer Graphics: The Select Rectangle and Lasso

The select rectangle picks up all pixels within the rectangle including white space. The lasso picks up only black pixels and enclosed white pixels. Thus, some of the pixels within a lassoed selection are transparent. Pasting the lasso over a background will have a very different effect from pasting a selected rectangle over an area.

Scripts That Use Layers

HyperCard's dual graphics layers allow creation of special visual effects in scripts. The background layer allows one to simulate the nondestructive motion of object-oriented graphics. That is, a graphic object in the card layer can appear to move without affecting the pixels underneath. Also, actions in the foreground can cause images in the background to appear mysteriously. The following examples hint at some of the possibilities.

Simulation of Object-oriented Graphics

An image in the card layer does not affect images in the background. A card layer image can be selected and moved around via *drag* commands. The object in Figure 12.7 will appear to move over the background.

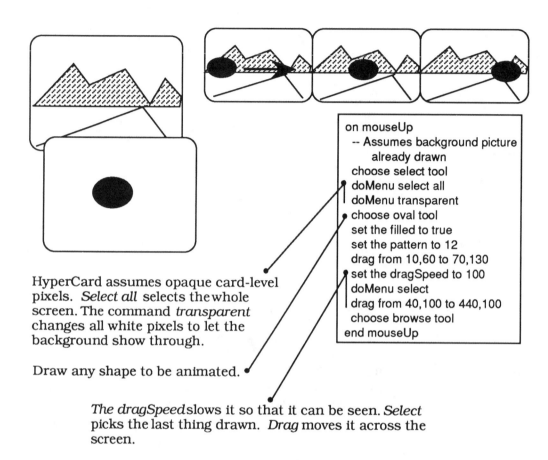

HyperCard assumes opaque card-level pixels. *Select all* selects the whole screen. The command *transparent* changes all white pixels to let the background show through.

Draw any shape to be animated.

The dragSpeed slows it so that it can be seen. *Select* picks the last thing drawn. *Drag* moves it across the screen.

Figure 12.7   Movement of Card-Level Graphics over the Background

The dragSpeed

The speed with which the *drag* command operates is not fixed. It is a HyperCard property that can be set in scripts or through the Message Box. The value of *the dragSpeed* represents the number of pixels per second that it moves. One can set it by use of the *set* command — for example, *set the dragSpeed to 200.* HyperCard uses the convention of 0 as the fastest speed possible. Slow to fast stretches from 1 to larger numbers. Figure 12.8 moves an oval across the screen at five increasing speeds.

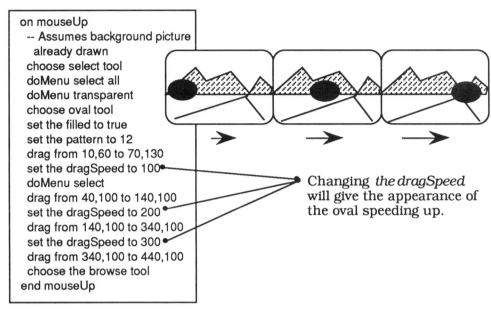

```
on mouseUp
 -- Assumes background picture
   already drawn
 choose select tool
 doMenu select all
 doMenu transparent
 choose oval tool
 set the filled to true
 set the pattern to 12
 drag from 10,60 to 70,130
 set the dragSpeed to 100
 doMenu select
 drag from 40,100 to 140,100
 set the dragSpeed to 200
 drag from 140,100 to 340,100
 set the dragSpeed to 300
 drag from 340,100 to 440,100
 choose the browse tool
end mouseUp
```

Changing *the dragSpeed* will give the appearance of the oval speeding up.

Figure 12.8   Use of the dragSpeed to Control the Speed of Motion

Scripts To Make Background Objects Appear

The fact that the card layer obscures the background can be used to create scripts to make graphics seem to appear. For example, a series of *erase* movements can make background graphics emerge.

Chapter 13
Scripts to Use Text

HyperCard provides many flexible ways to work with text. The text tool and text fields have been introduced earlier. This chapter explains them in more detail.

Text Tool

The text tool on the Paint Menu allows one to create graphics in the forms of letters. They become part of the bit-mapped graphics just like any other shape drawn with the paint tools. The graphics can be produced in a great variety of fonts, sizes, and styles. Chapter 6 on the paint tools explained the use of the text tool in hand interactive mode. Most of these features are available for use in scripts. Programs can be written in which text seems to appear mysteriously, move, and otherwise transform itself.

The *type* and *click at* Commands

The HyperCard command to cause automatic typing is *type*. A script needs merely to specify a location with the *click at* command. *Click at* specifies the coordinates of a location for the next HyperCard action. A *type* command will type whatever is specified in that location in the selected font, size, style, alignment, and height. The item to be typed can either be a string of characters or the name of a variable container that holds characters.

Figure 13.1 demonstrates the *type* command. Note the use of variables to store letters to be typed.

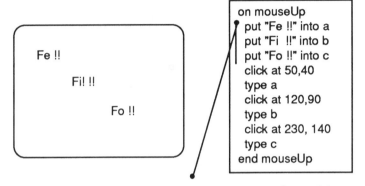

This example did not strictly require use of variables *a, b,* and *c*. For example, the line *type a* could have read *type "Fe !!"* without first putting the words into *a.* In more complex scripts, however, variables can be very useful.

Figure 13.1   Type Command

TextFont, textStyle, textSize, textAlign, **and** *textHeight*

Scripts can automatically set properties of the text to be typed. The syntax is fairly straightforward: *set (whatever property) to (whatever value).* These script lines accomplish the same results as clicking on the Text Style item in the Text Dialog Box accessed through the Edit Menu.

TextFont needs the name of the font and is limited to those fonts that happen to be installed in the system folder. *TextSize* refers to the size of the text in points. *TextStyle* refers to style attributes of the text such as *plain, bold, italic, outline,* and *shadow. TextAlign* can have the values of *left, right,* or *center* and refers to what axis a set of text lines align themselves to. *TextHeight* refers to the distance between lines of text in pixels. Figure 13.2 shows a script to create text in various sizes, styles, and fonts.

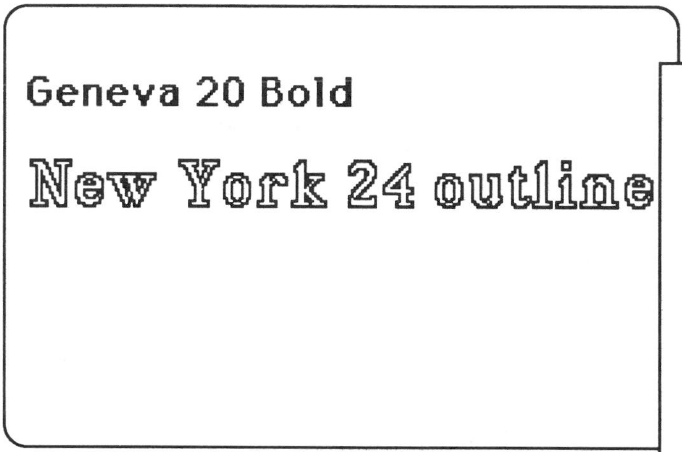

Geneva 20 Bold

New York 24 outline

```
on mouseUp
  choose text tool
  set the textFont to Geneva
  set the textSize to 20
  set the textStyle to bold
  click at 10,40
  type "Geneva 20 Bold"
  set the textFont to New York
  set the textSize to 24
  set the textStyle to outline
  click at 10,80
  type "New York 24 outline"
  choose browse tool
end mouseUp
```

Figure 13.2   Scripts to Set Text Characteristics

Text Fields

In addition to the text tool on the Paint Menu, text fields offer another major way to manipulate text. Text fields, like buttons, are HyperCard objects that can exist either on the card layer or the background layer. They are optimized for storing and displaying text. Visually, text field text can appear like text tool text, or it can hover in a variety of bordered rectangles. Because it is an object, however, it maintains its integrity and does not become fixed with confirmation. The text in a text field can be edited, moved, and changed in style, font, or size at any time, unlike text tool text, which becomes part of the picture once confirmed.

Text Field Creation

Text fields act much like buttons. They are created via the New Field item of the Objects Menu.   HyperCard automatically numbers them sequentially for each card or background. Clicking the New Field item brings forth a dotted rectangle on the screen representing the newly born field. Clicking on the Field Information item on the Objects Menu or clicking twice on the dotted rectangle opens up the Text Information Dialog Box (Figure 13.3).

The Field Information Dialog Box offers a set of choices to indicate and set properties of the field, including its name, its sequential number, and its unique ID number. One can set the LockText property to make it impossible for users to change text in the field, the Wide Margins setting to create more white space between the text and the field margins, and the Show Lines setting to put dotted guidelines across the field for text. The Font button brings forth the Font Information Box for setting the font, size, and style of the text in that field. All the text in one field can have only one setting, although the use of carefully positioned overlapping transparent fields can create the illusion of multiple fonts in one area of the screen. The Script button opens up the Script Creation Box, in which message handler scripts for that field can be created or edited. The OK button confirms the settings, and the Cancel button cancels any changes made.

Five field styles are available. Transparent allows the graphics beneath to show through, duplicating the appearance of text tool text. Opaque puts the text on a white field that obscures graphics below. Rectangle creates a rectangular border around the field. Shadow adds a drop shadow to the border. Scrolling creates a field with standard

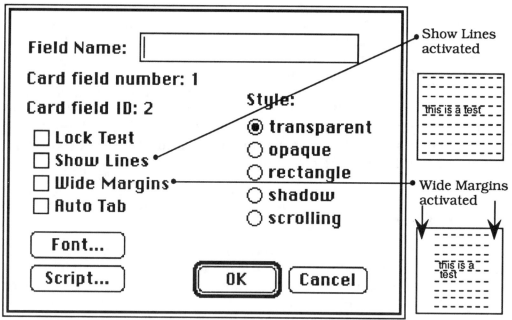

Figure 13.3   Field Information Dialog Box

Macintosh scroll bar on the right side to allow a user to scroll the window to move through text too long to be displayed in the field window (Figure 13.4).

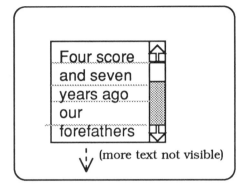

A scrolling style field allows the field to hold more information than can be displayed at one time. The scroll bar allows user to move through the information.

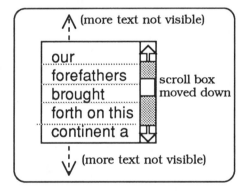

Figure 13.4   Scrolling Field

Text Field Editing

Users can edit field characteristics via the field tool icon on the Tools Menu. Clicking that icon puts dotted lines around all the fields on the current card. The field can be moved by clicking on the field and dragging the mouse with the mouse button held down. The field can be resized by clicking in the corners and dragging the borders. A user can select the field to edit by double-clicking on the desired field or selecting the Field

Information item from the Objects Menu. Since fields are sequential objects like buttons, their sequential order can be changed with the Bring Closer and Send Further commands on the Objects Menu.

Text Fields as Variable Containers

In addition to their use for displaying text, text fields provide a special kind of visible variable in which one can store information. For example, one could store a set of coordinates that describe a shape or animation path or a list of names. HyperCard provides a powerful set of commands for accessing the information in the fields.

Information can be put into fields in interactive hand mode by conventional Macintosh text-editing techniques. For example, clicking in a field (that does not have the *lock text* property set) changes the cursor to an I beam. One can move the position by clicking anywhere in the text in the field. Cutting and deleting text can be accomplished by clicking at the starting point of the text to be worked with and dragging the mouse over the desired text, which turns inverse. After the text is thus selected, it can be replaced by typing new text or cut or copied via the Edit Menu or keyboard equivalents.

Information can also be put into fields by use of the *put...into* command — for example, *put "This is a sample of text" into card field 3*. Scripts can thus automatically control the contents and displays of card fields. The *get* command will put the contents of the indicated field into a special variable called *it*. For example, *get card field 3* would put the words *This is a sample text* into the variable *it*, which could then be used in a script.

The *find* Command

The *find* command will search a field for a specified string of characters. For example, *find "apple" in card field 3* would return with the word *apple* highlighted in the field.

Elements of Fields and Other Containers: Characters, Words, Items, Lines, Chunks, and *the Number of*

As an aid to working with text, HyperCard understands how to find and manipulate particular elements of fields and other containers. It can work with characters, groups of characters, words, items, lines, and combinations of these called chunks.

> • Characters: It can find particular characters by their order in a field — for example, *put character 7 of card field 3 into the message box* or sequences of characters (*character 2 to 7*).
> • Words: It can find particular words — for example, *put word 2 of background field 3 into the message box.* HyperCard uses spaces to demarcate the boundaries of words. Figure 13.5 illustrates a script that uses this capability.

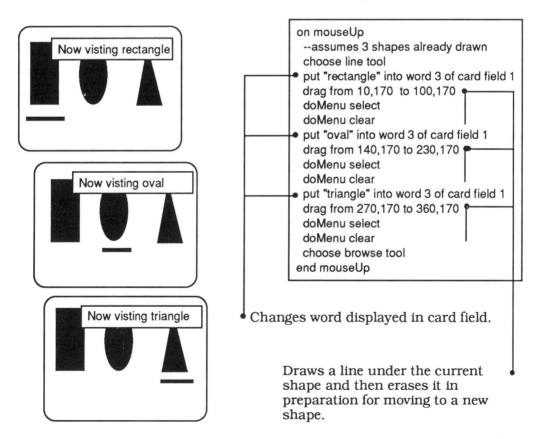

```
on mouseUp
  --assumes 3 shapes already drawn
  choose line tool
  put "rectangle" into word 3 of card field 1
  drag from 10,170  to 100,170
  doMenu select
  doMenu clear
  put "oval" into word 3 of card field 1
  drag from 140,170 to 230,170
  doMenu select
  doMenu clear
  put "triangle" into word 3 of card field 1
  drag from 270,170 to 360,170
  doMenu select
  doMenu clear
  choose browse tool
end mouseUp
```

Changes word displayed in card field.

Draws a line under the current shape and then erases it in preparation for moving to a new shape.

Figure 13.5   Script to Change Words in a Field

- Items: It can find particular items — for example, *find item 2 of card field 3.* HyperCard uses commas to demarcate items — for example, item 2 of a field containing *cars, dogs, apples* is dogs.
- Lines: It can find particular lines in a scrolling field — for example, *put line 5 of card field "addresses" into the message box.* It uses carriage returns to demarcate the lines of a field.

These elements can be combined — for example, *find character 4 of word 2 of background field 3.* The ordinal words from *first* to *tenth* can also be used, as can *last* and *middle* — for example, *put the sixth word of the card field "shapes" into message box.* Any can be used to find a random element — for example, *put any word of card field 2 into message box.* The *length of* function returns the number of elements in a field — for example, *put the number of words in card field 3 into message box.* All of these functions work just as well with variables as with fields. That is, you can manipulate a particular character, word, or item of a variable that is not a field.

Chapter 14
Data Structures and Randomness

Data Structures

Data structure is a fancy name for an ordered set of information. A sentence or a book could be thought of as a data structure. The alphabetical listing of names, addresses, and phone numbers in the phone book, the notes of a musical composition arranged into a score, and the vertices of a geometric shape are all data structures. The memory values that represent the display on a computer screen are a data structure. People constantly create and use data structures every day without calling them this name.

Data structures are important to programming because the computer must know explicitly where to get its instructions. Careful design of the way information is stored can enable computer programs to be speedy and efficient in what they do. This chapter will demonstrate ways to order information to affect visual, sound, and text events.

The text fields described in earlier chapters are most useful in creating HyperCard data structures. Other computer languages have even more powerful ways to order information.

Creation of Data Structures in a Field or in a Variable: Sequencing Cards

As with all computer programming, the first step is careful analysis of what is desired. Then one must find a way to realize the idea within the limitations of the programming language.

Chapter 10 on navigation in HyperCard demonstrated creation of a button script to sequence through a set of cards. What if one wanted to control the sequence differently — for example, to move backward or to move in a specified nonsequential order? A script to do this could be created by use of a data structure in a variable or in a field.

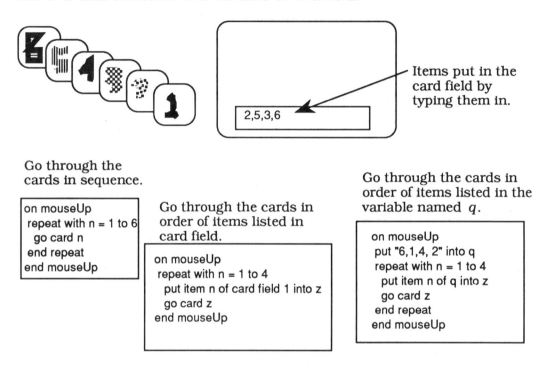

Items put in the card field by typing them in.

2,5,3,6

Go through the cards in sequence.

```
on mouseUp
  repeat with n = 1 to 6
    go card n
  end repeat
end mouseUp
```

Go through the cards in order of items listed in card field.

```
on mouseUp
  repeat with n = 1 to 4
    put item n of card field 1 into z
    go card z
end mouseUp
```

Go through the cards in order of items listed in the variable named q.

```
on mouseUp
  put "6,1,4, 2" into q
  repeat with n = 1 to 4
    put item n of q into z
    go card z
  end repeat
end mouseUp
```

Figure 14.1   Controlling the Sequence of Displayed Cards

One could create a card text field arbitrarily named "card order" (as a reminder of the field's function). One could then enter the order of the cards to be displayed by entering their names or ordinal numbers into the field. These names could be separated by spaces or commas. If they are separated by spaces, HyperCard will consider them each a separate word of the field. If they are separated by commas, HyperCard will consider them each a separate item. This distinction becomes important for the script that will make use of the information.

A button script can then be written to retrieve the card names systematically and navigate through them in that order. Assuming that the names have been stored with commas between them, the script to be discussed uses a repeat loop that moves through the field, retrieving each name in order. *The length of* function is used to tell HyperCard automatically how many items are in the field.

The same effect could be accomplished by using a variable instead of a field. The contents of the variable would not be visible, and the script would need a command line to put the values into the variable because interactive hand editing is available only with fields.

Creation of Data Structures in a Field or in a Variable: Coordinates for Shapes

The same approach could be used to automate drawing. An earlier example (Figure 4.5) demonstrated a script to draw a triangle by including three lines in the script, each of which specified the coordinates for the drag command. The process can be automated by use of simple data structures; this is useful for complex shapes requiring many lines.

One can create a data structure either via interactive mode in a card field or via script mode in a variable. Assume that one wants the computer to draw a complex shape automatically. In the analysis stage, one needs to determine the coordinates of the endpoints of all the lines. These coordinates can then be entered into the field or variable separated by spaces. Each set of coordinates then becomes a word in HyperCard parlance. A script can then access each word in turn to draw the lines.

In Figure 14.2, a repeat loop drags from word z to word $z+1$. This means it moves from 1 to 2. Next time through, it goes from 2 to 3. The z and $z+1$ are symbolic names to represent the relationship. The name z was arbitrary; it could have been anything desired. The loop stops at 1 less than the length of words in the variable because it is set up to drag to the next word. If the loop were allowed to go all the way to the last word, there would be no next word to drag to. To complete the image, the script drags from the last word back to the first word.

Note that this script will work with shapes made of any number of lines. The script uses the symbolic variable of *storelist* to store all the coordinates, the function number of *storelist* to determine the number of co-ordinate pairs, and z and $z+1$ to identify the elements of *storelist* to use for dragging. Because it is stated in the most generic terms, it is an algorithm for drawing a shape from a data structure of any number of coordinate pairs.

Only the data structure needs to change when a shape changes. The program to generate the image stays absolutely the same for all shapes made of straight lines. In this example, one could very well have written a script with command lines for each drag. With much more complex shapes, however, the abstraction of this script can save a lot of labor.

In fact, many computer-aided design and computer animation programs create data structures such as this one. The coordinates of each point are stored, as well as information about line style, patterns, and the like. These programs use computer languages that allow them to redraw the image very quickly.

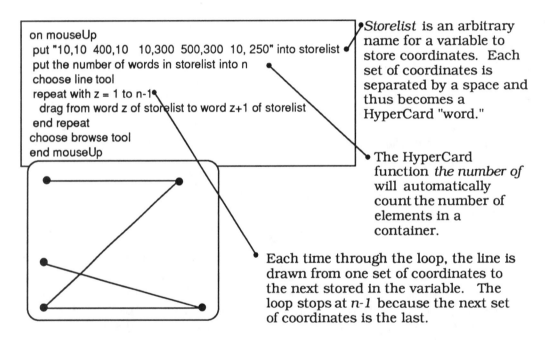

```
on mouseUp
  put "10,10  400,10   10,300  500,300  10, 250" into storelist
  put the number of words in storelist into n
  choose line tool
  repeat with z = 1 to n-1
    drag from word z of storelist to word z+1 of storelist
  end repeat
  choose browse tool
end mouseUp
```

Storelist is an arbitrary name for a variable to store coordinates. Each set of coordinates is separated by a space and thus becomes a HyperCard "word."

The HyperCard function *the number of* will automatically count the number of elements in a container.

Each time through the loop, the line is drawn from one set of coordinates to the next stored in the variable. The loop stops at *n-1* because the next set of coordinates is the last.

Figure 14.2   Script to Draw Lines Using Coordinates Stored in a Variable

Object-oriented graphics as described in Chapter 6 depend upon these algorithms. The graphics are stored not as pixel values in memory but rather as data structures of coordinates and lines. Anytime they are moved or scaled, the computer goes to the data structure to get the information to redraw them. It does this so fast that one is unaware of the process. Every graphic object on the screen has its own data structure, which maintains the independence of the objects. One can change them at any time by changing the data structures.

Creation of Data Structures in a Field or in a Variable: Complex Drawing Instructions

Any kind of information can be stored in HyperCard variables. For example, one could automate an entire drawing session using multiple tools and patterns — for example, choose black and draw a filled oval at these coordinates, then choose the bamboo pattern and draw a rectangle at these coordinates, and so on. Note that this data structure approach to using HyperCard tools works with many but not all of the tools. Many lasso, curve, and irregular polygon tool hand interactive actions cannot be simulated with a sequence of drag commands in a script.

One would need to create a data structure that contained information about tool, pattern, and coordinates to use. There are many ways to accomplish this. One could have a single data structure in which each entry contained a tool, pattern, and coordinate. One could just as well create three data structures for each of the aspects. Whatever the choice, the script to use the data structures would have to be customized to the way the information was stored. Figure 14.3 stores the information in three fields.

Randomness: Aesthetic Bases of Computer-mediated Art

Complaints are often raised that computer graphics are too regular and predictable. Often the images are seen as "geometric" and "mathematical." It is easy to see that the built-in functions of a language can affect the nature of the images created.

HyperCard's rectangle, oval, regular polygon, and other tools seductively make it easy to create images using these components. Similarly, the algorithms for generating grid scripts showed how easy it was to generate images built of actions with regular relations to each other. Many early examples of program-generated computer art indeed had this feel. One response is to emphasize the tendency toward regularity. Some commentators believe that the ability of computers to build images on abstract

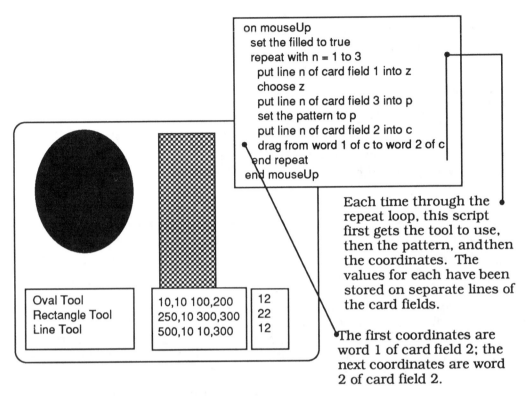

```
on mouseUp
  set the filled to true
  repeat with n = 1 to 3
    put line n of card field 1 into z
    choose z
    put line n of card field 3 into p
    set the pattern to p
    put line n of card field 2 into c
    drag from word 1 of c to word 2 of c
  end repeat
end mouseUp
```

Oval Tool	10,10 100,200	12
Rectangle Tool	250,10 300,300	22
Line Tool	500,10 10,300	12

Each time through the repeat loop, this script first gets the tool to use, then the pattern, and then the coordinates. The values for each have been stored on separate lines of the card fields.

The first coordinates are word 1 of card field 2; the next coordinates are word 2 of card field 2.

Figure 14.3   Data Structure with Complex Drawing Instructions

mathematical relationships is a unique aesthetic worth exploring in more detail. For example, see Herbert Franke's book *Computer Graphics* (Springer-Verlag, 1988) and Frank Dietrich's 1987 article in the journal *Leonardo* on algorithmic art ("The Computer: a Tool for Thought Experiments"). Every art form is shaped by the capabilities of its tools, so why should art generated with computers be different?

Other approaches emphasize the importance of randomness. Randomness is useful in creating art that has a less geometric feel. Much of the organic feel of nature comes from the fact that shapes and events combine predictability and order. For example, all the leaves of a tree will share some common qualities, but they will also vary in certain random ways. Many twentieth-century artists have introduced randomness into their visual, sound, and performance work. Also, this randomness is seen as essential for capturing essential elements of life in the contemporary world. Events are not as predictable as the medieval church or Enlightenment philosophers would have us believe.

Randomness in HyperCard: *the random of* Function

Some artists who use computers maintain that computer art does not need to highlight its mathematical tendencies. HyperCard, for example, allows hand drawing of images with the mouse or importation of images captured by a scanner. These kind of images are hardly mathematical in feel and can be easily manipulated in HyperCard scripts as in the sequencing of cards described in Chapter 10.

Many computer languages offer access to random functions. These routines generate random numbers that can be used in scripts to control shapes, movement, sequences, or whatever. Computers generate random numbers in different ways. Some use action on the keyboard or changes in components to generate values electronically. Many generate a random number table that lists numbers mathematically. Unfortunately, these numbers will repeat if they are accessed too many times. Although functionally these numbers work as random numbers, purists complain that they are not good enough for some kinds of work.

HyperCard provides a function called *the random of.* One can use it in scripts to generate random numbers between 1 and 32767. The upper limit of random numbers desired is indicated by the syntax *the random of (number of upper limit).* Larger or smaller numbers can be obtained by multiplication or division. Usually, scripts that use *the random of* function put the number returned into a variable that can then be used in a program.

HyperCard also provides access to randomness with the word *any,* which can be used in scripts. For example, *go to any card* will randomly pick one card in the current stack. *Put any word of card field 2 into the message box* will produce a word randomly selected out of those stored in card field 2.

Use of *the random of* Function with Drawing Commands

The example in Figure 14.4 draws seven random lines on the screen. It accomplishes this by randomly creating coordinates for the *drag* command. Since coordinates consist of two numbers, the script must randomly generate two random numbers, and then they must be put together into the proper form to represent a coordinate — that is, separated by a comma with no spaces.

HyperCard provides the ampersand (&) function to put things together. *Put "joe"&"jane" into q* will store the string of characters *joejane* in the variable *q*. Double ampersand (&&) puts things together with a space between them. *Put "joe"&&"jane" into q* will store the characters *joe jane* in variable *q*. In Figure 14.4, the script generates a random number for the horizontal coordinate (out of the possible 512 pixels) and another random number for the vertical coordinate (out of the 342 possible) and puts them together with a comma in between. This creates a coordinate in acceptable HyperCard syntax. It then creates another set of coordinates and drags from one to the other. Two samples are shown because the script will probably generate a different image each time it runs.

A very similar program (Figure 14.5) randomly draws shapes. It picks the coordinates in the same way, but it also randomly accesses tool names from a data structure variable that has names of tools stored in it. It also picks the number of shapes to draw randomly. It thus draws a random number of randomly sized, randomly shaped graphics.

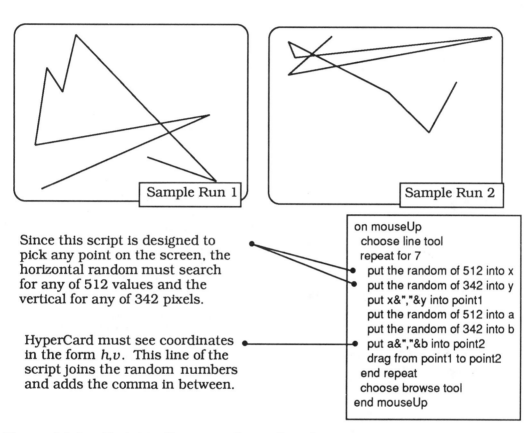

Since this script is designed to pick any point on the screen, the horizontal random must search for any of 512 values and the vertical for any of 342 pixels.

HyperCard must see coordinates in the form *h,v*. This line of the script joins the random numbers and adds the comma in between.

```
on mouseUp
  choose line tool
  repeat for 7
    put the random of 512 into x
    put the random of 342 into y
    put x&","&y into point1
    put the random of 512 into a
    put the random of 342 into b
    put a&","&b into point2
    drag from point1 to point2
  end repeat
  choose browse tool
end mouseUp
```

Figure 14.4   Script to Generate Seven Random Lines

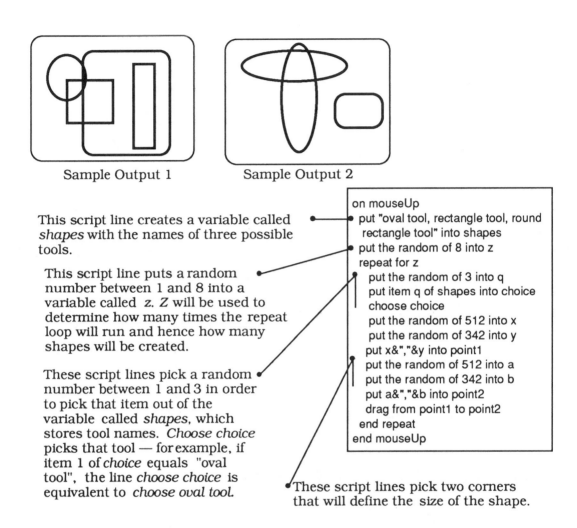

Sample Output 1   Sample Output 2

This script line creates a variable called *shapes* with the names of three possible tools.

```
on mouseUp
  put "oval tool, rectangle tool, round
    rectangle tool" into shapes
  put the random of 8 into z
  repeat for z
    put the random of 3 into q
    put item q of shapes into choice
    choose choice
    put the random of 512 into x
    put the random of 342 into y
    put x&","&y into point1
    put the random of 512 into a
    put the random of 342 into b
    put a&","&b into point2
    drag from point1 to point2
  end repeat
end mouseUp
```

This script line puts a random number between 1 and 8 into a variable called *z*. *Z* will be used to determine how many times the repeat loop will run and hence how many shapes will be created.

These script lines pick a random number between 1 and 3 in order to pick that item out of the variable called *shapes*, which stores tool names. *Choose choice* picks that tool — for example, if item 1 of *choice* equals "oval tool", the line *choose choice* is equivalent to *choose oval tool.*

These script lines pick two corners that will define the size of the shape.

Figure 14.5   Script to Generate a Random Number of Random-Sized, Randomly Chosen Shapes

Controlling the Range of Random Numbers

The function *the random of* function itself generates random numbers between 1 and its upper limit (32767). But a user is not stuck with this range; scripts can be adjusted to produce any numbers desired.

For example, in Figure 14.5, if one wanted random lines to appear only in a particular area rather than just anywhere on the screen, one could adjust the random numbers. In Figure 14.6, they are adjusted to appear only in an area bounded by horizontal coordinates 250 and 450 and vertical coordinates 100 and 200.

To do this first requires assessment of the number of possible numbers between the lower and upper limits. In this example, horizontally there are 200 possible numbers (450 minus 250). Vertically there are 100 possibilities (200 minus 100). These are the totals of random numbers possible in each case.

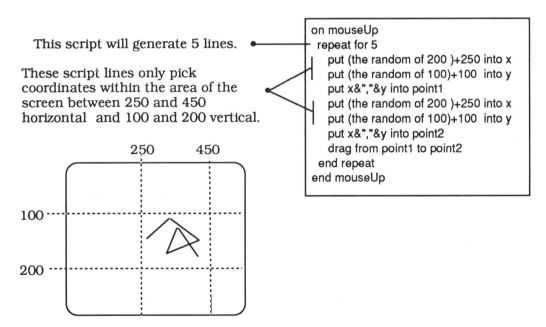

This script will generate 5 lines.

These script lines only pick coordinates within the area of the screen between 250 and 450 horizontal and 100 and 200 vertical.

```
on mouseUp
  repeat for 5
    put (the random of 200 )+250 into x
    put (the random of 100)+100  into y
    put x&","&y into point1
    put (the random of 200 )+250 into x
    put (the random of 100)+100  into y
    put x&","&y into point2
    drag from point1 to point2
  end repeat
end mouseUp
```

Figure 14.6   Limits on Random Numbers

Use of the function *the random of 200* will indeed produce any of 200 possible random numbers. The only problem will be that they start at 1 and go to 200 instead of starting at 250. One can adjust the range by adding 249 to each number produced. Thus if the random number produced is 1, the adjustment will kick it up into the acceptable range. The same thing is done with the vertical coordinate, although the adjustment requires adding 100 to each one.

Random Text

The function *the random of* function can be combined with data structures to create forms that randomly vary among particular possibilities. This approach is often effective for creation of works that exhibit a tension between order and disorder. It can also translate the random numbers into random words, commands, or whatever.

Figure 14.7 shows how to create random sentences. English has certain basic syntactic structures that transcend the particular words contained. For example, subject—verb—object is a fundamental structure. This can be used to create a script that will make random sentences that may or may not make sense. Twentieth-century artists, beginning with the Dadaists, have been fascinated with randomly organized text.

The script creates two data structures — one for verbs and one for nouns. In this example, the words are separated by spaces so that HyperCard defines them as words. The script picks a random noun, then a random verb, and then a random noun. It puts them together into a sentence, types them into a transparent card field, waits two seconds, and then puts the next sentence in the field. The wait is achieved by use of the HyperCard *wait* command which needs to be followed by a specified number of seconds. For more on the *wait* command, see Chapter on time-based art.

Randomness is a powerful tool if used carefully. Again, novice computer artists often go random-crazy. It is important to constrain programs so that the randomness functions well both conceptually and visually.

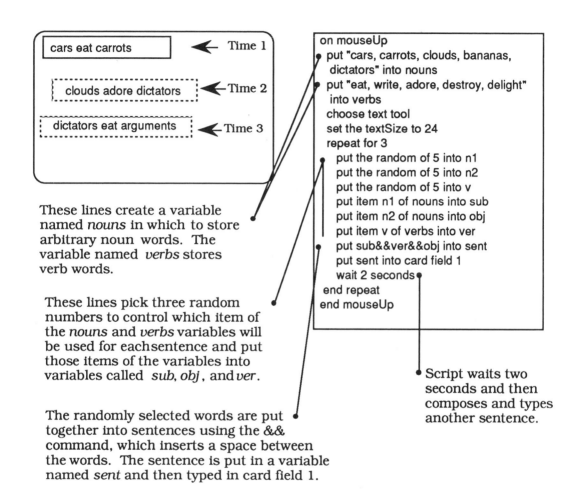

cars eat carrots ← Time 1

clouds adore dictators ← Time 2

dictators eat arguments ← Time 3

```
on mouseUp
  put "cars, carrots, clouds, bananas,
    dictators" into nouns
  put "eat, write, adore, destroy, delight"
    into verbs
  choose text tool
  set the textSize to 24
  repeat for 3
    put the random of 5 into n1
    put the random of 5 into n2
    put the random of 5 into v
    put item n1 of nouns into sub
    put item n2 of nouns into obj
    put item v of verbs into ver
    put sub&&ver&&obj into sent
    put sent into card field 1
    wait 2 seconds
  end repeat
end mouseUp
```

These lines create a variable named *nouns* in which to store arbitrary noun words. The variable named *verbs* stores verb words.

These lines pick three random numbers to control which item of the *nouns* and *verbs* variables will be used for eachsentence and put those items of the variables into variables called *sub, obj,* and *ver*.

The randomly selected words are put together into sentences using the **&&** command, which inserts a space between the words. The sentence is put in a variable named *sent* and then typed in card field 1.

Script waits two seconds and then composes and types another sentence.

Figure 14.7   Script to Create Three Nonsense Sentences

CHAPTER 15
INTERACTIVITY

Audience as Co-creators

The dark view of current technological developments such as mass media, telecommunications, and surveillance is that they represent decays in living standards, not advances. Analysts who hold this position point out that technology allows increasing centralization and control of society and encourages passivity. The bright view of the technological future points to increased opportunities for individual choice and expression made possible by the technologies.

The technology itself guarantees neither future: Both kinds of capabilities are inherent in the tools. Artists can help to develop the bright option by creating art that explores the interactive capabilities of the technology. They can create works that require audiences to act as cocreators rather than as passive appreciators.

Creation of interactive artworks is somewhat unprecedented in art history and will require the learning of new conceptual and technical skills. Traditionally, artists have created works that stay the same for all of history, except for unpreventable decay. An artist creating an interactive work must create a structure that will have many manifestations, depending on the choices audiences make. It must be capable of producing whole families of events instead of just one manifestation. The psychology of the audience and the nature of the context become essential design elements.

Work with computers provides good preparation for the creation of interactive events. The technology is easily adapted to the creation of interactive programs.

Interactivity in HyperCard

HyperCard is especially well adapted as a computer language and an environment for the creation of interactive events. Its structure and commands allow easy ways to monitor and respond to the user's actions. Scripts can make instant use of keyboard and mouse actions.

Mouse Location

Even when HyperCard appears to be doing nothing, it is reading the mouse and keyboard. It is reading the mouse pointer's location on the screen.   The function *the mouseLoc* continuously returns the coordinates of the pointer. The function *the mouseV* returns the vertical coordinate, and *the mouseH* returns the horizontal coordinate. Scripts can easily be written to make use of this information.

Figure 15.1 continuously reads and prints the location of the mouse in the Message Box for a specified period of time. With this example and the following ones, there is no way to stop the script until it has finished. Later examples will demonstrate how to stop these actions whenever one wants. The command key followed by the period (.) will stop a program if you want to stop it before the loop is done. In the example, after clicking the button,

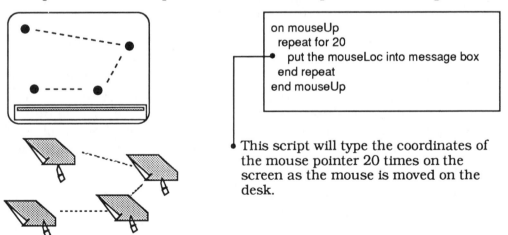

```
on mouseUp
  repeat for 20
    put the mouseLoc into message box
  end repeat
end mouseUp
```

This script will type the coordinates of the mouse pointer 20 times on the screen as the mouse is moved on the desk.

Figure 15.1   Script to Print Out the Mouse Location Continually

one can drag the mouse around and watch the coordinates change.

In Figure 15.2, a card field follows the mouse around. The program prints the coordinates of the mouse, *the mouseLoc*, in the field as it moves around. This is accomplished by using the property of a field called *the loc*. *The loc* returns the coordinates of a field or a button. *The loc* can also be changed by scripts. The example continually resets *the loc* to be the same as *the mouseLoc*, and the field seems to follow the mouse around.

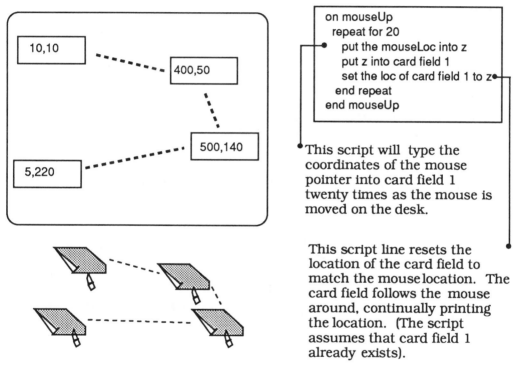

```
on mouseUp
  repeat for 20
    put the mouseLoc into z
    put z into card field 1
    set the loc of card field 1 to z
  end repeat
end mouseUp
```

This script will type the coordinates of the mouse pointer into card field 1 twenty times as the mouse is moved on the desk.

This script line resets the location of the card field to match the mouse location. The card field follows the mouse around, continually printing the location. (The script assumes that card field 1 already exists).

Figure 15.2   Script to Make the Card Field Follow the Mouse

The *if* Command

The *if* command allows scripts to act intelligently. If the script is clever enough, it can give the appearance of almost human understanding. The *if* command checks for a specified situation. If the situation is true, the script will do one thing. If it isn't true, it will do something else. The syntax requires *if* to be followed by the word *then* followed by the desired action. If HyperCard tests the *if* situation and finds it false, it forgets about the *then* part and goes to the next line.

The *repeat until* and *repeat while* commands met in Chapter 9 show a similar intelligence. In fact, almost any script created with a *repeat until* or *repeat while* command could be built in an alternative way using the *if* command.

Combination of the *if* command with the interactive mouse commands can create programs that seem quite intelligent. Figure 15.3 reads the mouse's vertical position for a period of time and beeps at users if they cross over the borderline. The *if* command beeps only if the mouse's vertical position (*the mouseV*) becomes greater than the 100 vertical position where the line is drawn.

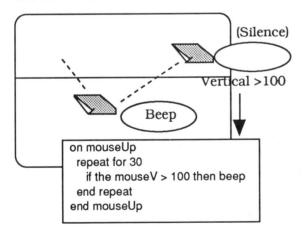

Figure 15.3   The if Command

The *if* command can have varying syntaxes. In Figure 15.3, *if* and *then* are on the same line. They could have been on separate lines. If there are many command lines to be executed if the test situation is true, each must be on its own line, and the whole set of lines must be ended with the phrase *end if.*

To illustrate an *if* construction that includes several command lines, Figure 15.4 elaborates on the preceding example. It beeps and draws a line from the mouse position to the 250,340 point on the bottom of the screen if the mouse is moved below the line.

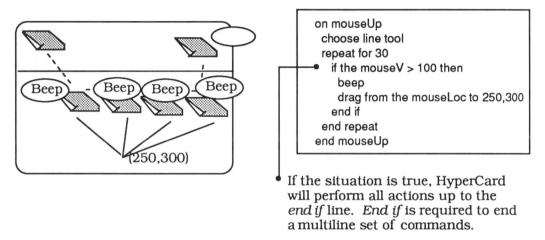

If the situation is true, HyperCard will perform all actions up to the *end if* line. *End if* is required to end a multiline set of commands.

Figure 15.4   The Multiline if Command

The *if* command can have an *else* phrase after the *then* phrase to specify what should be done if the test situation is not true. Normally, HyperCard just goes on to the next command. Figure 15.5 illustrates the use of the *if...then...else* construction by drawing a line to one place if the mouse is above the line and another place if it is below the line.

Mouse Clicking: A Simple Drawing Program

HyperCard keeps track of whether a user has clicked the mouse button. If the button has been clicked, HyperCard records the location of the pointer when the button was clicked. The HyperCard function *the mouse* returns *up* if the mouse button is not being pressed and *down* if the button is being pressed. The HyperCard function *the mouseClick* returns *true* if the mouse button is down and *false* if it is up. The function *the clickLoc* returns the location of the last time the mouse button was clicked regardless of the current position of the mouse.

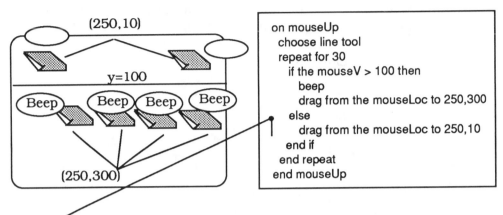

(250,10)

```
on mouseUp
  choose line tool
  repeat for 30
    if the mouseV > 100 then
      beep
      drag from the mouseLoc to 250,300
    else
      drag from the mouseLoc to 250,10
    end if
  end repeat
end mouseUp
```

y=100

Beep   Beep   Beep   Beep

(250,300)

The only way this script differs from the previous one is the *else* clause. If the mouse is below vertical position 100, it beeps and draws a line to 250,300 at the bottom of the screen. Else, if it is above vertical position 100, it draws a line to 250,10 at the top of the screen. In the previous example, it did nothing if it was above the line.

Figure 15.5   The if...then...else Command Structure

These commands can be used to give the user considerable control over a program. The button example in Figure 15.6 will beep continually after the screen button is activated until the mouse button is clicked. The example shows an equivalent script that uses the *repeat until* construction. In both of these, the situation being tested for is *the mouseClick* being true. That will happen only when the user pushes down on the mouse button.

The *mouseDown* message can be used in similar ways. In Figure 15.7, lines are drawn to the current mouse location only while the mouse button is held down.

Figure 15.8 demonstrates the elegant power of these commands. Almost all beginning Macintosh users marvel at the power of paint and draw programs such as MacPaint and MacDraw. Actually, the core ideas are fairly simple and easy to realize with these interactive commands.

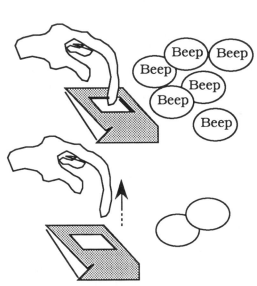

```
on mouseUp
  repeat forever
    beep
    if the mouseclick = true then exit repeat
  end repeat
end mouseUp
```

Both of these will continue beeping indefinitely once the original screen button is pushed until the user pushes on the mouse button. When the mouse button is pushed, HyperCard changes the value of *the mouseclick* to *true* and the script stops.

```
on mouseUp
  repeat until the mouseclick = true
    beep
  end repeat
endmouseUp
```

15.6   Endless Beeping until the Mouse Button Is Clicked

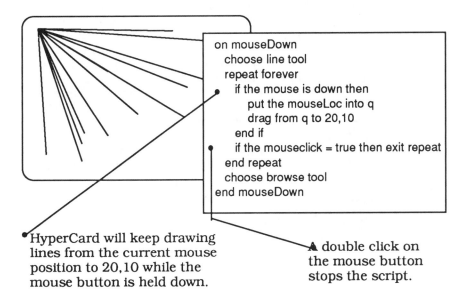

```
on mouseDown
  choose line tool
  repeat forever
    if the mouse is down then
      put the mouseLoc into q
      drag from q to 20,10
    end if
    if the mouseclick = true then exit repeat
  end repeat
  choose browse tool
end mouseDown
```

HyperCard will keep drawing lines from the current mouse position to 20,10 while the mouse button is held down.

A double click on the mouse button stops the script.

Figure 15.7   Endless lines While the Mouse Button Is Down

The script in figure 15.8 creates a simple drawing program. The program will draw lines between clicks of the mouse. It uses the function *the clickLoc* to determine where the mouse is clicked. It draws a line from the postion of the last click and then stores the present click's location in a variable so that the next click can be used. One can stop the program by moving the mouse pointer to the right side of the screen.

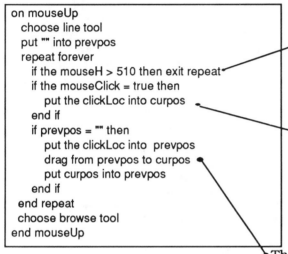

```
on mouseUp
    choose line tool
    put "" into prevpos
    repeat forever
        if the mouseH > 510 then exit repeat
        if the mouseClick = true then
            put the clickLoc into curpos
        end if
        if prevpos = "" then
            put the clickLoc into  prevpos
            drag from prevpos to curpos
            put curpos into prevpos
        end if
    end repeat
    choose browse tool
end mouseUp
```

Stop the drawing process when the mouse is moved over to right screen.

If the mouse button is clicked, put the location of the mouse at that time (*the clickLoc*) into a variable called *curpos*.

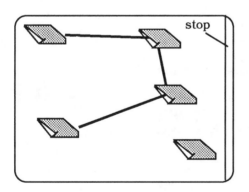

The script will draw a line from the position of the last click to the current position. It does this by putting the current position into a variable called *prevpos* when it is done with a line. Thus, it is ready for the next click. The script line *if prevpos = ""* checks for the situation at the very beginning where there is no previous click. It puts the current position into the variable so that the first line is a dot. If it did not, HyperCard would return an error because it wouldn't know where *prevpos* was.

15.8   *Simple Draw Program Using mouseClicks*

All examples so far have been single-button scripts. Variables have been used within the same script in which they were created. This restriction has avoided the complication of worrying how scripts can share variable information. The next example uses global variables to store an array of coordinates.

HyperCard assumes that all variables created are local variables unless instructed otherwise. This means that HyperCard remembers the value of a variable only for the duration of the script in which it appears. Another script or the Message Box would not know what the value was. For example, in the script in Figure 15.8, the location of *the clickLoc* is stored in a variable. Requesting the last value of that variable from the Message Box would result in an error message. The Message Box does not know what the variable is because it appeared in another object.

On the one hand, the fact that HyperCard "forgets" between scripts can be very useful because one does not need to keep track of what names have been given to variables in other scripts in the stack. In a large stack with lots of scripts, it could be a nightmare to try to keep track of names.

On the other hand, it is often useful for scripts and objects to share the values of variables. HyperCard can be forced to remember by declaring a variable to be global. The syntax for that is the word *global* followed by the names of the variables to be treated that way, separated by commas. A variable must be declared as global before it is used in each message handler script that is to share the value.

The example in Figure 15.9 builds on the previous draw program. Instead of drawing lines, it stores the series of coordinates where the mouse button has been clicked in a variable. Another button on the card animates a word to move through those locations. The scripts of the two buttons share the same global variable containing the series of locations. It creates the animation effect by typing the word and then undoing before the next word is typed.

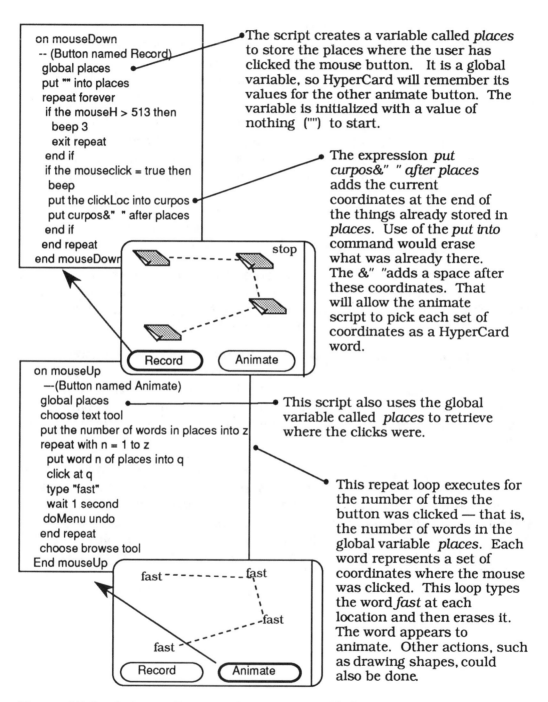

```
on mouseDown
 -- (Button named Record)
 global places
 put "" into places
 repeat forever
  if the mouseH > 513 then
   beep 3
   exit repeat
  end if
  if the mouseclick = true then
   beep
   put the clickLoc into curpos
   put curpos&" " after places
  end if
 end repeat
end mouseDown
```

The script creates a variable called *places* to store the places where the user has clicked the mouse button. It is a global variable, so HyperCard will remember its values for the other animate button. The variable is initialized with a value of nothing ("") to start.

The expression *put curpos&" " after places* adds the current coordinates at the end of the things already stored in *places*. Use of the *put into* command would erase what was already there. The &" "adds a space after these coordinates. That will allow the animate script to pick each set of coordinates as a HyperCard word.

```
on mouseUp
 ---(Button named Animate)
 global places
 choose text tool
 put the number of words in places into z
 repeat with n = 1 to z
  put word n of places into q
  click at q
  type "fast"
  wait 1 second
  doMenu undo
 end repeat
 choose browse tool
End mouseUp
```

This script also uses the global variable called *places* to retrieve where the clicks were.

This repeat loop executes for the number of times the button was clicked — that is, the number of words in the global variable *places*. Each word represents a set of coordinates where the mouse was clicked. This loop types the word *fast* at each location and then erases it. The word appears to animate. Other actions, such as drawing shapes, could also be done.

Figure 15.9   Animate Program Using mouseClicks to Determine the Path

Button and Field Messages

HyperCard objects are designed to receive messages. Many of these messages result from user-interactive actions. For example, all the button scripts in the examples in the previous chapters have checked for the user action of releasing the mouse button — *on mouseUp*. HyperCard is designed to send a *mouseUp* message up the hierarchy whenever the user releases a button. It is constantly watching for this kind of user action. All the standard HyperCard objects — buttons, fields, cards, backgrounds, and stacks — have the capacity of responding to this message if a message handler is written.

mouseUp, mouseDown, mouseStillDown

Scripts can be written for a variety of mouse actions. A *mouseUp* handler reads the act of the mouse button going up. A *mouseDown* handler reads the action of putting the mouse button down. A *mouseStilldown* handler reads whether the button is still currently down.

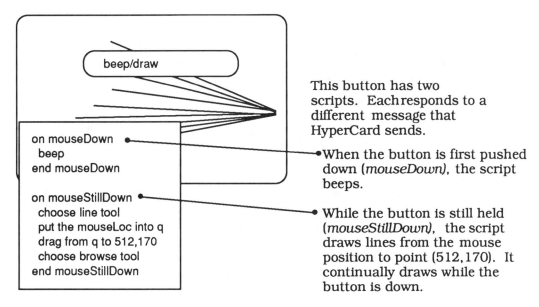

beep/draw

on mouseDown
  beep
end mouseDown

on mouseStillDown
  choose line tool
  put the mouseLoc into q
  drag from q to 512,170
  choose browse tool
end mouseStillDown

This button has two scripts. Each responds to a different message that HyperCard sends.

When the button is first pushed down (*mouseDown*), the script beeps.

While the button is still held (*mouseStillDown*), the script draws lines from the mouse position to point (512,170). It continually draws while the button is down.

Figure 15.10 MouseDown, mouseStillDown, mouseUp Messages

The button script in Figure 15.10 makes use of the *mouseDown* and *mouseStilldown* messages. The button beeps when the button is first pushed down, it keeps drawing while the mouse is still down, and it quits when the button is released. Again, there could be other scripts to accomplish the same goal using repeat structures and other functions.

mouseEnter, mouseWithin, and *mouseLeave:* An Enhanced Drawing Program

These three messages make use of the mouse's position rather than actions on the mouse button. *MouseEnter* is the message HyperCard automatically sends to the button or the other object when the mouse pointer enters anywhere in its bordering rectangle. *MouseLeave* is the message that is sent to the object when the mouse pointer leaves the rectangle. *MouseWithin* is the message that is constantly sent while the pointer is within the rectangle. Scripts can be written to make highly interactive programs based on these messages. One needs to exercise some care with the *mouseLeave* and *mouseEnter* messages because very busy scripts can miss the actions if they are engaged in other actions.

The sample button scripts in Figure 15.11 build on the simple random line program introduced previously. In this enhanced program, the user can choose what shapes will be drawn and can change the result of subsequent *drag* commands merely by moving the pointer in and out of buttons representing different shapes. The set of buttons acts as a kind of palette, just like the tools palettes of most paint and draw programs.

The basic button to draw random shapes remains. The process will continue until the mouse button is clicked. In this button's script, however, there is a global variable named *whichtool* that tells which tool to use in the dragging action. *Whichtool* gets its value from the user dragging the mouse to point at the tool buttons. Using *mouseEnter,* each button changes the value of *whichtool* to be its target tool. The user does not have to click the button, only to drag the pointer into the visual rectangle of that particular button. The continual drawing instantly reflects the change of shape.

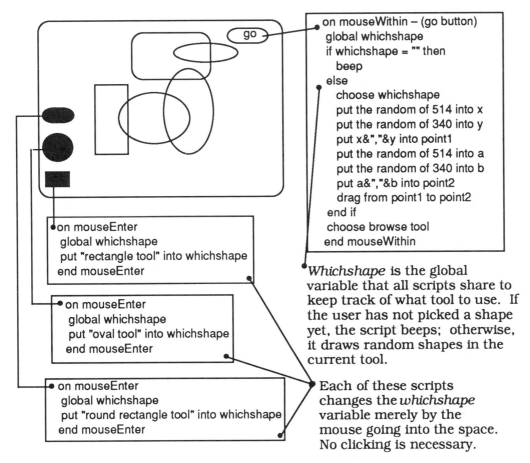

```
on mouseWithin – (go button)
  global whichshape
  if whichshape = "" then
    beep
  else
    choose whichshape
    put the random of 514 into x
    put the random of 340 into y
    put x&","&y into point1
    put the random of 514 into a
    put the random of 340 into b
    put a&","&b into point2
    drag from point1 to point2
  end if
  choose browse tool
end mouseWithin
```

```
on mouseEnter
  global whichshape
  put "rectangle tool" into whichshape
end mouseEnter
```

```
on mouseEnter
  global whichshape
  put "oval tool" into whichshape
end mouseEnter
```

```
on mouseEnter
  global whichshape
  put "round rectangle tool" into whichshape
end mouseEnter
```

Whichshape is the global variable that all scripts share to keep track of what tool to use. If the user has not picked a shape yet, the script beeps; otherwise, it draws random shapes in the current tool.

Each of these scripts changes the *whichshape* variable merely by the mouse going into the space. No clicking is necessary.

Figure 15.11   MouseEnter and mouseWithin Messages

This example could be enhanced with additional functions to simulate all the simple features available in computer paint programs. The reader is encouraged to add to this program to make it perform other graphics operations.

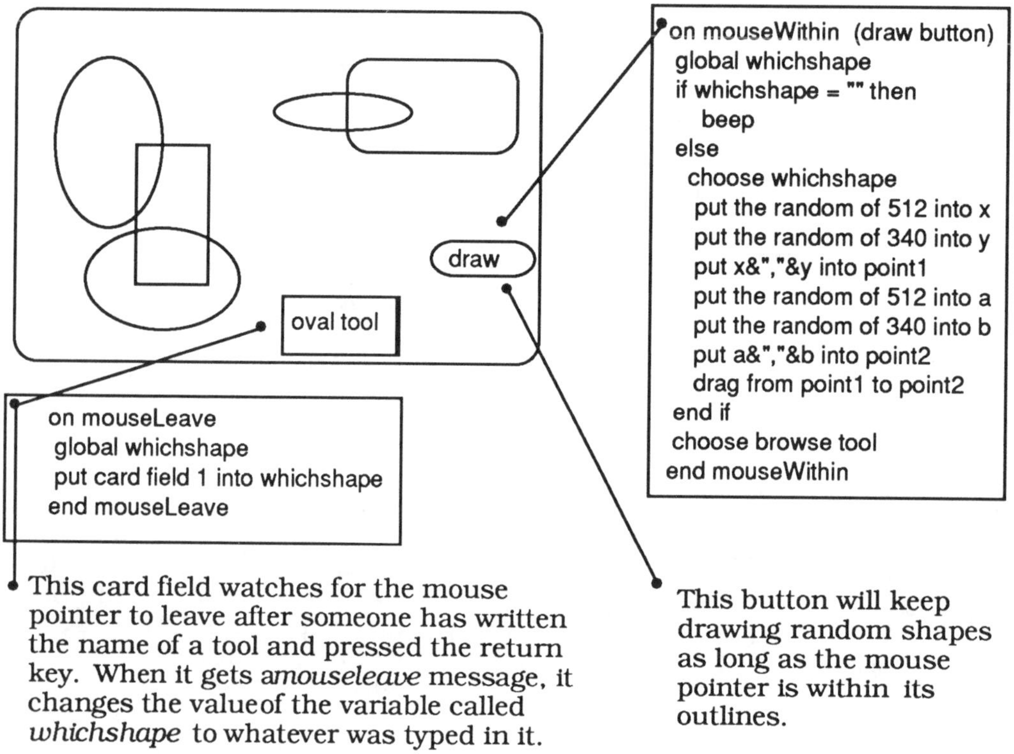
draw
oval tool
on mouseWithin (draw button)
global whichshape
if whichshape = "" then
beep
else
choose whichshape
put the random of 512 into x
put the random of 340 into y
put x&","&y into point1
put the random of 512 into a
put the random of 340 into b
put a&","&b into point2
drag from point1 to point2
end if
choose browse tool
end mouseWithin
on mouseLeave
global whichshape
put card field 1 into whichshape
end mouseLeave
This card field watches for the mouse pointer to leave after someone has written the name of a tool and pressed the return key. When it gets amouseleave message, it changes the valueof the variable called whichshape to whatever was typed in it.
This button will keep drawing random shapes as long as the mouse pointer is within its outlines.

Figure 15.12 Using Card Fields for Interactions

Interactions With the Keyboard

In HyperCard, fields are instrinsically interactive. HyperCard also continually monitors the keyboard and provides easy ways to process typed information. The information typed can be assessed by message handlers, and scripts can proceed on that information.

The script in Figure 15.12 performs the same actions as the previous one except that it has replaced the shape buttons with a field. The user is asked to type desired tool modes — *line, oval, rectangle, polygon* — into the field and press the return key when done. This request is placed in a card field that hovers above the screen so that it will not get obscured by the drawing shapes.

The message handler for the recipient field waits for the user to push the return key. When that happens, it changes the global variable *whichtool.* The drawing action then changes to use the new tool. The script also checks for other words besides those allowed using *if* statements. If the word typed in is not one of those allowed, it beeps, clears the field, and asks for another word.

The *answer* Command

HyperCard provides commands that produce preconfigured dialog boxes to collect information. *Answer* produces a box that asks the user a question and provides one, two, or three buttons to indicate an answer. HyperCard then puts the user's answer into the special *it* variable. The *it* variable is a general-purpose global variable that is used by HyperCard as a temporary storage area. The syntax of the command is *answer* (what the question is) *with* (response) *or* (response) *or* (response).

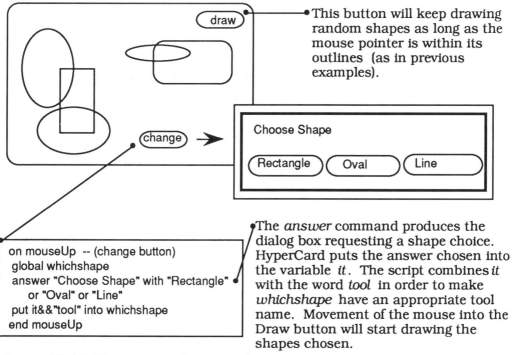

draw

•This button will keep drawing random shapes as long as the mouse pointer is within its outlines (as in previous examples).

change →

Choose Shape

Rectangle   Oval   Line

```
on mouseUp -- (change button)
  global whichshape
  answer "Choose Shape" with "Rectangle"
    or "Oval" or "Line"
  put it&&"tool" into whichshape
end mouseUp
```

•The *answer* command produces the dialog box requesting a shape choice. HyperCard puts the answer chosen into the variable *it*. The script combines *it* with the word *tool* in order to make *whichshape* have an appropriate tool name. Movement of the mouse into the Draw button will start drawing the shapes chosen.

Figure 15.13 The answer Command

Figure 15.13 builds on Figure 15.12. It replaces the script with an Answer Dialog Box that gives the user a chance to pick a shape. Drawing then proceeds using the tool chosen.

The *ask* and *ask password* Commands

The *ask* command does not force the user to choose among prespecified options. It produces a dialog box that asks the user to type the requested information in a response field. The script creator can provide the question and the default response that will be put in the response field. Users can check OK or erase that default and substitute their own answer. Whatever the user types is put into the special *it* variable. The stack creator's script must provide the commands that specify what to do with the response. The syntax of the command is *ask* (whatever the question is) *with* (reply). The default specification of reply is optional.

The *ask password* command takes the user's answer and converts it into a code-modified number representing the response, which is returned in the *it* variable. This coded version can be compared with previously stored versions to see if the person is a valid user. The stack creator's script must provide the intelligence about what to do with given matches or mismatches.

Figure 15.14 demonstrates use of the *ask* command. The program asks users to type their name in the response field. The script then proceeds to draw their name in random fonts, styles, and sizes. Note the use of the *it* variable to convert their answer into the text to be typed.

This chapter has introduced HyperCard's interactive features. Combinations of these features with other graphic potentials can produce engaging programs.

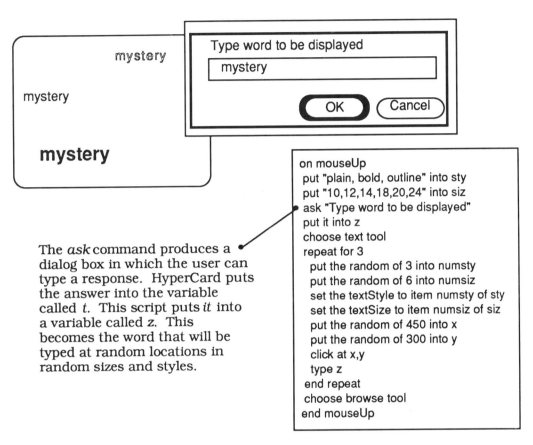

The *ask* command produces a dialog box in which the user can type a response. HyperCard puts the answer into the variable called *t*. This script puts *it* into a variable called *z*. This becomes the word that will be typed at random locations in random sizes and styles.

```
on mouseUp
  put "plain, bold, outline" into sty
  put "10,12,14,18,20,24" into siz
  ask "Type word to be displayed"
  put it into z
  choose text tool
  repeat for 3
    put the random of 3 into numsty
    put the random of 6 into numsiz
    set the textStyle to item numsty of sty
    set the textSize to item numsiz of siz
    put the random of 450 into x
    put the random of 300 into y
    click at x,y
    type z
  end repeat
  choose browse tool
end mouseUp
```

Figure 15.14 The ask Command

Chapter 16
Self-running Stacks and Animation

Interactive versus Self-running Programs

HyperCard is optimized for the creation of interactive programs. In almost all of the previous examples, the scripts create objects that can be activated by the viewer. Users can cause the computer to perform certain options by clicking on buttons or writing in fields. In more traditional computer programming environments, programs are often conceived differently. They are self-running, with user interactions requested only at specific times. Once started, the program moves through its sequence of preprogrammed steps.

Traditional art forms are similar to traditionally developed programs in the following way: The creator of a book, cinema, or musical piece has predetermined the sequence of audience experiences. The task for the creator of an interactive event is more complicated. Each audience member is free to pick a unique sequence. The experiences must make sense and be engaging in a variety of orders. This distinction, between preprogrammed and user choice will undoubtedly become a major aesthetic design issue in the future.

Although HyperCard is ideally suited for the creation of interactive events, it also has several features that allow creation of completely self-running programs. That is, once a user initiates a program, it can completely take over — presenting images and sounds in the precise, predetermined order that the creator has designed.

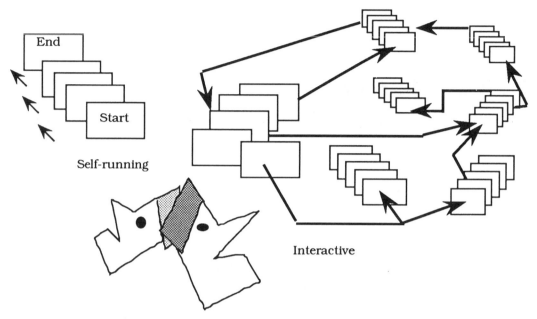

Figure 16.1   Self-running and Interactive Events

The *open* Message Handler

HyperCard objects (stacks, backgrounds, cards) have the built-in capability to undertake certain actions whenever they are first started. For example, a stack creator can write a script that will be automatically activated each time someone chooses to enter the stack. In HyperCard lingo, the stack is said to understand the *open* message. Similar scripts can be attached to backgrounds and cards.

The effects can be similar to traditional art forms. Starting a stack can produce a series of predesigned image/sound events over which the viewer has no control. Of course, it is possible to create mixed designs in which automatic sequences are interspersed with viewer options or in which a certain limited viewer set of actions (such as terminating the sequence) are allowed throughout.

The *openStack* message handler can be used to set up features of a stack that will pertain throughout a viewer's visit. For example, a script can set *the userLevel* to adjust the interactivity. If the stack creator does not want a viewer to be able to change the script, the level can be set to painting or lower. A scriptor can arrange for features such as the menuBar or the Message Box to be visible or invisible. HyperCard commands *hide* and *show* can accomplish the same effect. Almost all objects in HyperCard can be hidden or made visible under stack control. Buttons, fields, and pictures can similarly be hidden or shown.

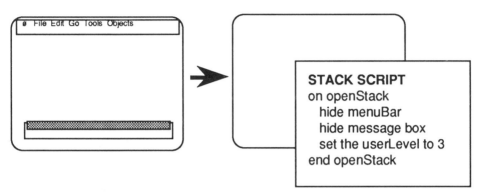

Figure 16.2   OpenStack Script to Hide MenuBar and Message Box and to Set the UserLevel

The *on open(Object)* message handlers can be used expressively to arrange for certain animations to occur each time a person opens the stack. A common example is the opening credits that are commonplace in cinema and video. In Figure 16.3, the *openStack* handler hides the menuBar and all the buttons and fields and runs an animated credit sequence. The name of the work moves across the screen by a loop that types itself at a particular location and then erases itself and moves on to another. The *open* sequence takes over until it is completed; the buttons are not available until that time.

Another *open* script might take the viewer through a sequence of cards in the stack. For example, one might use this approach as a teaser or introduction to the interactive possibilities of the stack or a cel animation created by rapid sequencing through a set of cards.

Note that the *open* message handler could dominate all the actions of the stack. That is, a stack could consist entirely of a sequence of presentations activated by the *open* message handler. In this approach the stack functions just like traditional art forms and computer language environments that do not emphasize interactivity.

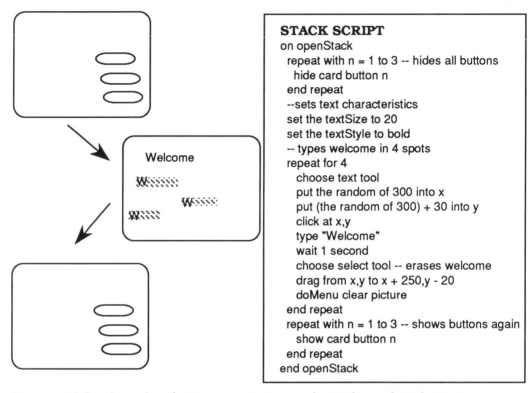

```
STACK SCRIPT
on openStack
  repeat with n = 1 to 3 -- hides all buttons
    hide card button n
  end repeat
  --sets text characteristics
  set the textSize to 20
  set the textStyle to bold
  -- types welcome in 4 spots
  repeat for 4
    choose text tool
    put the random of 300 into x
    put (the random of 300) + 30 into y
    click at x,y
    type "Welcome"
    wait 1 second
    choose select tool -- erases welcome
    drag from x,y to x + 250,y - 20
    doMenu clear picture
  end repeat
  repeat with n = 1 to 3 -- shows buttons again
    show card button n
  end repeat
end openStack
```

Figure 16.3   OpenStack Menu to Animate the Title and Hide Buttons

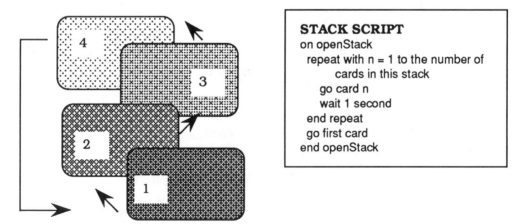

```
STACK SCRIPT
on openStack
  repeat with n = 1 to the number of
           cards in this stack
    go card n
    wait 1 second
  end repeat
  go first card
end openStack
```

Figure 16.4   OpenStack Script to Cycle through All Cards in the Stack

The *open* message can be used with cards and backgrounds also. Upon entering a card, the *open* message handler can arrange events as designed by the stack creator. For example, each card could have animations that were activated by the choice of that card. A stack might contain a home card consisting of buttons leading to various cards, each of which contained self-running animations.

The *close* Message Handler

The *on close(Object)* message works in a parallel fashion to the *open* message handler. Scripts can be written to activate whenever a card, background, or stack is quit, either interactively by the user or automatically. The syntax parallels the use of the *open* message handler.

For example, the *close* handler can be used to activate an animation that visually indicates the termination of a sequence, or it could start animated text to thank the browser. The *close* message handler can be used to check whether the user really wants to quit or offer options for the next activities available in the stack.

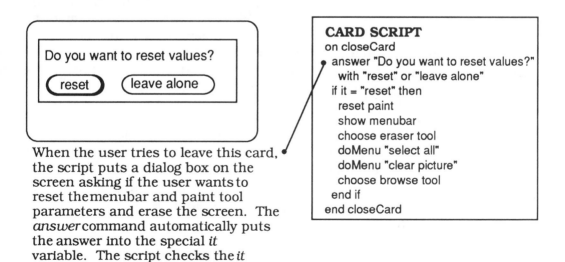

When the user tries to leave this card, the script puts a dialog box on the screen asking if the user wants to reset the menubar and paint tool parameters and erase the screen. The *answer* command automatically puts the answer into the special *it* variable. The script checks the *it* variable and acts accordingly.

Figure 16.5   Script to Reset Parameters When Card Is Quit

Often the *close* handler is used to reset changes made with the *open* handler. For example, if buttons or pictures have been hidden when a particular card became active, they can be reshown with the close action. Similarly, if *the userLevel* has been set to a value that doesn't allow interactivity, it can be reset when the stack, card, or background is exited. Similarly, paint properties such as *draw filled* or *the lineSize* can also be reset. The *reset paint* command will reset all paint properties to their default values. Because one cannot be sure what stack a browser will go to next, it has become customary to reset any global system properties that one's stack has changed. Since HyperCard remembers all settings when moving from stack to stack, changes can play havoc with other stacks that worked according to default settings — for example, all lines being drawn in 8-pixel size instead of the default 1-pixel size.

The *idle* Message Handler: Animation Examples

Even when nothing seems to be happening, HyperCard is automatically sending constant *idle* messages. Message handlers can be placed at any level (card, background, or stack) to intercept and respond to the *idle* message. Thus, scripts can appear to be self-activating other than at the opening and closing times. *Idle* message handlers can be used to give the screen life while HyperCard is waiting for the browser to do something. A later chapter will show how the *idle* message can be used in conjunction with time and date functions to create time-based art forms that create image and sound events, which respond to the passing of time.

Idle message handlers can be used to create animations that are in some ways more flexible than those built with the repeat loop command structures illustrated in earlier chapters. In most common designs, repeat loops take over and do not allow for other actions until they complete. *Idle*-based animations can move objects as long as nothing else is happening and then yield to other HyperCard message handlers, such as clicks on buttons, when they are activated.

Figure 16.6 illustrates a stack that automatically sequences through its cards until the user clicks a button to focus on the current display. This stack script illustrates some of the difficulties of working with the *idle* command.

The rate at which HyperCard sends *idle* messages varies with the level of other script activity. Thus, one can't be certain about the timing with which the scripts will execute. With the card-sequencing script example, the cards might pass too quickly (if no other scripts were executing) or too slowly. A script therefore needs to include timing commands such as the *wait* command to adjust the flow.

In Figure 16.6, the *idle* message-handling script is placed in the stack or background level because it must apply to many cards. The script must continue to operate no matter what card the viewer chooses. In the example, the *on idle* message handler continues to display the next card. A *wait* command ensures that each card will be displayed for approximately the same amount of time during the sequencing.

A button is placed in the background that allows the viewer to stop the display when an interesting card is displayed and to restart the sequencing. All the cards in the sequence are designed to share one common background so that the background button will show through all cards in the sequence.

The *idle* handler will be activated each time HyperCard automatically sends its *idle* message. Some method must therefore be devised to turn it off when the viewer wants to inspect the current card. This capacity to stop and start is accomplished by use of an *if* phrase in the script, which checks

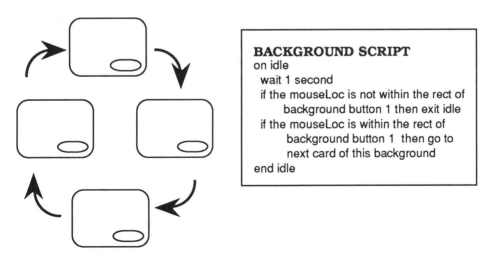

```
BACKGROUND SCRIPT
on idle
  wait 1 second
  if the mouseLoc is not within the rect of
      background button 1 then exit idle
  if the mouseLoc is within the rect of
      background button 1  then go to
      next card of this background
end idle
```

Figure 16.6   On idle Script to Cycle through Cards

whether the viewer has moved out of the boundaries of the button that says to keep displaying cards. The sequencing of cards stops whenever the viewer moves the mouse away.

In Figure 16.7, an *idle* message handler continues to draw random lines unless stopped by the viewer. Control is accomplished with a single button that changes its name and effect, depending on its previous status. Each time the button is clicked, the button script determines the present value of the global variable arbitrarily named "status" and changes it to its opposite. Also the button makes use of HyperCard's ability to change button names in the middle of actions. If the stack is currently in drawing mode, the button's name is Stop Drawing. If it's in stop mode, its name is Start Drawing. Thus, the button changes its action according to the currently active function and uses its name to alert users to what will happen if they click the button.

The script makes use of the HyperCard function *the name of* and the special object indicator called *me*. When used in scripts, the term *me* automatically fills in the name of whatever object contains a script that uses

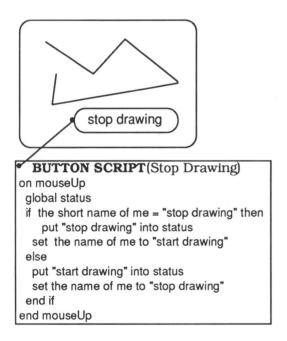

```
BUTTON SCRIPT(Stop Drawing)
on mouseUp
  global status
  if  the short name of me = "stop drawing" then
      put "stop drawing" into status
    set  the name of me to "start drawing"
  else
    put "start drawing" into status
    set the name of me to "stop drawing"
  end if
end mouseUp
```

```
CARD SCRIPT
on openCard
  global status,x,y
  put 0 into x
  put 0 into y
end openCard

on idle
  global status,x,y,x1,y1
  if status = "stop drawing" then exit idle
  if status = "start drawing" then
    put the random of 512 into x1
    put the random of 340 into y1
    choose line tool
    drag from x,y to x1,y1
    put x1 into x
    put y1 into y
    choose browse tool
  end if
end idle
```

Figure 16.7   Idle Script to Draw Random Lines That Can Be Controlled by a Button That Changes Its Name

the term. This generic way of automatically getting a name is very useful for several reasons. It allows one to create objects with scripts that will operate correctly in any context. It allows creation of buttons that can be widely distributed and copied — for example, there are companies that sell stacks full of special buttons that work in widely varying stacks. The function of generic reference is especially useful in this script because the button's name keeps changing. The *name of* function returns the name of whatever object is specified. *Set the name of (an object) to (a new name)* changes the name of the object.

Another example illustrates use of the *on idle* handler to animate objects on a single card. Each time HyperCard sends an *idle* message the script will change the location of the object in accordance with a specified pattern.

In order to accomplish this movement, *global* variables must be declared that will determine the desired location. They must be *global* variables rather than local variables so that they can store the last values. This is necessary because local variables are initialized each time Hyper-Card exits from the handler in which they reside.

In Figure 16.8, a filled circle moves across the screen with *idle* messages. Each time the card is entered, the animation picks up from where it was when the card was closed. The variables x and y store the location of the circle.

Animation requires that an image be erased or drawn over in the background pattern before it is redrawn at the new spot. The sequence of drawing, erasing, and redrawing is what gives the appearance of motion (if the drawing and erasing happen quickly enough). The *idle* script draws in white at the current location and adds an increment to x and/or y to specify the next location, changes the pattern to black, and then draws at the new location.

As illustrated with the repeat loops in an earlier chapter, positive increments to x move the item to the right. Negative increments move it to the left. Positive increments in y move it down, and negative increments in y move it up. Combined increments move it in diagonal directions. Increment size controls the speed and smoothness of motion. X and y are arbitrary names given to the horizontal and vertical position, respectively.

The *if* commands in the *idle* message handler check for the situation in which the object has moved to the border of the screen. If an *x* or *y* should exceed the edges, the script resets *x* and *y* to the opposite side. The object appears to come back or "wrap around."

The other sample script shows how to make the object appear to bounce back and start moving in the opposite direction. It accomplishes

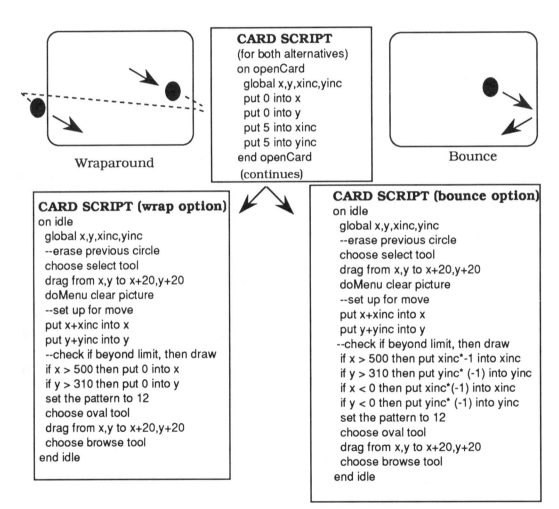

```
CARD SCRIPT
(for both alternatives)
on openCard
  global x,y,xinc,yinc
  put 0 into x
  put 0 into y
  put 5 into xinc
  put 5 into yinc
end openCard
(continues)
```

Wraparound   Bounce

```
CARD SCRIPT (wrap option)
on idle
  global x,y,xinc,yinc
  --erase previous circle
  choose select tool
  drag from x,y to x+20,y+20
  doMenu clear picture
  --set up for move
  put x+xinc into x
  put y+yinc into y
  --check if beyond limit, then draw
  if x > 500 then put 0 into x
  if y > 310 then put 0 into y
  set the pattern to 12
  choose oval tool
  drag from x,y to x+20,y+20
  choose browse tool
end idle
```

```
CARD SCRIPT (bounce option)
on idle
  global x,y,xinc,yinc
  --erase previous circle
  choose select tool
  drag from x,y to x+20,y+20
  doMenu clear picture
  --set up for move
  put x+xinc into x
  put y+yinc into y
  --check if beyond limit, then draw
  if x > 500 then put xinc*-1 into xinc
  if y > 310 then put yinc* (-1) into yinc
  if x < 0 then put xinc*(-1) into xinc
  if y < 0 then put yinc* (-1) into yinc
  set the pattern to 12
  choose oval tool
  drag from x,y to x+20,y+20
  choose browse tool
end idle
```

Figure 16.8   Idle-controlled Script to Move a Circle with Wraparound and with Bounce

this by changing positive increments to negative and vice versa when the shape comes up against the edge. Changing the sign in the variables (and hence the direction of movement) is accomplished by the mathematical fact that negative numbers multiplied by negative numbers result in positive numbers. Thus, a positive increment multiplied by a negative one becomes negative (and hence changes direction). Similarly, a negative increment number multiplied by a negative one becomes positive (changing into the other direction).

These scripts activate as long as one is looking at cards that have the *on idle* message handler as part of their script. The only way to start or stop them is to leave or enter the card. Other arrangements, such as buttons to turn the idle handler off or on, could be easily arranged.

Animation of Buttons and Fields

In this example, simple shapes were moved. Practically all the other graphic forms (for example, filled forms or polygons) can also be moved in a similar way. In addition, any other objects that can have their location specified can similarly be moved — for example, buttons and fields.

In Figure 16.9, a field moves across the screen in various ways. It creates an animated opening credit similar to Figure 16.3. These animations can be very effective because the buttons and fields appear to hover above picture levels. If a graphic icon has been attached to the button, the

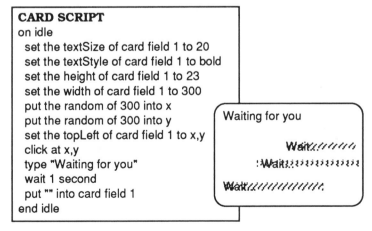

CARD SCRIPT
on idle
  set the textSize of card field 1 to 20
  set the textStyle of card field 1 to bold
  set the height of card field 1 to 23
  set the width of card field 1 to 300
  put the random of 300 into x
  put the random of 300 into y
  set the topLeft of card field 1 to x,y
  click at x,y
  type "Waiting for you"
  wait 1 second
  put "" into card field 1
end idle

Figure 16.9   Idle Script to Move Fields Around

icon can be animated in this way. Animation of fields full of text makes animation of text easy. Other computers optimized for computer graphics have a similar capacity to animate small blocks of image, sometimes called sprites or blocks.

Oscillating Icon Animation

The icon feature of HyperCard buttons allows for more complex animations combining gross movement with internal movement. Hyper-Card allows dynamic assignment of icons within scripts. Thus, the icon can appear to change as it moves along. To accomplish this, one must select an appropriate family of visually related icons. In Figure 16.10, the arrow seems to rotate as it moves along. This approach to internal motion is similar to the classic cycling of images in traditional film animation, as described in an earlier chapter.

To accomplish this combined linear and internal motion, one must determine the icon numbers of the icons that will be used to make up the

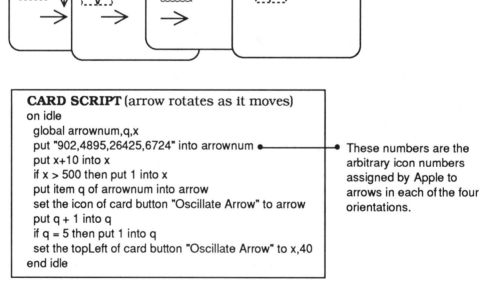

CARD SCRIPT (arrow rotates as it moves)
```
on idle
  global arrownum,q,x
  put "902,4895,26425,6724" into arrownum
  put x+10 into x
  if x > 500 then put 1 into x
  put item q of arrownum into arrow
  set the icon of card button "Oscillate Arrow" to arrow
  put q + 1 into q
  if q = 5 then put 1 into q
  set the topLeft of card button "Oscillate Arrow" to x,40
end idle
```
These numbers are the arbitrary icon numbers assigned by Apple to arrows in each of the four orientations.

Figure 16.10 Idle-controlled Button with Rotating Icon

cycling images. HyperCard scripts can change the icon of a button by use of syntax such as the following: *Set the icon of card button 1 to 733.*

In Figure 16.10, the set of icons depicts arrows in various positions. The location of the button is controlled by global variables *x* and *y*. The *idle* message handler increments these each time, and the button appears to move.

This script also changes the icon each time by creating a global variable containing the list of icon numbers that represent the arrow in each position when the card is first opened. Another global variable is created to keep track of which icon is currently being displayed. Each time through the loop, a particular icon number out of the set of items in the global variable is incremented — for example, item 1 of the list, then item 2 of the list and so on. This technique was described in Chapter 14. The *if* statement checks for the situation in which the last item in the list is selected and resets the *keeptrack* variable to point at the first icon.

One is not limited to using just the icons provided with HyperCard. Public domain and commercial programs such as Icon Factory and Resedit allow design of custom icons that can then be created specifically for the animation effect. These programs are available from the sources described in Chapter 20.

Simultaneous Animation of Several Objects

Animations so far have illustrated the movement of single objects. The *idle* message handler can easily be designed to move several objects each with its own path. Separate variables must be created to keep track of the horizontal and vertical positions of each and of the horizontal and vertical increments of motion.

With each *idle* message, the position of each object is adjusted separately. This script is only an extension of the earlier one with the bouncing shape. Object 1 starts to move right and down while object 2 starts moving up and left.

Theoretically, this approach could be extended to any number of items. Practically, this is not possible. HyperCard cannot compute quickly enough to move many objects seamlessly. Complex animations require use

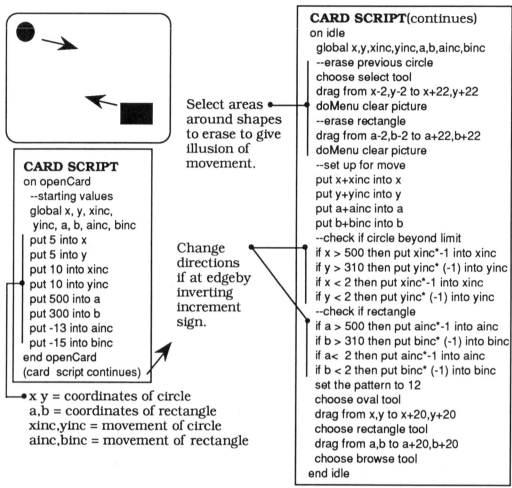

Figure 16.11 Idle-controlled Movement of Two Objects

of extensions to HyperCard like the special drivers to use animations created in programs such as Videoworks™ discussed in Chapter 20.

Animation of Complex Drawn Images

All examples so far have illustrated movement of standard Hyper-Card objects — buttons, fields, and graphics provided by the tool palette. The techniques described are not limited to these standard shapes. Judicious use of the selection tools in scripts can animate any shape drawn on the screen. These shapes can be drawn by hand with the paint tools, imported from MacPaint or from other paint programs or imported in MacPaint format from a scanner or other sources. Although this section will illustrate these techniques used with *idle* message handlers, they could also be used with *repeat* loops and other scripting approaches.

The strategy for animating these shapes duplicates the process for moving hand-drawn shapes.

- A bit-mapped, paint-format image must be created or imported.
- The image must be selected using one of the selection tools — the selection rectangle or lasso.
- Click within the object while holding down the mouse button. As one drags the mouse, the object appears to follow the mouse movements.

This is the kind of movement that can be duplicated by scripts — within certain limitations determined by the nature of the image and the limitations of the HyperCard selection tools.

The selection rectangle and lasso work quite differently, as described in Chapter 6. The rectangle chooses everything within its boundary, including white space. The moving rectangle appears like an opaque card moving over any other graphics. All white areas included in the rectangle obscure other graphics.

The *lasso* works differently. In interactive hand mode, dragging a mouse around a graphic object causes the object to be selected apart from its white surrounding area. In addition, internal white areas appear transparent. Once an object is selected, clicking inside the area with a mouse button causes the object to follow the movements of the mouse. This animation, which does not obscure other graphics, appears much different from the moving opaque rectangle.

Scripts to accomplish movement of selected areas are quite easy. The script needs only to use the coordinates of the rectangle surrounding the object. The script then chooses the selection rectangle by clicking inside the rectangle *with the option key,* as one must do by hand. The object may then be moved around the screen with the *drag* command. The timing must be adjusted for *idle* message irregularities, and *the dragSpeed* must be changed appropriately.

The use of the lasso in scripts is not so straightforward. There is no way to duplicate the free-form dragging of the hand-controlled mouse under script control. In interactive hand mode, the mouse button is held down while the mouse is moved from coordinate to coordinate around the object

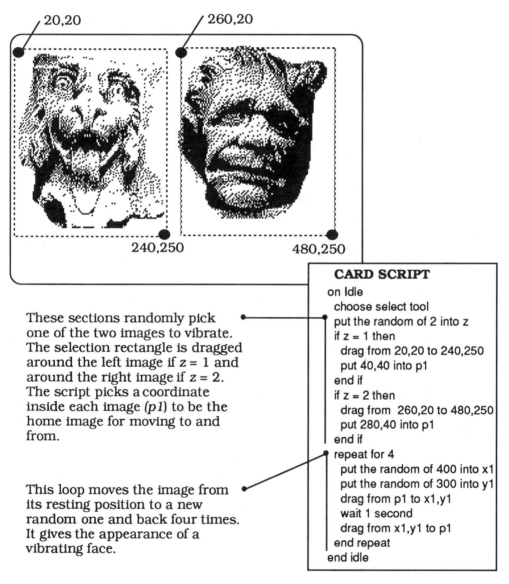

These sections randomly pick one of the two images to vibrate. The selection rectangle is dragged around the left image if *z* = 1 and around the right image if *z* = 2. The script picks a coordinate inside each image *(p1)* to be the home image for moving to and from.

This loop moves the image from its resting position to a new random one and back four times. It gives the appearance of a vibrating face.

```
CARD SCRIPT
on Idle
  choose select tool
  put the random of 2 into z
  if z = 1 then
    drag from 20,20 to 240,250
    put 40,40 into p1
  end if
  if z = 2 then
    drag from  260,20 to 480,250
    put 280,40 into p1
  end if
  repeat for 4
    put the random of 400 into x1
    put the random of 300 into y1
    drag from p1 to x1,y1
    wait 1 second
    drag from x1,y1 to p1
  end repeat
end idle
```

Figure 16.12 Idle Script to Move a Digitized Image

to be selected. Unfortunately, HyperCard supplies an automatic *mouseUp* message each time a *drag* command executes in a script. Thus, it is impossible to duplicate the unbroken movement of a hand-controlled mouse around an object. HyperCard acts as though one line was dragged, then let go, and another dragged and so on. This same lapse in HyperCard prevents scripts from duplicating other actions, such as drawing irregular polygons.

Animation Opportunities with Option and Command Key Enhancements

Luckily, HyperCard provides some possibilities to approximate these kinds of hand-dragging actions. In hand mode, dragging the selection rectangle while holding down the option key results in an object being hugged with the smallest rectangle that can surround it. Dragging a selection rectangle with the command key results in HyperCard automatically selecting the item, as if someone had precisely selected the item with a lasso drawn to hug its border. In lasso tool mode, clicking inside an object with the command key causes HyperCard automatically to seek the closest contiguous border and select it.

On graphic objects with clean borders and no overlapping, these techniques can duplicate the lasso. Once selected, the objects can be animated under script control. For these techniques to work, one must know precisely where the coordinate boundaries are in order to simulate clicks and drags at the right location.

Using *idle* to Keep Track of the Mouse

Often it is useful to know the exact coordinates of the mouse. For example, when one is planning animations, it is sometimes necessary to know the exact top left and bottom right coordinates in order to use the selection rectangle accurately. Similarly, placement of buttons and fields sometimes requires information about coordinates. An example in Chapter 15 showed how *the mouseLoc* function could be typed at any time to ascertain the mouse's current location. Figure 16.14 illustrates the usefulness of the *idle* command in automating this process. The script gives a

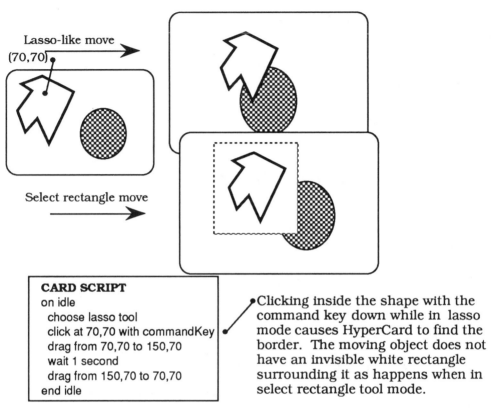

Lasso-like move
(70,70)

Select rectangle move

```
CARD SCRIPT
on idle
  choose lasso tool
  click at 70,70 with commandKey
  drag from 70,70 to 150,70
  wait 1 second
  drag from 150,70 to 70,70
end idle
```

•Clicking inside the shape with the command key down while in lasso mode causes HyperCard to find the border. The moving object does not have an invisible white rectangle surrounding it as happens when in select rectangle tool mode.

Figure 16.13 Idle-controlled Lassolike Animation

constant readout of the mouse's location as it is moved about, which eases the planning and visual design of cards.

HyperCard is famous for its interactive capacities. The self-running features described in this chapter enable HyperCard to simulate computer languages that are not focused on interactivity. They also enhance the possibilities for stack design by allowing integration of interactive and self-running structures and by facilitating the design of animations.

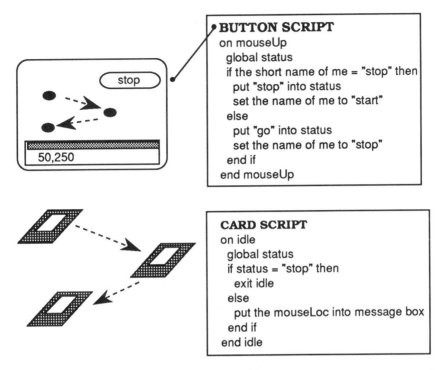

BUTTON SCRIPT
```
on mouseUp
  global status
  if the short name of me = "stop" then
    put "stop" into status
    set the name of me to "start"
  else
    put "go" into status
    set the name of me to "stop"
  end if
end mouseUp
```

CARD SCRIPT
```
on idle
  global status
  if status = "stop" then
    exit idle
  else
    put the mouseLoc into message box
  end if
end idle
```

Figure 16.14 Script to Print the Mouse Location Continuously

Chapter 17
Sound Programming

New Possibilities for Multimedia Art

The original Macintosh computer included a sophisticated electronic sound-generating integrated circuit chip and speaker as part of its basic hardware. This chip was capable of producing respectable sound effects, speech, and music. Newer models provide even more sophisticated sound possibilities, including stereo. The computer also provides an audio line-out connector jack through which an audio signal can easily be routed to any common amplifier such as is used for home music systems. The computer sound is considerably enhanced when amplified.

HyperCard provides easy access to sound-generating possibilities. Built-in commands allow generation of precisely timed musical notes tuned to traditional Western scales. Digitally recorded sounds can be used in scripts in conjunction with relatively inexpensive sound digitizers such as the MacRecorder®. The addition of special external commands allows scripts to talk with a synthesized voice or to control MIDI-compatible music synthesizers. These external commands will be explained more in following sections.

Such capabilities have opened up unprecedented possibilities for artists to work across media. Programming environments such as Hyper-Card invite artists to create multimedia events that integrate image with music, speech, and sound effects. Computers are expanding the ranks of those who can work with music and sound. They are enabling many artists to work with sound who may not have the performance skills but do have sophisticated expressive ideas they want to explore.

The reader should be aware that although HyperCard's sound capabilities are interesting for interactive event creation, they are primitive compared to the specialized music software available specifically for working with sound. Interested readers are urged to consult magazines aimed at Macintosh users for descriptions and reviews of these programs.

Introduction to Sound

Although a detailed presentation of sound synthesis theory is beyond the scope of this text, some background knowledge will be useful for readers wanting to work with computer sound. Readers can get some additional details in my book *Using Computers to Create Art*, and in specialized texts.

For humans, sound is experienced when air vibrates the eardrum and the connected sensory organs of the ear. With computers, the sound is originated by the electronic control of the rubber or cardboard diaphragm of a speaker, which vibrates the air; ultimately the air vibrates the eardrum. In a Macintosh, the speaker is controlled by the sound chip.

Sound can be characterized by certain analytical features. These characteristics are important to understand because computers often give the artist discrete control over their values. Artists can "sculpt" sound by controlling these characteristics. The amount of energy used in creating a sound determines its amplitude, or loudness. A great deal of movement is perceived as a loud sound. For example, with string instruments it is the distance the string moves in its vibrations. With an audio speaker, it is the distance the diaphragm moves each time it vibrates.

The speed with which the vibrations occur is called the frequency or pitch. This is what is commonly called the "highness" or "lowness" of a sound. Frequency is measured with a unit called the *hertz* (abbreviated *Hz*), which means vibrations per second. Thus, a sound might be described to be at 100 hertz (the speaker and eardrum vibrating 100 times a second). Normal human hearing can pick up sounds between 20 and 20,000 Hz. Musical notes are essentially standardized shorthand names for particular frequencies. Middle C is internationally defined as 261.6 Hz. The note A in the same octave is defined as 880 Hz. Thus, the bell of a trumpet playing middle C will be vibrating 261 times a second, as will the eardrum hearing that sound.

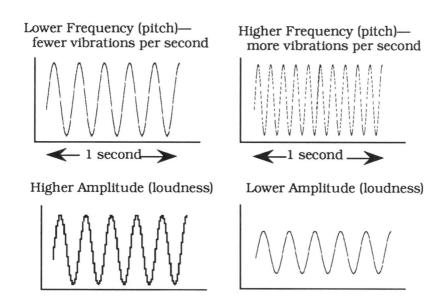

Figure 17.1   Basic Characteristics of Sound: Frequency and Amplitude

Obviously, a voice, a trumpet, and a violin playing the same note do not sound the same. These differences result from a variety of other characteristics of sound.   Materials in nature rarely vibrate purely at one frequency. While one frequency may dominate, other frequencies with less energy also occur. These are called overtones or harmonics. In a related fashion, the way each vibration occurs can differ. For example, each vibration can build up slowly, and recede slowly or each vibration can come and go almost instantaneously. The variations are called wave shapes. Figure 17.2 shows three common wave shapes.

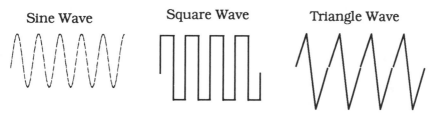

Figure 17.2   Wave Shapes

Finally, the way in which a sound ebbs and flows in volume over time can differ. The shape of this variation is called the ADSR envelope (for attack, decay, sustain, release). For example, the sound in a trumpet note comes up in volume quickly and dies quickly. A piano note, by contrast, dies out slowly. The envelopes are thus different. This combination of features is called the timbre or color of the sound.

Sophisticated computer chip–activated sound synthesizers allow artists and musicians to discretely manipulate each of these qualities of sound. Whereas the internal sound chip in the Macintosh does not offer this level of discrete control, it does allow some, as will be explained.

The *beep* Command

HyperCard provides a very basic *beep* command to output the standard beep that the Macintosh uses for warnings and aural feedback. A script can specify any number of beeps. Use of this command can very simply add sound to animations or be used as feedback for user actions. The following illustrate the format:

```
beep       beep 5
beep z     (assuming that  z is a variable container that has a number in it)
```

The *play* Command and the Function *the sound*

The *play* command is HyperCard's workhorse for sound generation. It allows the playing of a variety of sounds as musical notes (that is, in different frequencies) in various tempos (speeds). Figure 17.3 illustrates its format. Everything except the sound parameter is optional. That is, scripts using the *play* command do not have to specify these other values if it is not necessary.

The sound parameter specifies a particular sound definition (sound wave and color) that will be used to create the sound generated by the *play* command. HyperCard comes with four built-in sounds: harpsichord, boing, silence, and dialing tones. The section on sound digitizers will demonstrate how to increase its repertoire of sounds.

The *tempo* parameter specifies the speed with which the notes are played if there is a sequence of notes indicated in the *notes* parameter. Otherwise, HyperCard will use the last tempo specified or the default value

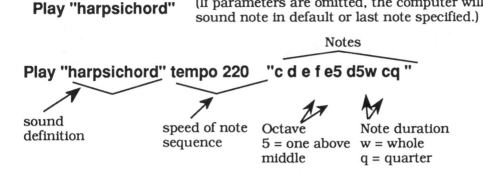

Figure 17.3   *HyperCard's play Command with Parameters*

of 200. One would need to experiment to match these numbers up with traditional musical tempos.

The *notes* parameter uses the traditional letter names of notes in the Western scale — A,B,C,D,E,F,G. It assumes the natural form of each note unless flats (b) or sharps (#) are specified. A *play* command will assume middle C if no specific notes are specified.

Because the note names repeat for each octave, the play command requires the script to specify the octave if the notes are not in the octave around middle C. This octave is given the number 4, and it is the default if no other octave is specified.

An alternative method of naming notes uses numbers to indicate each note. Middle C is given the value 60, and every note (including sharps and flats) is given a sequential number. Figure 17.4 shows the note names, octave numbers, and number equivalents for notes as indicated on a piano keyboard and on a standard musical notation stave.

The *duration* parameter can be assigned to each note. It represents the standard musical notation values associated with notes. HyperCard understands the following values for note duration:

w = whole note	e = eighth note
h = half note	s = sixteenth note
q = quarter note	t = thirty-second note

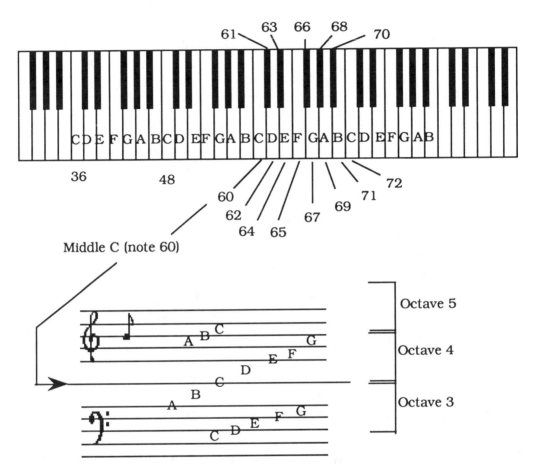

Figure 17.4   Notes, Note Numbers, and Octaves

With these parameters, it is easy to direct HyperCard to play just about any single-voice music. Single-voice means that only one note at a time can sound, and harmonies are not possible. One needs only to convert the sheet music notation to the letter and octave notation that HyperCard understands. Ironically, the sound chip inside the Macintosh is capable of simulating multivoice music, but the initial versions of HyperCard do not allow the user to control this feature. The sound digitizers described in following sections will allow the use of prerecorded multivoice sounds but will not allow scripts to control each voice independently.

Figure 17.5 shows HyperCard scripts to play musical notes using the note notation just described.

Script using note letter

Play "harpisichord" "ce cs dq cq fq eq   ce cs dq cq gq   fq cq   ce cs ae f3e e3q dq
          bbe bbs aq fq gq fq "

Notes do not need duration indication if the note has the same
duration as previous note.

Script using note number

Play "harpsichord" 60e 60s 62q 60 65 64   60e 60s 62q 60 67 65   60e 60s 60q 57 55
64 62 58 58 57 65 67 65

Figure 17.5   Script to Play "Happy Birthday to You"

When one needs only a simple sound, all the parameters can be
dropped except the name of the sound. For example, *play boing* will play the
boing sound in its default pitch and speed.

The *Play stop* Command

The command to stop whatever sound is currently playing is *play
stop.*

The Function *the sound*

HyperCard provides one other sound-related function that allows
scripts to assess where the sound chip is in its action. Using *the sound*

function, a script can ask the current value of the sound. HyperCard will return either the name of the current sound (for example, harpsichord), or the word *done* if nothing is playing or if the last *play* command has finished. The word *the* is a necessary part of using the function. Commands are scripts' ways of telling HyperCard what to do. Functions are HyperCard's way of communicating back the results of actions or inquiries. For example, the command line *put the sound into message box* will put the name of the currently playing sound in the Message Box.

Readers might wonder why *the sound* function is necessary. If one issues a *play* command, obviously the sound playing is the sound issued by the *play* command.

It is necessary for several reasons: The sound chip is actually a sort of computer on its own. After HyperCard sends it a sequence of sounds to play (such as a series of notes), it will take over the responsibility for playing the sounds. The next commands in the script will then be executed as the sound plays simultaneously. If coordination between these commands (for example, graphics) and sound is necessary, the script needs a way to assess when sounds are done. Combining the sound function with appropriate commands to check the status of playing sounds (for example, *if, repeat until,* or *repeat while*) allows for coordinated action.

The function is also necessary because other commands following the *play* command might need to access the disk. A disk access on floppy disks or some hard disks will interfere with the quality of the sound generated. HyperCard is designed to access the disk frequently — for example, a *go to next card* command might well need to load the card from disk storage. Using *the sound* function to check for completion of the *play* sequence before allowing the other commands to proceed guarantees no interruption to the sound quality.

Checking the status of the sound also allows precise sequencing. A sequence of *play* commands in a script can cause problems because HyperCard will not automatically interrupt the previous sounds. Also, repeated calls to the *play* command before playing sounds are stopped can cause HyperCard to crash and cease to function.

Coordination of Sound with Other Script Actions

Some care is necessary in scripts to coordinate sound and graphics because of the peculiarities of the *play* command. In Figure 17.6, a schematic ball bounces down some schematic stairs with the notes getting lower on each stair. A *play stop* command is used to stop the previous sound when the ball hits the next stair.

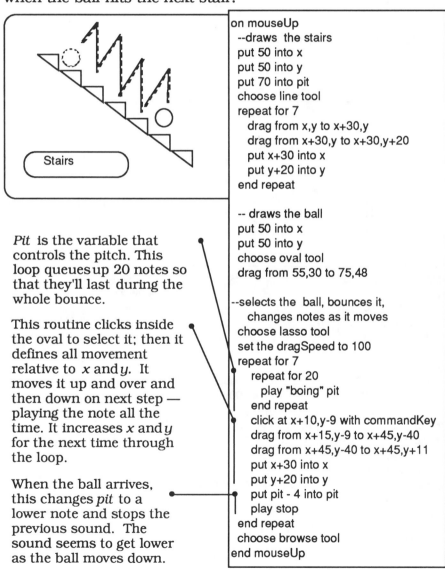

```
on mouseUp
  --draws the stairs
  put 50 into x
  put 50 into y
  put 70 into pit
  choose line tool
  repeat for 7
    drag from x,y to x+30,y
    drag from x+30,y to x+30,y+20
    put x+30 into x
    put y+20 into y
  end repeat

  -- draws the ball
  put 50 into x
  put 50 into y
  choose oval tool
  drag from 55,30 to 75,48

  --selects the ball, bounces it,
    changes notes as it moves
  choose lasso tool
  set the dragSpeed to 100
  repeat for 7
    repeat for 20
      play "boing" pit
    end repeat
    click at x+10,y-9 with commandKey
    drag from x+15,y-9 to x+45,y-40
    drag from x+45,y-40 to x+45,y+11
    put x+30 into x
    put y+20 into y
    put pit - 4 into pit
    play stop
  end repeat
  choose browse tool
end mouseUp
```

Pit is the variable that controls the pitch. This loop queues up 20 notes so that they'll last during the whole bounce.

This routine clicks inside the oval to select it; then it defines all movement relative to x and y. It moves it up and over and then down on next step — playing the note all the time. It increases x and y for the next time through the loop.

When the ball arrives, this changes *pit* to a lower note and stops the previous sound. The sound seems to get lower as the ball moves down.

Figure 17.6   Coordination of Animation and Sound

Figure 17.7 combines the *play* command with attention to user action. The script plays a fixed sequence of notes. The viewer can choose which instrument sound will be used to generate the sound. The script keeps the sequence of sounds in a global variable called *whichnotes*. It uses a repeat loop to sequence through the notes. It uses a global variable called *instrument* to control the nature of the sound. Movement in and out of buttons changes the value of the variable called *instrument*—thus changing the sound. Moving higher or lower within the button areas controls the octave pitch of the notes being played.

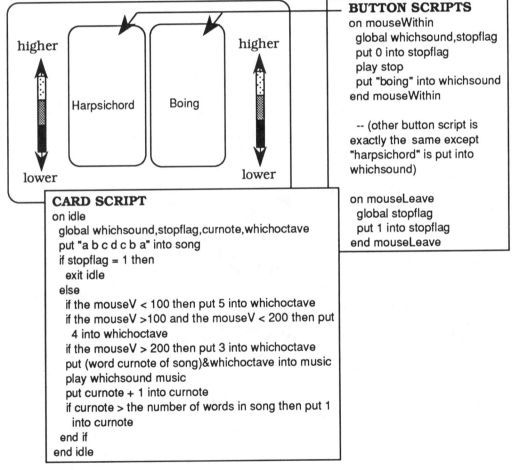

```
BUTTON SCRIPTS
on mouseWithin
  global whichsound,stopflag
  put 0 into stopflag
  play stop
  put "boing" into whichsound
end mouseWithin

-- (other button script is
exactly the same except
"harpsichord" is put into
whichsound)

on mouseLeave
  global stopflag
  put 1 into stopflag
end mouseLeave
```

```
CARD SCRIPT
on idle
  global whichsound,stopflag,curnote,whichoctave
  put "a b c d c b a" into song
  if stopflag = 1 then
    exit idle
  else
    if the mouseV < 100 then put 5 into whichoctave
    if the mouseV >100 and the mouseV < 200 then put
      4 into whichoctave
    if the mouseV > 200 then put 3 into whichoctave
    put (word curnote of song)&whichoctave into music
    play whichsound music
    put curnote + 1 into curnote
    if curnote > the number of words in song then put 1
      into curnote
  end if
end idle
```

Figure 17.7   *Script to Change the Instrument Sound Used by the play Command*

Synthesized Speech

Many computer sound chips are capable of synthesizing human speech. That is, they can create sounds that match the sound patterns of voice by using sounds to approximate the phonemes (basic sound building blocks of speech). Often these speech sounds are robotlike and sometimes difficult to understand. However, they can be intriguing additions to programs. A following section on sound digitizers presents details on generating higher-quality speech sounds.

To use synthesized speech, one needs software to instruct the sound chip to generate the phoneme sounds. Early in the development of the Macintosh, Apple Computer created a special system facility called MacIn-Talk™ that gave the user control if one had a program to access it. Apple decided, however, to offer MacInTalk as a developer's research tool rather than as a commercial product. As a consequence, Apple does not give any official support to its use, and it is not as easy to use as other products.

Independent developers have developed special additions to Hyper-Card that allow scripts to make use of MacInTalk. These special additions are called external commands (XCMDs) and external functions (XFCNs). The designers of HyperCard made it very easy to add new features via these kinds of additions. Once they have been added, they can be activated through command words and functions just as if they were intrinsic parts of HyperCard. Because they are so useful, Chapter 20 explains their use in more detail.

Synthesized speech capability does *not* come with the standard HyperCard. One must take easy but specific actions to prepare HyperCard. The following steps are necessary:

1. The special MacInTalk system facility must be placed in the system folder of the system that will be used to start up the computer. If one starts up off a floppy disk, MacInTalk must be dragged into the folder there. If one uses a hard disk, MacInTalk must be dragged into the system folder on the hard disk. One must therefore obtain a copy of MacInTalk. It can be obtained from national sources such as Com-puServe or the Berkeley Macintosh Users Group (BMUG). For more details on these, see Chapter 20.

2. The special external commands to access MacInTalk from inside HyperCard must be added to HyperCard. Again, one must find a source for these external commands; they are available from many of the same sources as MacInTalk.

3. To install these external commands inside HyperCard, one must use one of the special resource utilities designed for this kind of activity. The external commands are called program resources. Common programs for working with resources are ResEdit™ and ResCopy™. These programs are available from the same sources as MacInTalk. Their use is described in more detail in Chapter 20.

4. Because of HyperCard's hierarchial structure, one has some choice about where to install these external commands. One can place them in HyperCard, the home stack, or a particular user-created stack. Because of HyperCard's hierarchical structure, this decision controls how widely the external commands will apply. If the external command is put into HyperCard, every stack run with that copy will have the ability to use the new commands. Placement of the external commands in a particular stack means that only scripts in that stack will be able to use those commands.

Normally MacInTalk requires a user to specify the phonemes that make up speech sounds. This process can be tricky because one must learn the standard notation system for the approximately 60 basic phonemes that linguists use to specify the repertoire of normal sounds used in English. The phonetic spelling of the word heavy is *h, eh1, v, y.*

The external commands simplify the process of synthesizing speech. The external command software contains algorithms that embody normal rules of English pronunciation. They scan the text presented and convert it into the phonemes that MacInTalk can understand. For example, the commands know that syllables with *a* vowel followed by a consonant followed by an e generally give the vowel a long sound and the last *e* is silent — for example, mute, late, vote.

The algorithms, of course, make mistakes on words that do not follow the rules. For example, foreign words can come out sounding funny. To illustrate, *lasagna* comes out as la- sag-na. Also, the algorithms are not very good at dealing with the inflections, stresses and differential emphases that play a surprisingly important part in making speech understandable.

After practice, however, one can get skilled at adjusting the spelling of words to move closer toward desired sounds. For example, adjusting lasagna to le- zan-ya makes it sound more like its English pronunciation.

The commands are very easy to use. In the external commands, two new commands are added to HyperCard — *talk* and *speak*. *Talk "(whatever text)"* pronounces the words as best as the algorithm can judge. *Speak "(whatever text)"* allows a script to adjust the frequency and tempo of the words.

In Figure 17.8, a series of buttons talk about themselves whenever a viewer moves a mouse into their perimeter. The second part speaks whatever a viewer types into a card field.

Digitized or Sampled Sound

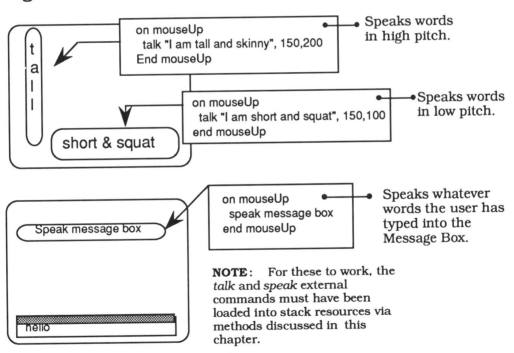

Figure 17.8 *Buttons That Use the talk and speak External Commands to Generate Synthesized Speech*

Digitized or sampled sound represents a radically different way for computers to generate sound from the synthesized sound methods. In synthesized methods, the software mathematically creates waveforms that instruct the sound chip to make sounds. Analytical information about the sound structure of tones or phonemes is converted into the different energies and frequencies that our ears read as sound.

Digitized sound methods do not attempt to create sound artificially. Instead, they digitally record real sounds in the world in a form that can be used to control the sound chip. To accomplish this, they need special software and electronic hardware to convert sound signals from a source such as a microphone or a tape recorder into a form that the computer can work with.

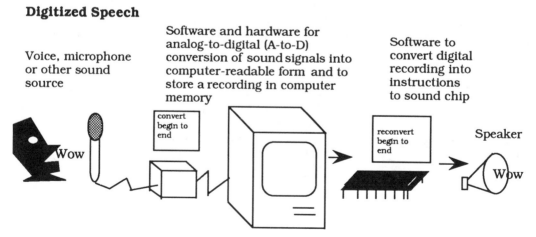

Synthesized Speech

Software to convert text into instructions to control the sound chip to synthesize speech sounds

Sound Chip

Speaker

Text

oxxxx
ssssdas

Text

Digitized Speech

Voice, microphone or other sound source

Software and hardware for analog-to-digital (A-to-D) conversion of sound signals into computer-readable form and to store a recording in computer memory

Software to convert digital recording into instructions to sound chip

Wow

convert begin to end

reconvert begin to end

Speaker

Wow

Figure 17.9   Synthesized and Digitized Speech

To understand how digitized sound works, one needs to understand a little about how computers store and process information internally. In everyday life, human sensory information is characterized by what is called analog representation. For example, humans see light in continuous variations of intensity and hue and hear sound in continuous variations of loudness and frequency. Biologists believe that sense organs physiologically create internal body signals that are analog representations of these physical events in the world. The retina sends nerve signals directly in proportion to the changing intensity of the light seen in the world.

Traditional electronic devices also store and communicate information in analog fashion. The voltage a video camera puts out follows the pattern of light intensity focused by its lens on its sensor. The pattern of grooves created in a phonograph record faithfully copies the original patterns of amplitude and frequency variations of the original sound. Each representation is an analog of other forms of the same event.

Computers do not store information in continuous analog forms. The electronic chips are designed to work with only two levels of voltage. The information is said to be processed in binary or digital form. "Digital" means that information is stored in discrete number units rather than in continuously varying quantities. Thus, when a computer is storing information about sound or light recorded from the world, the original analog information must be converted into digital form. This process is called analog-to-digital (A-to-D) conversion, and it requires special electronic hardware. For more detailed information, see *Using Computers to Create Art* or other specialized texts.

Digitized sound recording is accomplished by a process called sampling. The electronic A-to-D device takes an ongoing series of quick, regular "snapshots" of the frequencies and amplitudes of an incoming sound signal and stores digital representations of those values in the computer's memory. If the sampling is quick enough, this record of values captures much of the information of the original sound. The reverse process is necessary for a computer to play a digital sound. An electronic digital-to-analog (D-to-A) device must convert the discrete values stored in memory back into electronic pulses that can move a speaker diaphragm in the pattern to cause the original vibrations. The sound chip inside the Macintosh can do exactly that.

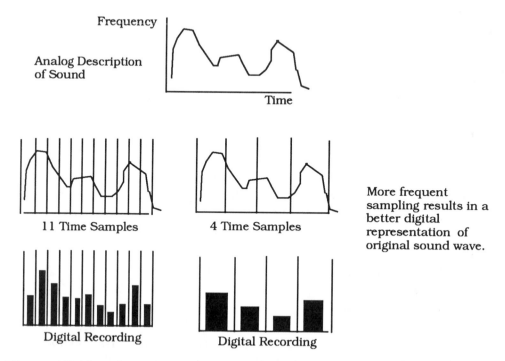

Figure 17.10 Relationship of Sampling Frequency to Faithfulness of Digital Recording

Unlike synthesis methods, digitization can preserve much of the nuance and color of the original sound. Indeed, contemporary Compact Disc recording methods use these digital processes to capture original sounds even more accurately than older analog methods. Increasing the faithfulness of digital recording, however, necessitates increasing the rate of sampling and the resolution (fineness of variations) captured. These increases require more computer memory and processing speeds. Thus, there is a trade-off in digital methods between the quality of sound and the amount of memory required to store the sound.

HyperCard's *play* command can play any digitized sound that has been recorded in the appropriate format. This capability introduces enormous potentials for the creation of multimedia events that include relatively high-quality sound. Stacks can incorporate music, sound effects, and non-robotic speech in naturalistic ways. Only the storage space required for sound limits the amount of sound that can be included. To

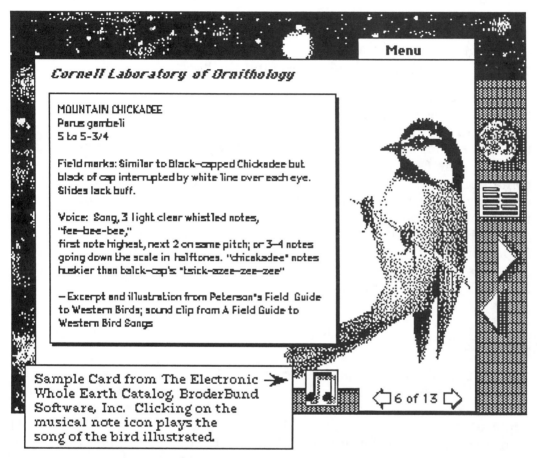

Figure 17.11 Bird Identification Card Which Includes Bird Song Sounds as Part of Its Information

illustrate, Figure 17.11 shows a card from one stack containing a field guide to birds. Each card in this stack includes a picture of the bird, text about its behavior, and a button that plays its song.

Sound Digitizers and MacRecorder®

The use of digitized sound requires that somehow the sound has been previously recorded in the appropriate digital format. One can obtain such sounds in two ways. Many independent developers have used A-to-D sound digitizers to prerecord sounds that can be bought, generally at low prices. These can be obtained from the user groups and information services as described in Chapter 20. These disks contain sound effects, instrument sounds, animals, clips from movies, and the like.

The other way to use digital sound is to create it oneself. This requires use of one of the electronic sound digitizers designed for the Macintosh such as the built in digitizer on some models of Macintosh, the Digidesign™ board, the Voice Navigator® from Articulate Systems, or the MacRecorder® from Farallon Computing, Inc. This relatively inexpensive device is a self-contained A-to-D sound digitizer that can record via its built-in microphone, or through jacks that can take a signal from an external microphone, or by means of just about any sound source, such as a stereo amplifier. The device plugs into a Macintosh as easily as a printer. The SoundEdit™ and HyperSound™ software packages come with it. These software packages allow easy recording and manipulation of digital sounds that can be used later in HyperCard scripts.

SoundEdit™

Because digital sound recording and manipulation will be an increasingly important tool for multimedia artists, this section offers a brief introduction to this software. SoundEdit is a specialized sound-editing application. It is not a HyperCard stack. Figure 17.12 shows the basic recording window of SoundEdit. The sound wave illustrated is the word *Hyperspace* digitally sampled and recorded by the device.

Clicking on the Record button (microphone icon) causes MacRecorder to record digitally any signal coming into its microphone or sound jack. SoundEdit places a dialog gauge on the screen showing the amount of time available for recording and a bar graph of elapsed time. Moving the mouse stops the recording process and places an image of the recorded sound's waveform in the window. The Scroll Bar on the bottom allows moving through long waveforms.

Clicking the Play button (speaker icon) causes the Macintosh to play the recorded sound. Dragging the indicator on the Zoom control changes the view of the waveform to show more or less information at one time. For example, in speech one can identify specific words, syllables, or sound components, depending on the zoom level.

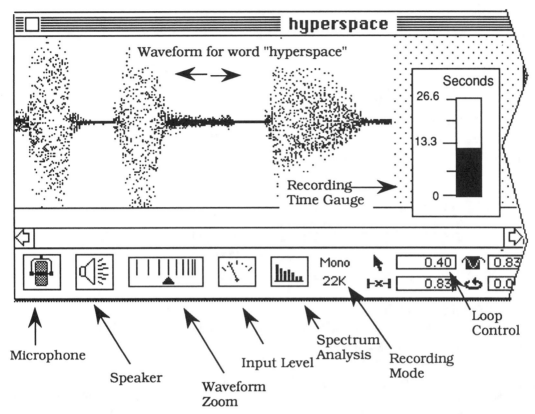

Figure 17.12 Basic Editing Window from SoundEdit

The Input Level button (gauge icon) allows continuous real-time testing of sound levels to adjust the input volume level on the source or the sensitivity control on the digitizer device. Clicking the Spectrum Analysis button (bar chart icon) presents a display that visually separates the real-time incoming sound into frequency bands. The indicators on the right side show the portion of the sound wave selected (if any), and the loopback shows the current settings for SoundEdit's *repeating* function, if it is activated.

The sound can be edited much like text. Clicking and dragging in the waveform window selects the part of the waveform. It can then be cut or copied into the clipboard and be pasted in other places if desired. For example, words can be removed just as easily as blemishes are removed in photo retouching. For instance, the word *not* could be removed from the phrase *I am not guilty.*

The Settings menu allows one to change recording and display options. MacRecorder is capable of recording sounds at various sampling rates of 22, 11, 7, and 5 kilohertz. Kilohertz (abbreviated kHz) is the technical term for the frequencey (in thousands of times a second) that a sound sample is captured. As discussed previously, there is a trade-off between quality of sound and amount of memory required to store a sound. The table shows the calculation of the memory that will be required to store 10 seconds of information at each rate. MacRecorder stores each sample in 1 byte of computer memory.

Amount of Memory Required to Store 10 Seconds of Sound

Sampling Rate	Amount of Memory
22 kHz	10 x 22000 = 220000 bytes
11 kHz	10 x 11000 = 110000 bytes
7 kHz	10 x 7000 = 70000 bytes
5 kHz	10 x 5000 = 50000 bytes

Digital recording can require enormous amounts of memory. The amount of RAM available in the computer can thus limit the length of a sound that can be recorded at one time. The storage space available on the floppy or hard disk can limit how much can be stored. The dialog box that appears after pushing the Record button shows the length of time that can be recorded given the sampling rate and the memory in the computer. For example, a standard 1-megabyte Macintosh can store approximately 27 seconds of sound at the 22 kHz sampling rate.

High-quality music requires higher sampling rates in order to faithfully record high frequencies and other nuances. Generally, lower sampling rates are allowable for voice. There are, however, no iron-clad rules. Each user needs to find the appropriate mix of sampling rate and memory requirements. Later versions of SoundEdit provide additional compression options that maintain sound quality while reducing memory requirements. These compression methods produce a digitally recorded sound in a non-standard format that HyperCard's *play* command cannot use. If one uses compressed sound, one must install special external commands provided with the HyperSound™ software that work much like the *play* command. One can select which sampling rate is used via the Recording Options item on the Menu Bar. New versions of the operating system allow new kinds of compression that can be activated with the standard play command. The Connection item allows changing the serial port to which the MacRecorder will be connected.

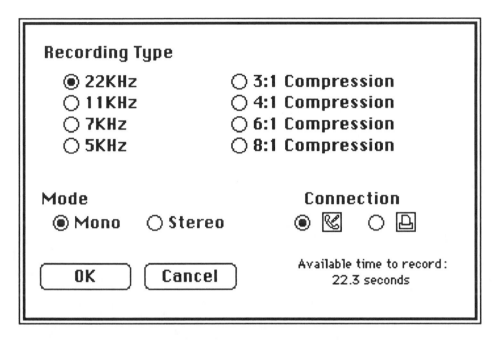

Figure 17.14 Effects Menu and Sample Option Dialog Boxes

The HyperSound software that comes with MacRecorder provides a HyperCard version of SoundEdit that allows control of the basic recording and playback functions from within a stack. It also provides external commands and functions that allow one to create stacks that record and manipulate sound files within a HyperCard environment. HyperSound does not provide access to the visual sound analysis or the sophisticated sound manipulation facilities that are available in the full SoundEdit.

Sound Manipulation

SoundEdit gives the artist an unprecedented ability to manipulate sound almost as freely as text or graphics. Sounds can be transformed and collaged in myriad ways. One has the equivalent of a sound studio that a few years ago would have cost tens of thousands of dollars. This section briefly introduces some of the possibilities.

SoundEdit allows one to modify recorded sounds or parts of sounds in the following ways:

Amplify — make louder or softer
Backwards — reverse a sound
Bender — add an artificial pattern of changing frequency to the sound
Echo — add a user-determined pattern of echo to a sound
Envelope — add an artificial pattern of changing loudness to the sound

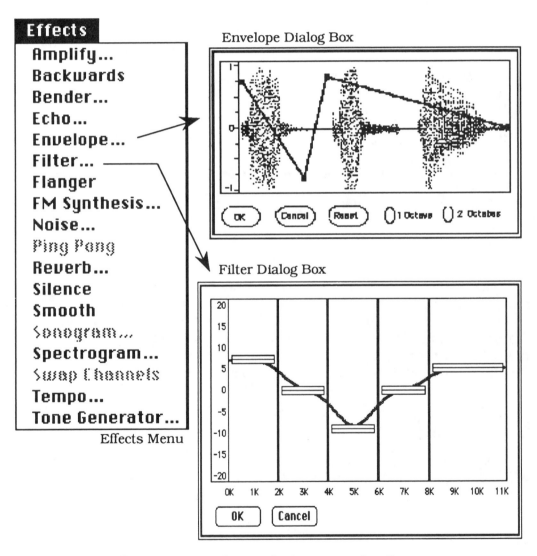

Figure 17.14 Effects Menu and Sample Option Dialog Boxes

Filter — differentially control various frequency ranges for the sound
Flanger — add a sense of pitch to unpitched sounds
Ping Pong — gradually swap sounds between the two stereo channels
Reverb — add a pattern of smooth decay to sound
Smooth — remove sharp sounds
Swap Channels — interchange sounds from two stereo channels
Tempo — change the speed of a sound without changing pitch (for
　　　example, allows accelerated speech playback)

SoundEdit provides three sound synthesis options.

Tone generator — produces a tone of user-determined frequency and am-
　　　plitude for a specified duration (selectable from sine wave, square
　　　wave, or triangle wave)
Noise — provides a random "white noise" sound for a specified duration
FM — produces a frequency modulated synthesized tone that changes in
　　　frequency in accordance with a user specification of pattern

SoundEdit provides two visual sound analysis tools. The Sonogram and Spectogram options (Figure 17.15) create varying technical analysis graphs of the recorded sound. Parameters can be changed to vary the display. On a color monitor, these graphs provide beautiful representations of the underlying qualities of the recorded sound.

The Set Pitches option allows playback of the sound at various frequencies. The Set Mixer option (Figure 17.16) simulates the action of a mixing studio in allowing the combination of up to four recorded sounds into a single composite waveform. The pattern of relative volumes of the waveforms can be modified as the user wishes.

The Save and Save As commands on the File Menu control the format that the sound will be saved in. Choices are SoundEdit, Instrument (needed by some of the special music applications), Resource (the format needed by HyperCard), and Audio IFF. Choice of the Resource format is absolutely necessary if a sound is to be used in HyperCard.

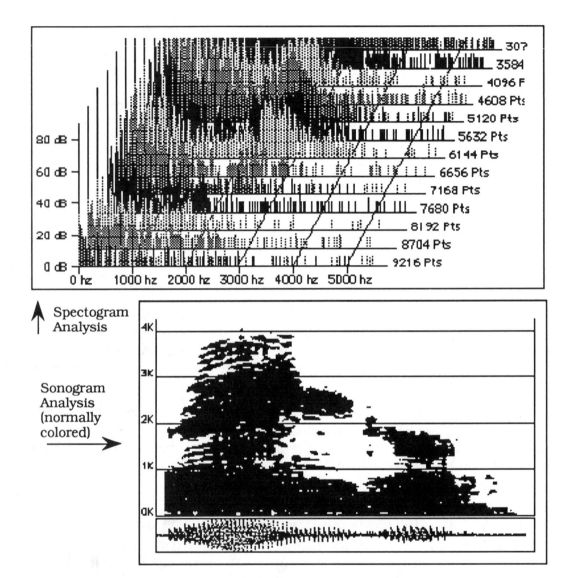

Figure 17.15   Sonogram and Spectrogram Displays

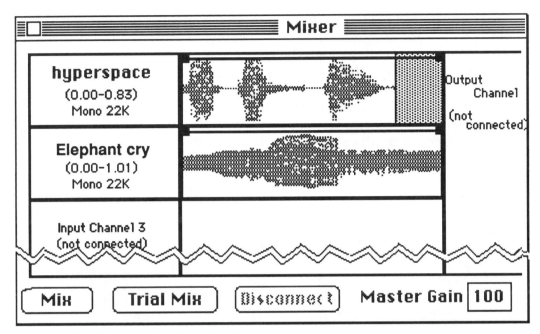

Figure 17.16 Mixer Option Display

Comparisons of Synthesized and Digitized Sound Use

Each approach has its strengths and weaknesses. Synthesized sounds are very efficient in memory usage and extremely flexible. For example, use of synthesized speech requires only storage of the text representing the words. Digital speech, by contrast, requires that the full representation of all the sounds be stored in digital form. In addition, synthesized speech can be generated on the run (as illustrated by the earlier example in which the button spoke whatever a user typed). But digitized speech must have prerecorded all the phrases or sounds that will be used. Digitized sound's main advantage is its ability to store and recreate the nuance of complex sounds. The following table summarizes these strengths and weaknesses.

Comparison of Strengths and Weaknesses of
Digitized and Synthesized Sound

	Memory Use	Flexibility	Quality
Digitized Sound	High	Low	High
Synthesized Sound	Low	High	Low

The situation is changing as developers work to enhance the ability of microcomputers to use sound. The memory requirements for digitized sound are being reduced through the use of new compression schemes that preserve the original quality of the sound. The flexibility is being enhanced by mixed methods that use digital components of sound assembled like synthesized sounds. On the other side, the quality of synthesized sounds is being improved through development of more sophisticated electronic chips optimized for synthesizing speech and music.

Introduction to MIDI

MIDI (Musical Interface for Digital Instruments) is an international standard developed to allow flexible interconnection of electronic musical instruments from any manufacturer and the computers of any manufacturer. Previously, each electronic keyboard or other instrument required its own custom interface to each computer and its own specialized software. Electronic music was a complex and expensive undertaking.

Now, almost all professional and near-professional electronic keyboards are made with connections for the standard MIDI computer interface. These interface devices are generally inexpensive (around $100) and easy to connect. Since developers can assume a standard interface, music software can be sold to a wide market, and hence it is relatively inexpensive. As a result, there is a great flowering of interest in computer-mediated music.

MIDI synthesizers are high-quality devices that generate musical sounds. Many of them allow a wide range of sound manipulations, such as key and tempo changes, sound effects, and multivoice sounds. Most allow control over their musical "voice." Some come with hundreds of instrument voices built in: They can simulate the sound of pianos, violins, drums, flutes, guitars, xylophones, gamelans, sitars, or whatever. Many allow artificial sound construction through control of sound elements such as sound envelopes and harmonic structures. Synthesizers can create sounds of instruments that don't exist. Some MIDI instruments called samplers take another approach: The sounds they manipulate are based originally on digital recordings of real instruments.

Many are designed with keyboards so that they can be played with or without a computer. Some varieties of new MIDI devices resemble drums, saxophones, and guitars in addition to keyboards. As long as they have a MIDI interface built in, however, they can be controlled by a computer. Indeed, it is sometimes eerie to see a MIDI instrument played by a human and then played exactly the same by the computer, which has recorded the human's musical choices.

Obviously, this chapter can only offer the briefest introduction to the world of MIDI music. Readers are encouraged to consult other specialized texts for more detail. We will now concentrate on software that allows control of MIDI instruments from HyperCard scripts.

HyperCard and MIDI

As with the recording of digitized sound, HyperCard requires the addition of hardware and special external commands to use MIDI. The following are required:

- An electronic instrument with MIDI interface built in
- An electronic MIDI interface box designed for use with the Macintosh along with connecting cables
- Software containing the external commands necessary to put out appropriate MIDI compatible signals from the Macintosh

MIDI standards require communication with MIDI devices to be sent in accordance with a strictly defined format and timing. The external commands for HyperCard take parameters indicated in HyperCard commands and convert them to a form that controls the electronic chips sending signals out from the modem serial port. As with the *talk* and *speak* commands described previously, one must obtain the external commands from a source such as user groups or information utilities. There are several sets of the external commands written by independent developers. Then one must use ResEdit or ResCopy to add these external commands to the resources for HyperCard or to a particular stack.

One such set of commands is part of the MIDI Recorder Stack written by Kunihito Koike. This stack allows both the sending and receiving of MIDI information. We will focus on the sending of control information to MIDI instruments. The format for these commands is quite simple. After loading the external command into a stack, one can use the command *MIDI out,* "*(data)*" anywhere in a script. The phrase "*(data)*" stands for a string of numbers that make sense in terms of MIDI conventions. For example, the following script would sequentially play the notes middle C and D each for 1 second on a MIDI instrument set up to receive instructions on channel 1:

MIDI out, "144 60 127"	turns C on
wait for 1 second	
MIDI out, "144 60 0"	turns C off
MIDI out, "144, 62 127"	turns D on
wait for 1 second	
MIDI out, "144 62 0"	turns D off

To use any of the MIDI external commands, one must understand some background about MIDI data conventions.

MIDI Data Conventions

MIDI instruments are designed with chips that look for particular strings of digital voltage pulses. When the chips receive these pulses, they activate internal electronics to generate the appropriate sounds. The numbers placed in the HyperCard commands are converted by software into the appropriate string of pulses.

As with most computer-related instruments, MIDI electronics are designed to work with binary digital electronics. The structure of MIDI is most clear if one understands binary numbers, although one can use the MIDI commands without understanding all the details.

In computer communication, information is often sent in digital bits of information. Each bit is a pulse of voltage. Bits can assume only one of two binary values — either high or low voltage. High is often represented by a 1 and low by a 0. Bits are usually communicated in groupings of eight called bytes. Binary numbers are a shorthand way of describing these patterns of bits. Binary numbers work on a base 2 system where each position represents a power of 2. The examples in Figure 17.17 show the bits, the bytes and the binary, base 2 ways of describing the patterns.

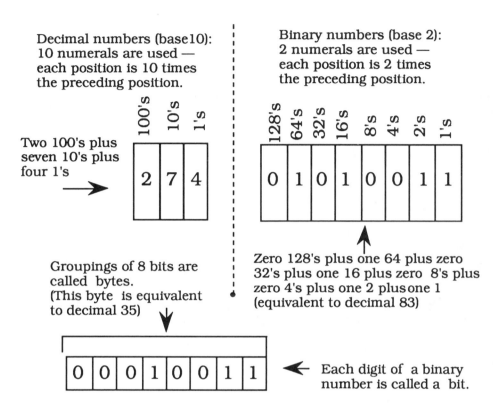

Figure 17.17 Binary Numbers, Bits, and Bytes

MIDI makes use of the binary nature of these patterns to set up conventions for communication. MIDI controls consist of a string of bytes that carry information about which instrument should act, what note should be affected, and what action the instrument should take. The conventions are arbitrary but systematic.

The first byte sent is usually called the status byte. It contains information about which channel is the intended recipient of the message and what it is supposed to do. (Each instrument can arbitrarily be given a channel number.) In Figure 17.18, the command string to turn on the note C is "144 60 127".

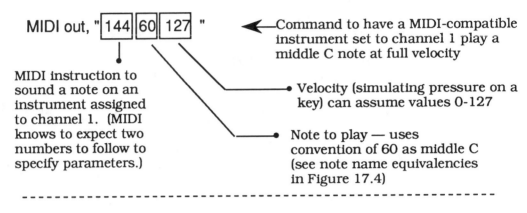

MIDI out, "144 60 127"

MIDI instruction to sound a note on an instrument assigned to channel 1. (MIDI knows to expect two numbers to follow to specify parameters.)

Command to have a MIDI-compatible instrument set to channel 1 play a middle C note at full velocity

Velocity (simulating pressure on a key) can assume values 0-127

Note to play — uses convention of 60 as middle C (see note name equivalencies in Figure 17.4)

MIDI convention for using binary structure of numbers:

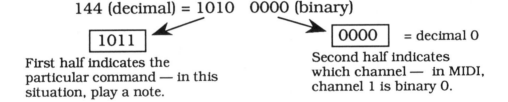

MIDI out, "144 60 127"   This command plays note 60 (middle C) on an instrument set to channel 1.

144 (decimal) = 1010   0000 (binary)

1011   0000   = decimal 0

First half indicates the particular command — in this situation, play a note.

Second half indicates which channel — in MIDI, channel 1 is binary 0.

MIDI out, "147 62 127"   This command plays note 62 (D) on an instrument set to be channel 4.

147 (decimal) = 1010 0011 (binary)   0011 binary = decimal 3 — in MIDI, channel 4 is binary 3 because numbering starts at 0.

144 = ch1 149 = ch5 154 = ch9   159 = ch13
145 = ch2 150 = ch6 155 = ch10 160 = ch14
146 = ch3 151 = ch7 156 = ch11 161 = ch15
147 = ch4 152 = ch8 157 = ch12 162 = ch16

Figure 17.18 Expanation of the MIDI Command Structure

The 144 is the status byte. It is made up of two 4-bit halves — the performance instruction and the channel number. The decimal number is just a shorthand for the total binary pattern.

In MIDI work, each instrument is designed so that it can be assigned a channel number. Each instrument has its own way of being given a channel number — for example, on the Casio CZ101 synthesizer, a button called Channel can be pushed, and then an arrow key can set the number on the display to anything from 1 to 16. It is important to read the instruction manual for each instrument to learn how to assign channel numbers. MIDI is designed to work with up to 16 instruments daisy-chained together (Figure 17.19). Its adjustability allows one easily to change which channel each device will identify itself with via some kind of hardware switch. A MIDI instrument set to a channel will, from that point on, ignore signals sent to other channels and jump to action upon receiving signals addressed to its channel. Theoretically, one could have a complete orchestra of 16 electronic instruments being controlled by one computer-MIDI interface. Sometimes a synthesizer capable of generating multiple simultaneous instrument sounds might simulate four instruments by assigning each internal instrument voice to a different channel. Thus, channels 1 through 4 might be responded to physically by the same synthesizer.

The first half of the status byte contains performance instructions, which are arbitrary bit patterns set by the international standard. 144 is the code to play a note. 128 is the code to turn a note off. 224 is the code for a pitch blend — a kind of slur between notes. 192 is the code for a program change. Other numbers control other actions, which can be learned from any text on MIDI. In addition, each brand of synthesizer has the ability to respond to "system-exclusive" messages. The code 240 lets MIDI know that codes that follow are idiosyncratic to a particular brand and model of synthesizer. The manual for each synthesizer explains its particular system-exclusive codes.

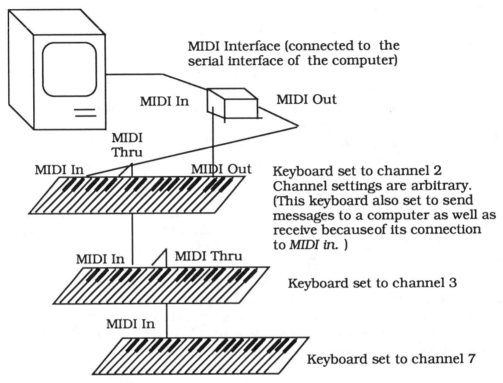

MIDI Interface (connected to the serial interface of the computer)

MIDI In

MIDI Out

MIDI Thru

MIDI In   MIDI Out   Keyboard set to channel 2
Channel settings are arbitrary.
(This keyboard also set to send messages to a computer as well as receive becauseof its connection to *MIDI in.*)

MIDI In   MIDI Thru

Keyboard set to channel 3

MIDI In

Keyboard set to channel 7

Figure 17.19 MIDI Performance Setup with Three Keyboards Daisy-chained Together

In the example, 144 instructs the synthesizer to play the following note on whatever synthesizer has been set to channel 1. 145 would mean to turn on the following note on the synthesizer set to channel 2. Once the MIDI interface sees a 144 performance instruction, it knows to look for two following bytes. The first one indicates a note number to act on and the second one indicates a velocity. The notes are numbered in the same convention as HyperCard's intrinsic notes — i.e., in accordance with the standard keyboard position with 60 as middle C.

Velocity simulates the speed with which a finger would press a key: 64 is medium pressure, 127 is fastest press, and 0 is no pressure at all and in fact causes the note to stop playing. Some inexpensive synthesizers do not have the capability to respond to different velocities.

Figure 17.20 illustrates a display of buttons simulating a keyboard. Each piano key is a HyperCard button that controls a note on a MIDI-compatible keyboard. The example assumes that a MIDI keyboard is connected via a MIDI interface device and that the keyboard is assigned to channel 1. It also assumes that external commands to control MIDI have been loaded in by the methods described in Chapter 20.

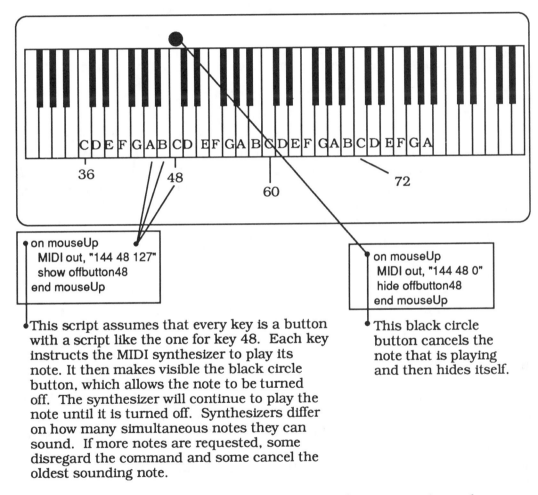

```
on mouseUp
  MIDI out, "144 48 127"
  show offbutton48
end mouseUp
```

```
on mouseUp
  MIDI out, "144 48 0"
  hide offbutton48
end mouseUp
```

• This script assumes that every key is a button with a script like the one for key 48. Each key instructs the MIDI synthesizer to play its note. It then makes visible the black circle button, which allows the note to be turned off. The synthesizer will continue to play the note until it is turned off. Synthesizers differ on how many simultaneous notes they can sound. If more notes are requested, some disregard the command and some cancel the oldest sounding note.

• This black circle button cancels the note that is playing and then hides itself.

Figure 17.20 Computer Screen Keyboard Full of Buttons to Control a MIDI Synthesizer

		These are some of the preset
1 Brass Ensem.	9 Brass Ens2	instrument defintions
2 Trumpet	10 Vibraphone	("programs") built into one
3 Violin	11 Crispy Xylophone	inexpensive synthesizer, the
4 String Ensem.	12 Synthetic Strings	Casio CZ-101. Issuing a MIDI
5 Elec. Piano	13 Fairy Tale	command to change a program
6 Elec. Organ	14 Accordion	to sound definition 14 would
7 Flute	15 Whistle	make subsequent notes sound
8 Syn Bass	16 Percussion	like an accordion.

The synthesizer also allows the user to "sculpt" sound by controlling sound characteristics described earlier to create totally unique sounds.

Figure 17.21 Sample MIDI Instrument Definitions

Program change deserves some special mention. The program (also called the patch from the old days) is the instrument sound definition. As previously mentioned, most synthesizers come with instrument sounds built in. Each sound is assigned a number — for example, 1 might be flute, 2 might be electronic piano. User-created sounds can also be assigned these numbers. Synthesizers differ on how many definitions they can have and what particular sounds are assigned to each sound. A *change program* message tells the synthesizer to interpret any following *play note* commands to come out in the new instrument sound. Many synthesizers are capable of having instrument definitions downloaded into them; these sound definitions can be bought from commercial and independent sources.

Sample Script

In the sample script, an *idle* command placed at the card level generates random notes to be played on a MIDI synthesizer. In this script, each note plays for 1 second. Four buttons on the screen each represent one of the instrument definitions available in the synthesizer. Clicking on any button makes its instrument the active one for subsequent random notes.

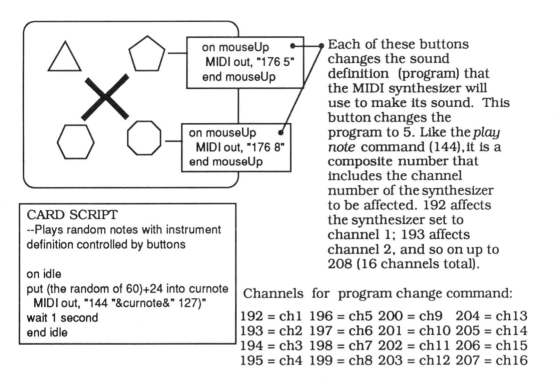

The text content within the figure reads:

```
on mouseUp
MIDI out, "176 5"
end mouseUp
```

```
on mouseUp
MIDI out, "176 8"
end mouseUp
```

Each of these buttons changes the sound definition (program) that the MIDI synthesizer will use to make its sound. This button changes the program to 5. Like the *play note* command (144), it is a composite number that includes the channel number of the synthesizer to be affected. 192 affects the synthesizer set to channel 1; 193 affects channel 2, and so on up to 208 (16 channels total).

```
CARD SCRIPT
--Plays random notes with instrument
definition controlled by buttons

on idle
put (the random of 60)+24 into curnote
  MIDI out, "144 "&curnote&" 127)"
wait 1 second
end idle
```

Channels for program change command:

192 = ch1	196 = ch5	200 = ch9	204 = ch13
193 = ch2	197 = ch6	201 = ch10	205 = ch14
194 = ch3	198 = ch7	202 = ch11	206 = ch15
195 = ch4	199 = ch8	203 = ch12	207 = ch16

Figure 17.22 Script That Allows Mouse Movements to Change the MIDI Instrument Defintion

New Possibilities

It is hoped that this brief introduction has whet the appetite. Electronic sound is an art form with a long and illustrious history. There are many excellent books on general issues of electronic sound, although few focus specifically on HyperCard and sound. Sound and music are becoming increasingly available to artists. New kinds of art forms will undoubtedly appear, ones that explore computer-mediated speech and the integration of graphics and sound. Speech recognizers such as the Voice Navigator™ from Articulate Systems open the possibilities even more to art that seems to understand the viewer's voice. Programs such as HyperCard make the computer control of these events relatively easy.

CHAPTER 18
TIME-BASED ART

Time, Date, and Duration as Artistic Focus

Most contemporary computer systems incorporate battery-backed electronic circuitry that provides constant access to the date and time accurate often to the millisecond. This also allows for accurate determination of duration — for example, the time elapsed since a program was started.

These features are obviously beneficial to business and technical programs. For example, word processors allow for the automatic dating of letters, and scientific research programs facilitate the accurate analysis of time-based phenomena such as calculations in astronomy.

These capabilities also give birth to opportunities for artists to create new kinds of events conceptually linked to date and time. For example, an

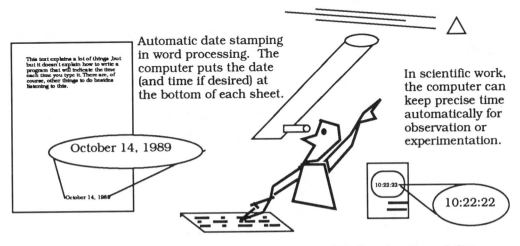

Automatic date stamping in word processing. The computer puts the date (and time if desired) at the bottom of each sheet.

In scientific work, the computer can keep precise time automatically for observation or experimentation.

Figure 18.1   Conventional Uses of the Time and Calendar Capabilities of Computers

artist can create events that change their imagery with the seasons or the day of the week. Other events can key to time of day or duration since some previous event.

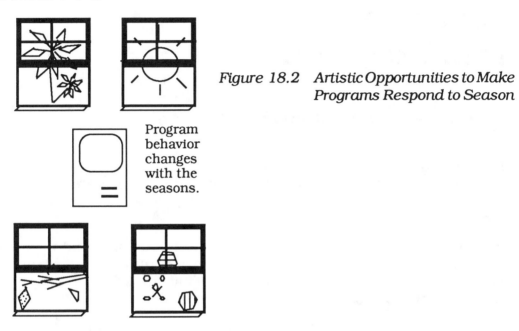

Figure 18.2   Artistic Opportunities to Make Programs Respond to Season

Program behavior changes with the seasons.

The aesthetics of time-based art is underdeveloped. Certainly many traditional and media art forms such as music, drama, cinema, and video consider duration a critical compositional element. Similarly, many arts metaphorically reflect on time of day or change of season.

The new technologies encourage contemporary extension of these artistic focuses. Artists can create dynamic image and sound systems that actively sense time. Moreover, these works can focus conceptually on changing time. That is, they can help the viewer to experience the time, date, or duration phenomena in new and provocative ways.

Anthropologists and cultural historians who compare modern urban cultures with those of other peoples often note accelerated pace and heightened time awareness as important distinguishing characteristics. It is fitting for artists in urban cultures to find ways to reflect on the features of modern life.

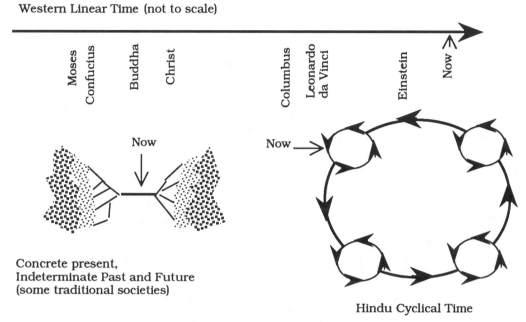

Figure18.3   Cultural Variations in Concepts of Time

Date Functions

HyperCard features built-in functions called *the date, the abbreviated date,* and *the long date.* Any reference to these functions in a script creates access to the built-in electronic calendar, which then supplies the date.   Different formats can be specified by the script.   The following examples demonstrate the variations:

the date	10/14/89
the abbreviated date	Sat, Oct 14, 1989
the long date	Saturday, October 14, 1989

Each subsequent version provides a fuller rendering of the date text. The abbreviated function can be shortened to *the abbrev* or *abbr date.*   These can be tested by typing them into the Message Box. After one presses the return key, HyperCard types back the correct date (assuming that the correct date has been set through the Alarm Clock Desk Accessory feature located under the Apple Menu.)

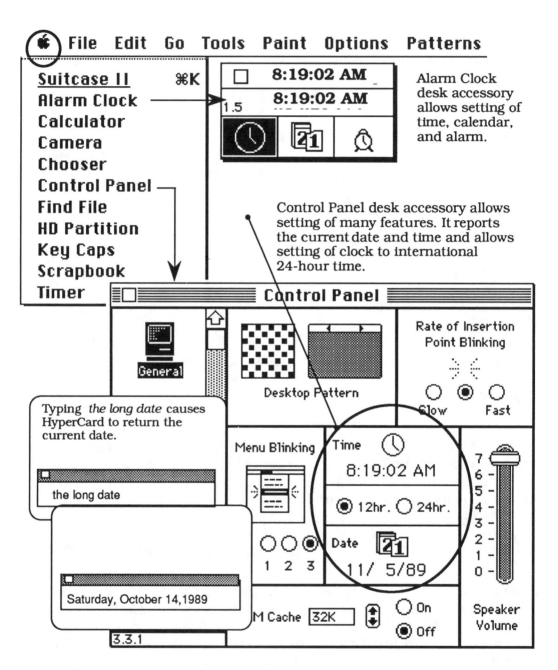

File   Edit   Go   Tools   Paint   Options   Patterns

Suitcase II   ⌘K
Alarm Clock
Calculator
Camera
Chooser
Control Panel
Find File
HD Partition
Key Caps
Scrapbook
Timer

8:19:02 AM
8:19:02 AM
1.5

Alarm Clock
desk accessory
allows setting of
time, calendar,
and alarm.

Control Panel desk accessory allows
setting of many features. It reports
the current date and time and allows
setting of clock to international
24-hour time.

Control Panel

General

Desktop Pattern

Rate of Insertion
Point Blinking

Slow   Fast

Typing *the long date* causes
HyperCard to return the
current date.

the long date

Menu Blinking

Time

8:19:02 AM

● 12hr. ○ 24hr.

7
6
5
4
3
2
1
0

Saturday, October 14, 1989

1 2 3

Date

11/ 5/89

M Cache 32K   ○ On
                      ● Off

Speaker
Volume

3.3.1

*Figure 18.4   Time-related Desk Accessories and HyperCard Date and
Time Functions*

Breaking the Date Apart

A script can use part or all of the date — for example, just the day of the week or the month. To do this, a script makes use of HyperCard's ability to identify parts of expressions such as a certain word, item, or character. Since the elements of *the abbr date* and *the long date* are separated by commas, each one is an item. The second item —"October 14" — is composed of two elements separated by a space; thus, each one is a word. These examples illustrate how elements of *the long date* or *the abbreviated date* can be separated.

the long date	Saturday, October 14, 1989
the abbr date	Sat, Oct 14, 1989
item 1 of the long date	Saturday
item 3 of the long date	1989
item 2 of the long date	October 14
word 1 of item 2 of the long date	October
word 2 of item 2 of the long date	14
item 1 of the abbr date	Sat

Sometimes one wants the number of the month rather than the text name — for example, *10* instead of *October*. Breaking apart *the date* function that uses number rather than text format (10/14/89) can be more difficult because the items are not separated by commas or spaces. HyperCard allows easy breaking apart for comma-separated elements (items) and space-separated elements (words). One could build a routine to use the *char* function to break apart the date in this format; for example:

the date	10/14/89
char 1 to 2 of the date	10
char 4 to 5 of the date	14 (/ is char 3)
char 7 to 8 of the date	89 (/ is char 6)

This method is not foolproof, however, because one can't always predict how many characters will exist in the date. If the month or the day of the month is a number less than 10, the characters would be different from those illustrated because one-digit months or dates make the illustration that assumes two-digit dates wrong. One could build elaborate scripts to correct the format — for example, by searching *the date* for slashes and replacing them with commas.

The Convert Command

HyperCard provides an easier method in the *convert* command, which can be used to change formats in dates and times. It automatically allows switching between formats. The command is used in scripts as follows:

convert (*container*) to (*format*)

A container is any HyperCard structure such as a field or a variable that can contain values. Format is the generic name of the alternative forms that HyperCard provides for expressing dates and times. One of the formats, *dateItems*, provides each element as a number item separated by commas. This makes it easy for scripts to use parts of dates and items. (Details about time formats will be discussed later.)

the long date	Saturday, October 14,1989
the long time	9:30:22 AM
the dateItems	1989,10,14,9,30,22,7

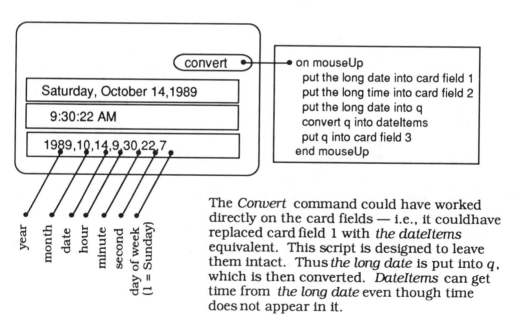

The *Convert* command could have worked directly on the card fields — i.e., it couldhave replaced card field 1 with *the dateItems* equivalent. This script is designed to leave them intact. Thus *the long date* is put into *q*, which is then converted. *DateItems* can get time from *the long date* even though time does not appear in it.

Figure 18.5   Conversion of Date and Time Formats

The format of *the dateItems* is as follows: year, month, day of month, hour, minute, second, day of week (1 = Sunday). It is very easy to access any part of the date and time in this format. To use the command some form of the date or time must be put into a container (field or variable). The script then asks the *convert* command to operate on whatever is in that container and replace it with the new format. Figure 18.5 creates a variable called *q*, puts *the long date* into it, and then converts it to *the dateItems* format.

Graphic Calendar

Figure 18.6 demonstrates a new form of calendar that displays graphics for the month, date, and day of the week. Month is displayed on the top line. Each month is represented by a polygon with the number of sides corresponding to the number of the month — for example, March (month 3) is represented by a triangle (3 sides), June (month 6) with a hexagon (6 sides). Because there are no polygons with 1 or 2 sides, January (month 1) is illustrated with a large dot and February with a thick line.

The script in Figure 18.6 is put in an *openCard* message handler — whenever anyone accesses that card, it displays the calendar. It could also have been put in a button handler. For the sake of clarity, the routines to draw month, date, and day of the week are created as separate subroutines. The master routine uses the *convert* command to create number variables *mon*, *date*, and *dayweek* to use later. The *drawMon* subroutine draws polygons across the screen to represent the months (except for the January and February exceptions). It then fills in the shape for the current month with a pattern. It uses the number of the month to automatically calculate a position for the polygon. Each month is placed at its date number (for example, October = 10) times 40 horizontal pixel position.

The *drawDate* subroutine draws an array of polygons (shaped in accordance with the scheme described). The day of the month is again filled in with a pattern. The positions are again calculated by multiplying the date times a standard pixel separation. The *drawDayweek* subroutine flashes the day of the week name in an appropriate place in the display.

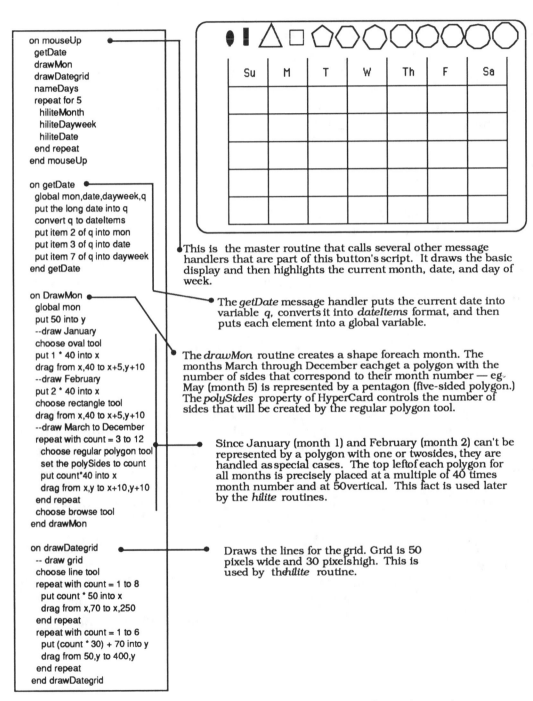

```
on mouseUp
  getDate
  drawMon
  drawDategrid
  nameDays
  repeat for 5
    hiliteMonth
    hiliteDayweek
    hiliteDate
  end repeat
end mouseUp
```

```
on getDate
  global mon,date,dayweek,q
  put the long date into q
  convert q to dateItems
  put item 2 of q into mon
  put item 3 of q into date
  put item 7 of q into dayweek
end getDate
```

```
on DrawMon
  global mon
  put 50 into y
  --draw January
  choose oval tool
  put 1 * 40 into x
  drag from x,40 to x+5,y+10
  --draw February
  put 2 * 40 into x
  choose rectangle tool
  drag from x,40 to x+5,y+10
  --draw March to December
  repeat with count = 3 to 12
    choose regular polygon tool
    set the polySides to count
    put count*40 into x
    drag from x,y to x+10,y+10
  end repeat
  choose browse tool
end drawMon
```

```
on drawDategrid
  -- draw grid
  choose line tool
  repeat with count = 1 to 8
    put count * 50 into x
    drag from x,70 to x,250
  end repeat
  repeat with count = 1 to 6
    put (count * 30) + 70 into y
    drag from 50,y to 400,y
  end repeat
end drawDategrid
```

This is the master routine that calls several other message handlers that are part of this button's script. It draws the basic display and then highlights the current month, date, and day of week.

The *getDate* message handler puts the current date into variable *q*, converts it into *dateItems* format, and then puts each element into a global variable.

The *drawMon* routine creates a shape for each month. The months March through December each get a polygon with the number of sides that correspond to their month number — eg. May (month 5) is represented by a pentagon (five-sided polygon.) The *polySides* property of HyperCard controls the number of sides that will be created by the regular polygon tool.

Since January (month 1) and February (month 2) can't be represented by a polygon with one or two sides, they are handled as special cases. The top left of each polygon for all months is precisely placed at a multiple of 40 times month number and at 50 vertical. This fact is used later by the *hilite* routines.

Draws the lines for the grid. Grid is 50 pixels wide and 30 pixels high. This is used by the *hilite* routine.

Figure 18.6   Calendar with Flashing Month, Day of Week, and Date

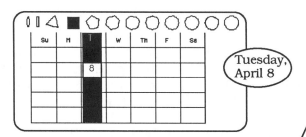

```
on nameDays
  -- name days
  put "Su,M,T,W,Th,F,Sa" into
    nameWeek
  choose text tool
  put 90 into y
  repeat with count = 1 to 7
    put item count of nameWeek
      into z
    put (count * 50) +20 into x
    click at x,y
    type z
  end repeat
end nameDays
```

The *nameDays* routine puts the abbreviations for the
day of the week in the right place in the grid. It puts the
abbreviations into a variable called *nameweek* so that
each initial is a separate item. Then it places item 1
(Su) in the right position between grid lines 1 and 2 by
using the fact that all grid lines are 50 pixels beyond
the previous one. It adds 20 to that coordinate in order
to center the date.

```
on hiliteMonth
  global mon,date,dayweek
  put mon*40 into x
  put 50 into y
  set the filled to true
  set the pattern to mon+1
  if mon > 2 then
    choose regular polygon tool
    set the polySides to mon
    drag from x,y to x+10,y+10
  end if
  if mon = 1 then
    choose oval tool
    drag from x,40 to x+5,y+10
  end if
  if mon = 2 then
    choose rectangle tool
    drag from x,40 to x+5,y+10
  end if
  doMenu select
  repeat for 2
    doMenu invert
  end repeat
  choose browse tool
end hiliteMonth
```

The *hiliteMonth* routine gets the current month and
fills the polygon representing that month with the
pattern that has the same number + 1. (The 1 is added to
avoid pattern 1, which is white and would look no
different from the normal display. Months 1 and 2 are
again handled differently because they were originally
drawn differently.)

This part of the routine selects the shape just drawn, inverts it,
and inverts it back to create a flashing effect.

The *hiliteDayweek* routine determines the appropriate
rectangle representing the current day. It can do this because
each grid line is 50 pixels to the right of the other. Day 2
(Monday) is therefore represented by the rectangle between
100 (2*50) and the line 50 to the right (150).

```
on hilitedate
  global date,dayweek
  put dayweek * 50 into x
  put (date div 7) into temp
  put (temp*30) + 100 into y
  choose text tool
  click at x+20,y+20
  type date
  choose select tool
  drag from x,y to x+50,y+30
  repeat for 2
    domenu invert
  end repeat
  choose browse tool
end hilitedate
```

The *hiliteDate* routine
determines where in the
grid the date is by
determining how many
units of 7's must be
skipped. It then uses the
pixel sizes of the grid to
determine the precise
box, types the date, and
then flashes the box.

```
on hiliteDayweek
  global dayweek
  put 70 into y
  put dayweek * 50 into x
  choose select tool
  drag from x,y to x+50,250
  repeat for 2
    doMenu invert
  end repeat
end hiliteDayweek
```

Figure 18.6   Calendar (continued)

Time Functions

HyperCard also provides easy access to the current time accurate to the second. Duration can be measured with even greater accuracy, if needed, down to the sixtieth of a second. This creates artistic opportunities to create events that make use of duration or focus on time.

HyperCard provides the time in several formats. The function *the time* provides a standard hour-and-minute time indication separated by a colon with the AM or PM designation at the end. The function *the long time* returns hour, minutes, and seconds.

The seconds (or *the secs*) provides the number of seconds that have elapsed since 0:00:00 January 1, 1904. For example, at the moment this text is being written, 2706859282 seconds have elapsed since that moment. Each second in time thus has a unique number description based on the date (number of days elapsed since that date) and time (number of seconds since midnight). This date was arbitrarily selected most likely because the designers assumed that most calculations about elapsed time would deal with dates since that year.

the time	9:21 AM
the long time	9:21:22 AM
the seconds	2706859282

The reader may be wondering why this function is provided. Time calculations can be difficult because of the repeating hour numbers and the nondecimal (i.e., 60-minute, 24-hour) basis for time calculation. Often calculation of time duration can be a difficult task because the program script must assess whether the noon or day boundaries have been crossed. For example, to calculate the time elapsed from 11:30 AM to 2:45 PM, one must add 12 to the hour figure and otherwise adjust the minutes. To calculate the time that has elapsed between 9:47 PM to 2:15 AM, one must take into account that the hour numbering started over at midnight.

International standard or military time (the 24-hour clock) was developed to solve some of these problems. On the 24-hour clock, each minute of the day has a unique description. This is accomplished by adding 12 to each of the hours after noon and thus not repeating hours. 1:00 PM becomes 13:00 (usually pronounced "thirteen hundred hours"). Most computers with clocks provide a way to set the time format. The Macintosh requires the format to be set via the Alarm Clock desk accessory under the Apple Menu (Figure 18.4). The format cannot be set by a HyperCard script. The following examples illustrate the equivalencies between the 12-hour system and 24-hour system.

12-Hour System	24-Hour System
3:15 AM	3:15
12:00 AM (midnight)	0:00
4:45 PM	16:45
11:10 PM	23:10

One can write an easy script to convert times. One needs only to read the last two characters provided by *the time* function. If those characters are *PM*, the script can add 12 to the hour (represented as the first or first and second characters).

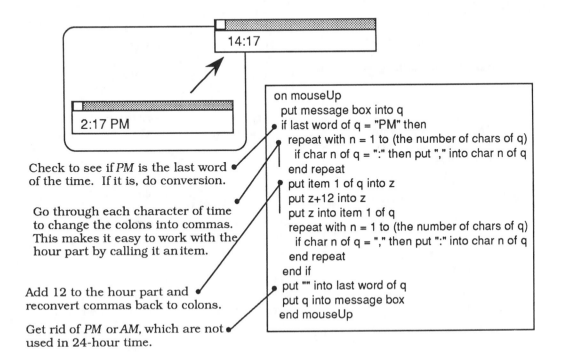

14:17

2:17 PM

Check to see if *PM* is the last word of the time. If it is, do conversion.

Go through each character of time to change the colons into commas. This makes it easy to work with the hour part by calling it an item.

Add 12 to the hour part and reconvert commas back to colons.

Get rid of *PM* or *AM*, which are not used in 24-hour time.

```
on mouseUp
  put message box into q
  if last word of q = "PM" then
    repeat with n = 1 to (the number of chars of q)
      if char n of q = ":" then put "," into char n of q
    end repeat
    put item 1 of q into z
    put z+12 into z
    put z into item 1 of q
    repeat with n = 1 to (the number of chars of q)
      if char n of q = "," then put ":" into char n of q
    end repeat
  end if
  put "" into last word of q
  put q into message box
end mouseUp
```

Figure 18.7   Converting 12-Hour Time to International 24-Hour Time

The cleanest method to determine elapsed time, however, is to use the function *the secs* because these numbers are purely sequential. Duration in seconds can be easily determined by subtracting the beginning time and date (in seconds) from the stop time. This subtraction yields the number of elapsed seconds between these two points. The seconds can be

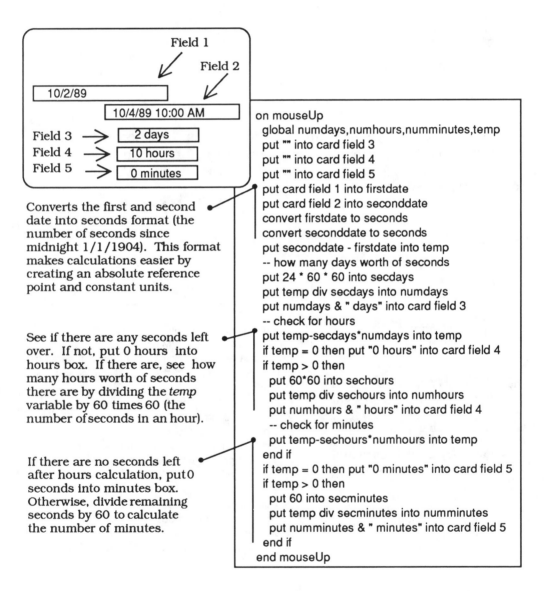

Field 1

Field 2

10/2/89

10/4/89 10:00 AM

Field 3 → 2 days
Field 4 → 10 hours
Field 5 → 0 minutes

Converts the first and second date into seconds format (the number of seconds since midnight 1/1/1904). This format makes calculations easier by creating an absolute reference point and constant units.

See if there are any seconds left over. If not, put 0 hours into hours box. If there are, see how many hours worth of seconds there are by dividing the *temp* variable by 60 times 60 (the number of seconds in an hour).

If there are no seconds left after hours calculation, put 0 seconds into minutes box. Otherwise, divide remaining seconds by 60 to calculate the number of minutes.

```
on mouseUp
 global numdays,numhours,numminutes,temp
 put "" into card field 3
 put "" into card field 4
 put "" into card field 5
 put card field 1 into firstdate
 put card field 2 into seconddate
 convert firstdate to seconds
 convert seconddate to seconds
 put seconddate - firstdate into temp
 -- how many days worth of seconds
 put 24 * 60 * 60 into secdays
 put temp div secdays into numdays
 put numdays & " days" into card field 3
 -- check for hours
 put temp-secdays*numdays into temp
 if temp = 0 then put "0 hours" into card field 4
 if temp > 0 then
  put 60*60 into sechours
  put temp div sechours into numhours
  put numhours & " hours" into card field 4
  -- check for minutes
  put temp-sechours*numhours into temp
 end if
 if temp = 0 then put "0 minutes" into card field 5
 if temp > 0 then
  put 60 into secminutes
  put temp div secminutes into numminutes
  put numminutes & " minutes" into card field 5
 end if
end mouseUp
```

Figure 18.8 Number of Days, Hours, and Minutes between Two Dates

reconverted to minutes, hours, and days by dividing the elapsed time by the number of seconds in a minute, hour, or day. Figure 18.8 determines the number of seconds between any two dates and times.

The Function *the ticks*

HyperCard provides another time function to keep track to sixtieths of a second. *The ticks* provides the number of sixtieths of a second since the last system start up (the last time the operating system was booted up).

Figure 18.9 illustrates a simple reaction time event. The viewer clicks on a start button. After a random period of time, the script places another invisible target button at a random position on the screen and then makes it visible. The script records *the ticks* at the moment the button becomes visible, in an arbitrarily named global variable called *starttime*. The viewer is invited to move the mouse from the home position to click the mouse on the appearing button as quickly as possible. When the viewer clicks, the script records *the ticks* at that time in a global variable named *endtime*. The script then subtracts *starttime* from *endtime* to obtain the number of sixtieths of a second since the button appeared. The script then prints out the time and resets by making the target button disappear.

An *if* statement checks if the viewer has moved away from the home button (trying to cheat by anticipating the appearing button). If the mouse is moved outside the Home button, the script beeps and tells the viewer to get back.

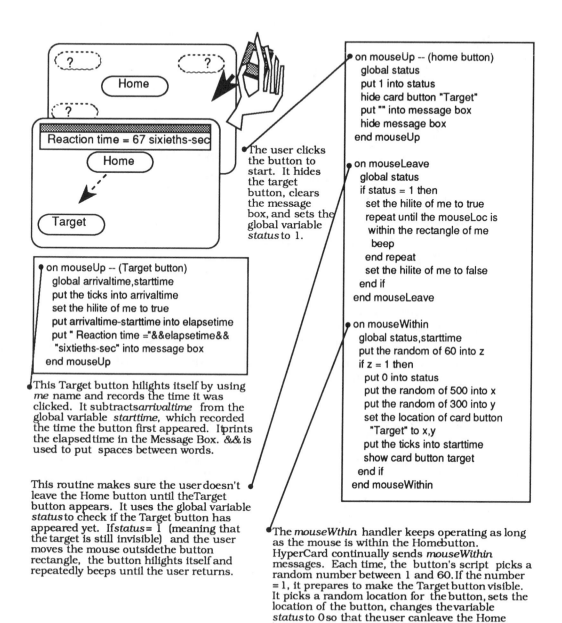

The user clicks the button to start. It hides the target button, clears the message box, and sets the global variable *status* to 1.

```
on mouseUp -- (home button)
  global status
  put 1 into status
  hide card button "Target"
  put "" into message box
  hide message box
end mouseUp

on mouseLeave
  global status
  if status = 1 then
    set the hilite of me to true
    repeat until the mouseLoc is
    within the rectangle of me
      beep
    end repeat
    set the hilite of me to false
  end if
end mouseLeave

on mouseWithin
  global status,starttime
  put the random of 60 into z
  if z = 1 then
    put 0 into status
    put the random of 500 into x
    put the random of 300 into y
    set the location of card button
      "Target" to x,y
    put the ticks into starttime
    show card button target
  end if
end mouseWithin
```

```
on mouseUp -- (Target button)
  global arrivaltime,starttime
  put the ticks into arrivaltime
  set the hilite of me to true
  put arrivaltime-starttime into elapsetime
  put " Reaction time ="&&elapsetime&&
    "sixtieths-sec" into message box
end mouseUp
```

This Target button hilights itself by using *me* name and records the time it was clicked. It subtracts *arrivaltime* from the global variable *starttime*, which recorded the time the button first appeared. It prints the elapsed time in the Message Box. && is used to put spaces between words.

This routine makes sure the user doesn't leave the Home button until the Target button appears. It uses the global variable *status* to check if the Target button has appeared yet. If *status* = 1 (meaning that the target is still invisible) and the user moves the mouse outside the button rectangle, the button hilights itself and repeatedly beeps until the user returns.

The *mouseWthin* handler keeps operating as long as the mouse is within the Home button. HyperCard continually sends *mouseWithin* messages. Each time, the button's script picks a random number between 1 and 60. If the number = 1, it prepares to make the Target button visible. It picks a random location for the button, sets the location of the button, changes the variable *status* to 0 so that the user can leave the Home button, makes the Target button visible, and records the time in sixtieth's of a second ticks in global variable *starttime*.

Figure 18.9   Reaction Time Recorder

Script to Draw a Clock

The script in Figure 18.11 draws a traditional clock with hour, minute, and second hands. This clock will always be functioning as long as the card is visible (not requiring clicks on any button). Two special issues complicate this script. The requirement that it always be functioning necessitates use of an *idle* message handler to constantly read the time. Also, since traditional clocks are circular, the script must convert the information about time into appropriate positions for the hands.

In figure 18.11, an *openCard* message handler draws the basic clock outline centered at 250,150 with a radius of 100. An *idle* message handler placed at the card level constantly reads the time. A *convert* command changes *the time* into a *dateItems* format so that the hours, minutes, and seconds can be easily ascertained. Each of these time items is put into a global variable so that the clock-drawing routines can use the information to draw the hands.

DrawHrhand, drawMinhand, and *drawSechand* subroutines convert the time into position. To do this, the subroutines use a trigonometric computer algorithm to convert circular angle information into horizontal and vertical coordinates. The heart of this algorithm is a pair of formulas that use information about center position, radius, and angle in the circle to determine the coordinates of points on the edge. A description of the reasons these formulas work can be found in *Using Computers to Create Art.* In addition, Chapter 19 explains more on the application of mathematics to computer graphics.

To use the formulas, the scripts must convert time to angle. The conversion is actually easy because minutes and seconds are indicated on a 60 unit basis that can be converted to the 360 degrees basis of circles. Each number on a normal clock is at a predictable angle position in the circle. Figure 18.10 shows the degree equivalencies of the hour positions on a circular clock. For example, the 3 on a clock is at 90 degrees, the 6 at 180 degrees, the 9 at 270 degrees.

The three conversion scripts in Figure 18.11 take the time and calculate the equivalent angle. They get the time from the global variables provided by the *idle* command. For the seconds and minutes this conversion is an easy matter of figuring out the angular fraction of the circle defined by the particular hand's relationship to the 0-degree line. The script

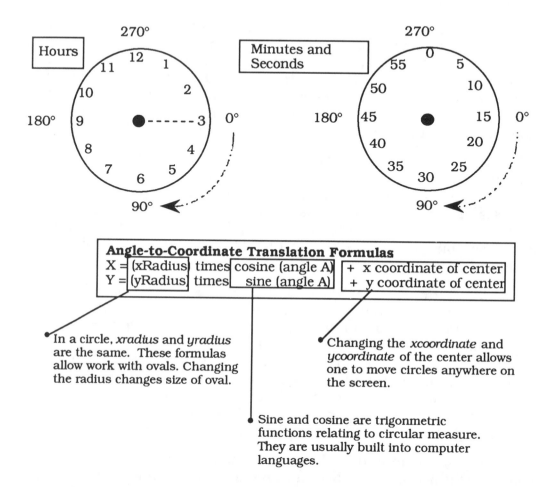

Angle-to-Coordinate Translation Formulas

X = (xRadius) times cosine (angle A) + x coordinate of center
Y = (yRadius) times sine (angle A) + y coordinate of center

In a circle, *xradius* and *yradius* are the same. These formulas allow work with ovals. Changing the radius changes size of oval.

Changing the *xcoordinate* and *ycoordinate* of the center allows one to move circles anywhere on the screen.

Sine and cosine are trigonmetric functions relating to circular measure. They are usually built into computer languages.

To calculate the drawing of clock hands, one must take certain steps:
• Translate time into angle measures.
• The degree angle measures must then be converted into radians, which are another way of measuring angles that computers use.
• These angles must then be converted into horizontal and vertical Cartesian grid coordinates so that lines can be drawn representing the hands. This conversion is accomplished by using trignometric formulas. (These formulas asume that 0-degrees is at the right instead of the conventional position at top.)

Figure 18.10 Conversion of Time into Coordinates on the Screen

creates a fraction of the current time divided by 60 multiplied by 360. For example, a hand pointing at 20 minutes (visually at the 4 on the clock) represents 20/60 of a circle. To determine degrees, this fraction is multiplied by 360 (the total degrees in a circle). To convert the hour, the fraction is a proportion of 12. For example, the 8 o'clock hour defines an angle of 8/12 of a circle, or 240-degrees.

The script then must convert the degree measurement of angle into another method of measuring angle called radians, which is the unit required for computer calculations. In a circle there are approximately 6.29 radians (2 times the mathematical quantity *pi*) instead of 360 degrees. Conversion is an easy ratio determination. In the scripts in Figure 18.11, the number of radians is determined by multiplying the number of degrees defined by the particular hand position by the fraction of 6.29 divided by 360. Because the formulas assume that 0 is at the right of the circle while clocks assume that it is at the top, 90-degrees is subtracted from each angle before conversion to adjust for the difference.

The script then uses the trigonometric formulas to determine the coordinates. The subroutines then draw lines from the center to the position on the perimeter to represent the hands on a clock. Before they draw the hands each time, they erase the previous line.

Although this script will accomplish the desired drawing, it could be improved in certain ways. In scripts doing other work besides drawing the clock, the clock routine may not be able to draw evenly at every second — HyperCard is not fast enough to do the calculations, erase, and draw all within a second. Also, the script may redraw the same hands several times if nothing else is going on. It may make sense to create routines in the script to check if there is a change before redrawing — for example, many second hands will be redrawn before it is absolutely necessary to redraw a minute hand. Strategic *if* commands in the *drwMin* script can check if the minute has changed before actually redrawing the minute hand.

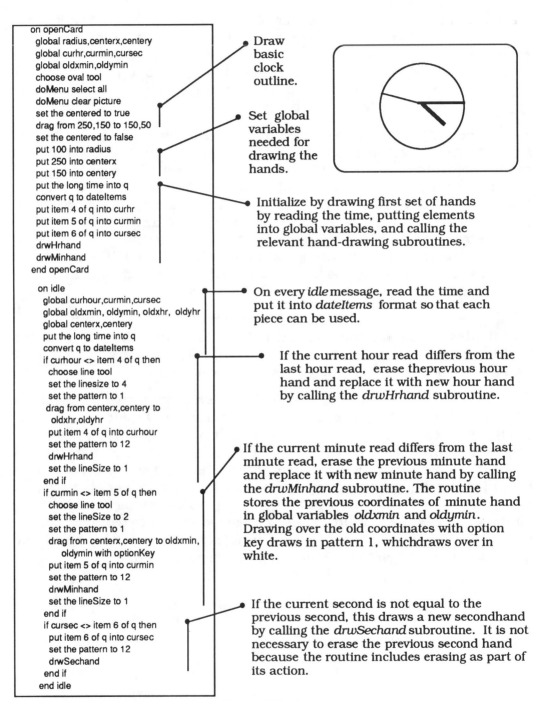

```
on openCard
  global radius,centerx,centery
  global curhr,curmin,cursec
  global oldxmin,oldymin
  choose oval tool
  doMenu select all
  doMenu clear picture
  set the centered to true
  drag from 250,150 to 150,50
  set the centered to false
  put 100 into radius
  put 250 into centerx
  put 150 into centery
  put the long time into q
  convert q to dateItems
  put item 4 of q into curhr
  put item 5 of q into curmin
  put item 6 of q into cursec
  drwHrhand
  drwMinhand
end openCard

  on idle
    global curhour,curmin,cursec
    global oldxmin, oldymin, oldxhr, oldyhr
    global centerx,centery
    put the long time into q
    convert q to dateItems
    if curhour <> item 4 of q then
      choose line tool
      set the linesize to 4
      set the pattern to 1
      drag from centerx,centery to
        oldxhr,oldyhr
      put item 4 of q into curhour
      set the pattern to 12
      drwHrhand
      set the lineSize to 1
    end if
    if curmin <> item 5 of q then
      choose line tool
      set the lineSize to 2
      set the pattern to 1
      drag from centerx,centery to oldxmin,
        oldymin with optionKey
      put item 5 of q into curmin
      set the pattern to 12
      drwMinhand
      set the lineSize to 1
    end if
    if cursec <> item 6 of q then
      put item 6 of q into cursec
      set the pattern to 12
      drwSechand
    end if
  end idle
```

Draw basic clock outline.

Set global variables needed for drawing the hands.

Initialize by drawing first set of hands by reading the time, putting elements into global variables, and calling the relevant hand-drawing subroutines.

On every *idle* message, read the time and put it into *dateItems* format so that each piece can be used.

If the current hour read differs from the last hour read, erase theprevious hour hand and replace it with new hour hand by calling the *drwHrhand* subroutine.

If the current minute read differs from the last minute read, erase the previous minute hand and replace it with new minute hand by calling the *drwMinhand* subroutine. The routine stores the previous coordinates of minute hand in global variables *oldxmin* and *oldymin*. Drawing over the old coordinates with option key draws in pattern 1, whichdraws over in white.

If the current second is not equal to the previous second, this draws a new secondhand by calling the *drwSechand* subroutine. It is not necessary to erase the previous second hand because the routine includes erasing as part of its action.

Figure 18.11 Drawing a Traditional Clock

This subroutine takes the hour and converts it into coordinates so that a hand can be drawn from the center to the correct place to represent the angle corresponding to the hour. It calculates the proportion of the circle represented by the hour — for example, 3 o'clock uses 3/12 of the circle, or 90 degrees. It then uses the trigonometric formulas to convert angle into horizontal and vertical coordinates (see text). Since HyperCard needs whole numbers, it rounds off the calculated numbers. It sets the *lineSize* to 4 in order to draw a thick line. It stores the calculated coordinates in *oldxhr* and *oldyhr* so that the line can be erased when the hour changes by drawing over it in white.

```
on drwHrhand
  global curhr
  global radius,centerx,centery
  global ranglehr,x,y
  global oldxhr,oldyhr
  if curhr = 12 then put 0 into curhr
  put (curhr/12)*360 into anglehr
  put anglehr-90 into anglehr
  put anglehr*(3.1416/180) into ranglehr
  put (radius-50) *cos (ranglehr) + centerx into x
  put (radius-50) *sin (ranglehr) + centery into y
  put round(x) into x
  put round(y) into y
  choose line tool
  set the lineSize to 4
  drag from centerx,centery to x,y
  put x into oldxhr
  put y into oldyhr
  set the lineSize to 1
  choose browse tool
end drwHrhand
```

This subroutine functions much like the hour hand routine. The proportion of the circle occupied by the minutes uses 60 as part of the ratio — for example, 20 minutes is 20/60 of a circle, or 1/3 of 360 degrees, which equals 120 degrees. All of these routines must subtract 90 degrees from the calculated angle because the trigonometric formulas assume that the circle measurement starts at the right instead of at the top.

```
on drwMinhand
  global curmin
  global radius,centerx,centery
  global ranglemin,x,y
  global oldxmin,oldymin
  put (curmin/60)*360 into anglemin
  put anglemin-90 into anglemin
  put anglemin*(3.1416/180) into ranglemin
  put radius*cos (ranglemin) + centerx into x
  put radius*sin (ranglemin) + centery into y
  put round(x) into x
  put round(y) into y
  choose line tool
  set the lineSize to 2
  drag from centerx,centery to x,y
  put x into oldxmin
  put y into oldymin
  set the lineSize to 1
end drwMinhand
```

```
on drwSechand
  global cursec
  global radius,centerx,centery
  global ranglesec,x,y
  global oldxsec,oldysec
  put (cursec/60)*360 into anglesec
  put anglesec-90 into anglesec
  put anglesec*(3.1416/180) into ranglesec
  put radius*cos (ranglesec) + centerx into x
  put radius*sin (ranglesec) + centery into y
  put round(x) into x
  put round(y) into y
  choose line tool
  drag from centerx,centery to x,y
  doMenu undo
  put x into oldxsec
  put y into oldysec
  choose browse tool
end drwSechand
```

This second hand routine works exactly like the minute hand routine except that it automatically erases itself after each draw. The *doMenu undo* erases the line just drawn. It can be set up this way because the second hand just needs to be on the screen for a second. Because of HyperCard's slowness, this routine occasionally misses a second.

Figure 18.11   (continued)

Alternative Time-based Art

Much space has been given to describing the creation of a traditional clock script because it is a good learning experience for working with HyperCard. Readers are encouraged to strike out beyond traditional clocks to design their own time-sensitive imagery. There is nothing sacred about the shape and functioning of the traditional circular clock. Indeed, sculptors are beginning to create new kinds of timekeepers that are visually appealing and conceptually intriguing. The computer's ability to provide easily manipulable information about time and date invites artists to work with these entities.

Figure 18.12 illustrates a tree that mourns the passing of time. It is full of leaves that look like eyes. The tree loses one leaf each time approximately 1 second passes. The tree groans in one of four distinct sounds each time a leaf goes away. At the end of the minute, leaves are put back on the tree and the process starts again. Readers are encouraged to design their own innovative time-sensitive events.

```
CARD SCRIPT
on openCard
  global t
  put 0 into t
  spreadButstart
end openCard


on idle
  global qhours, qseconds, qminutes,
    curtime
  put the long time into curtime
  convert curtime to dateitems
  put item 4 of curtime into qhours
  put item 5 of curtime into qminutes
  put item 6 of curtime into qseconds
  secEye
end idle

on secEye
  global qseconds,t
  if qseconds > 57 then
    spreadButstart
  else
    if qseconds <> 0 then
      put qseconds into t
      hide card button t
      put the random of 4 into q
      play stop
      play "oh"&q
    end if
  end if
end secEye


on spreadButstart
  repeat with n = 5 to 57
    put (the random of 475) + 25  into x
    put (the random of 135) + 65   into y
    set the location of button n to x,y
    show card button n
  end repeat
end spreadButstart
```

The *idle* routine constantly reads the time and puts components into variables *qhours*, *qminutes*, and *qseconds*. Each time it activates the *secEye*, subroutine which makes another of the eye-shaped leaves disappear from the tree. The tree loses one leaf each second approximately and sighs. Other routines could be added to indicate minutes and hours.

When the seconds count reaches 57, this *spreadButstart* routine spreads the leaves on the tree again in preparation for their disappearing during the next minute.

Each second, another one of the eye buttons is made to disappear by hiding the button as an indication of passing time. The computer randomly plays one of four sigh sounds (oh1, oh2, oh3, oh4) that have been previously recorded via a sound digitizer.

The *spreadBut* routine is activated at the end of each minute to put new eyes on the tree in random locations. It only goes from 5 to 57 because it takes HyperCard from second 57 of one minute to second 5 of the next minute to complete putting the eyes on the tree. (This routine assumes that buttons 5 to 57 have been previously created and assigned the icon of the eye.)

Figure 18.12 Clock in Which Falling and Sighing Leaves Indicate Passing Seconds

CHAPTER 19
A PRAGMATIC INTRODUCTION TO THE MATHEMATICS OF COMPUTER GRAPHICS

This chapter pragmatically introduces the reader to some basic analytical geometry that might be interesting for graphics work in Hyper-Card. Although HyperCard's relative slowness and lack of support for advanced mathematical functions make it less appropriate than some other computer languages for some mathematics-based graphics work, there are still interesting possibilities to explore.

Unfortunately, many artists shy away from mathematics because of their prior experience of it in schools. Too often, mathematics study became the memorization of formulas and their dull, repetitive application in problems without life. The mathematics of exploration and imagination is quite different. Theoretical mathematics is an enterprise that shares important attributes with the arts. Both the mathematical theorist and the artist develop internally consistent artificial worlds. Both are rewarded for original thought. Both celebrate human imagination and willingness to inquire in realms often without immediate utilitarian goals. This chapter will not be able to introduce the provocative world of theoretical math. Readers are encouraged to reconnect with this other mathematics. For more on connections between art and mathematics, see *Using Computers to Create Art* and issues of the *Journal Leonardo*, the international journal of art and science (address in Chapter 20).

Contemporary hardware and software tools allow artists to use computers quite comfortably without formally engaging in mathematical analysis. Users can draw images merely by selecting tools from a palette and moving a mouse around. Actually, this is not so far removed from the mathematics of graphics as one might imagine. The computer software that allows the mouse to draw images and move shapes around makes use of the mathematical analysis of graphics. Similarly, the animation and 3-D design programs described in later chapters rely heavily on the image transformation algorithms developed over several centuries by mathematicians. This software could not exist without building upon the history of mathematical inquiry.

Most computer science-based graphics courses focus almost exclusively on the mathematics of graphic image manipulation — topics such as the geometry of two-dimensional representation, transformation of images (translation, scaling, and rotation), methods for creating three-dimensional illusion, and the mathematics of chaos and fractals. The previous chapters have demonstrated ways artists can use HyperCard's graphic drawing commands in an intuitive fashion — moving from visual ideas to the set of commands to realize the ideas on the computer screens. Actually, the development of some of these scripts represents an application of mathematical principles. In devising logical systems for the manipulation of symbols, readers may have been developing mathematical algorithms without calling them such.

Equation of the Line

Analytical geometry is a branch of mathematics that attempts to systematize and analyze the relationships of objects in space. It codifies the relationships into symbolic statements that can represent the whole family of related objects. The statements are often presented in the form of equations that summarize the relationships.

For example, the straight line is a fundamental object in geometry. It is the shortest distance between two points. Lines appear to differ greatly from one another. They start and stop in different places and go in all kinds of directions. Analytical geometry asks, "Is there some way to represent the underlying similarity?"

Using the Cartesian coordinate system for mapping space, geometricians developed an equation for the straight line that describes the underlying relationship of all lines. Each line has a unique equation that describes its position in space, its slant, and its direction. Yet the form of the equations is the same for all straight lines.

The equation allows one to determine the vertical position of each point if one knows the horizontal position. Conversely, it also allows the determination of the horizontal position if one knows the vertical position.

The key elements in the equation are the symbolic value *m*, which stands for the slant of the line, and *b*, which stands for the place the line crosses the vertical *y* axis in the Cartesian coordinate system. Slant is measured in the number of vertical units changed for each change in horizontal units. For example, a line with the *m* value 3 would change 3 vertical units for each horizontal unit. A steeper line with the *m* value 10 would change 10 vertical units. Minus values mean that the line slants in the other direction (down 3 vertical units for each *x*).

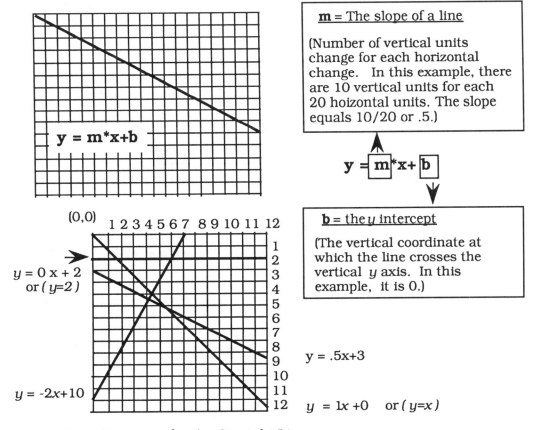

m = The slope of a line

(Number of vertical units change for each horizontal change. In this example, there are 10 vertical units for each 20 hoizontal units. The slope equals 10/20 or .5.)

$$y = m^*x + b$$

b = the *y* intercept

(The vertical coordinate at which the line crosses the vertical *y* axis. In this example, it is 0.)

$y = .5x + 3$

$y = 1x + 0 \quad or\ (y=x)$

$y = 0x + 2$ or (*y*=2)

$y = -2x + 10$

Figure 19.1   Equation for the Straight Line

Application of this equation can be used to generate interesting images in HyperCard, such as families of parallel lines or lines with systematically changing slants. Although all of these images could be drawn by hand movement of the mouse, these scripts are sometimes easier and allow for script-controlled image generation. To use the equation in a script, one uses the equation to generate the vertical value for the endpoints with predetermined horizontal positions. One then connects the points. Figure 19.2 illustrates some of the possibilities.

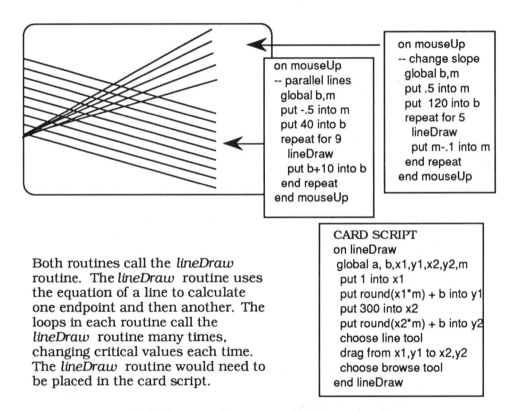

Both routines call the *lineDraw* routine. The *lineDraw* routine uses the equation of a line to calculate one endpoint and then another. The loops in each routine call the *lineDraw* routine many times, changing critical values each time. The *lineDraw* routine would need to be placed in the card script.

Figure 19.2   Parallel Lines and Lines with Changing Slopes

Equations for Ovals, Circles, and Spirals

The definition of a circle is a set of points, all of which are equally distant from one point. Unfortunately, this definition does not provide the detail necessary in a Cartesian coordinate system to specify the coordinates of the points on the circumference of the circle when one knows the center and the radius. Analytical geometry, however, builds on the definition to generate equations that can provide the coordinates.

The equation is built on geometric understanding of the relationship between lengths of sides and angles in right triangles. As with straight lines, all right triangles have systematic underlying qualities that can be used. This trigonometric knowledge allows one to determine missing information when some information is known — e.g., the length of one of the sides when one angle and one side are known. This knowledge is frequently applied in surveying and navigation. The ratios of sides to each other are known for all angles and have been codified into functions called the sine, cosine, and tangent. One can find tables of these ratios in the back of all geometry and trigonometry books. Most computer systems also provide these functions

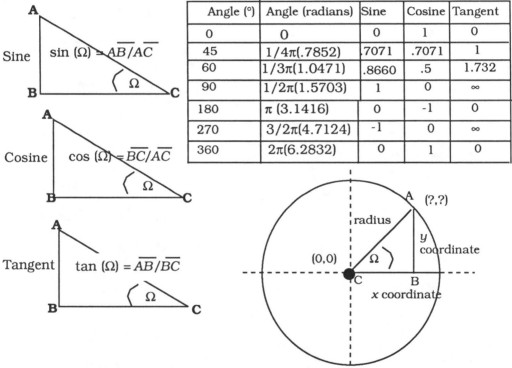

Angle (°)	Angle (radians)	Sine	Cosine	Tangent
0	0	0	1	0
45	1/4π(.7852)	.7071	.7071	1
60	1/3π(1.0471)	.8660	.5	1.732
90	1/2π(1.5703)	1	0	∞
180	π (3.1416)	0	-1	0
270	3/2π(4.7124)	-1	0	∞
360	2π(6.2832)	0	1	0

The trigonometric functions can be used to calculate the unknown coordinates of a point on the circle. Because of the constraints of right triangles, unknown lengths can be calculated if one angle and one side are known. In the example, the angle Ω is arbitrarily selected, and the line AC equals the known radius. The x coordinate equals CB, and the y coordinate equals AB. Sin(Ω) =y/radius. Cos(Ω) = x/radius. X and Y can be determined using knowledge of the standard sine and cosine values for angle Ω and simple algrebra.

Figure 19.3   Use of Trigonometric Functions in Computer Graphics

automatically. For more details on derivation of these, see any trigonometry book.

With computers, this knowledge is useful for calculating the points on a circle when the coordinates of the center and the length of the radius are known. The relationships are codified into two equations that can generate the horizontal and vertical coordinates for each angle in a circle, expressed in radian measure. The separation of a horizontal and vertical radius allows for the generation of ovals. In a circle, the horizontal and

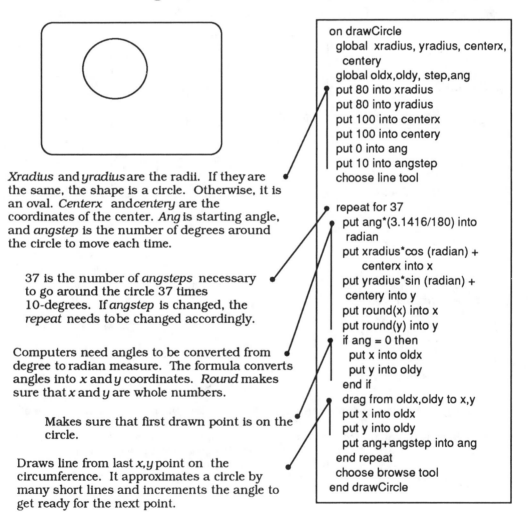

Xradius and *yradius* are the radii. If they are the same, the shape is a circle. Otherwise, it is an oval. *Centerx* and *centery* are the coordinates of the center. *Ang* is starting angle, and *angstep* is the number of degrees around the circle to move each time.

37 is the number of *angsteps* necessary to go around the circle 37 times 10-degrees. If *angstep* is changed, the *repeat* needs to be changed accordingly.

Computers need angles to be converted from degree to radian measure. The formula converts angles into *x* and *y* coordinates. *Round* makes sure that *x* and *y* are whole numbers.

Makes sure that first drawn point is on the circle.

Draws line from last *x,y* point on the circumference. It approximates a circle by many short lines and increments the angle to get ready for the next point.

```
on drawCircle
  global  xradius, yradius, centerx,
    centery
  global oldx,oldy, step,ang
  put 80 into xradius
  put 80 into yradius
  put 100 into centerx
  put 100 into centery
  put 0 into ang
  put 10 into angstep
  choose line tool

  repeat for 37
    put ang*(3.1416/180) into
      radian
    put xradius*cos (radian) +
      centerx into x
    put yradius*sin (radian) +
      centery into y
    put round(x) into x
    put round(y) into y
    if ang = 0 then
      put x into oldx
      put y into oldy
    end if
    drag from oldx,oldy to x,y
    put x into oldx
    put y into oldy
    put ang+angstep into ang
  end repeat
  choose browse tool
end drawCircle
```

Fgiure 19.4   Algorithm for Drawing a Circle or an Oval

vertical radius would be the same. For more on angular measure, see Chapter 18.

A circle can be generated, using these equations, by creation of a loop (Figure 19.4). Each time through the loop, the script changes the angle. The equations generate the horizontal and vertical coordinates of the point on the circumference for that angle. The script then connects that point with the previous point on the circumference. Depending on the angle increment each time, one gets an approximation of a circle built on many short sides. For example, a 10-degree (.17-radian) increment would provide a 36-sided approximation that would be almost indistinguishable from the best circle that could be displayed on the computer screen. Remember that the digital nature of the computer screen means that no true circle can be displayed. One is limited by the resolution of the screen. For the sake of illustration, Figure 19.4 assumes that the center is 100,100 and the x radius and y radius are both 80. The *if* command script line for angle 0 causes the first point to be drawn on the circle rather than coming from 0,0.

A reader might be wondering, "Why bother?" HyperCard provides an instant circle/oval drawing command. For plain circles and ovals, one does not need this formula, and the intrinsic commands are quicker. (Note, however, that the underlying software is built precisely on this kind of analysis.) The formulas become useful, however, when one wants to create graphics based on circles and ovals that cannot use the intrinsic commands. HyperCard's oval command does not provide any detailed information about the points on the circumference such as this algorithm can.

This basic routine provides the means for generation of all of the following:

- A circle or an oval that slowly draws itself rather than popping onto the screen
- Circles or ovals that connect spokes to their centers or other points
- Arcs rather than full circles
- Spirals
- Animated motion of objects that move in a circular motion

Readers are urged to explore extensions beyond the examples.

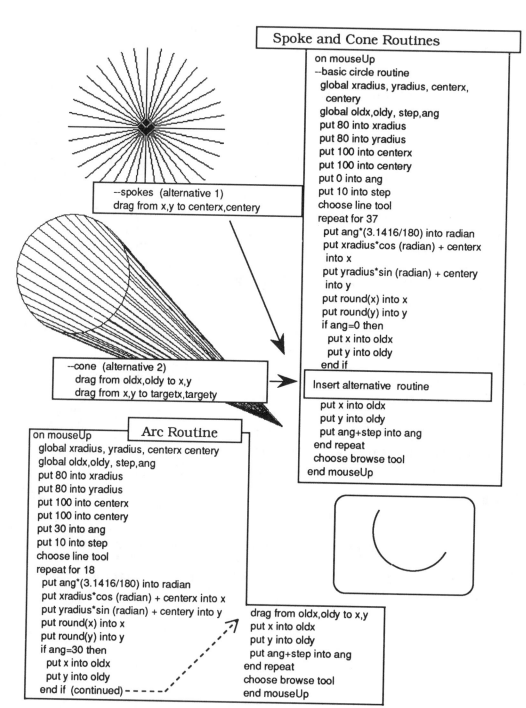

Spoke and Cone Routines

```
on mouseUp
--basic circle routine
 global xradius, yradius, centerx,
  centery
 global oldx,oldy, step,ang
 put 80 into xradius
 put 80 into yradius
 put 100 into centerx
 put 100 into centery
 put 0 into ang
 put 10 into step
 choose line tool
 repeat for 37
  put ang*(3.1416/180) into radian
  put xradius*cos (radian) + centerx
  into x
  put yradius*sin (radian) + centery
  into y
  put round(x) into x
  put round(y) into y
  if ang=0 then
   put x into oldx
   put y into oldy
  end if
```

```
Insert alternative routine
```

```
  put x into oldx
  put y into oldy
  put ang+step into ang
 end repeat
 choose browse tool
end mouseUp
```

--spokes (alternative 1)
drag from x,y to centerx,centery

--cone (alternative 2)
drag from oldx,oldy to x,y
drag from x,y to targetx,targety

Arc Routine

```
on mouseUp
 global xradius, yradius, centerx centery
 global oldx,oldy, step,ang
 put 80 into xradius
 put 80 into yradius
 put 100 into centerx
 put 100 into centery
 put 30 into ang
 put 10 into step
 choose line tool
 repeat for 18
  put ang*(3.1416/180) into radian
  put xradius*cos (radian) + centerx into x
  put yradius*sin (radian) + centery into y
  put round(x) into x
  put round(y) into y
  if ang=30 then
   put x into oldx
   put y into oldy
  end if (continued)- - - - -
```

```
 drag from oldx,oldy to x,y
 put x into oldx
 put y into oldy
 put ang+step into ang
 end repeat
 choose browse tool
end mouseUp
```

Figure 19.5   Variations on the Circle Routine: Spokes, Cone, Arc

```
on mouseUp
  global xradius,yradius,centerx,centery
  global oldx,oldy, step,ang
  put 80 into xradius
  put 80 into yradius
  put 100 into centerx
  put 100 into centery
  put 0 into ang
  put 10 into step
  choose line tool

repeat for 4* 37
  put ang*(3.1416/180) into radian
  put xradius-.5 into xradius
  put yradius-.5 into yradius
  put xradius*cos (radian) + centerx into x
  put yradius*sin (radian) + centery into y
  put round(x) into x
  put round(y) into y
  if ang = 0 then
    put x into oldx
    put y into oldy
  end if
  drag from oldx,oldy to x,y
  put x into oldx
  put y into oldy
  put ang+step into ang
end repeat
choose browse tool
end mouseUp
```

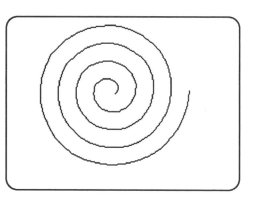

This routine varies from the standard circle routine in 2 ways:

• It must go around more than once to create the spiral effect. The 4 indicates the number of cycles and can be changed as long as one adjusts the decrement to the radius.

• Each time a point is calculated, the radii are decreased a standard amount. The value of this decrement controls the tightness of the spiral.

Spiral of boxes alternative

```
choose rectangle tool
  drag from x,y to x+10,y+10
```

The spiral of boxes can be accomplished by replacing the boxed section of the script with the new script lines. Instead of connecting each point on the spiral, the routine uses the points as the corners of a rectangle.

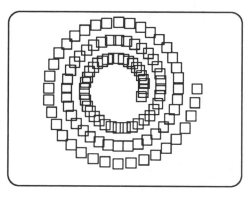

Figure 19.6   Spirals

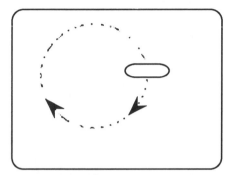

```
on mouseUp
  global xradius,yradius,centerx,centery
  global oldx,oldy, step,ang
  put 80 into xradius
  put 80 into yradius
  put 100 into centerx
  put 100 into centery
  put 0 into ang
  put 10 into step

repeat for 37
  put ang*(3.1416/180) into radian
  put xradius*cos (radian) + centerx into x
  put yradius*sin (radian) + centery into y
  put round(x) into x
  put round(y) into y
  if ang = 0 then
    put x into oldx
    put y into oldy
  end if
  set the location of card button 1 to x,y
  put x into oldx
  put y into oldy
  put ang+step into ang
  end repeat
  choose browse tool
end mouseUp
```

This animation moves a button in a circular path. Instead of drawing lines, the routine uses the calculated points to set the location of a button.

*Figure 19.7   Animation in a
              Circular Path*

Equation of the Sine and Parabola

Physicists use mathematical expressions to represent principles about the world symbolically. These expressions are codified into equations that can be used to represent the underlying relationships graphically. Computer graphic artists can use these equations either to build works based on the underlying physical realities or to explore the visual poetry of the curves created. This section explores both the sine and the parabola curve.

Sine Wave. Many phenomena in nature can be characterized by their regular periodic repetition. This vibration, however, is not a simple "go one way and then another" movement. The movement can be characterized by a constantly changing velocity that then reverses itself. One can see this movement in the pendulum. The pendulum moves quickest as it moves through its lowest position. As it moves up to the highest point on one side, it slows until it stops and reverses. Its speed then accelerates until it crosses the bottom. when it begins to slow again, and so on. A pen attached to the pendulum would describe a sine wave on a moving piece of paper. As described in Chapter 17, vibrating materials that produce sound also move in this sine pattern.

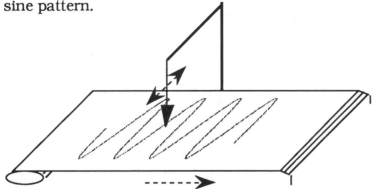

Figure 19.8   A Swinging Pendulum Draws a Sine Wave as Paper Moves at a Constant Speed beneath It

HyperCard provides access to a built-in sine function. The sine function yields a value based on the angle it is given. Angles must be expressed in radians. Computer images can be generated by mapping the angles to one axis and the sine value to the other axis. Images are created by connecting calculated points with lines.

The sine function returns a minimum of -1 (for 270 degrees or 4.717 radians) and a maximum of +1 (for 90 degrees or 1.572 radians). Since the sine wave is symmetrical around 0 degrees and computer screens have no negative values, the whole curve must be centered high on the screen in order to see both sides of the curve. The routine in Figure 19.9 accomplishes this adjustment by adding a vertical constant to each result. Similarly, the variation of 1 pixel on either side of the center line would not show much variation. The equation magnifies the curve by multiplying each outcome by a vertical constant. One complete sine variation is accomplished in movement of angles from 0 to 360 degrees (6.29 radians). The equation can generate more cycles by moving to angle values greater than 6.29. In fact, an exact number of cycles can be generated by multiplying 6.29 by the desired number of changes. Finally, the entire variation occupies only 6.2 horizontal pixels if angles are mapped directly on the horizontal axis. Greater spread can be accomplished by multiplying each horizontal coordinate by a constant before drawing.

```
on mouseUp
global oldx,oldy, step,ang
  put 0 into x
  put 0 into ang
  put 1 into numberwaves
  put 3 into xstep
  put 10 into angstep
  put 100 into ypos
  put 90 into ymag
  choose line tool
  repeat for  37 * numberwaves
    put ang*(3.1416/180) into radian
    put sin (radian) into y1
    put (y1* ymag) + ypos into y
    put round(y) into y
    if ang = 0 then
      put x into oldx
      put y into oldy
    end if
    drag from oldx,oldy to x,y
    put x into oldx
    put y into oldy
    put ang+angstep into ang
    put x+xstep into x
  end repeat
  choose browse tool
end mouseUp
```

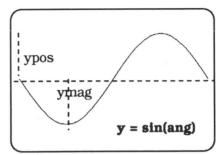

$$y = sin(ang)$$

Since the sine value ranges only between the values of -1 and +1 for all angles, the routine must adjust it to be displayed on a computer screen.

- *ypos* moves it vertically so that negative values will appear on the screen.
- *ymag* magnifies each sine value so it will make a wider curve.
- *angstep* controls how finely the curve will be drawn by controlling the number of points that will be calculated.
- *xstep* magnifies the curve in the horizontal direction.
- *numberwaves* controls the number of cycles to be displayed. *xstep* must be adjusted accordingly.

```
on mouseUp
 global oldx,oldy, step,ang
   put 0 into y
   put 0 into ang
   put 1into numberwaves
   put 3 into ystep
   put 10 into angstep
   put 100 into xpos
   put 90 into xmag
   choose line tool
   repeat for  37 * numberwaves
     put ang*(3.1416/180) into radian
     put sin (radian) into x1
     put (x1* xmag) + xpos into x
     put round(x) into x
     if ang = 0 then
       put x into oldx
       put y into oldy
     end if  (continued)
```

The vertical sine wave requires that angles be mapped on the vertical (*y*) axis and the resulting values be plotted on the horizontal (*x*) axis.

```
drag from oldx,oldy to x,y
put x into oldx
put y into oldy
put ang+angstep into ang
put y+ystep into y
end repeat
choose browse tool
end mouseUp
```

Figure 19.9   Basic Sine-drawing Routine

Judicious use of the sine routine can be used to create other kinds of related graphics. As with the oval routine, all the following are possible:

- Families of sine waves
- Sine waves with changing horizontal or vertical components
- Sine waves connected with other graphic objects
- Objects moving along a sine wave path

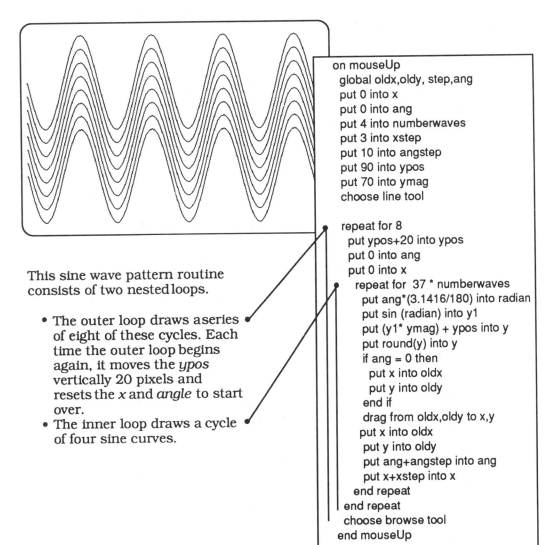

```
on mouseUp
  global oldx,oldy, step,ang
  put 0 into x
  put 0 into ang
  put 4 into numberwaves
  put 3 into xstep
  put 10 into angstep
  put 90 into ypos
  put 70 into ymag
  choose line tool

  repeat for 8
    put ypos+20 into ypos
    put 0 into ang
    put 0 into x
    repeat for  37 * numberwaves
      put ang*(3.1416/180) into radian
      put sin (radian) into y1
      put (y1* ymag) + ypos into y
      put round(y) into y
      if ang = 0 then
        put x into oldx
        put y into oldy
      end if
      drag from oldx,oldy to x,y
      put x into oldx
      put y into oldy
      put ang+angstep into ang
      put x+xstep into x
    end repeat
  end repeat
  choose browse tool
end mouseUp
```

This sine wave pattern routine consists of two nested loops.

- The outer loop draws a series of eight of these cycles. Each time the outer loop begins again, it moves the *ypos* vertically 20 pixels and resets the *x* and *angle* to start over.
- The inner loop draws a cycle of four sine curves.

Figure 19.10 Family of Sine Waves

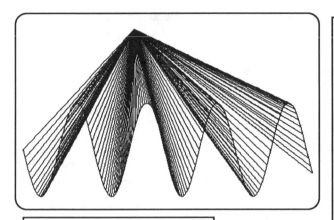

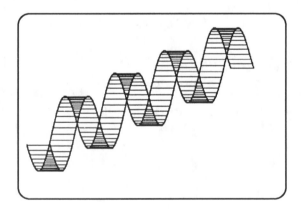

```
on mouseUp
 --undulation
 global oldx,oldy, step,ang
 put 0 into x
 put 0 into ang
 put 4 into numberwaves
 put 3 into xstep
 put 10 into angstep
 put 200 into ypos
 put 70 into ymag
 choose line tool

 repeat for  37 * numberwaves
   put ang*(3.1416/180) into radian
   put sin (radian) into y1
   put (y1* ymag) + ypos into y
   put round(y) into y
   if ang = 0 then
     put x into oldx
     put y into oldy
   end if
   drag from oldx,oldy to x,y
   drag from x,y to 170,20
   put x into oldx
   put y into oldy
   put ang+angstep into ang
   put x+xstep into x
 end repeat
 choose browse tool
end mouseUp
```

```
on mouseUp
 --ribbon
 global oldx,oldy, step,ang
 global x,y
 put 0 into x
 put 0 into ang
 put 4 into numberwaves
 put 3 into xstep
 put 10 into angstep
 put 250 into ypos
 put 50 into ymag
 choose line tool

 repeat for  37 * numberwaves
   put ang*(3.1416/180) into radian
   put sin (radian) into y1
   put (y1* ymag) + ypos into y
   put round(y) into y
   if ang = 0 then
     put x into oldx
     put y into oldy
   end if
   set the lineSize to 2
   drag from oldx,oldy to x,y
   drag from oldx+50,oldy to x+50,y
   set the lineSize to 1
   drag from x,y to x+50,y
   put x into oldx
   put y into oldy
   put ang+angstep into ang
   put x+xstep into x
   put ypos-1 into ypos
 end repeat
 choose browse tool
end mouseUp
```

Figure 19.11 Variations on Sine Waves

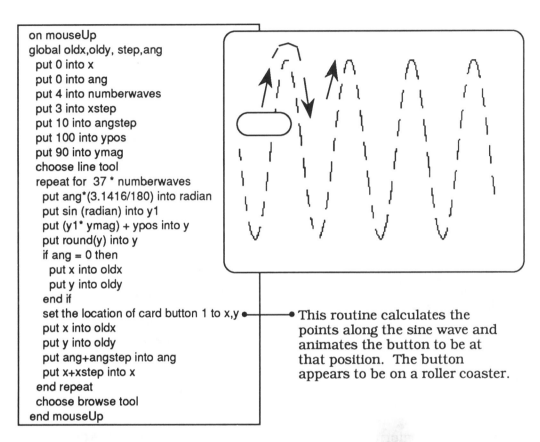

```
on mouseUp
global oldx,oldy, step,ang
  put 0 into x
  put 0 into ang
  put 4 into numberwaves
  put 3 into xstep
  put 10 into angstep
  put 100 into ypos
  put 90 into ymag
  choose line tool
  repeat for 37 * numberwaves
    put ang*(3.1416/180) into radian
    put sin (radian) into y1
    put (y1* ymag) + ypos into y
    put round(y) into y
    if ang = 0 then
      put x into oldx
      put y into oldy
    end if
    set the location of card button 1 to x,y
    put x into oldx
    put y into oldy
    put ang+angstep into ang
    put x+xstep into x
  end repeat
  choose browse tool
end mouseUp
```

This routine calculates the points along the sine wave and animates the button to be at that position. The button appears to be on a roller coaster.

Figure 19.12 Animation along a Sine Wave

Parabola: Physical objects subjected to constant acceleration move along a characteristic path called a parabola. One obvious example is a rock thrown into the air. Subjected to the force of gravity, it falls in a predictable way. An equation can be generated to describe the universal characteristics of these relationships (with air friction temporarily ignored). This equation will be true for all objects anywhere in the universe subjected to gravitation acceleration as it is currently understood. One would only need to change the value of the gravitational constant for the new planet. Again, this equation can be used to give animated objects a realistic motion or to explore the visual qualities of the curve apart from any representation.

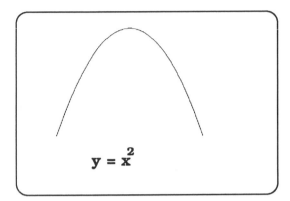

Since the parabola is symetrical about the y (vertical) axis, its horizontal *xpos* position must be adjusted so that it can be displayed. Similarly, *xstep* controls how wide the curve is horizontally.

```
on mouseUp
  global oldx,oldy
  put 0 into oldx
  put 0 into oldy
  put 160 into xpos
  put 20 into ypos
  put 10 into xstep
  choose line tool
  repeat with x1 = -16 to 16
    put x1^2 into y
    put x1*xstep into x
    put x+xpos into x
    put y+ypos into y
    if x1 = -16 then
      put x into oldx
      put y into oldy
    end if
    drag from oldx,oldy to x,y
    put x into oldx
    put y into oldy
  end repeat
end mouseUp
```

Figure 19.13 Parabola Drawing

Transformations: Moving, Scaling, Rotating

Computer graphics systems would not be very valuable if objects could not be transformed through movement, changes in size, and rotation. Again, HyperCard provides efficient routines to accomplish all of these via tools and commands. For example, the combination of selecting an object and dragging the mouse can move anything on the screen. Similarly, the selection of an object and dragging the mouse with the command key can scale objects to be bigger or smaller than the original. The selection of an object followed by the Rotate command from the Paint Menu can rotate objects in increments of 90 degrees. Most of these operations can be accomplished by scripts with appropriate commands.

As with other commands in the HyperCard graphics repertoire, these actions are dependent on underlying software that uses classic geometric and mathematical routines. This section briefly introduces some of this analysis because it will help readers understand advanced computer graphics systems and 3-D graphic manipulations. Readers will probably want to continue to use the HyperCard commands for most simple applications.

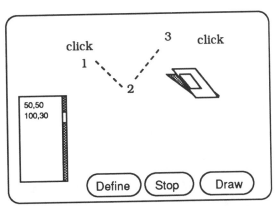

This routine stores all the coordinates where the mouse button was clicked in a card field. It stops when the mouse is moved within the Stop button area. The object is conceptualized as an array of coordinates on which transformations can later be done.

```
on defineObject
   put "" into card field 1
   choose select tool
   doMenu select all
   doMenu clear picture
   choose browse tool
   put "go" into status
   put 1 into q
   -- click stop button to stop"
   type "please click at vertices"
   repeat forever
       if the mouseLoc is within rectangle of
                     card button stop then
          set the hilite of card button stop to true
          set the hilite of card button stop to false
          exit repeat
       end if
       if the mouseClick = "true" then
          put the clickLoc into line q of card field 1
          choose text tool
          click at  the clickLoc
          type q
          put q+1 into q
          choose browse tool
       end if
   end repeat
end defineObject
```

```
on drawObject
   put the number of lines in card field 1 into q
   choose line tool
   repeat with n = 1 to q-1
     put line n of card field 1 into a
     put line n+1 of card field 1 into b
     drag from a to b
   end repeat
   choose browse tool
end drawObject
```

This routine draws an object whose coordinates are stored in a card field.

Figure 19.14 Visual Object Conceptualized as an Array of Coordinates

Most computer graphics systems analyze graphic objects as a series of vertices connected by lines. Objects can be transformed — for example, moved — by systematically adjusting all the vertices and then reconnecting them with lines. This way of thinking about objects simplifies the transformations because much less calculation is necessary to change just the vertices than all the points in between.

A two-dimensional object can then be thought of as a family of coordinate pairs representing each vertex. Usually these families of values are stored together in a special kind of structured list called an array. HyperCard does not provide much support for arrays, so the examples will use fields and variables as pseudoarrays. A generic draw routine will draw any array by systematically moving through and connecting each element with the next.

```
on mouseUp
  global xtrans,ytrans
  ask "how far in horizontal?"
  put it into xtrans
  ask "how far in vertical?"
  put it into ytrans
  put the number of lines in card field 1 into q
  repeat with n = 1 to q
    put item 1 of line n of card field 1 into oldx
    put item 2 of line n of card field 1 into oldy
    put oldx+xtrans into newx
    put oldy+ytrans into newy
    put newx&","&newy into line n of card field 1
  end repeat
  drawObject (from Figure 19.14)
end mouseUp
```

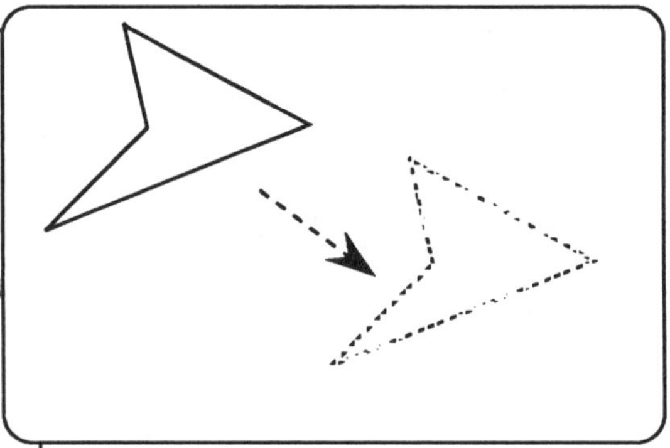

This routine assumes that an object has been drawn with a routine to store all its coordinates in an array in card field 1 (as in Figure 19.14). It asks for a translation factor in the x and y directions. It then adds the factor to each coordinate in the array. The drawObject routine (as in Figure 19.14) then draws the object in the new position. The original coordinates should be saved in another field because this routine changes the values in card field 1.

Figure 19.15 Translation of an Image Stored as an Array of Coordinates

Translation. Translation is defined as the movement of a graphic object in the horizontal or vertical direction. Algorithmically, this can be accomplished by moving each vertex in the desired direction. Pragmatically, this can be accomplished by adding or subtracting a constant to the target component of each coordinate pair in the array. For example, movement to the right could be accomplished by adding a constant value to each horizontal coordinate. Movement up is accomplished by subtracting a constant from each vertical coordinate. These changes can be accomplished by a loop that moves through all pairs. After the value changes are accomplished, the generic draw routine draws the object in the new position.

Scaling. Scaling is accomplished by multiplying the target component of each coordinate pair by a constant factor. For example, doubling the size in the horizontal direction can be accomplished by multiplying the horizontal component of each pair by 2. Halving the size vertically can be accomplished by multiplying each vertical coordinate by .5.

This algorithm has some noteworthy idiosyncrasies. Halving the size of an object in both directions cannot be accomplished by multiplying both the horizontal and vertical components by .5. Because of the two dimensions involved, this change would result in an object one-fourth of the size. It can be accomplished by multiplying each component by the square root of 2 (.707). Other changes require similar adjustments. Also, this scaling routine moves objects toward the 0,0 point. A further transformation would be needed to readjust.

Rotation. Rotation requires a similar approach. New rotated coordinates of each target component of the array of coordinate pairs must be calculated. The line-drawing routine then connects the new points. As with scaling, this routine rotates the object in relation to the 0,0 point. If one wants the object to change orientation but not position, translation routines must be applied after the rotation to bring the object back.

```
on mouseUp
  global xscale,yscale,oldpos
  ask "what scaling in horizontal?"
  put it into xscale
  ask "what scaling in vertical?"
  put it into yscale
  put line 1 of card field 1 into oldpos
  put the number of lines in card field 1 into q
  repeat with n = 1 to q
    put item 1 of line n of card field 1 into oldx
    put item 2 of line n of card field 1 into oldy
    put oldx*xscale into newx
    put oldy*yscale into newy
    put round(newx) into newx
    put round(newy) into newy
    put newx&","&newy into line n of card field 1
  end repeat
  bringBack  (calls subroutine below )
  drawObject (from Figure 19.14)
end mouseUp

on bringBack
  global xtrans,ytrans,xscale,yscale,oldpos
  put line 1 of card field 1 into newpos
  put (item 1 of oldpos) - (item 1 of newpos)
    into xtrans
  put (item 2 of oldpos) - (item 2 of newpos)
    into ytrans
  put the number of lines in card field 1 into q
  repeat with n = 1 to q
    put item 1 of line n of card field 1 into oldx
    put item 2 of line n of card field 1 into oldy
    put oldx+xtrans into newx
    put oldy+ytrans into newy
    put newx&","&newy into line n of card field 1
  end repeat
end bringBack
```

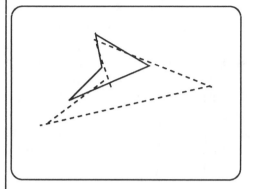

This routine assumes that an object has been drawn with a routine to store all its coordinates in an array in card field 1 (Figures 19.14 and 19.15). It asks for a scaling factor in the *x* and *y* directions. It then multiplies each coordinate in the array by the factor. The *bringBack* routine repositions the object to be roughly in the same place by translating it back. The *drawObject* routine (as previously) then draws the object in the new position. The original coordinates should be saved in another field because this routine changes the values in card field 1.

Figure 19.16 Scaling of an Image Stored as an Array of Coordinates

```
on mouseUp
  global xrotate,yrotate,oldpos
  ask "what angle to rotate in degrees;
      clockwise = positive numbers"
  put it into ang
  put ang*(3.1416/180) into radian
  put line 1 of card field 1 into oldpos
  put the number of lines in card field 1 into q
  repeat with n = 1 to q
    put item 1 of line n of card field 1 into oldx
    put item 2 of line n of card field 1 into oldy
    put oldx*cos(radian) + oldy sin(radian)
        into newx
    put oldy *cos(radian)- oldx*sin(radian)
        into newy
    put round(newx) into newx
    put round(newy) into newy
    put newx&","&newy into line n of card field 1
  end repeat
  bringBack (from Figure 19.16)
  drawObject (from Figure 19.14)
end mouseUp
```

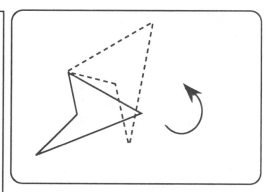

This routine assumes that an object has been drawn with a routine to store all its coordinates in an array in card field 1 (as in previous examples). It asks for a rotation factor. It then uses trigonometric functions to calculate new rotated positions for each coordinate in the array. The *bringBack* routine repositions the object to be roughly in the same place by translating it back. The *drawObject* routine then draws the object in the new position. The original coordinates should be saved in another field because this routine changes the values in card field 1.

Figure 19.17 Rotation of an Image Stored as an Array of Coordinates

The Illusion of Three Dimensions and Perspective

HyperCard provides no intrinsic three-dimensional-perspective graphics routines. Chapter 20 will describe ways of importing images from 3-D design programs that are optimized for the creation of 3-D representation on a computer screen. Here we introduce some theory about 3-D representation and some pragmatic ways to use them within HyperCard.

The computer screen is intrinsically two-dimensional. One must resort to illusions to suggest three dimensions. The search for 3-D illusion predates computers and has been a long-standing quest of both Eastern and Western art. Artists have searched for ways to suggest the three dimensions of real life within the limits of two-dimensional canvases.

Size and atmospheric effects can suggest distance. To the eye, closer objects look bigger than more distant objects. One can use this fact to create displays with both, although other cues must be offered to suggest difference in distance and not just difference in size. Atmosphere also cues distance. Eastern art built on the fact that objects in the distance often seem more indistinct, as if clouded in haze or fog. Both of these techniques can be used in computer graphics.

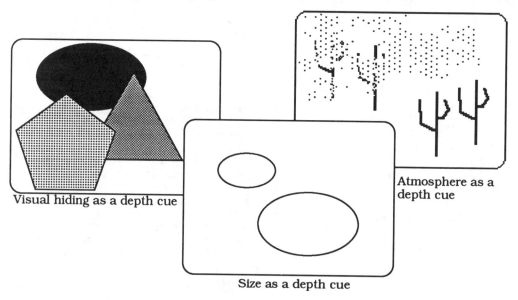

Visual hiding as a depth cue

Atmosphere as a depth cue

Size as a depth cue

Figure 19.18 Visual Conventions to Suggest Three Dimensions

Obscuring surfaces also suggests depth. Opaque closer objects hide distant objects. HyperCard provides a natural graphics model to accomplish this, since buttons and fields hover above each other in accordance with their priority. Similarly, the card picture hovers above the background. Selected objects appear to hover above the picture as they are moved. Filled objects drawn over other objects appear to be closer. All of these effects can be used to suggest three dimensions.

The main technique used in Western art, however, has been perspective. Perspective builds on the notion that more distant objects seem to get smaller and recede toward vanishing points on the horizon. One-, two-, and three-point perspective systems have been developed. The 3-D design programs described in Chapter 20 make extensive use of these conventions. Curiously, although they seem normal and believable to visually literate twentieth-century people, perspective images do not suggest three dimensions to other peoples from traditional cultures who see them for the first time.

The basic theory of one-point perspective is quite simple. All points behind the plane of the screen or canvas are moved toward the vanishing point in proportion to their distance behind the screen plane and the distance of the hypothetical viewer's eye or camera lens. Straight lines going perpendicularly into the screen appear to move diagonally toward the vanishing point.

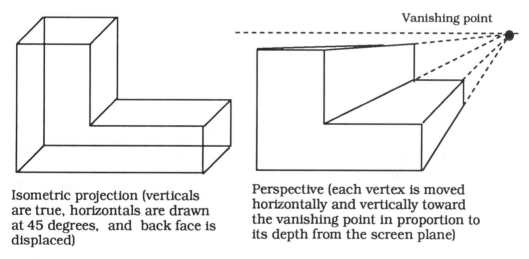

Isometric projection (verticals are true, horizontals are drawn at 45 degrees, and back face is displaced)

Perspective (each vertex is moved horizontally and vertically toward the vanishing point in proportion to its depth from the screen plane)

Figure 19.19 Isometric and One-Point Perspective

The amount each point needs to move toward the vanishing point can be expressed in precise mathematical terms. Computer algorithms can be generated to calculate the new screen coordinates of the points that are behind the plane of the screen. Again, these routines make use of the concept of adjusting the coordinates of vertices stored in an array.

For 3-D routines, one must know the real-world horizontal, vertical, and *depth* coordinate of each vertex. Thus, just as two coordinates can describe the exact position of every point in a 2-D Cartesian coordinate system, three coordinates are needed to describe the exact position of every point in a 3-D Cartesian coordinate system. The basic concept of 3-D space follows logically from the concepts of 2-D space, and the same mathematical rules apply with logical extensions. For example, translation in 3-D space is accomplished by changes in the horizontal, vertical, and depth coordinates.

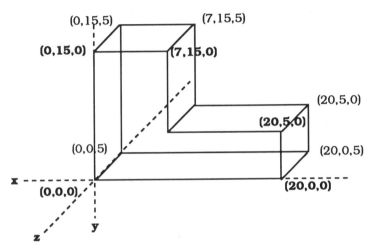

Figure 19.20 Each Vertex Can Be Described by Three Coordinates in a 3-D Cartestian Coordinate System

Interestingly, the extensions from three to four dimensions (and above) seem logically just as natural mathematically, although we lack conventions for picturing four- or *N*-dimensional space. *Flatland,* the classic book and film, investigates the difficulties of conveying information about higher dimensions. Twentieth-century artists have been much taken by these problems of representing *N* -dimensional space (for more information, see the journal *Leonardo*).

One computer algorithm to generate perspective transformations uses the depth information stored in the third coordinate to adjust the horizontal and vertical coordinates to move them toward the vanishing point. A loop is constructed to adjust each coordinate trio stored in an array. The generic draw routine then draws the new object with perspective transformations included.

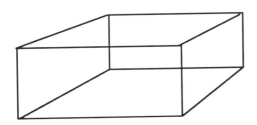

```
on mouseUp
  put -200 into d
  put 200 into xe
  put 150 into ye
  put 500 into xv
  put 10 into yv
  put the number of lines in card field 1 into q
  repeat with n = 1 to q
    put item 1 of line n of card field 1 into x
    put item 2 of line n of card field 1 into y
    put item 3 of line n of card field 1 into z
    put xv + (xv-x) * (d/(z-d)) into newx
    put yv + (yv-y) * (d/(z-d))into newy
    put round(newx) into newx
    put round(newy) into newy
    put newx&","&newy&","& z into line n of
    card field 1
  end repeat
  drawObject3d
end mouseUp
```

This routine assumes that the 3-D coordinates of an object are stored in card field 1. It then uses the indicated perspective transformation formulas to change each *x* and *y* coordinate based on its depth coordinate. More distant coordinates move closer to the vanishing point. Coordinates should also be stored in another field because the routine changes those in card field 1. The *drawObject3d* routine is a limited drawing routine to draw objects with the same number of vertices on the front and back face.

```
on drawObject3d
  global a, b
  put the number of lines in card field 1
    into q
  choose line tool
  put q/2 into q2

  -- front
  repeat with n = 1 to q2-1
    put line n of card field 1 into a
    put item 1 of a &","& item 2 of a into a
    put line n+1 of card field 1 into b
    put item 1 of b &","&item 2 of b into b
    drag from a to b
  end repeat
  put line 1 of card field 1 into a
  put item 1 of a &","& item 2 of a into a
  drag from b to a

  --back
  repeat with n = q2+1 to q-1
    put line n of card field 1 into a
    put item 1 of a &","& item 2 of a into a
    put line n+1 of card field 1 into b
    put item 1 of b &","&item 2 of b into b
    drag from a to b
  end repeat
  put line q2 + 1 of card field 1 into a
  put item 1 of a &","& item 2 of a into a
  drag from b to a

  --connectors
  repeat with n = 1 to q2
    put line n of card field 1 into a
    put item 1 of a &","& item 2 of a into a
    put line n+q2 of card field 1 into b
    put item 1 of b &","&item 2 of b into b
    drag from a to b
  end repeat
  choose browse tool
end drawObject3d
```

Figure 19.21 Drawing a Simple Object with Its Coordinates Transformed to Represent Perspective Projection

Fractals and the Mathematics of Chaos

Fractals are perhaps best known to readers as exotic computer graphics images generated on high resolution systems. These organic-looking shapes can be rendered as either abstract or representational forms. Indeed, the commercial cinema's computer graphics industry has seized on fractals as one way to algorithmically generate realistic-looking landscapes like the "Genesis" sequence in *Star Trek III*. Many artists who use computers have become enchanted, intrigued, and confused by fractals.

Actually, fractal images are just the tip of a theoretical iceberg. They are representations of structures generated by equations used to study the behavior of dynamic chaotic systems. Many aspects of nature appear not to subscribe to the simplified models created by scientists to illustrate basic principles. Many phenomena in nature result from the interlinked workings of predictable principles and feedback from slight imperfections — for example, weather patterns, air turbulence, flows around obstructions, and the growth of biological organisms and populations. One cannot predict their ultimate states because of feedback that amplifies slight differences at every stage. A branch of mathematics called the study of chaotic systems attempts to understand and formalize the systemic regularities of such behavior. For more information, see *The Beauty of Fractals* by H. Peitgent and P. Richter (Springer-Verlag, 1986).

One fascinating property of these systems is self-same cyclicity. As one looks at structures at all levels, one finds repeating patterns. The example of the seashore is offered — the view from an airplane and from eye level are similar. The study of these systems would be almost impossible without the computer, which allows simulation of the outcomes resulting from iterations with feedback.

The computer graphics images called fractals do not magically appear from the behavior of these equations. The renderer must make decisions about the parameters introduced into the equations and the method for assigning computer graphics colors or tones to the values that result. Changes in either result in radically different images.

A fractal is a graph of the values that result in a plane in which the values for each position are determined by the combination of randomness and order. Thus, as one moves through the plane, the results of past

This fractal is created by mapping each pixel of the screen to the dwell of repeated squaring of complex numbers (see below for a description of dwell). In this example, an arbitrary 100-by-100 pixel area of the screen is mapped to a complex number plane stretching from -2 to +2 in the x and y directions. Thus, the range of complex numbers (4) is mapped onto the pixels in the x and y dimensions. Each pixel represents a move of .04 in the complex number plane. The nested loops do 100 columns of 100 rows, each time incrementing the complex number by .04 (cx and cy). Each time, the *getDwell* routine is called to discover the behavior of that particular place in the complex number plane. The *getDwell* routine comes back with the dwell represented by the *numtimes* variable. This dwell is arbitrarily assigned to a color. The phrase *numtimes mod 2* returns 0 if the dwell is divisible by 2 and 1 if it is not. If it is not divisible by 2, a black pixel is plotted. In a color system, even division by other numbers would each be assigned a different color.

These formulas continually calculate the squares of complex numbers to determine if they move toward some limit or run off toward infinity. The number of times they can be squared before escaping to infinity is called the dwell. In this plane, defined to be 4by4, moving beyond the value of 4 is a good estimation of moving toward infinity. In this computer algorithm, the number of times the loop runs (*numtimes*) equals the dwell. The variable *numtimes* is incremented by 1 each time through the loop. *Maxtimes* is an arbitrary number set to limit the number of times the loop will run before assuming that the calculation will not go to infinity. The exit repeat occurs if the value of zx^2+zy^2 exceeds 4 or when the loop has run the *maxtimes*. *Numtimes* is a global variable containing the number of times the loop ran (called the dwell). In this example, it will have a value between 0 and 51 (because of the *maxiter* of 50, which stops the loop after 50 times).

```
on mouseUp
  choose line tool
  global x,y,cx,cy,numtimes
  put -2 into cx
  put -2 into cy
  repeat with x = 1 to 100
    repeat with y = 1 to 100
      getDwell
      if numtimes mod 2 = 1 then
        drag from x,y to x,y
      end if
      put cy +.04 into cy
    end repeat
    put -2 into cy
    put cx + .04 into cx
  end repeat
end mouseUp


on getDwell
  global maxtimes, result, temp,
    cx, cy, zx, zy, numtimes
  put 0 into numtimes
  put 50 into maxtimes
  put cx into zx
  put cy into zy
  repeat forever
    put zx*zx - zy*zy + cx into temp
    put 2*zx*zy + cy into zy
    if zx*zx + zy*zy > 4 then exit
      repeat
    if numtimes> maxtimes then exit
      repeat
    put numtimes+1 into numtimes
    put temp into zx
  end repeat
end getDwell
```

Figure 19.22 Generation of a Mandelbrot Set Fractal

computations (feedback) help to determine the next outcomes. The shapes suggest biological and natural forms. The best-known fractals rely heavily on color to highlight the different areas of common values and the borders between them. The Mandelbrot set of fractals is one of the most explored.

HyperCard is not an ideal environment for explorations of fractals. It offers no color, and it is slow at the time-consuming calculations necessary when each pixel must be based on the value of previous pixels. For example, Figure 19.22 took one hour to calculate. Nonetheless, HyperCard does offer some possibilities for experimentation.

The Relinking of Mathematics and Art

Mathematics is an area of study often neglected by artists. This chapter has illustrated some of the concrete usefulness of analytic routines in the generation of computer graphics. Mathematics' greatest potential asset for artists, however, is its approach to using imagination for creating internally consistent artificial worlds and symbol systems for representation of real and imaginary worlds. Increasing computer literacy may well reconnect artists with mathematical inquiry.

Chapter 20
External Resources, User Groups, and Telecommunications

Modular Programming Environments and Openness to the Future

Human nature often leads to vanity about present accomplishments. Each era often believes that it is approaching the boundaries of knowledge. For example, scientists in the nineteenth century marveled at the accomplishments of science and believed that new scientific work would be needed only to polish up some of the rough edges of missing knowledge. This danger of vanity can sometimes blind users of the sophisticated machines and programming environments that are available in any era. Users believe that the computing environment is sufficiently comprehensive to support just about anything anyone will ever want to do. History usually shows these vanities to be wrong.

The tremendous versatility and richness of HyperCard might tempt one to think that it is almost sufficient as a programming environment. It provides a treasure house of visual, sound, and interactive capabilities for artistic exploration. Nonetheless, readers who engage HyperCard's possibilities will quickly imagine enhancements and new capabilities that they wish were included. Such pushing against boundaries is a venerable feature of artistic experimentation.

Fortunately, HyperCard's designers tried to anticipate an unpredictable future and the exploratory aspects of human nature. They built an environment that was easily extensible so that new capabilities could be added as desired. In doing this, they made HyperCard uniquely responsive to artistic tendencies toward experimentation by imbuing it with an object-oriented philosophy. HyperCard objects can be designed to stand on their own in any HyperCard environment. Thus, one can transfer appropriately conceived buttons, fields, and cards from stack to stack. Images created in external specialized graphics programs can be easily imported and will function just like graphics created with HyperCard's own tools.   As explained earlier, sounds can be imported and played with the standard HyperCard *play* command.   User groups and commercial suppliers offer disks full of HyperCard objects already programmed to operate in interesting ways.   Similarly specialized disks of images (often called clip art) and sounds can be obtained.

The designers also included the capabilities to easily add new commands and functions that allow HyperCard to act in new ways The commands are called external commands (XCMDs) and external functions (XFCNs).   Once added as a resource to HyperCard or one of its stacks via a special resource-moving program, these features function just like intrinsic commands.   Some allow control of specialized devices, such as digitizers or videodiscs.   Some allow easy links with other programs, such as the VideoworksII or Studio 1 animation program.   HyperCard can grow as needed.   This chapter and the next offer more details on sources, methods of adding external resources to stacks, and samples of what is available.

There are some questions about how far an extensible environment can stretch.   When is HyperCard with special additions no longer Hyper-Card?   I once owned a sports car that went through many changes over its 12-year life.   At various times its motor, transmission, electrical system, brakes, tires, and parts of its body were replaced.   At the end, was it still the same car?

Other questions concern efficiency and standardization.   Will a heavily supplemented HyperCard run as efficiently as an environment built from the ground up to contain the new capabilities?   The standardized nature of HyperCard is one of its greatest appeals.   With heavy reliance on specialized XCMD, however, it becomes probable that people will not be able to use other people's HyperCard-created objects unless they happen to have the required external commands installed in their stacks.

Programs such as Plus and Supercard created by other companies work much like HyperCard and add capabilities such as color, object-oriented graphics, and the ability to resize, move, and use multiple windows. New updates of HyperCard also include new capabilities.   Indeed, some analysts are speculating that computer manufacturers may one day include HyperCard-like environments as their basic operating system so that nonspecialists will be able to use it as the functional control center for everything else that uses the computer.

Resource-moving Programs: Font/DA Mover®

The Macintosh desktop metaphor is famous for offering an intuitively clear presentation of available applications and documents. Icons each usually represent something that can be used. The visual array on the screen reveals what is present.

This metaphor is not complete, however: Many resources used by programs do not show up on the desktop in most early versions of the Macintosh operating system. These hidden resources include fonts, desk accessories (DAs), sounds, icons, and, for HyperCard, external commands and functions.   One must use specialized utility programs to see and manipulate these resources.

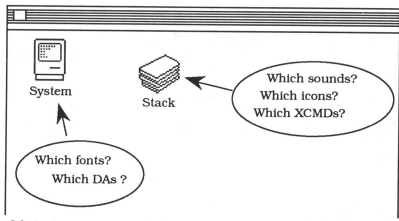

Figure 20.1   Resources Inside System Programs and Stacks Are Not Clear from Desktop Icons

Desk Accessories (DAs). Desk accessories are mini-programs that can be accessed under the apple symbol on the Menu Bar. These programs are usually available no matter what other applications are running. Thus, one can temporarily run them without quitting the currently active application, such as HyperCard. They allow necessary kinds of activity to be completed, which can then be copied and pasted into the main application.

The Macintosh operating system provided by Apple usually includes many DAs already installed. The following are some examples: the alarm clock (which allows setting of the calendar, clock, and alarm), the calculator (which simulates a simple hand calculator), the chooser (which allows the selection of an output device), the control panel (which allows the setting of features such as speaker volume, number of colors displayed, and key repeat rate), the scrapbook (which allows convenient storage and retrieval of text, sound, and images), and the key caps (which shows symbols to be displayed when various keys are pressed). Commercial and shareware developers have created a host of other DAs that provide useful functions.

The system program icon in the System Folder provides no clue to what DAs are installed. One cannot click on the icon to see what is inside, nor can one easily remove or add other DAs.

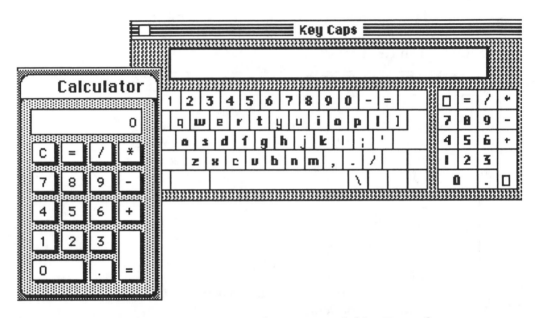

Figure 20.2   Desk Accessories Are Always Available, Even from within HyperCard

Fonts. As described in an earlier chapter, one of the Macintosh's claims to fame has been its capability to display text in a wide range of fonts, sizes, and styles. In fact, many other computer manufacturers have now introduced that capability. The range of options available is determined by which fonts and font sizes have been "installed" in the system program. At any given time, one's font choices are determined by the system that was used when the Macintosh was started up. It is thus possible to find that font choices that were available at one time while using HyperCard (because a certain system disk was used to boot up) will not be available at another time (if a different system disk was used to start up).

This variability will be no problem if one always uses the same system disk to start up, because the same system program will be used with its same set of hidden font resources. It becomes a problem if someone attempts to run the stack in another environment, in which a system disk with different fonts has been used to start up the computer.

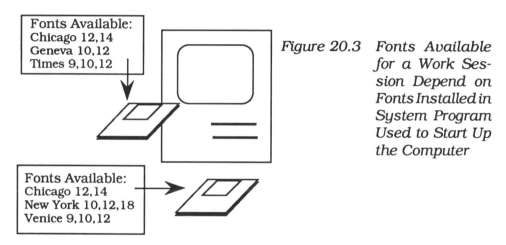

Fonts Available:
Chicago 12,14
Geneva 10,12
Times 9,10,12

Fonts Available:
Chicago 12,14
New York 10,12,18
Venice 9,10,12

Figure 20.3   Fonts Available for a Work Session Depend on Fonts Installed in System Program Used to Start Up the Computer

The potential problem is somewhat alleviated by the standardization of system disks that come with HyperCard when obtained from a dealer before any modifications. The standard system has installed the following fonts and font sizes:

Font Name		Font Size			
Chicago			12		
Courier		10	12		
Geneva	9	10	12	14	18
Helvetica		10	12		
Monaco	9				
New York	9	10	12	14	18
Times		10	12		18

HyperCard also alleviates the problem in its flexible approach to fonts. If it cannot find the specific font used in the creation of a stack, it will substitute the best fit it can achieve. If it cannot find the size indicated, it will use a mathematical algorithm to create a resized version of the font in the specified size. If a text using a certain font is created using the text painting tool, the font image will become a fixed pattern of bits just as though it had been drawn with a paintbrush. Thus, it will keep that shape no matter what fonts are installed in the system disk. (This solution of treating text as painted graphics will not solve the problem of needing a particular font to appear as users interactively type fresh text.)

Unfortunately, the approximations may not be aesthetically satisfactory. The font substitutions can play havoc with careful designs and placements. The size approximations can create raggedy stairstep images. Finally, text that is created with a font installed in the system tends to print out on a printer much more cleanly than the approximations.

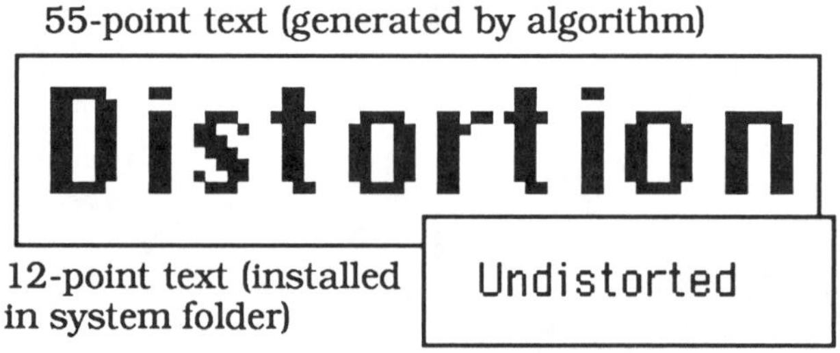

55-point text (generated by algorithm)

Distortion

12-point text (installed   Undistorted
in system folder)

*Figure 20.4   HyperCard's Attempt to Generate Text in a Size Not Installed in
the System Folder Results in Distortions*

For users who are interested, there are thousands of fonts that can be obtained from commercial and shareware developers. These custom fonts greatly expand the visual options available to stack designers. Fonts can convey subtle conceptual and emotional meanings that enhance the manifest message of the text. Readers wanting more details are urged to consult any of the excellent texts available on typography and design with typography. The examples show just a few of the alternative fonts available.

Font/DA Mover. Fonts, like DAs, do not show up as icons in the desktop display and cannot be manipulated by the usual clicking and dragging conventions. One must use a special utility program such as Font/DA mover, which Apple provides on the system utility disk provided when one buys a Macintosh. This easy-to-use program makes visible the fonts and DAs installed in particular applications and makes it possible to add, copy, and remove these resources.

Running the Font/DA Mover program brings up the dialog box illustrated in Figure 20.6. At the top are two radio buttons for determining whether one wants to work with fonts or with desk accessories. Once the type of resource is selected, a list of currently installed resources of that type

Figure 20.5 A Small Sample of the Variety of Fonts Available

appears in the left of two scrollable boxes. The name of the application along with the name of the volume on which it is located appears below the box. Usually the name listed will be the system program of the disk that was used to boot the disk. Another line of text lists the amount of space remaining on that volume.

Font/DA Mover essentially offers two choices. One can either remove a resource or copy a resource from one place to another. Font/DA Mover dims the Remove and Copy choices until the user has selected one of the resources to act on. Selection involves clicking on one of the names listed. The box will invert the selection and indicate the size of the selected resource in bytes. Dragging the mouse with the shift key depressed allows selection of more than one resource at a time and makes the Remove option accessible. To remove a resource, one needs only click on the Remove button.

To copy a resource, one must have two files open. The Open and Close buttons below the resource-listing boxes allow one to pick any file to

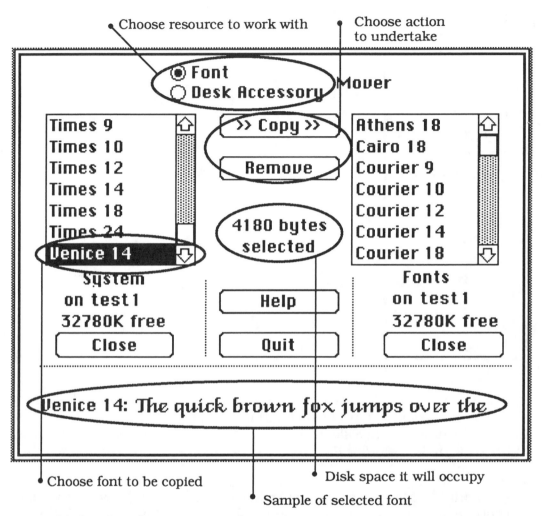

Choose resource to work with • Choose action to undertake

Choose font to be copied • Disk space it will occupy

Sample of selected font

Figure20.6   Font/DA Mover Dialog Box

act on via the standard Macintosh Open File Dialog Box. With two files open, the Copy and Remove option buttons both become available. At the bottom of the display, Font/DA Mover shows a sample line of text in the font chosen. To copy a font or a DA, click on a resource and then click on the Copy button. Font/DA Mover then installs the specified resource in the other file.

   The reader may wonder what is wrong with installing every possible font and DA that one might want in the system program. One major problem is that each resource takes up disk space. Multiple fonts in multiple sizes can eat space quickly. People not working with an extensive hard disk storage will need to make compromises between space and resources installed. Also, multiple disk accessories can sometimes interfere with one another. Developers have created alternative utility programs for managing fonts and DAs. For example, the Suitcase and Juggler programs allow access to multiple sets of DAs and fonts without actually installing them in the system program. These utilities can access resources stored in other locations and make them available as if they were installed.

Versions of the Macintosh operating system beyond version 6 make the management of fonts and DAs much easier. These resources have visible representations and are easier to manipulate. Also, a new font technology called outline fonts does away with the need to install each size font to be used. Outline fonts are improved graphic algorithms that tell the computer how to create good-looking fonts at any size. Thus, only one resource needs to be installed for each font.

Finally, there are font design programs — such as Fontagrapher — for artists who are not happy with any available font. These allow users to custom-design their own fonts (Figure 20.7). For each letter, the user is offered a blown-up grid in which the details of each letter can be drawn. When done, the font is stored just like professional fonts and can be installed via the Font/DA or other font utilities. Typing the *a* key, for example, will produce the *a* that the designer created when using the custom-created font.

Resource-moving Programs: ResCopy®

Every Macintosh application makes heavy use of what are called resources. These resources include sounds, icon and cursor designs, external commands and functions (for HyperCard), and several other kinds of program elements. Professional programmers use a utility program called ResEdit, which gives them control over editing and manipulating these resources. ResEdit is somewhat complicated to use and allows users to seriously mess up essential system resources, so it is not often used by novices.

Steve Maller of Apple Computer wrote a utility program that allows manipulation of HyperCard resources through an easily understandable

Figure 20.7   Font Design Software Allows Users to Create Custom Fonts

dialog box that looks much like Font/DA Mover. With this utility, one can view, hear, copy, and remove resources. The ResCopy® program is obtainable from the sources listed at the end of this chapter.

Running ResCopy brings up the dialog box shown in Figure 20.8. Like the Font/DA Mover, this box consists of two scrollable boxes that can list resources in stacks and an Open/Close button beneath each that allows selection of stacks and files to work on and Copy and Remove buttons that allow one to manipulate resources. The text below each box shows the file and volume being worked with. Selection of a resource brings forth a line of text that indicates the size (in bytes) of the resource selected and undims the appropriate Copy and Remove buttons.

The list that appears in each box shows the resource type, the arbitrary ID number that was assigned when it was created, and the name of the resource. ResCopy offers some additional features. If the selected resource is a sound, the *play* button undims; clicking the button plays the sound (provided that it was recorded in a standard Macintosh type 2 sound format) through the Macintosh speaker. If the selected resource is an icon, ResCopy shows a visual image of the icon in the box below the Edit button. If the selected resource is a mouse cursor, the currently active cursor that follows mouse movement changes to the selected cursor resource. XCMDs

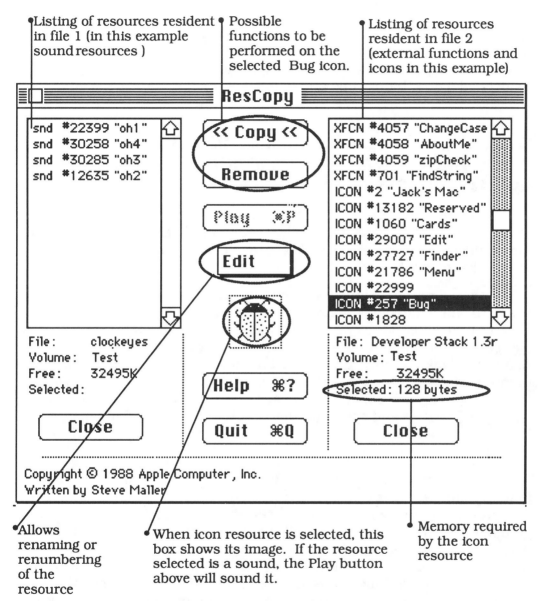

Listing of resources resident in file 1 (in this example sound resources)

Possible functions to be performed on the selected Bug icon.

Listing of resources resident in file 2 (external functions and icons in this example)

Allows renaming or renumbering of the resource

When icon resource is selected, this box shows its image. If the resource selected is a sound, the Play button above will sound it.

Memory required by the icon resource

Figure 20.8   ResCopy Dialog Box Allowing Removal and Copying of Stack Resources

and XFCNs are also listed but cannot be tried out from ResCopy. The Edit box allows one to rename or renumber a selected resource.

As mentioned earlier, specialized programs also allow creation and manipulation of these resources. For example, the SoundEdit program described in Chapter 17 allows one to copy and remove sound resources in stacks. A program called Icon Manager allows easy creation of button-associated icons that can be added to HyperCard's standard icons.

Sources: Commercial Companies, User Groups, Shareware, Public Domain, Electronic Bulletin Boards, Information Utilities, and Telephone Modems

Where does one find programs like ResCopy and the external resources described here and in other chapters? There are several sources including regular computer software dealers and many other kinds of alternative networks.

User Groups. Since its inception, the microcomputer community has been characterized by grass-roots organizations called user groups that offer mutual support to people working with microcomputers. In fact, pioneers such as Steve Jobs and Steve Wozniak, who founded Apple Computer, acknowledge the nurturing role of the legendary Homebrew Computer Club in stimulating them and many of the others who gave birth to this technology. Ideologically, these clubs were based on the fundamental principle of free and open information exchange. New developers would bring their ideas to these forums for supportive critique. New software was freely shared.

The spirit of user groups continues; although the folk culture of the industry has been weakened by the new emphasis on commercial success and proprietary information, the spirit of user groups continues on. User groups have come into existence all over the world. They have matured to offer diverse services for very reasonable prices. Because of HyperCard's orientation to empowering the average user and support for multimedia work, many groups have focused special attention on HyperCard-related topics. Also, many of the groups have a special fondness for graphics and sound work, topics of interest to artists, designers, and musicians. The addresses of several user groups are listed at the end of this chapter. Much of the noncommercial HyperCard-enhancing software described in this book is available from user groups.

To illustrate the typical activities of user groups, this section will describe some of the resources available through one club called BMUG (the Berkeley Macintosh Users Group) in Berkeley, California. BMUG was one of the first user groups to focus explicitly on the Macintosh. Since then it has achieved a reputation as one of the best-organized Macintosh user groups. It offers the following resources:

- Weekly meetings focusing on issues and new products.
- A telephone help line that will try to answer any Macintosh-related questions.
- Special-interest groups (SIGs) such as Beginners, Music, Design/ Graphics, HyperCard Scripting, and HyperCard Browsing.
- A massive semiannual newsletter with articles on a wide range of topics. For example, one recent newsletter included these articles: "Beginners Guide," "Fax on the Mac," "Computer-aided Design," and a section on HyperCard including "Animation in HyperCard," "Three Medium-sized Hypertexts on CD–ROM," and "Making Special Cursors in HyperCard."
- An electronic bulletin board that one can access by a telephone modem attached to a computer. The bulletin board presents ongoing electronic conferences in which a person can electronically converse with others interested in the same topics. There are conferences on a variety of topics including several related to graphics, sound, and HyperCard. The bulletin board also allows one to download and upload programs and stacks. (See following section on modems and electronic bulletin boards for more on these ways of obtaining software.)
- A software library consisting of public-domain programs, shareware, and demoware available very inexpensively on a wide range of topics. BMUG publishes a catalog of the software available from the group. Each disk can be bought for a few dollars.

Shareware, Demoware, and Public-Domain Software. Continuing the spirit of the early days of the microcomputer era, many developers have sought ways to share the fruits of their labor. Public domain software is offered to the community for free. Sometimes there are requirements that a user include an acknowledgment of the author if the material is used. Shareware is offered with the requirement that a user pay a shareware fee to the author if the material is found useful. Users are invited to try out the software and pay a (usually small) fee directly to the author if the user decides to use the material regularly. Middleman expenses of distribution and advertising are thus eliminated. Demoware is any special version of commercial software offered on the networks that has been crippled in some crucial way — for example, by not allowing saving of work to disk or printing. Again, users are invited to test the software and to buy full versions if they like what they see.

Shareware and public-domain software are a unique resource. Much in the way of computer-related graphics, sound, and interactive events that would otherwise not be available is shared in this way. Often the authors work like artists. They have a passion to create something that they personally find interesting or challenging. They then generously offer it to the community. HyperCard authors especially have worked in this way. Readers are encouraged to become part of this shareware network both as users and creators.

Unfortunately, there has been some problem of users not sending in their shareware fees. Authors report that they get fees from only a small proportion of those who are using their programs. Readers who become active as shareware users are urged to promptly send their fees to the authors or this alternative system of sharing work may fail.

Electronic Bulletin Board Systems (BBSs) and Information Utilities. In addition to user groups, electronic bulletin boards and commercial information utility companies can serve as sources. A device called a modem (to be described more fully) allows computers to communicate with each other via telephone lines. Special communications software makes it easy for computers to talk to each other, using this device. Bulletin board software allows a single computer to become a completely automated operation that can answer the phone, connect several callers simultaneously, and respond with a variety of services.

Many noncommercial bulletin boards have been established that take advantage of this technology. A single individual or a small group can inexpensively set up one of these systems that offer electronic mail between people who become members, conferences in which people can have ongoing multiperson electronic conversations about topics of interest, and file libraries. Many user groups have established electronic bulletin boards as part of their services.

Bulletin boards have been developed for all kinds of special interests. Some focus on services for people who use a particular computer or kind of software. Others offer more topical focuses. Here is a sample of some of the systems available nationally and in the Northern California area (For addresses of some of the art-oriented ones, see the end of the chapter):

- FAST/Electronic Bulletin Board and Fine Arts Forum (these are sponsored by the journal *Leonardo*; they cover topics such as art and computers, artificial intelligence, vision research, holography, new music technology, video, telecommunications, new materials, and space art)
- The Well (This electronic conference space was created by the group that was responsible for the *Whole Earth Catalog*)
- ART COM (A service trying to explore new electronic ways for artists to share their work. It bills itself as the electronic magazine of the future)
- AIDS BBS (AIDS epidemic information)
- Asian Exclusive Act (Asian-American community information)
- Back Door (Alternative lifestyles)
- Blind Users Group (Blind computer users)
- Buccaneer Bay Man O' War (Computer gaming)
- Public Utilities Commission BBS (Citizen input to state commission)
- Catholic Information (Issues relevant to the Catholic religion)
- Dating Tree (Matchmaking for singles)
- Earth Rite (New age and pagan philosophy)
- EconNet (Focus on ecology issues)
- Flea Market (Classified ads)
- Freedom BBS (Political debate for thinking liberals and conservatives)
- Guideboard (Cabbies' guide to city — restaurants, etc.)
- Lunatik Laboratories (Cyberpunk, occult, suppressed technologies)
- Nightingale (Nursing issues)
- OASIS (Focused on recovery from obesity and other eating disorders)
- Opportunity Network (Job hunters' and recruiters' bulletin board)
- PeaceNet (International network of peaceful coexistence)
- Railbird's Racing (Racing and other sporting news)
- SF Robotics Society (Robotics issues)

Software libraries are especially important because they are a major distribution channel for shareware and public-domain materials. These libraries allow telephone callers to upload or download programs and stacks. In downloading, the communications software on an individual's home computer can systematically copy a program from the library. Once copied, that program becomes useful just as though someone had physically given the caller a disk.   Some visionaries believe that almost all distribution of computer-based materials (which will one day ultimately include even mainstream movies and music) will come via telecommunications channels.   Currently, one must purchase communication software such as Red Ryder to use bulletin boards and file libraries, although new developments in HyperCard may make telecommunications possible with the simplicity of HyperCard commands.

Information Utilities. Several commercial operations offer similar electronic communications for a fee. This fee usually consists of a monthly charge and/or a per-hour connect fee. Some of the best known services are Applelink, CompuServe, GENIE, Prodigy, and America OnLine. Like the non commercial bulletin boards, they offer electronic mail, topic forums, and file libraries for downloading and uploading. They usually have a wide variety of HyperCard-relevant discussions and files among their offerings.

In addition, they offer a wide variety of other services. Here is a sample of services available on America Online, which are similar to those available on other systems:

- People Connection (ability to chat in real time with strangers who happen to be signed on)
- Entertainment (news and gossip from Hollywood, comedy and trivia club, sports, games)
- News & Finance (business news and stock quotes)
- Lifestyle & Interests (cooking, genealogy, science fiction, other topic groups)
- Learning & Reference (classes, tutors, college database)
- Travel & Shopping (airline schedules and reservations, travel destinations, on-line shopping)
- Computing &Software (computer news and troubleshooting, software libraries)

*Figure 20.9   Basic Navigation Screen from America Online
Information Utility*

Modems and Electronic Communication.   A modem and communications software are necessary for using a computer to communicate via
telecommunications networks. A modem is a special electronic device that
converts the signals inside a computer into a form that can be sent over the
telephone system. Similarly, it can convert the sound signals from the
telephone system into a form that can be used by a computer.

The word *modem* comes from the first two letters of terms **MO**dulator
and the first three letters of **DEM**odulator. Computers use groupings of bits
as the main form of internal communication. Bits are voltage pulses either
at 5 volt or 0 volt levels. Usually they are grouped into units of eight called
bytes. A modem converts these groups of 8 bits into serial sequences of

sound frequencies that can be sent over the phone lines. This process of creating sound frequencies is called modulation. At the other end, the modem receives the frequencies, reconverts them back to voltage pulses, and reassembles them back into 8-bit bytes.

With the Macintosh, modern modems, and communications software, this process is fairly transparent to the user. One needs only to plug the modem into one of the serial ports on the back of the computer. The software presents a Macintosh graphics interface that allows choices through the menu and mouse movement conventions. Usually there is a Dial option in the software that allows the user to specify a telephone number to dial. The computer then dials the number and establishes contact with the modem on the computer at the other end. The communications software on the host computer sends text via the telephone line to the user's screen. This text asks questions that users can answer by typing on their keyboard.

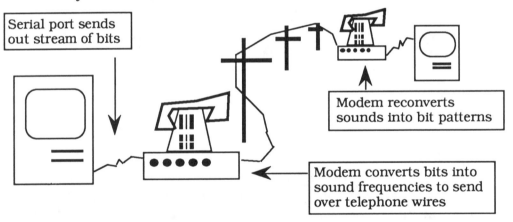

Serial port sends out stream of bits

Modem reconverts sounds into bit patterns

Modem converts bits into sound frequencies to send over telephone wires

Figure 20.10 Modems Allow Computer to Communicate over the Telephone System

Some communications software may require the user to set the baud rate. Baud rate is the speed at which modems send information — usually measured in bits per second. This speed is important because clean communication requires synchronization between receivers and senders or information can get lost. Current technology offers typical settings of 1200 and 2400 baud. Future systems anticipate speeds of 9600 or more. The top speed of a modem is determined by its electronic design. Faster speeds require more sophisticated electronics to filter out the inevitable noise that accompanies telephone communication, and hence faster modems are more expensive. Some communications software will automatically determine the speed capabilities of the data being sent and set the user's modem automatically.

Each bulletin board or information utility has its own structure for navigation. Usually there are help screens that explain the possibilities and the conventions for using the system. Eventually there will be communications software specifically designed to work in the HyperCard environment. The host system will look just like a card with buttons and fields within the sender's stack. Pointing toward this future, HyperCard includes a command called *dial,* which will dial a specified telephone number.

HyperCard Resources Available from Commercial Software Developers, User Groups, and Telecommunications Sources

A cornucopia of resources from commercial and noncommercial sources await anyone who wants to work with graphics, sound, and multimedia. To illustrate, this section will briefly describe a very small sample of HyperCard-relevant resources available, with a focus on noncommercial sources. The resources include complete stacks, HyperCard objects such as buttons, cursors, useful scripts, external commands and functions (XCMDs and XFCNs), clip art, fonts, and sounds.

Apple stimulated the development of resources by offering the stacks called Stack Ideas, Button Ideas, and Art Ideas with the standard HyperCard set of disks. Several independents have worked to provide clearinghouses for these resources. Examples include DeveloperStack, StackBuilder, Acme Button Factory, and Heizer Software.

Stacks. Users can obtain finished stacks that integrate sound and graphics and illustrate interesting HyperCard potentials. The following are examples.

- HyperComposer presents a graphic piano keyboard that allows intuitive entry of musical information, which is then automatically converted to the HyperTalk commands to play the sounds.
- MIDI Recorder is a stack that allows control of MIDI instruments.
- Manhole is an artist's artificial world of sound and animated graphics in which one can wander.

- Inigo Adventures is another set of interactive sound and graphic free exploration fantasies.
- Macsody in Blue offers an integrated visual/sound poem based on the "Rhapsody in Blue."
- Animation Help demonstrates a variety of HyperCard animation techniques.
- Hyperalarms is a stack that will automatically alert the reader to deadlines and appointments that have been previously entered.
- Russian 1–5 teaches the Russian language with images and digitized speech to pronounce the words.
- Mr. Potato Head simulates the children's game of the same name.
- ResMover allows the copying and removing of resources.

Scripts. Developers have written scripts that users can insert into their stacks wherever they need them.

- Cardmover will automatically move multiple cards from one stack to another.
- Stacksplitter and Stackmerge will either divide a stack into several stacks or merge several stacks into one.
- Compactor will automatically compact a stack when it is needed.
- Scrolling Fields will cause several fields to scroll in unison.
- Show Script allows quick access to script editing.

Buttons and Cursors. Disks are available offering a great variety of buttons and cursors that differ in appearance and behavior. Some are animated. These resources are thus combinations of scripts to control the behavior and actual icons to control the appearance. The animated buttons require a set of icons that are looped through to give the appearance of motion. Possible button styles offered include on-off light switches, push buttons, sliders, dogears, dials, and self-naming buttons. The cursors replace the standard HyperCard cursors such as the arrow and the crossbeam and follow the mouse around as it is moved. The careful design of these buttons and cursors often shows elegance and humor. Figure 20.11 shows simple illustrations of an on-off button and a slider button.

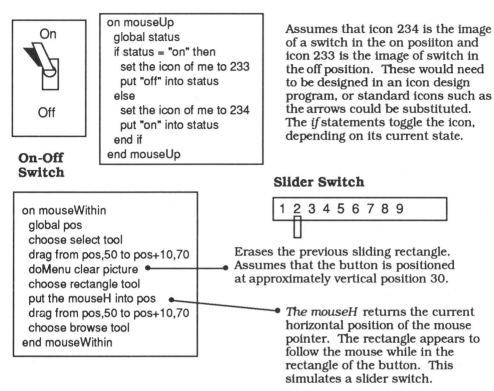

Figure 21.11 Samples of Special Kinds of Buttons

External Commands(XCMDs) and Functions(XFCNs). External commands and functions are routines written in computer languages such as Assembler, Pascal, and C that can more quickly and directly make use of the Macintosh's hardware capabilities. HyperCard itself was written in these kinds of languages. Most of the stacks, scripts, buttons described in this chapter can be written strictly within a HyperCard context. XCMDs and XFCNs, however, require access to and knowledge of one of these outside languages.

HyperCard's designers made it easy to write external routines in one of these external languages that can be integrated into HyperCard in a way that is invisible to the casual user. HyperCard's guidelines allow a creator of an external command or function to pick the name for the command and a specification of parameter values to be sent in and out of HyperCard. For this to work, the creator of the command must follow the guidelines that tell how to have one of these other languages communicate with HyperCard.

XCMDs and XFCNs must be installed in a stack by using a utility program such as ResCopy. If someone tries to run a stack with scripts that use the new commands without first having installed them as resources, HyperCard will come back with a dialog box saying it doesn't understand the command.

The *speak* command discussed in Chapter 17 illustrates the use of an external command. The developer of that command picked the name *speak* for the command and the order of values to be sent to the command — the words to be spoken, the rate of speech, and the pitch of speech. When HyperCard sees the command *speak*, it searches its resources to see if it has been installed. If it has, it sends the values to the routine, which then takes over — in this situation, causing the speaker to sound the words. It then returns control to HyperCard. An external function performs an action and then returns a value that HyperCard's script can use. It returns the value in the special variable called *it*.

Developers usually invent external commands and functions to do things that HyperCard doesn't do or to do them in some improved fashion. Here is a sample of some of the external commands and functions available via the noncommercial networks.

- *changeCase* quickly exchanges upper- and lowercase letters in text
- *fontSize* returns the size of fonts installed in the system
- *popUpMenu* allows one to use Macintosh pop-up menus that are not usually available in HyperCard
- *sort* does a very quick sort of values stored in a field
- *thePixel* returns information on whether the pixel at a particular location is black or white
- *color* allows limited use of single colors in HyperCard run on a color-capable Macintosh model
- *clipToPict* allows HyperCard to make limited use of graphics stored in the PICT rather than paint format
- *shutDown* allows HyperCard scripts to turn off the Mac just as though a user had selected Shut Down from the System Menu

Sounds. Macintosh sound resources can be used in all kinds of programming environments and are thus not restricted to HyperCard. There are two major sound formats for the Macintosh, however, so one needs to be sure that the sounds are in the resource format that HyperCard can use. An individual can create sounds using a sound digitizer such as MacRecorder. Prerecorded sounds are available, however, for those who lack this equipment and for sounds that would be difficult to generate for the digitizer. The following list illustrates the kinds of sounds available.

- Animals   • Instruments
- Movie and TV sounds   • Music
- Household objects
- Sound effects such as floors squeaking and waterfalls

Clip Art and Fonts. As with sounds, graphics resources and fonts are not restricted in application to HyperCard. These resources can be used in a wide variety of Macintosh environments. In fact, the richest graphics and font resources have been developed for professional graphic artists working with professional illustration applications such as Illustrator or Freehand. Extensive commercial and noncommercial clip art disks are available with a great variety of images.

To use clip art with HyperCard, one needs only activate the Import Graphics command in the File Menu that becomes available when one is in the paint tool mode. This command will bring in any image that was saved in the MacPaint bit-mapped format. Images from other paint or draw programs can also be brought into HyperCard via the clipboard. For more details, see Chapter 21

Apple's Art Ideas stack, which comes with HyperCard illustrates well the range of images available. These are the categories used in that stack:

- Address cards   • Geography   • People
- Animals   • Holidays   • Restaurants
- Books   • Home   • Science
- Business   • Letters   • Symbols
- Calendars   • Macintosh   • Telephone
- Filing cards   • Money   • Tools
- Fonts   • Music   • Transportation

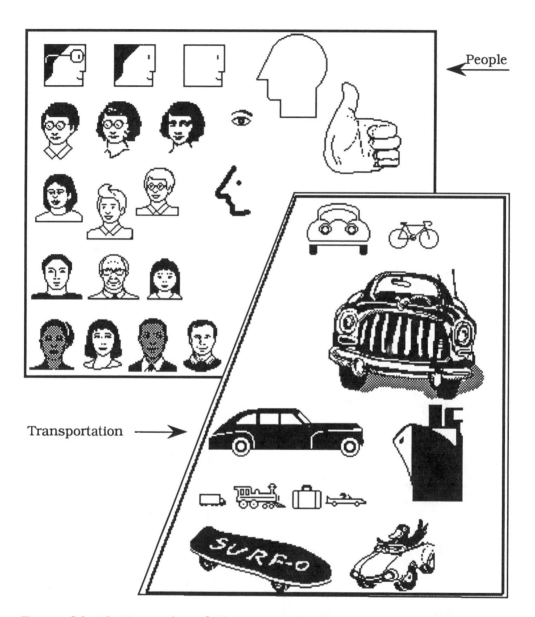

Figure 20..12   Examples of Clip Art Available on Apple's Art Ideas Stack

Copyright Issues

Use of resources raises important unresolved copyright issues. Copyrights are legal structures designed to protect the creative work of writers, artists, programmers, and others who produce intellectual work. In the United States, copyrights can be easily and inexpensively obtained on creative work. No one has the right to use someone else's copyrighted work without permission.

HyperCard and digital materials in general complicate copyrights. Unlike traditional methods of copying, digital methods can produce *exact* duplicates of original work. For example, a digital copy of a computer graphic can be pixel for pixel the same as the original. In traditional copying methods such as photographic reproduction or audio tape recording, each generation loses some information. Continued copying of copies can lead to total degeneration into noise. This degeneration served as a natural protector of original creative work by putting a premium on obtaining access to a version least removed from the original.

HyperCard's object-oriented structure also makes copying easy and effective. HyperCard is designed for the almost effortless incorporation of graphics, sounds, scripts, and functional objects (such as buttons) obtained from external sources. No attached information about the creator is intrinsically transmitted in the copying process. For example, a sound resource provides nowhere for the original creator to attach his or her name. Even where there is — for example, an author's name placed in a comment line in a script — the information can get omitted as stacks go through the process of copying and development.

Ownership can get confused in the modification process. HyperCard invites users to extrapolate and elaborate on resources. Thus, one might start with a button, sound, script, or picture obtained from an external source but later add to it or otherwise modify it. When does the resource become the creative work of the person who has done the modifications?

There are no clear-cut answers to these questions. The situation promises to get even cloudier with the increasing spread of object-oriented environments, the improvement of copying technologies such as scanners and digitizers, the expanding density of optical storage capabilities to the point where they can provide instant on-line access to a world's worth of creative work, and the increasing reach of computer networks. All of these promote the easy flow of creative work from place to place.

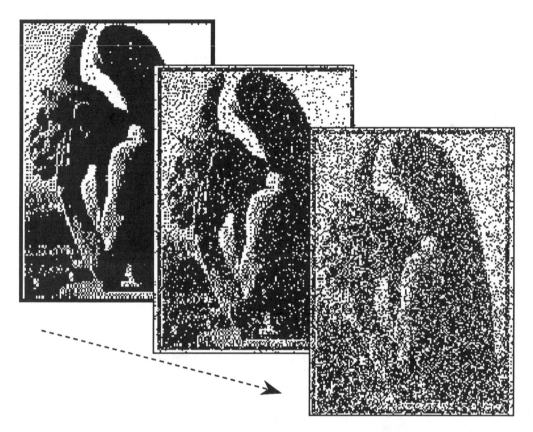

Figure 20.13 Decay Resulting from Analog Copying Methods

Readers, who themselves are producers of creative work, are urged to be especially conscientious in this world of copyright acknowledgment. Every attempt should be made to discover the creators of resources and to acknowledge their contribution when appropriate. Creators deserve to reap the rewards of their efforts.

At the same time, however, readers are urged to remember the seventeenth century scientist Isaac Newton's comment that his accomplishments were dependent on his "standing on the shoulders of giants." Readers are encouraged to freely share their creative work because the open exchange will ultimately enrich everyone working in these fields.

Sources of Resources and Information

<u>User Groups and Journals</u>.

AHUG (Apple HyperCard Users Group)
Apple Computer
20525 Mariani Ave
MS-27-AHUG
Cupertino, CA 95014

APDA (Apple Programmers and Developers Association)
Apple Computer
20525 Mariani Ave.
MS-33G
Cupertino, CA 95014
(800) 282-2732

ART COM
70 Twelfth Street
San Francisco, CA 94103

BMUG (Berkeley Macintosh Users Group)
1442A Walnut St. #62
Berkeley, CA 94709
(415) 549-2684

Boston Computer Society
1 Central Plaza
Boston, MA 02108

Leonardo (International Journal of Art and Science)
2030 Addison St.
Berkeley, CA 94704
(415) 845-8298

MacUser
950 Tower Lane
Foster City, CA 94404
(303) 447-9330

MacWorld
501 Second St.
San Francisco, CA 94107
(800) 288-6848

New York Macintosh Users Group
245 West 25th Street
New York, New York 10001

Telecommunications Resources.

CompuServe
P.O. Box 20212
5000 Arlington Center Blvd.
Columbus, OH 43220
(800) 848- 8990

FAST (Fine Arts, Science and Technology) Bulletin Board
Fine Arts Forum
c/o *Leonardo*
2030 Addison St.
Berkeley, CA 94704
(415) 845-8298

GENIE
401 N. Washington St.
Rockville, MD 20850
(800) 638-9636

Online
Quantum Computer
8619 Westwood Center Dr.
Vienna, VA 22182
(703) 448-8700

Prodigy
P.O. Box 7243
Portsmouth, NH 03801

The Well
27 Gate Five Rd.
Sausalito, CA 94965
(415) 332-4335

CHAPTER 21
IMPORTING GRAPHICS AND CONTROLLING EXTERNAL DEVICES SUCH AS VIDEODISCS AND CD ROM

In addition to the added resources described in Chapter 20, there are many other specialized applications, such as animation and 3-D design programs, that offer powerful capabilities of interest to artists. Also many computer-controllable devices such as scanners and videodisc players invite artisitic exploration. HyperCard makes it easy to work in conjunction with other programs and devices.

Paint and Draw Programs, Multifinder, Scrapbook, Clipboard

Although HyperCard provides a wide array of graphics tools, it does not offer the flexibility and depth of applications specialized for graphics work. Paint programs such as MacPaint, Studio1, Pixel Paint, and Modern Artist each offer unique capabilities missing from HyperCard — for example, a variety of filling methods and transformations. Object-oriented drawing programs such as MacDraw, Illustrator, and Freehand offer other features such as the ability to treat each graphic element as separate and independent. Each element can be flexibly repositioned, filled, and transformed until the resulting total graphic is satisfactory. Programs such as SuperPaint and Canvas offer the integrated advantages of both approaches.

Many artists prefer to work in their favorite graphics program and then import the graphics into HyperCard. This process is relatively straightforward. There are two methods of getting images into HyperCard:

1. Importing an image via the Import Picture command available when in paint tool mode
2. Using the clipboard and scrapbook

When in paint tool mode, the Import Picture and Export Picture

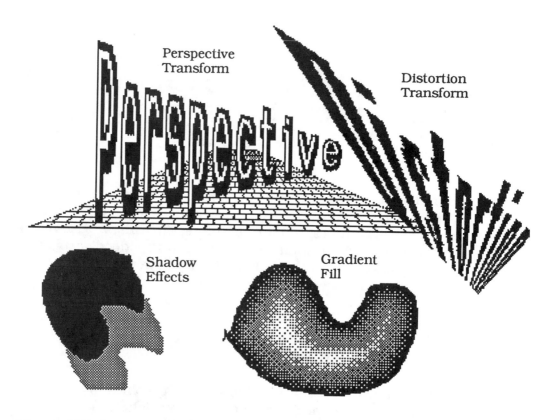

Figure 21.1   Image Possiblities in External Paint Programs

commands become available under the Files Menu. Clicking on Import Picture will bring up a standard Macintosh File Location Dialog Box that allows one to indicate the picture (in bit-mapped paint format) to import. HyperCard will then copy the picture from its storage location and place it as a card picture on the currently displayed card. The Export Picture command reverses the process. It takes the currently displayed card picture and stores it on disk as a paint-formatted graphic, under a name given in a standard File Dialog Box.

The clipboard and scrapbook provide another easy way to move images back and forth between HyperCard and graphics programs. One needs to select an image while in the graphics program, copy or cut it to the clipboard, then quit the graphics program and open HyperCard. With enough RAM memory, Multifinder can be used such that both the graphics program and HyperCard can be open simultaneously. Quitting the program

CLIPBOARD METHOD

3. Quit paint program, start HyperCard, choose any paint tool, and choose Paste Picture.

4. Image appears as though drawn in HyperCard.

1. Start the graphics application and draw the image.

2. Cut or Copy automatically puts the item into clipoard memory.

SCRAPBOOK METHOD

1. and 2. Same as above.

3. Open the Scrapbook desk accessory located under the Apple symbol.

4. Paste the image into the scrapbook using the command-*V* keyboard equivalent for Paste. Continue working in the paint program if desired. Repeat for other images.

5. Image is now stored in the scrapbook file inside the system folder on disk. It is available at any time while in HyperCard by opening the scrapbook desk accessory. It does not go away like the clipboard when the machine is turned off.

IMPORT PAINT METHOD

1. Create as many pictures as desired while in graphics applications. Save each image in paint format.

2. Open HyperCard, choose any paint tool, and activate the Import Paint command. It will ask for the name of the image file and bring it into HyperCard.

Figure 21.2 Methods of Importing Images into Hypercard from Other Graphics Applications

is therefore not necessary as one can switch active application merely by clicking in various windows. Since Multifinder is known to ocassionally crash, one must be careful to back up frequently.

Selection of any paint tool while in HyperCard will put it into the mode to receive a picture. Choice of Paste Picture from the Edit Menu will then plop a copy of the picture on the currently displayed card. As long as one does not turn off the Macintosh or copy anything else to the clipboard, that image will be waiting in the clipboard. Since the clipboard is really an area of electronic RAM memory, it will lose anything stored if the power goes off.

If one wants to create several pictures in the paint program without quitting each time to bring them into HyperCard, the Scrapbook desk accessory can be used. This accessory, which can be opened from within any program without quitting, allows one to cut, paste, and copy graphics and text. The Scrapbook uses disk storage instead of electronic RAM memory, so it does not lose information when the machine is turned off. One needs to be sure, however, that the same system folder is in use when the target program is opened, or one will access a scrapbook belonging to a different system folder and hence not find the picture.

Exchange of graphics into HyperCard requires awareness of some limitations:

- HyperCard is capable only of using images in MacPaint bit-mapped format. Since the sophisticated graphics programs have the ability to save in several higher-resolution formats, one must be careful to select the MacPaint format in setting the form of output from a program.
- The bit-mapped format also means that object-oriented images (as described in Chapter 6) will lose that capability when imported into HyperCard. They will be changeable only via the usual HyperCard methods of selection tool manipulation.
- HyperCard's bit-mapped format is capable only of displaying a 72-dots-per-inch (dpi) image. The images will not look as good as the higher-resolution images that several of the programs can produce on high-resolution printers.
- HyperCard's image space is limited to the 5-by-7-inch size of the standard Macintosh screen. Larger images can be cut off in the importation process. It is essential while in the graphics program to account for size limitations and to prepare the image as fully as possible for its ultimate HyperCard presentation.

Three-dimensional Design Programs

Specialized computer-aided design programs for the Macintosh allow creation of realistic three-dimensional objects. Programs such as Swivel and Super3D can render objects as wire frames or as fully shaded forms. The user has multiple ways of moving from an idea to something that approaches the solidity of objects in three-dimensional space. The position of the eye viewpoint and light sources can be manipulated. The objects can be animated to move and rotate in three-dimensional space.

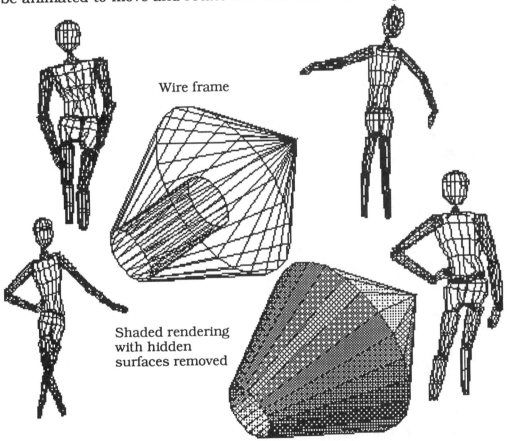

Wire frame

Shaded rendering with hidden surfaces removed

Figure 21.3   Three-dimensional Images Created with a 3-D Design Program

Since these images can be saved in bit-mapped paint format, they can be easily used in HyperCard. They are loaded into HyperCard by the Import Paint and clipboard methods described previously. 3-D images can offer a dramatic addition to HyperCard stacks.

3-D animation can be created in the following way. 3-D programs allow consecutive saving of the views of an image as it is animated. The mathematics of 3-D object animation is complex and time-consuming and can take even these specialized programs several seconds for each move. Each view, however, can be saved as a separate image. These images can each be imported to HyperCard and placed on a separate card. A loop script can be written to sequence the cards, achieving the appearance of 3-D animation within HyperCard. Unfortunately, this approach to animation consumes much memory space if the images are complex.

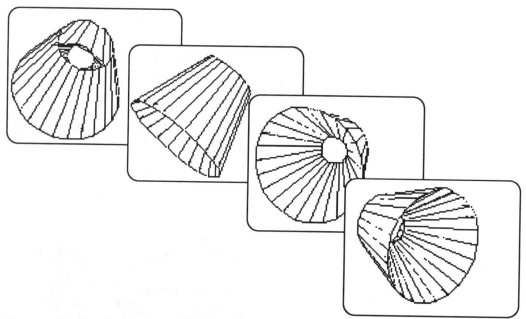

Figure 21.4   Illusion of 3-D Animation Created by Importation of a Sequence of Images from a 3-D Design Program

3-D image generation is an important artistic tool because this is where reality and creative imagination dance together. Ever since the Renaissance, artists have searched for methods of creating 3-D illusions of reality as a way of adding impact to their work. Contemporary 3-D computer design capabilities continue this quest.

Animation Control Programs

Developers have created programs such as VideoWorks™ and Director™ that are optimized for the creation of moving two-dimensional animations. These programs make it easy to create precisely timed animations in which several objects move in predetermined pathways accompanied by sound. The process for creating these animations is easy to learn and use.

First, one creates "cast members" with the included paint tools or by importing graphics from other graphics applications. Each of these images can be an independently moving graphic entity. The actual movement of the object can be set by dragging the object around the screen while the program records the movement or by requesting a "tween" process. In tweening, a user specifies "key frames" and the number of steps desired between frames. The program then calculates the precise placement of the object on the frames in between the keys. Each object's motion is recorded on an animation channel score. Synchronization can then be edited by manipulating this score.

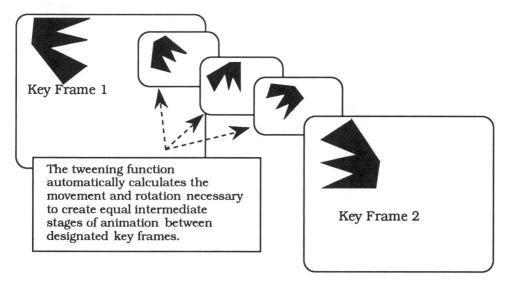

Key Frame 1

The tweening function automatically calculates the movement and rotation necessary to create equal intermediate stages of animation between designated key frames.

Key Frame 2

Figure 21.5   Importation of Animation Frames from a Specialized Animation Application Such as Director

Again, the calculations for smoothly moving many simultaneous objects would quickly overwhelm a program such as HyperCard. This difficulty was seen in the sample script in Figure 16.11 illustrating simultaneous movement of objects.

Typically, animations created by Director or other similar applications require their host programs or special free-standing play programs in order to be viewed. There are, however, ways these programs can be used in conjunction with HyperCard to achieve desired animation effects. As with the 3-D programs just described, these programs can save each of the frames in a sequence in paint format. These frames can then be imported into HyperCard to be placed on a sequence of cards.

Fortunately, an even better method exists. Developers of these programs have created special programs called HyperCard drivers that allow activation of animations from within HyperCard. These drivers, which must be bought separately, consist of a stand-alone animation player that can respond to a set of external commands that function like intrinsic HyperCard commands. These external commands must be added as resources to the stack via a special installation program provided with the drivers or one of the resource-moving methods described previously, such as ResCopy. Use of these commands calls the special program to run an animation that was previously prepared in one of the animation programs.

The animation runs with all the smoothness and complexity that these specialized programs can generate. Furthermore, the animations are not limited to HyperCard's restrictions and can thus use color and move anywhere on the screen, even outside HyperCard's standard windows (on Macintoshes with bigger screens). This approach to animation is memory-expensive, however. The driver, the external commands, and the previously prepared animations can take up a great deal of memory, both in electronic

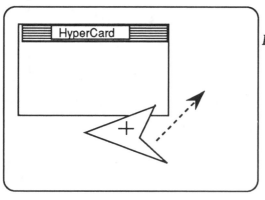

Figure 21.6   Animation Driver Allows Animation to Take Place outside the HyperCard Window

RAM and in disk storage. Some small memory systems cannot use these methods to full advantage.

Here is a sample of some of the external commands added through the Videoworks driver:

VWclick (stop the animation if the user clicks the mouse button)
VWlocation (where to place the animation on the screen)
VWloop (play the animation over and over)
VWnoSound (turn off the animation's sound)
VWtempo (how fast to play the animation)

Image Digitizers and Scanners

In working with computer graphics, one is not limited to using only images drawn by hand or generated by design programs — special electronic devices called digitizers and scanners allow the digital capture of image information from the world. These devices can convert the information of a photograph, hand drawing, or video image into a form that can be worked on by graphics programs. The scanned image retains the photographic realism of the source.

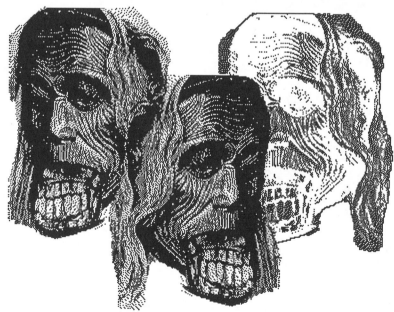

Figure 21.7 Manipulation of Scanned Images

For example, one could import a photograph via a scanner to one of the graphics programs described earlier. Once in the paint program, it is possible to manipulate the image by drawing on it, duplicating portions of it, distorting it, or collaging with other scanned or drawn images. One could then import the image to HyperCard, in which it would function just as though it were created with HyperCard's paint tools.

Image scanners work by optically capturing the pattern of dark and light that make up an image. Usually, they mechanically move a sensor lens line by line through the image. Each line of dark and light is converted into the bit pattens that a computer can understand. Thus, black might be converted into the high 5-volt-pulse and white might be converted into the low-voltage pulse. These streams of bits are stored in the computer's memory in the format expected for graphics. Once stored, the image is indistinguishable from any other graphic created. Video digitizers work similarly, by converting the electronic video signals to the patterns of bits in the correct format. Video digitizers can work with images coming from

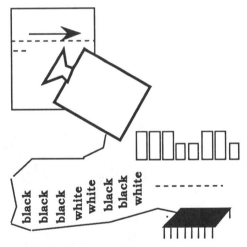

Scanner systematically passes over each line of an image, sending voltage pulses that correspond to the image tones seen in the sensor. Software transfers the values to screen memory to recreate the image inside the computer.

Figure 21.8   Scanner Converts Patterns of Dark and Light into Computer-readable Forms

any standard video source such as a camera or a VCR.

Some digitizers are capable of recording and storing color and full gray scale information about the images they capture. The gray scale provides tonal information about variations between black and white. Scanners are usually described by the amount of gray scale variations they can record — for example, 16 or 256 levels. These scanned images can appear very realistic. Unfortunately, they take a lot of memory. A full-color or 256 gray level scan of an 8-by-10-inch image can require several megabytes of storage, which is more than many systems have. The image cannot even fit on a single floppy disk.

HyperCard can only work with paint format images (two levels — black and white). Usually, scanner control programs allow a choice of recording formats. In fact, Apple's scanner includes a HyperCard stack called HyperScan that allows flexible control of scanner settings. No matter what scanner one is using, one should select the paint format if the ultimate goal is importation into HyperCard. Once the image is in paint format, it can be brought in via the Import Graphics command or clipboard cut-and-paste methods, as described previously.

Computer Control of Videodiscs

Videodiscs, which have been on the consumer market for several years, provide a high-quality medium for storage and playback of video information. They can store information with great density, packing half an hour of action video or 54,000 still images on a single videodisc. They offer certain critical disadvantages and advantages over videotape players. The major disadvantage is they are not an easy recording medium. Videodiscs require expensive, precisely engineered recording equipment. Thus, consumers are not able to record their own information. Rather, like a phonograph record, one would need to take video material to a specialized service center that would press a videodisc for a significant fee.

Videodiscs also offer advantages. Videodisc players read the discs by reading the changing reflections of a small laser beam bouncing off the surface. This optical reading method means that the head does not actually touch the surface. Consequently, there is much less abrasion of the surface compared to videotape; thus the discs last longer and the electronic signal is cleaner.

Even more significant, videodisc technology allows random access of images. If the locations of sequences are known, the videodisc player can very quickly jump to those places without needing to fast-forward through other images. A sequence can thus be determined on the fly and be varied with need. Unfortunately, even though videodiscs can change sequences quickly, the change is not instantaneous. There is a short noticeable pause while the controller moves the reading head to the proper physical spot on the disc to pick up the images.

Developers quickly realized that this technology would be useful for training and other presentations that required changing sequences. They built computer interfaces into videodisc players so that the sequence could be controlled by computer. They developed educational videodiscs with computer-aided instruction programs that changed the video sequence based on the user's responses. There is now an extensive specialty devoted to the production of these interactive videodiscs.

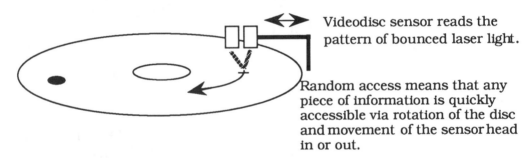

Videodisc sensor reads the pattern of bounced laser light.

Random access means that any piece of information is quickly accessible via rotation of the disc and movement of the sensor head in or out.

Figure 21.9   Videodisc Processes of Reading Information

These interfaces use the standard serial communication hardware and software that computers use for linkage with printers and modems. That is, one can plug a serial cable into the back of the computer and into the videodisc player if the physical plugs match. Each brand of player has an arbitrary set of commands it can understand built into its electronics. For example, a sequence of instructions such as the combination of the escape key followed by a *1* might make one videodisc player play backward. For another player, the sequence to make the player play backward might be the combination of the control key followed by *B*. The only way to learn these codes is to read the operating manual that comes with the player one is using.

A computer program can thus control a videodisc player by linking viewer actions with the correct codes to cause the videodisc players to act accordingly. Developers created a set of HyperCard external commands that allow this sending of codes back and forth between a computer and a videodisc player via the modem port.

Commercial developers such as Voyager have built on this capability to create special HyperCard stacks for controlling the players. For example, the Voyager company has created the Discovery stack with a well-designed visual control panel interface. The stack automatically loads in the specific commands that a particular brand uses to control events based on the user's answers to an inquiry made during initial setup. Each button on the screen can then control a specific function of the player. An Edit List card allows a user to try out various sequences of images and effects. It automatically assembles the corresponding instructions to the videodisc player and allows the user to test them. For this to work, one must identify the start and stop frame numbers of all the sequences one might want to sequence. Each of the approximately 54,000 frames on a videodisc has a unique identifying sequential number.

Currently, videodisc controls play the video on a video monitor separate from the computer screen. New technology has been developed that will allow the video to play in a window on the standard screen.

One can control a videodisc from Voyager's stack or import the external commands into one's own stack. Once these external commands

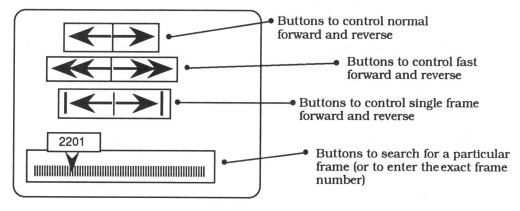

Figure 21.10 Example of a Videodisc Control Panel

are installed, one can create a unique HyperCard environment that controls the videodisc. An artist is totally free, within the limitations of HyperCard, to develop visual metaphors that can be integrated with the available videodisc information. Figure 21.11 shows a simple control card in which movement of the mouse controls a hypothetical videodisc.

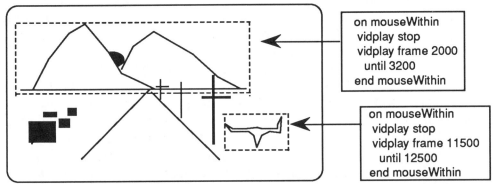

In this hypothetical videodisc control panel, the image acts as the controller of the videodisc player. It assumes that there are videodisc sequences metaphorically relevant to the mountains, the town, the road, and the animal skeleton. The sequences are activated by moving the mouse into the area of the image. A transparent button stops the previous sequence and starts the next sequence. For example, the sequence starting at 11500 poetically relates to the animal skeleton.

Figure 21.11 Use of an Image with Hidden Buttons as a Videodisc Controller

Videodiscs offer extraordinary opportunities to artists. Artists can create events that interactively control full-action video and sound. Pioneering artist Lynn Hershman experimented with videodiscs as an artistic medium even before computer interfaces were widely distributed. For example, in Hershman's *LORNA*, a viewer is given the chance to inquire about the main actor's thoughts and to exercise limited control on the order of sequences presented. Several artists' works that use interactive videodiscs under HyperCard control were described in Chapter 1.

Since the process of pressing a videodisc is complicated and expensive, artists can also use preexisting videodiscs. That is, artists can create interactive HyperCard events that resequence and recontextualize the images that already exist. Technically, this process is called repurposing. For example, the many movies that exist in videodisc format invite this kind of work. Remember, one would need to check the copyright situation if the works produced were to be displayed in public or commercial settings.

In addition to movies, there are many other kinds of videodiscs that could be explored for possible repurposing, for example:

- The Art Conservator (demonstration of art conversation techniques and a collection of stills of objects in the J. P. Getty collection)
- Tele-shop (consumer catalog done by Sears Roebuck)
- History Disquiz (questions about historical events based on newsreels of those events)
- Puzzle of Tacoma Narrows Bridge Collapse (discussion of the physics of wave motion and resonance related to the collapse)
- Mysterydisc (videodisc game offering 16 mystery stories that the viewer can try to solve)
- Planetary Image Videodisc (images from outer space)
- National Air & Space Museum Archive (images from the collection)
- National Gallery of Art (images of 1645 objects from the collection)
- BioSci Videodisc (complete visual library for the study of biology).

CD ROM, WORM, Erasable Optical Discs, and DVI

The information stored on videodiscs is analog video information, just like one would get from a videotape. Although the videodisc player can be controlled by a computer, the information itself cannot be manipulated digitally. For example, the images cannot be visually shrunk or composited, the sounds cannot be digitally edited, and the text cannot be searched for key words. Digitally stored information is much more flexible and much more intrinsically integratable into computer work. New optical digital technologies such as Compact Disc Read-Only Memory (CD ROM) promise to offer the advantages of both video imagery and digital manipulation.

Theoretically, one could convert an analog videodisc to digital form, as was described in the section on scanners and digitizers. However, the amount of memory required would be astronomical because of the way digital information must be stored. The digitization process requires high sampling rates to capture the nuance and detail of visual and sound information.

One can intuitively appreciate this resolution and storage issue by comparing a newspaper photo with a high-quality magazine photo. In part, the difference in clarity can be attributed to the high-resolution system's use of more dots to represent the image. The issue is also illustrated by the difference between a relatively high-resolution computer screen such as the Macintosh with 512-by-340 resolution with older, lower-resolution screens such as the Apple II with 280-by-180 resolution. In lower-resolution screens one can see the big pixel blocks that make up the image. The blocky staircase effect is most clearly seen in curves and diagonals. On color systems, the colors do not merge cleanly. This blockiness is called aliasing. Higher-resolution systems allow more subtle shapes and colors. They also take much more memory because each pixel needs more discrete locations in memory to represent it. More locations and more colors require more memory. For more information, consult my book *Using Computers to Create Art* (Prentice Hall, 1986).

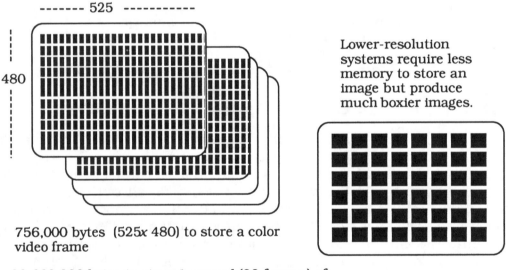

‑‑‑‑‑‑‑ 525 ‑‑‑‑‑‑‑‑‑‑‑

480

Lower-resolution systems require less memory to store an image but produce much boxier images.

756,000 bytes (525x 480) to store a color video frame

22,680,000 bytes to store 1 second (30 frames) of uncompressed video (30x 756,000)

Figure 21.12 Memory Requirements to Store High-Resolution Images

Live-action video is made up of frames that play 30 times a second. A standard video frame can be represented fairly well by a full-color 525-by-480 grid of pixels. With an assumption of full color, which requires 3 bytes of memory for each pixel, one frame would require 756,000 bytes of memory (525 times 480 times 3). One second of video would require 22,680,000 bytes of memory (756,000 times 30). One can easily see that live video would quickly fill up the biggest hard disk. Luckily, new optical storage methods are being developed.

CD ROM uses an optical laser–based recording and retrieval technology similar to videodisc to store very dense digital information. A three-and-a-half-inch CD is capable of storing 550 megabytes (MB) of information on a disc the same size as popular music CDs. This is the equivalent of storing 1500 books. Images and sound can be stored as well as text. These devices use standard hard disk interfaces so to the computer the CD ROM looks just like a big hard disk.

Furthermore, the information is in digital form, so the computer can search and manipulate it. One available optical disc offers the complete works of Shakespeare. One can do various kinds of searches — for example, instructing the computer to search for every instance of the word *rose* used within the same sentence as the word *death.*   Because the text is in computer-readable digital form, the computer can quickly generate the results of this search or any other other search.

Futurists are enthralled with the possibilities of this technology. Computers will be able to quickly access enormous stores of text, image, and sound information already in digitized form. They imagine all the libraries and museums of the world available at the tip of a finger. Furthermore, we all will be able to wander this information space, in our own way at our own pace. As described earlier, hypermedia browsing will be encouraged, to allow each person's nonlinear mental associations to be followed wherever they lead. Breakthroughs in synthesized knowledge can be expected.

HyperCard is often seen as a prototype for interfaces to guide navigation of this information space. Its flexible linking capabilities, its stress on interactive structure, and its ability to handle multimedia text, graphics, and sound information are all important. Experimental CD ROMs using HyperCard interfaces have already appeared that hint at the possibilities. Here are some examples:

- Grolier's Encyclopedia (access to all text and images of the encyclopedia)
- Electronic Whole Earth Catalog (access to descriptions of resources and tools such as appeared in the *Whole Earth Catalog* series)
- ABC's Interactive News (nonlinear access to the history and issues of the 1988 political campaigns)
- Microsoft's Office, which includes a dictionary, a thesaurus, Bartlett's quotations, style guides, and a zip code directory

There are some clouds in the sky of this information utopia. CD ROMs are read-only devices. This means that the user cannot change or add any information. Like videodiscs, they must be pressed with expensive equipment at specialized facilities. For some applications, such as reference works, this immutability is fine; for others in which the user needs more flexibility, this is unsatisfactory. Newer technologies are trying to remedy this situation. For example, WORM (write once, read many) discs allow a user to add to a disc but not make any changes. Also, erasable optical discs that allow reading and writing just like hard disks have been developed. They are still relatively slower than hard disks but promise improvements to the extent that they are expected ultimately to replace them.

Image storage represents another problem. In spite of their enormous storage capacity, CD ROMs can only store a limited number of images: approximately 720 full-color images. With this limited capacity, action video is out of the question. Research labs are working hard on methods of enabling CD ROM to digitally store video. Digital Video Interactive (DVI) is one promising approach. Special hardware and software are used to compress digital video information into a minimum storage size. Special decompression hardware can play the video by decompressing the digital information on the fly. Half an hour of low-resolution video can be stored on a regular-sized CD using these methods.

Perhaps the most important limitation is the lack of understanding of how to structure the unprecedented amounts of information for productive nonlinear hypermedia access. For example, some researchers have explored the concept of "agents." Agents are special intelligent programs that search and monitor the flow of information as a representative of the user. After having been made aware of the user's interests and needs, these programs locate and organize information of possible relevance to the user.

In the future design of hypermedia, deliberations on the following questions could benefit from artistic contributions. What visual metaphors can be developed to serve as maps and navigation aids for individuals using complex hypermedia spaces? What are appropriate ways for organizing the simultaneous presentation of text, image, and sound information so that it can be engaging and clear? How can computerized agents be designed so that they are welcomed by hypermedia browsers? Furthermore, new forms of art can be developed in which the variety of pathways through complex information spaces becomes as much the art as the information itself.

Control of Real-World Devices and Reading of External Conditions

Computers are capable of controlling real-world devices besides video screens and printers. Similarly, they are capable of reading real-world events beyond the pressing of keys and the movements of mice. Computers are regularly used in applications such as industrial control — for example, in factories, monitoring critical temperatures and liquid levels and responding with appropriate adjustments to valves and motors.

Typically, these kinds of computerized controls and sensors were available only via expensive specialized equipment. The equipment required sophisticated levels of knowledge to use. Recently, new HyperCard interfaces to inexpensive sensor and control equipment have become available. This equipment enables artists to use computers to control interactive installations that can read events such as human movement and respond with control of kinetic sculpture.

These devices use the serial communication port just like printers, modems, and videodisc players. The user installs a set of external commands that enable one to send signals out from HyperCard scripts. Like videodiscs, these devices may be activated by a set of arbitrary commands that are the keys to their actions. One learns these codes by reading the manuals. Scripts can then be written that send the appropriate signals out at the correct time.

For example, the Hyperboard™ allows HyperCard control of a single-board remote computer with wide capabilities. It is possible to buy add-on boards that allow this computer to turn relays off and on, convert analog information to digital form, and precisely control stepper motors. Setting electronic switches on them gives the boards specific addresses.   For example, a relay board might be given the addresses 1-16. Each relay is a switch that will turn on when the remote computer sends a voltage pulse. The script command in HyperCard to tell the computer to turn on relay 1 might be *sendSport 1,1*. A script can then be created in which movement into a series of buttons will turn on and off a series of lights.

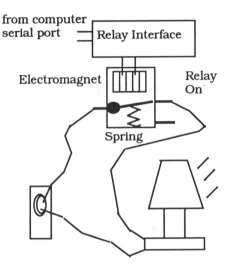

Special real-world interface devices that connect to the serial port allow HyperCard to control devices in the world.   Usually an external command must be installed in HyperCard that enables messages to be sent out to the device.

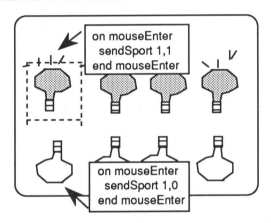

In this example, a relay interface board is connected.   A relay is an electrically operated switch. The board activates the electromagnet inside the target relay, which pulls a connector to close the circuit when the computer sends the proper voltage. When there is no voltage, the spring pulls the connector, so there is no complete circuit for the electricity.

Each relay is given an address by the designer of the device. The external command *sendSport 1* tells relay 1 to turn on if the mouse enters the button area of the lit bulb and tells relay 1 to turn off if the mouse enters the area of the unlit bulb.

Figure 21.13 Computer Control of Lights via a Relay Interface Board

HyperCard is a versatile program. It is even more powerful when it can be combined with other outside applications and devices. These frontiers await artistic exploration.

CHAPTER 22
HYPERCARD 2.0: ENHANCEMENTS, NEW OPPORTUNITIES, AND NEW CHALLENGES

HyperCard 2.0: Compatibility with HyperCard 1.x Series, System Requirements, Accessibility, New Features

HyperCard 2.0 corrects many of the shortcomings of the HyperCard 1.x series (1.0–1.2.5), although it does leave a few lacks unaddressed. It is downward-compatible with HyperCard 1.x. This means that all stacks created in version 1.x will run in version 2.0 (although some manipulations of the stack will be impossible until the stack is converted to a version 2.0 stack); conversely, HyperCard 2.0 stacks will not run in HyperCard 1.x. When a version 1.x stack is opened via the Open Stack item on the File Menu, the lock symbol appears, meaning that the stack is read-only. The Compact Stack item changes to Convert Stack (Figure 22.1). Once this conversion is done, however, the stack becomes a HyperCard 2.0 stack,

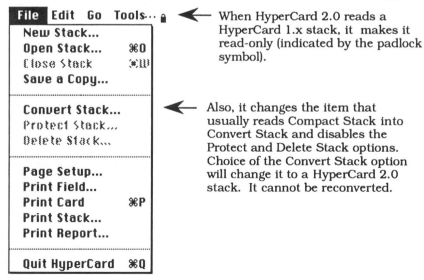

When HyperCard 2.0 reads a HyperCard 1.x stack, it makes it read-only (indicated by the padlock symbol).

Also, it changes the item that usually reads Compact Stack into Convert Stack and disables the Protect and Delete Stack options. Choice of the Convert Stack option will change it to a HyperCard 2.0 stack. It cannot be reconverted.

Figure 22.1   HyperCard 2.0 File Menu with Convert Stack Option

incapable of being run by HyperCard 1.0. There is no way to reconvert it. Archived copies of version 1.x stacks should be saved beforehand if they might be needed.

HyperCard 2.0 runs on all Macintoshes from the Plus on with at least 1 MB of memory. Large card sizes may not be possible with only 1 MB of memory and will be displayed in a default small screen size. HyperCard 2.0 requires System 6.05 or later and comes with every new Macintosh purchased. Updates are inexpensively available from Apple and user groups.

These are some of HyperCard 2.0's new features of special interest to people working with interactive multimedia:

- Increased speed
- Variable card sizes
- Screen display of multiple windows and dynamic sizing
- Control over menus in the Menu Bar
- Text field's ability to display a variety of text styles simultaneously
- Ability to treat text in fields like buttons (hot-linked text)
- Improvements and additions to visual effects: stretch and shrink
- Special paint transformations: rotate, slant, distort, perspective
- Limited ability to display color and grayscale pictures
- Built-in Icon Editor
- Control over inheritance hierarchies
- Improved script editing and debugging capabilities
- Improved printing features
- Ongoing stack activity with Multifinder
- Miscellaneous features: Title bar control, efficient searching, marking, security, scripts to avoid modal dialog boxes

Increased Speed

HyperCard 1.x was an interpreter. HyperCard 2.0 is a compiler. Each time an interpreter encounters a script line, it must convert it to computer machine language. By contrast, a compiler saves the conversion once it does it. As a consequence, compilers tend to be much faster than interpreters because they don't need to convert the program lines each time.

HyperCard 2.0 saves its compiled version of scripts in random-access memory until that memory is needed. It does not save the compiled version to disk, so the compilation must be done each time the script is freshly run. If timing is critical, a script must arrange to run through script handlers once before they are needed so that they will be precompiled.

Variable Card Sizes: *the rectangle of the card*

HyperCard 1.0 had only one card size available. Even if a large screen such as the Mac II 640-by-480 13-inch screen were used, HyperCard could only appear in a limited window. Thus, designers had little flexibility in determining card size and could not use the whole screen on larger screens. HyperCard stacks had a tendency to look uniform regardless of designer intentions.

HyperCard 2.0 allows stack creators to determine the card size of a stack, within certain limits. Cards can range anywhere from 64 by 64 to 1280 by 1280 (limited by available memory). Sizes can only be set in width multiples of 32 and height multiples of 8 (e.g., 128 by 104 but not 100 by 90) and all cards in a single stack must be the same size. The feature that allows dynamic sizing of the displayed Card window as opposed to the basic card size (explained later) allows a designer to create the illusion of different-sized cards. The full extent of large screens can now be used, and a uniform HyperCard look is no longer inevitable.

Card sizes can be set via the New Stack item on the File Menu, the Stack Info item on the Objects Menu, and a HyperCard command. A card size choice has been added to the New Stack Dialog Box (Figure 22.2). One can pick among standard sizes of windows by clicking on the Card Size item, which causes a pull-down menu to open. It is also possible to make a custom size by picking the Screen choice from the menu and dragging the handles on the Resizing Box. The dotted rectangle changes in 32-pixel width and 8-pixel height increments as it is dragged around, and the dimensions appear above the box.

The card size of an existing stack can be changed by picking the Stack Info item on the Objects Menu. A Resize button has been added to the Stack Info Dialog Box. Clicking on it opens a card sizing display similar to the one that is part of the New Stack Dialog Box. After a reduction of card size, graphics that were originally outside the new smaller card boundaries remain in the stack eventhough they cannot be seen.

Card size can be changed via a HyperTalk command to set the *rectangle* property of the card. For example, *set the rectangle of the card to 0,0,640,480* sets the size to fit a standard Mac II color monitor. With HyperCard 2.0, card size becomes a critical aesthetic design element.

New Stack Dialog Box

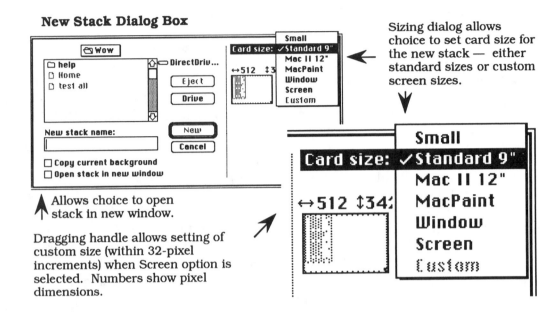

Sizing dialog allows choice to set card size for the new stack — either standard sizes or custom screen sizes.

▲ Allows choice to open
♠ stack in new window.

Dragging handle allows setting of custom size (within 32-pixel increments) when Screen option is selected. Numbers show pixel dimensions.

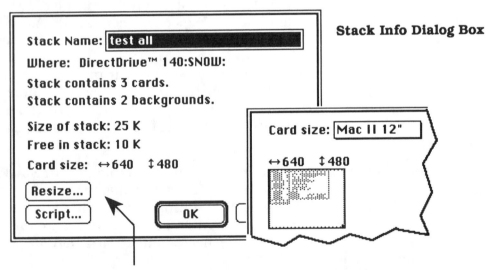

Stack Info Dialog Box

Stack Info item allows resizing of cards of existing stacks through Resize button, which presents Resizing Dialog Box similar to that presented in New Stack Dialog Box.

Figure 22.2   Card Sizing Options Available via the New Stack and the Stack Info Dialog Boxes

Screen Display of Multiple Windows and Dynamic Sizing: *open stack in new window, the rectangle of card window, suspend, resume, the scroll*

Opening Multiple Windows. The ability to open multiple windows on the screen simultaneously may be even more visually significant than card size. A designer can open as many stacks as RAM will allow. Each can appear in its own visible window. Stacks can be opened in new windows via the Open Stack item in the File Menu (Figure 22.3) or HyperTalk commands. The Open Stack Dialog Box has a new *Open stack in a new window* checkbox. If it is checked, the stack will appear in a separate window while the other stack continues to be displayed; otherwise, the stack to be opened will replace the previous stack display.

The Go Menu has a new Next Window item that allows switching between displayed windows of stacks that have been opened. It allows cycling through all the windows displayed on the screen.

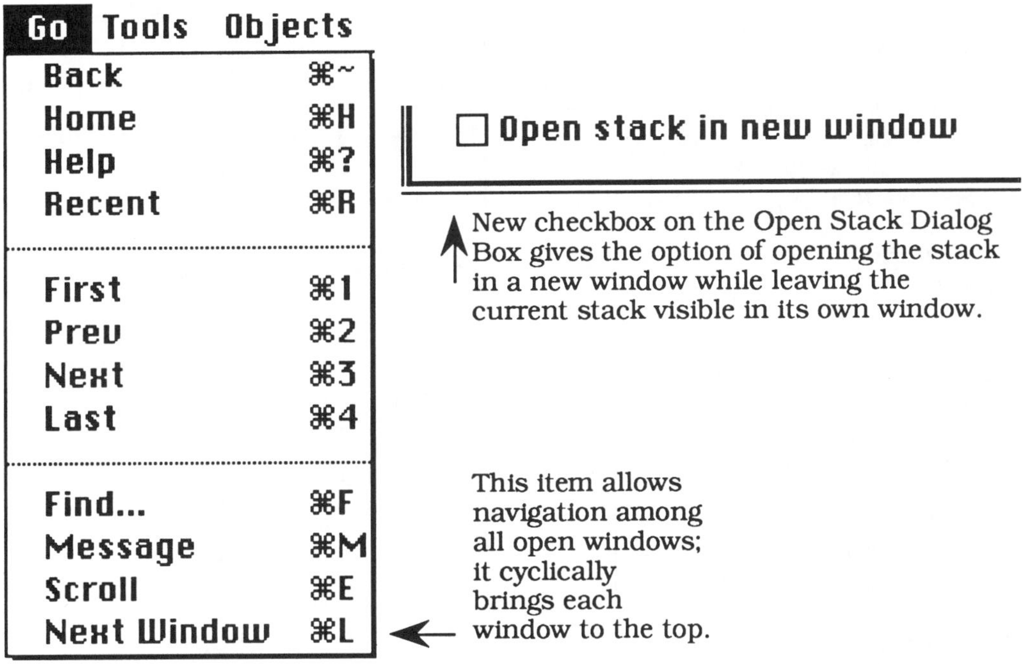

Go Tools Objects	
Back	⌘~
Home	⌘H
Help	⌘?
Recent	⌘R
First	⌘1
Preu	⌘2
Next	⌘3
Last	⌘4
Find...	⌘F
Message	⌘M
Scroll	⌘E
Next Window	⌘L

☐ **Open stack in new window**

New checkbox on the Open Stack Dialog Box gives the option of opening the stack in a new window while leaving the current stack visible in its own window.

This item allows navigation among all open windows; it cyclically brings each window to the top.

Figure 22.3   Open Stack Dialog Box and Go Next Window Option in the Go Menu

Only one card from a stack can be displayed on the screen at a time. Careful stack and script design allows one to work around this restriction. For example, two stacks can be created to work together. The script can open each stack in a different window and juggle the activity so that both windows seem to be part of a single stack and both seem to be active simultaneously (Figure 22.4). The *suspend* command allows the stopping

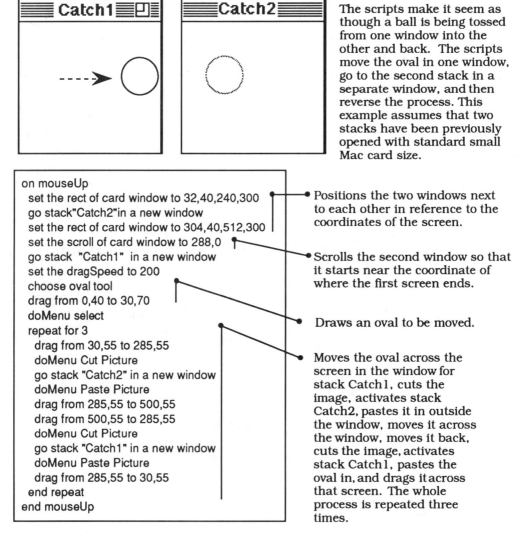

The scripts make it seem as though a ball is being tossed from one window into the other and back. The scripts move the oval in one window, go to the second stack in a separate window, and then reverse the process. This example assumes that two stacks have been previously opened with standard small Mac card size.

```
on mouseUp
  set the rect of card window to 32,40,240,300
  go stack"Catch2"in a new window
  set the rect of card window to 304,40,512,300
  set the scroll of card window to 288,0
  go stack  "Catch1" in a new window
  set the dragSpeed to 200
  choose oval tool
  drag from 0,40 to 30,70
  doMenu select
  repeat for 3
    drag from 30,55 to 285,55
    doMenu Cut Picture
    go stack "Catch2" in a new window
    doMenu Paste Picture
    drag from 285,55 to 500,55
    drag from 500,55 to 285,55
    doMenu Cut Picture
    go stack "Catch1" in a new window
    doMenu Paste Picture
    drag from 285,55 to 30,55
  end repeat
end mouseUp
```

Positions the two windows next to each other in reference to the coordinates of the screen.

Scrolls the second window so that it starts near the coordinate of where the first screen ends.

Draws an oval to be moved.

Moves the oval across the screen in the window for stack Catch1, cuts the image, activates stack Catch2, pastes it in outside the window, moves it across the window, moves it back, cuts the image, activates stack Catch1, pastes the oval in, and drags it across that screen. The whole process is repeated three times.

Figure 22.4　Two Stacks, Open in Separate Windows, Appear to Work Together

of stack actions, and the *resume* command allows the restarting of stack actions of stacks that are already open. The figure illustrates use of the commands to juggle action between stacks open in separate windows.

Resizing and Scrolling of Card Window Displays. In HyperCard 2.0, displayed windows can be resized up to the maximum of the basic card size for any given stack. Resizing must be done in 16-pixel width increments and 1 pixel height increments. There are several ways to resize and scroll windows: the Size Box, the Scroll window, the Zoom Boxes, and HyperTalk commands (see Figure 22.5). The keyboard combination command-shift-E makes the Size Box visible to allow scrolling and sizing by dragging the mouse. The box disappears when the mouse button is released.

The Scroll window is a floating window, like the Tool window and the Message Box, that does not get obscured by other windows as long as it is open. It displays a dotted rectangular frame representing the current window inside a white rectangle representing the standard card size chosen in a particular stack. Thus, it allows a user to see the current size of the displayed Card window and its scroll position relative to the total card. The cursor changes shape to indicate its function. Inside the dotted rectangle, the cursor becomes a hand; dragging it scrolls the display rectangle to make visible different parts of the card. Near the edges or corners, the cursor becomes a resizing double arrow; dragging it moves the edges in or out to change the size of the displayed Card window.

Clicking the Zoom Box in the Title Bar (see Figure 22.5) allows instant change between the current displayed Card window size and the standard card size. Double-clicking inside the frame rectangle of the Scroll window has the same effect.

The size of the displayed Card window and its scroll position can easily be controlled by HyperTalk scripts. This capability creates a new level of graphic control, since windows can be moved and sized under script control and the displayed Card window can be scanned across cards that may be larger than the Macintosh screen. Note that displayed window size is indpendent of the basic card size of the stack.

The property that controls the size and position of the displayed Card window is *the rectangle of card window*. The property that controls the horizontal and vertical scroll position of the displayed Card window relative to the underlying card is *the scroll of the card window*. Both of these can be changed via the *set* command: For example, *set the rectangle of card*

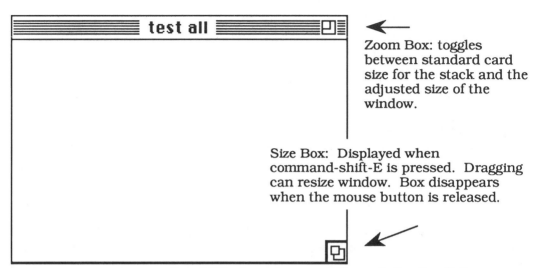

Zoom Box: toggles between standard card size for the stack and the adjusted size of the window.

Size Box: Displayed when command-shift-E is pressed. Dragging can resize window. Box disappears when the mouse button is released.

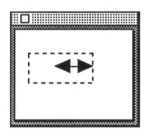

Scroll Window: Accessed through the Scroll item on the Go Menu. White rectangle shows the size of the standard card for the stack. Dotted rectangle shows the current size of the window. As the cursor moves inside the rectangle, it changes into a double-sided arrow. The boundaries can then be dynamically adjusted by dragging the mouse with the button pressed down.

Figure 22.5   Features for Resizing Displayed Card Windows: Size Boxes,
the Scroll Window, and Zoom Boxes

window to 96,100,304,200 would change the displayed Card window to occupy the position occupying horizontal pixels 96 to 304 and vertical pixels 100 to 200 in the absolute coordinates of the screen that puts 0,0 in the upper left corner of the physical monitor screen. If the command is *set the scroll of card window to 48,50*, the upper left corner of the card display will start at point 48,50 of the card regardless of where the window is positioned on the screen. Scroll must be set in 16-pixel horizontal increments.

Consider the analogy of a cardboard sheet with a cutout slot displaying a picture underneath. The cardboard is the actual screen of the monitor. *The rectangle of card window* property affects where the cutout is in the cardboard and how big it is. *The scroll of card window* property controls how the underlying picture is lined up with the slot — that is, what coordinate of the picture is aligned under the top left corner of the slot.

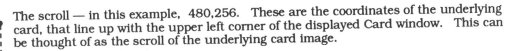

The scroll — in this example, 480,256. These are the coordinates of the underlying card, that line up with the upper left corner of the displayed Card window. This can be thought of as the scroll of the underlying card image.

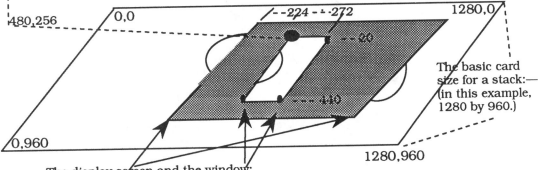

The display screen and the window:

The window's coordinates are expressed in the coordinates of the display screen. In this example, the window rectangle coordinates are approximately 224, 20, 272,440,assuming that the screen is a 640-by-480 display.

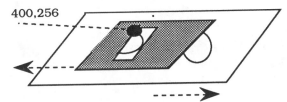

If the image were shifted to the right under the display screen or the cardboard were moved left, a different point of the underlying card would line up with the left top of the slot. The scroll might be something like 400,256. A different part of the image would appear in the window.

Figure 22.6   *The Metaphor of a Card with a Slot Cut Out Explains the Relationship of the rectangle of card window to the Visual Information on the Card*

This sizing and scrolling creates intriguing graphic possibilities. For example, windows can move around the screen, can appear to shrink and grow, and can appear to scan across a static image like a spotlight. Figure 22.7 illustrates two of these scripts.

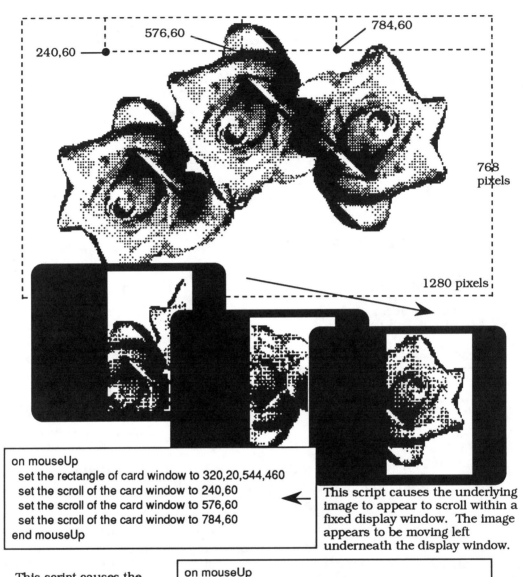

on mouseUp
  set the rectangle of card window to 320,20,544,460
  set the scroll of the card window to 240,60
  set the scroll of the card window to 576,60
  set the scroll of the card window to 784,60
end mouseUp

This script causes the underlying image to appear to scroll within a fixed display window. The image appears to be moving left underneath the display window.

This script causes the display window to move around, showing the same image in each place (not illustrated).

on mouseUp
  set the scroll of card window to 0,0
  set the rectangle of card window to 96,20,288,320
  set the rectangle of card window to 208,220,400,440
  set the rectangle of card window to 96,150,288,250
end mouseUp

Figure 22.7   Dancing Windows and Windows That Appear to Scan Across Images

Control over Menus in the Menu Bar: *Create, Delete, Put, the Name, Menu, MenuItem, Enable, Disable, the Enabled, Set, the cmdChar, the markChar, the checkMark, Reset*

One major complaint about the HyperCard 1.x series was its failure to uphold many standard Macintosh interface conventions. Menus were especially troublesome. Although the Menu Bar was a major interface feature of most Macintosh applications, HyperCard 1.x gave the script designer almost no control over the appearance and action of the Menu Bar. One was stuck with the standard HyperCard menus unless the *hide menubar* command was activated to completely hide it. As a result, HyperCard stacks did not look or act like many other applications.

HyperCard 2.0 gives the stack creator control over the Menu Bar. Stacks can be created that closely resemble standard Macintosh applications. HyperTalk commands allow a script to add new menus and associated menu items, delete unneeded standard HyperCard menus or menu items, enable and disable menus and menu items, assign command key equivalents to items, and control the appearance of menu items in accordance with Macintosh conventions (for example, by graying out items that can't be selected or putting check marks by default selections). Scripts can be written that check for the menu selections that users make and respond accordingly. No matter what changes are made, the command *reset menubar* will set everything back to the standard HyperCard menus.

Menus and menu items can be referred to by name or by number. The menus are numbered in their order across the Menu Bar, and the menu items are numbered in their order from top to bottom. *Create, put,* and *delete* are the commands to add or get rid of menus and menu items. *Create* makes new menus. *Put into* allows replacing, and *put before* or *put after* allows postioning of new menu items before or after other menu items. Names of menus and items can be changed by setting *the name* property to the desired name. Here are sample HyperTalk commands to manipulate menus and menu items:

```
create menu "Fish"
put "Salmon" into menu "Fish"
put "Tuna" before menu "Fish"
delete menu "Patterns"
delete menuItem 3 of menu "File"
delete menu 2
set the name of menu "Go" to "Transportation"
```

The *disable* command will gray out the specified menu or menu item and make it inactive. It still appears in the Menu Bar or menu but will not respond if the user should choose it. The *enable* command will activate the menu or menu item again and change it back to black. These changes can also be accomplished by setting *the enabled* property. *Set the enabled to true* results in an element being enabled; setting it to *false* results in an element being disabled.

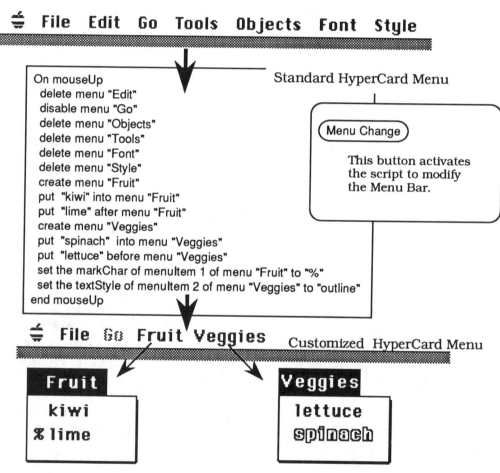

Figure 22.8   A Script Changes the Standard HyperCard Menu Bar

Scripts can set other aspects of menu items, including putting a checkmark by an item (*set the checkMark to true*), using another character to mark an item (*the markChar*), and changing the text style of a particular item. In addition, each menu item can have a keyboard shortcut equivalent assigned to it (*the cmdChar*).

> *Set the textStyle of menuItem "Home" of menu "Go" to bold*
> *Set the checkMark of menuItem 3 of menu "File" to true*
> *Set the markChar of menuItem "Last" of menu "Go" to "%"*
> *Set the cmdChar of menuItem 2 of menu "Options" to "Z"*

The Patterns, Tools, Apple, and Font menus can be disabled or deleted, but cannot be changed in other ways because of their special nature. Menu commands work on menus that don't visually appear on the Menu Bar (e.g., certain menus don't appear when paint tools have been selected). HyperTalk cannot execute *doMenu* commands on menu items that have been deleted, except for standard HyperCard menu items. Figure 22.8 demonstrates a script to change the standard menus.

To make actions result from choices of new menu items, the stack designer must add handlers to specify actions to be done if items are chosen. Actions can be specified by setting *the menuMessage* property of menu items or writing an *on doMenu* handler. Handlers for that message can then be placed at the card or higher levels to intercept and respond to it. Figure 22.9 illustrates the addition of a new menu and the scripts to activate it.

The window and menu features combined give the stack designer almost complete control. Stacks can be created that look and behave — within limits — like the standard Macintosh applications or like totally new creations. The opportunity of this easy-to-use development environment brings a challenge: Readers must now confront many complex interface design issues about aesthetic "look and feel" and psychological processes of interaction that were were not issues in HyperCard 1.0's constrained environment.

Text Field's Ability to Display a Variety of Text Styles Simultaneously

HyperCard 1.x allowed only one text font or style to appear in any given text field. HyperCard 2.0 allows free mixing of styles within fields. Each field has a default font, style, and size, but chunks can be changed from the default either through direct mouse and keyboard editing or

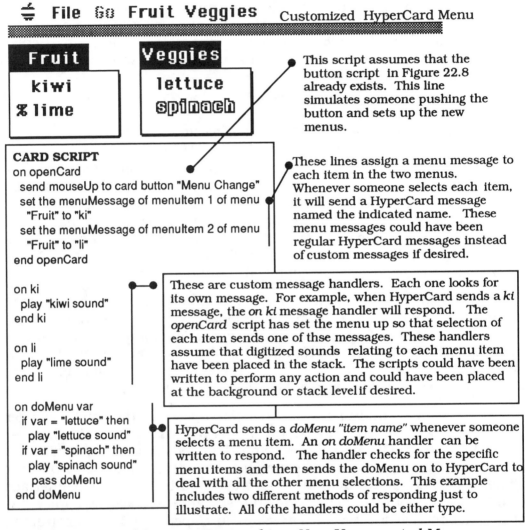

Figure 22.9   Card Script to Respond to a New User-created Menu

through HyperTalk scripts (see Figure 22.10). For example, in a field with plain text, the command *set the textStyle of word 5 of card field 1 to "outline"* would change just that one word to outline style. To facilitate the process of direct field editing, HyperCard 2.0 has added conventional Font and Style menus. Cutting and pasting styled text loses the variations and reverts the text to the default font in the pasted section. Also multiple styled text in fields slows HyperCard's display and should be used aparingly if speed is crucial.

With the advent of variable-sized text within a field, line heights can vary. HyperCard 2.0 has added a new field property called *the fixedLine-Height*. When it is set to *true*, all lines will be the same height regardless of variations in text size. When it is set to *false*, line heights will be allowed to vary in accordance with text size. The *fixedLineHeight* property can be set via a new checkbox in the Field Info Dialog Box or via HyperTalk commands. *Set the fixedLineHeight to false* allows line heights to vary. Also added are a *dontWrap* property, which disables HyperCard's automatic text wrap feature in fields, and a *sharedText* property, which makes background field text continue to appear in all cards that share that particular background.

Ability to Treat Text in Fields like Buttons (Hot-linked Text)

In traditional Hypertext systems, each word can act as a link to more information. Clicking on a word could lead to new text. However, in HyperCard 1.x this kind of text operation was difficult because no functions returned direct information about where a click occurred, although clever scripting could retrieve this information. HyperCard 2.0 has added functions that make it easy to write scripts to implement these hypertext features. When a field is locked, these functions return explicit information about what words were clicked on. If the field is not locked, HyperCard assumes that the user wants to edit or enter text since mouseclicking is the standard way to position the cursor.

The *clickText* function returns the actual text that was clicked on. *ClickChunk* returns a description of the chunk of characters that were clicked on (e.g., *char 5 to 9 of card field 2*). *ClickLine* returns a description of the line that was clicked (e.g., *line 2 of bkgnd field 4*). *MouseUp* scripts can be placed in the field, card, background, or stack to respond accordingly. HyperCard makes words the default chunk; thus, if one clicks in the middle of a word in a locked field, HyperCard will select that word. This default can be overridden by using the new *group* text style option — for example, to keep first and last names together in a list of names. To activate grouping, one selects the group of words to be joined and then selects the Group option from the Style Menu. Figure 22.11 illustrates the operation of these new functions.

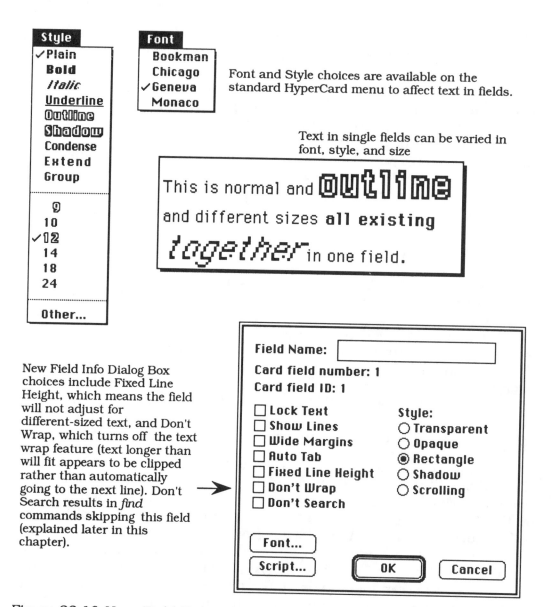

Font and Style choices are available on the standard HyperCard menu to affect text in fields.

Text in single fields can be varied in font, style, and size

New Field Info Dialog Box choices include Fixed Line Height, which means the field will not adjust for different-sized text, and Don't Wrap, which turns off the text wrap feature (text longer than will fit appears to be clipped rather than automatically going to the next line). Don't Search results in *find* commands skipping this field (explained later in this chapter).

Figure 22.10 New Field Properties (Varying Styled Text), New Choices in Field Dialog Box, and New Font and Style Menus

Bob Jones, Carol Smith, Hector Lopez, Gregory
Vlasic, Tiffany dePalma

Assume that the mouse button has been
clicked while the pointer is at the
indicated location in a field. The word
Lopez will invert, and the *click* functions
will yield these results:

>   *the clickText = Lopez*
>   *the clickChunk = char 32 to 36 of card field 1*
>   *the clickLine = line 2 of card field 1*

Style
✓ Plain
Bold
Italic
Underline
Outline
Shadow
Condense
Extend
Group

If the first and last names had been previously
selected and had the Group style applied to them,
clicking would yield the whole name. HyperCard uses
words as the default unit for the *click* functions
unless grouping is applied.

the clickText = Hector Lopez

Field Script
on mouseUp
  go card the clickText
end mouseUp

The *clickText* function can be used to create
hot-linked text. This script could be attached to
the field. It assumes that information cards had
been created for each person in the list. Clicking
on name would then display the card for the
person, assuming that the cards had been named
after the people. The *clickText* becomes the
name of the card in the *go* command line. This
script assumes that the field has been locked —
otherwise clicks would be interpreted as desires
to edit the text in the field.

*Figure 22.11 Hot-linked Text: the clickText, clickChunk, and click-
Line Functions; Grouped Text; and Scripts to Respond
to Hot-linked Text*

Improvements and Additions to Visual Effects: Stretch and Shrink

HyperCard 2.0 fixes the bug that required color systems to be set to the black-and-white, 1-bit monitor control panel setting in order for visual effects to work. Now the visual effects work on all settings and use the new card sizes if they are activated. Also, the Button Info Dialog Box has a new Effects option that allows automatic script generation of visual effects. This dialog box is accessed through the Button Info item of the Objects Menu. Clicking the Effects option opens up an Effects Selection Box that lets the user select a desired visual effect to add to a button script. HyperCard searches the script of the target button for the first *go* command and inserts the relevant *visual* command before it. If it can't find a *go* command, it adds the *visual* command and a *go this card* command to the button's script.

Two new visual effects are also added to the repertoire — *stretch* and *shrink*. These effects can be activated from the top, bottom, and center of cards. The stretch visually pulls the new card from the specified area (e.g., *visual stretch from top*). The shrink appears to fall into the specified area (e.g., *visual shrink to center*). As with all visual effects, the commands can optionally control the speed of the transition (e.g., *visual stretch from bottom very fast*) and the intermediate color (e.g., *visual shrink to bottom to black*). Figure 22.12 illustrates the new Effects Selection Box and the new shrink and stretch effects.

Paint Transformation Effects: Rotate, Slant, Distort, Perspective

New special effects have been added to the paint mode's Options Menu: Rotate, Slant, Distort, and Perspective. Like the other effects in this menu, these options require that the user first select some area of the screen via the select tool. These effects are not available through HyperTalk commands.

The Rotate effect allows free rotation of the selected area around the center point. The Slant effect allows symmetrical distortion of the selected area to a parallelogram form. The Distort effect allows pushing and pulling of any of its corners. The Perspective effect simulates one-point perspective along the vertical or horizontal axis.

New Visual Effects: Stretch and Shrink can be applied from bottom, top, and center.

visual shrink to top   *visual stretch from bottom*

Button Info Dialog Box (accessed through the Objects Menu) includes a new option to assign a visual effect to the button's script automatically. It is accessed through the Effects button on the dialog box, which brings up this Effects Dialog Box. Choice of an effect causes HyperCard to search for the first *go* command it can find and insert the appropriate *visual effect* script line. Users select from the list of possible effects and speeds.

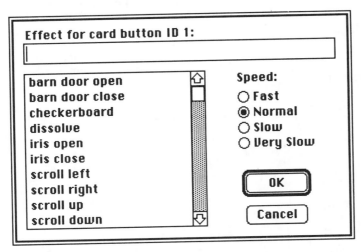

Figure 22.12   Shrink and Stretch Visual Effects and Effects Selection Box

Selection of any of these options makes visible four handles, one in each corner of the selected area. Clicking on one of these and dragging with the mouse button held down causes a dotted rectangle to indicate the new outline the transformed shape will take. Letting go of the mouse button implements the change. These effects are similar to options long available in specialized paint programs as described in Chapter 21. Conveniently, they are now built into HyperCard 2.0.

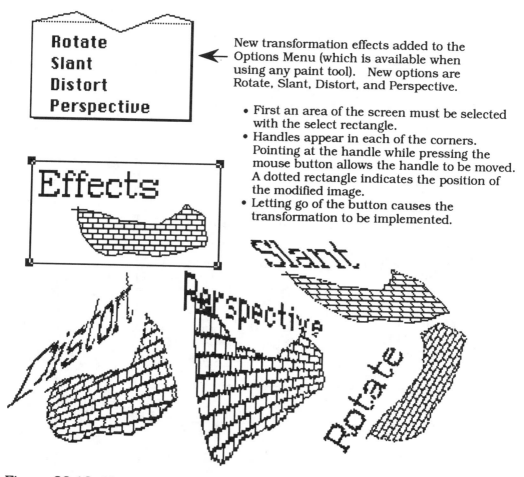

Rotate
Slant
Distort
Perspective

New transformation effects added to the Options Menu (which is available when using any paint tool). New options are Rotate, Slant, Distort, and Perspective.

- First an area of the screen must be selected with the select rectangle.
- Handles appear in each of the corners. Pointing at the handle while pressing the mouse button allows the handle to be moved. A dotted rectangle indicates the position of the modified image.
- Letting go of the button causes the transformation to be implemented.

Figure 22.13 New Paint Transformation Effects: Rotate, Slant, Distort, and Perspective

Limited Ability to Display Color and Grayscale Pictures via Picture XCMD

The lack of color was perceived as one of the most critical visual shortcomings in the HyperCard 1.x series. HyperCard 2.0 implements a special XCMD called *Picture* that allows the display of color and grayscale images in an external window. These pictures can be retrieved from the clipboard, from PICT or MacPaint files, or from PICT resources placed within stacks. Use of color and grayscale images requires at least two megabytes of memory and an appropriate video card and monitor.

This solution to color still has some limitations. Most significantly, HyperCard itself offers no way to edit or manipulate color or grayscale images — for example, none of the drawing or special effects tools can work with color. A user must prepare the images using external programs capable of color paint, draw, or image processing actions. HyperTalk real-time manipulations of images are not possible. Also, the images appear only in external windows. Thus, it is slightly more difficult to work with these images than classic HyperCard black-and-white images. Nonetheless, clever scripting and prior preparation of images can create stacks in which viewers will not be aware that the color images are not intrinsic. Here is the syntax to use the *Picture* XCMD to bring in images:

Picture sourceName, sourceType, windowStyle, windowVisible, windowBitDepth

sourceName: The name of the file or resource containing the picture. The name must be enclosed in quotes and be spelled exactly as it was originally stored. If the file is missing or misspelled, a standard Open File Dialog Box will open to request the information and will stop execution of a script.

sourceType: Identification of the type of image — resource, file, or clipboard. The default is file. Some readers might not be familiar with using pictures as resources. Pictures can be stored as external resources in a way similar to the way sounds (Chapter 17) and XCMDs and icons (Chapter 20) can be stored. They then become a hidden source that can be used in scripts. The reader must use the ResEdit or similar program (which can have dangerous effects if wrongly used) to convert PICT external file images into internal resources. This conversion is not absolutely necessary because the *picture* command will load images that exist as regular MacPaint or PICT files. The advantages of storing pictures as resources, however, are speed (a resource does not require a time-consuming disk access) and certitude about availability (installation as a resource guarantees its presence, whereas an external file might get separated from the stack that uses it). The disadvantage of using picture resources is their storage size. Color and grayscale images consume enormous amounts of memory space. One MacII-monitor-sized full-color image can require over 700 K of memory. Thus, one stack with several hidden color image resources could require many megabytes.

windowStyle: Type of window for the image to appear in — Plain, Document, Rect, Zoom, RoundRect, Dialog, Shadow, and Windoid. The default is Zoom. Plain, Rect, RoundRect, and Shadow all describe the visual nature of the window frame in accordance with standard Macintosh conventions. Zoom produces a window with the Zoom Box in the Title Bar and scroll bars on the right and left. Windoids are windows that will not go behind other windows. Dialog windows look like dialog boxes. Figure 22.14 illustrates some of the different types. Style also determines whether a window will disappear in response to a mouse click.

windowVisible: Visibility of the picture. Setting this parameter to *true* results in the picture being drawn on the screen immediately as the *picture* command is executed. *False* means the picture is stored in memory for later display. The advantage of non-visibility is the ability to set characteristics of the picture before its display — for example, its window size.

windowBitDepth. The amount of color or grayscale information displayed. In computer graphics, the number of binary bits of information allocated for each pixel determines the total number of different colors that can be simultaneously displayed. 1 bit allows 2 tones (black and white), 2 bits allows 4 colors or gray tones, 4 bits allow 16 tones, 8 bits allow 256 tones (the standard for Apple's color monitor) and 24 bits allow 16.7 million tones. This parameter allows one to display a picture with less color information than the original if one desires for visual effect, memory saving, or speed.

Here are some samples of the syntax:

picture "Flowers", file, plain, true, 8
picture "Tiger", clipboard, zoom, false, 2

HyperCard allows flexible script manipulation of the visual qualities of external picture windows by adjustment of the following properties.

the visible: Set the visible to true displays a hidden window; setting to *false* hides a visible window. The commands *hide* and *show window (name)* accomplish the same end. Optionally a location can be specified

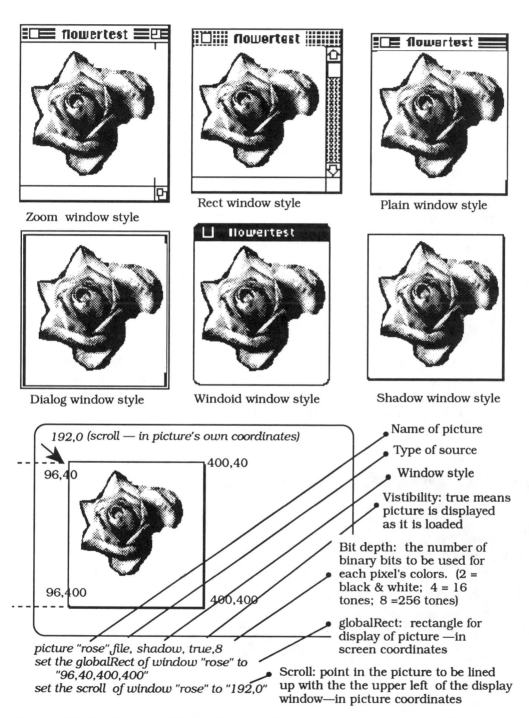

Zoom window style

Rect window style

Plain window style

Dialog window style

Windoid window style

Shadow window style

Figure 22.14 Picture XCMD Window Styles, Position, and Scroll

with the show command to locate the upper left corner — *show window "rose" at "100,100."* In scripts that set all of these properties, coordinates must be enclosed in quotes.

the loc: the coordinates of the uper left corner of the picture window relative to the top card window. *Set the loc of window "rose" to "100,100."*

the globalLoc: the coordinates of the upper left corner of the picture relative to the global coordinates of the display monitor. *Set the globalLoc of window "rose" to "320,100".*

the rect: the rectangle of the picture's window expressed in coordinates relative to the top card window. *Set the rect of window "flowers" to "50,50,320,300".*

the globalRect: the rectangle of the picture's window expressed in coordinates relative to the global coordinates of the display moniotr. *Set the globalRect of window "rose" to "100,50,250,250".*

the scroll: The point of the picture image (in its own coordinate system) to be lined up with the left top corner of the window. The default is "0,0". The *scroll* and *globalRect* work like the *scroll* and the *rect* property of card windows. The scroll controls the position of the underlying picture within the displayed window. For example, to line up the middle of a picture that was 100 pixels wide with the left side of the window, the command would be *set the scroll of window "rose" to "50,0".*

The picture XCMD brings in this external picture in a window that is placed within the rectangle of the card. The flower was prepared in an external program so it had a black background. The card also has a black background. Because of this design prethought, this color or grayscale picture seems to the viewer to be an intrinsic part of the HyperCard card.

picture "blackrose" , file, plain,true,8

Figure 22.15 Picture Command Used to Import Color or Grayscale Picture Carefully Designed to Integrate with Card Image

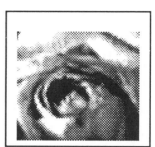

```
picture "rose",file,plain,true,8
set the scale of window "rose" to 1
set the scale of window "rose" to 2
```

Figure 22.16 Use of the scale property in Picture XCMD

the dithering: Indication of whether dithering should be applied to the image. *False* is the default. *True* means that dithering should be applied. The parameter takes effect only when Apple's 32-bit Quickdraw color drawing utility is installed. Dithering is the process of approximating colors or grayscales by dot patterns of available colors.

the scale: the magnification factor to be used in displaying a picture window. 0 is actual size. Negative numbers represent reductions; positive numbers represent magnifcations. Numbers represent powers of 2. For example, *set the scale of window "rose" to -3* would reduce it to one eighth actual size. *Set the scale of window "rose" to 1* would enlarge to twice size.

the zoom: indication of whether window is zoomed "in" or "out". *Set the zoom of window "rose" to "out"* displays the picture at its default rectangle size. *Set the zoom of window "rose" to "in"* displays it at whatever rectangle has been set by script.

The ability to control these aspects of color image window display allows stack designers to integrate imagery in a way that makes users unaware of its special nature. Also, these controls invite artistic exploration of color and grayscale in the HyperCard environment. Careful design of the original color pictures and the cards on which they are to be used are necessary for seamless integration.

Figure 22.15 illustrates a prototype to display color or grayscale pictures as part of the card. Note that the background of the external image is matched to the background of the area where the picture will be displayed.

```
on mouseUpInPicture theWindow,thePoint
    put "30,30,100,100" into head1
    put "300,0,370,80" into head 2
    if thePoint is within head1 then put "left
    gargoyle" into msg box
        if thePoint is within head2 then put "right
    gargoyle" into msg box
end mouseUpInPicture
```

HyperCard sends *a mouseUpinPicture* or *mouseDowninPicture* message whenever someone clicks the mouse button within external picture windows brought in by the *picture* command. It also sends parameters theWindow (to identify which window if several are showing) and thePoint (to identify the coordinates of the picture where the click occured. Position is expressed in the picture's own unmagnified coordinates). Thus a stack designer can make external pictures function just like regular stack pictures with areas defined to act like conventional HyperCard buttons.

In this example, the coordinates of the rectangles bounding each gargoyle's head are placed into variables head1 and head2. The script checks for thePoint parameter sent by HyperCard when a click occurs within the picture. It the click is inside the head of the left gargoyle's head, the script puts the words "left gargoyle" into the message box; it puts "right gargoyle" into the message box if a click is inside the right gargoyle's head If there were several external pictures showing, the script could identify the window in which the click occured.

Figure 22.17 Script to Use Picture XCMD's Ability to Pass on the Location of a Mouseclick

Figure 22.16 illustrates a script to create special animated effects with color or grayscale images via these messages sent to the Picture XCMD special window.

The Picture XCMD offers one additional extremely important feature: It can pass the location of the mouseclick. Thus, if an external image has been designed to have areas that resemble buttons, a stack designer can write scripts to respond to these clicks so that a viewer would get the impression of interacting with a standard HyperCard object. Figure 22.17 illustrates a script and image design necessary to achieve this effect.

Built-in Icon Editor

As explained in Chapter 5, visual icons can be associated with HyperCard buttons. Clicking on the Icon button on the Button Info Dialog

Box brings forth a window with a scrolling display of icons that can be linked to buttons. Many of these are quite useful in visually cuing the functions of buttons — for example, the house icon indicating a button that navigates to the home stack. Others in the display are visually interesting or delightfully whimsical and can be used for less utilitarian reasons. An attached icon follows its button around wherever the button may be moved. Since the location of a button is a property easily changed under script control, the button icon became a graphic sprite that could be animated. The script in Figure 16.10 demonstrates animation of an arrow by using button icons, and Figure 19.12 illustrates the animation of a button along the sine curve.

In HyperCard 1.x, the user was limited to the icons HyperCard provided, unless one obtained an external program that allowed easy creation and editing of icons. These icons then needed to be installed as external resources in the relevant stacks using a program such as ResMover.

In contrast, HyperCard 2.0 includes a built-in Icon Editor that facilitates custom design of icons for association with buttons. Access to the Icon Editor can be gained in three ways.

Icon Editor can be accessed via the Icon item on the Edit Menu.

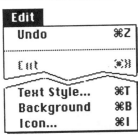

Each icon can be given a name or ID. The Icon Editor assigns automatic random rumbers that can be changed, if desired.

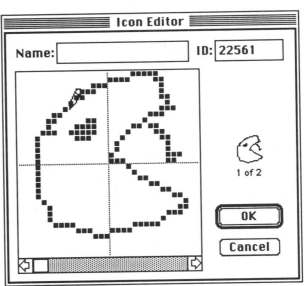

As the cursor moves into the blow-up grid, it changes into a pencil cursor. Pressing the mouse button while over a black dot erases it; pressing the button while over a white space registers a black pixel. The real-sized icon appears to the right of the blow-up.

Figure 22.18 The Icon Editor and Ways to Access It

- Choose the new Icon item from the Edit Menu (see Figure 22.18).
- Go to the scrolling display of button icons via the Icon button on the Button Info Dialog Box (accessed through the Objects Menu). At the bottom of this display is a new Edit button added to those that were already there.
- Select the button tool and click on a button with an icon associated. Choose the Icon item on the Edit Menu, or use the keyboard equivalent command-I.

The Icon Editor appears in a movable window that temporarily suspends HyperCard and installs its own special menus related to icon editing. Like the font editors described in Chapter 20, it presents an enlarged grid that allows pixel-by-pixel editing and shows a regular-sized image of the icon on the side. It also displays a box with the ID number and name of the icon. The editing display allows creation of a series of icons and presents a scroll bar on the bottom to allow movement among them.

As the cursor moves over the grid, it turns into a pencil. Clicking in a white grid box turns the pixel to black; clicking in a black grid box turns the pixel to white. The regular image on the side instantly reflects the change. Holding down the command key while the cursor is a pencil turns it into a selection tool. Dragging the corner with the mouse button down causes the familiar dotted selection rectangle to expand to cover the desired portion of the grid. If a selection has been made, actions chosen from the Edit and Special Menus (Figure 22.19) will then act only on the selected area.

When the Icon Editor is active, the File Menu allows creation of new icons, duplication of icons, closing the Icon Editor, and quitting HyperCard. The Edit Menu allows undoing of the last action, cutting of the icon and associated text, and copying, pasting, and clearing (erasing) of the icon (or of the section of the icon if a selection rectangle is active). Icons and icon parts that are cut or copied can be pasted back into the same stacks or different ones. A New Button item creates a new button with the edited icon already associated with it.

The Icon Menu offers these choices: New (creates a new icon, assigning a random ID in the range 128 to 32767; IDs in the range –32767 to 127 are reserved by Apple for other purposes); Duplicate (creates a duplicate of the current icon with the ID incremented by 1, if that number

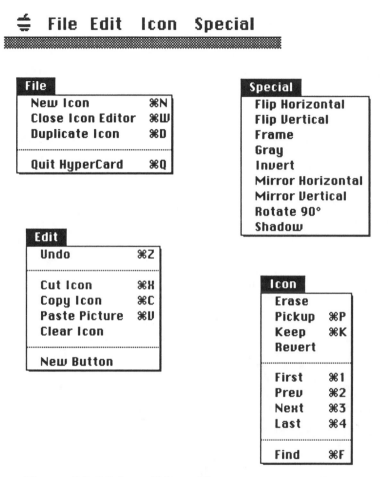

Figure 22.19 Icon Editor Menus

is not already taken); Erase; Keep (saves the current state of the icon); Revert (loads back in the last saved version of the icon); First (goes to the first icon in the stack and displays it); Prev (goes to the icon to the left of the current icon — based on a scheme that has all the icons in the stack lined up by ID number); Next (goes to the icon to the right of the current icon); and Last (goes to the last icon in the stack); Find (displays a Find Dialog Box that will search for an icon based on a typed-in ID number or name).

Pickup activates a 32-by-32-pixel box that can be dragged all over the screen (including areas outside the Icon Editor window). It dynamically places whatever image is underneath it into the Icon Editor grid as it is dragged. A mouseclick ends the process and the current 32-by-32-pixel area of the screen permanently replaces whatever was in the editing grid. In this way digitized or drawn images can be made into button icons (see Figure 22.20).

The Pickup item on the Icon Menu turns the cursor into a 32-pixel square to capture parts of the screen as an icon. Dragging the mouse with the button pressed dynamically puts part ofscreen into the Icon Editor. Releasing the button captures that area as an icon.

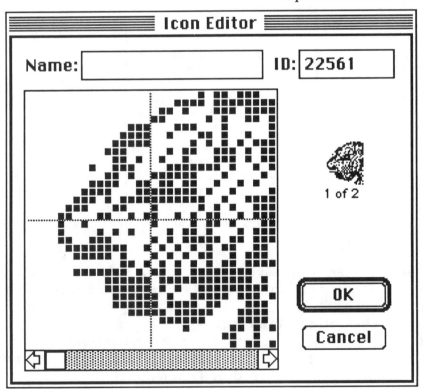

Figure 22.20 The Pickup Command Allows a Digitized Image to Become an Icon

The Special Menu allows transformations of the icon currently on the grid. If the selection rectangle has been activated, the transformations apply only to the selected area. Here are the choices: Flip Horizontal; Flip Vertical; Frame (draws a border around the icon); Gray (grays all black areas of the icon); Invert; Mirror Horizontal (mirrors the left half onto the right); Mirror Vertical (mirrors the top half onto the bottom); Rotate 90°; and Shadow (draws a shadow to the image along the right and bottom edges).

Icon images can be moved in the editing grid by pressing the option key. The pencil turns into a hand grabber cursor and the whole image can be shifted while the mouse button is held down — for example, to shift the image to the left or the right. If the image occupied the whole grid originally, part of the image will move outside the grid. When the mouse button is released, the image will get clipped, and the section outside the grid will be lost. Most of these menu choices and operations are accessible via keyboard shortcuts and power keys.

The Icon Editor invites stack designers to use animated button icons as visual elements. As Figure 16.10 demonstrated, scripts can be written that make the screen come alive with self-animated buttons cycling through carefully designed sets of icons.

Control over Inheritance Hierarchies

"Inheritance" is one of the main strengths of object-oriented programming. Once an object is given the capability to respond to messages, other derivative objects can inherit that capability. HyperCard 1.x implemented a variety of inheritance in the special status it gave the Home stack. In responding to messages or calls for external resources such as sounds, icons, pictures, or XCMDs in any stack, HyperCard would first search the stack where the script appeared. If it didn't find the handler or resource, it would then automatically search the Home stack. The Home stack was thus a part of the inheritance hierarchy. The Home stack could conveniently contain handlers and resources that were used by several descendant stacks; otherwise, these would need to be duplicated in every stack in which they were needed.

HyperCard 2.0 enhances this inheritance hierarchy. New HyperTalk commands allow the stack creator to dynamically add any stacks to the path that HyperCard will check (up to a limit of ten). Thus, one no longer needs to repeat the resources in every stack in which they are needed; similarly, the Home stack does not need to be loaded up with handlers and resources that are needed by only one particular group of stacks. One can customize archive stacks containing resources and handlers for particular sets of descendant stacks. For example, digitized sound resources, speech XCMDs, and MIDI XCMDs can be put into a stack arbitrarily named "Sound Archive". The stack designer can add this stack to the inheritance path for any stack that will need these resources. Other stacks that need particular picture resources can be stored in a stack called "Picture Archive". Figure 22.21 illustrates a sample organizational scheme.

One major danger in use of inheritance path stacks is the possibility that a stack can get separated from its essential resource stacks — for example, by someone copying just the target stack and not realizing that the resource stack is also needed. When the target stack is run, it will not understand the handlers and calls to resources that rely on the inheritance path.

The command to add a stack to the inheritance path is *start using stack "whatever"*. It will add the stack immediately above the current stack in the inheritance path. Another *start using* command will insert the next stack in between the current stack and the one previously added. The command *stop using stack "whatever"* will remove the stack from the inheritance path. The global property *the stacksInUse* returns a list of stacks in the inheritance path in the order in which they will be accessed.

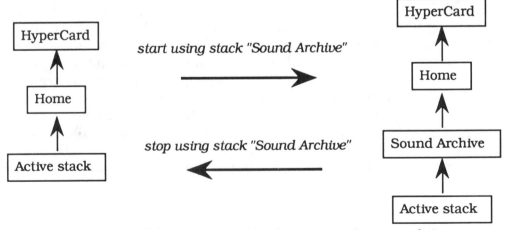

Figure 22.21 Use of Resource Stacks by Manipulations of the Inheritance Path

Improved Script Editing and Debugging Capabilities

HyperCard 1.x was primitive in its script editing and debugging capabilities. HyperCard 2.0 has added sophisticated capabilities that make script creation and troubleshooting much easier. Chapter 8 described a process of cyclic experimentation and refinement that is often a strength of work with computer programming and systems analysis. HyperCard 2.0 structurally encourages these systematic problem solving processes with these new features:

- Multiple scripts can be open at the same time in their own resizable windows, with cutting and pasting between them easily accomplished. Stack cards can be viewed at the same time.
- *Undo* works for editing and typing operations. Search and replace operations are available. A special script editing menu allows easy access to actions.
- Comments can be added to and taken away from script lines.
- Temporary and permanent checkpoints can be added to scripts for debugging. When a script is being run, a checkpoint causes the action to stop temporarily and activates the Script Editing window and the de-bugger. This controlled stopping is useful when one is trying to identify where problems occur in a script.
- A multifeatured Debugger includes line-by-line tracing of script actions; the Variable Watcher, which dynamically displays the changing value of variables; and the Message Watcher, which dynamically displays the messages being sent within HyperCard.

The Script Editor can be entered in several ways. As described in earlier chapters, the scripts for all objects can be accessed via the items on the Objects and Tools menus. Also, when HyperCard encounters a problem in running a script, it presents a dialog box explaining its problem with three buttons at the bottom — Cancel, Script, and Debug. Script opens a Script Editor window; Debug opens the Debugger. The Script Editor window can be resized and dragged anywhere on the screen. If the editor is not closed, a user can enter it at any time by clicking in one of the open script windows.

The editor can also be entered whenever a script encounters a checkpoint. Temporary checkpoints can be set anywhere in scripts via the Set Checkpoint item in the Script Menu in the Script Editor Menu Bar, or by clicking the mouse button while holding down the option key while in the Script Editor. These are toggles, so they can be removed in the same way.

A permanent checkpoint can be set by inserting the HyperTalk command *debug checkpoint* into a script. Temporary checkpoints are not saved to disk so they will not be present the next time the script is opened. Finally, the editor and Debugger can be entered by pressing command-option-period while a script is running.

Entering the editor causes HyperCard's standard menus to be replaced, pallette windows to be temporarily hidden, and message sending to be suspended. <u>Any changes made in the Script Editor must be explicitly saved to disk if they are to replace the original scripts</u>. This can happen via the Save Script item on the editor's File Menu or via the Close Dialog Box that appears when a Script Editor window is closed. Figure 22.22 illustrates the special menus that become available when in the Script Editor.

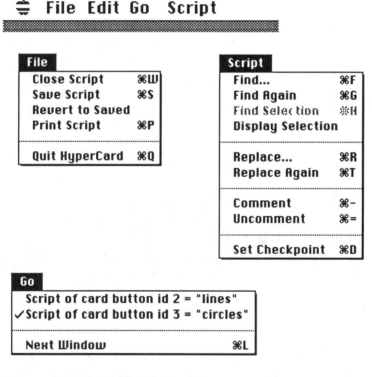

Figure 22.22 Script Editor Menus

The Debugger is a related, more specialized feature. It must be explicitly entered via checkpoints, selecting the Debug button on the Script Problem Dialog Box, or pressing the command-option-period key combination while a script is running. A special Debugger Menu is added to the Script Editor Menu Bar with these choices:

- Step: Steps to the next line of the script, puts a box around it, and executes it (skipping any calls to subroutines). If the card window is visible, the effects of the line can be watched.
- Step Into: Steps into all lines including subroutines that are called by the script.
- Trace: Follows the handler to completion, moving the box to surround each line as it is executed, without detailing any subroutines.
- Trace Into: Follows the handler to completion including subroutines.
- Go: Continues the script to its end.
- Clear Checkpoint: Clears the current checkpoint.
- Abort: Quits executing the current script.
- Variable Watcher: Toggles an external window that shows and allows editing of values of global and local variables used by the script. It can also be opened by the HyperTalk command *show Variable Watcher*, placed in either a script or the Message Box.
- Message Watcher: Toggles an external scrollable window that shows HyperTalk messages as they are sent. A checkbox titled "Hide unused messages" allows users to decide whether the window should show only messages that are intercepted by handlers or all messages — for example, without the Hide box checked, it will show the continuing stream of idle messages. Messages that are not intercepted are enclosed in parentheses. A "Hide idle" checkbox cuts all idle messages from the displays. The Scroll Bar allows viewing the approximately the last 150 lines of messages. The Message Watcher can also be toggled on or off by a HyperTalk command *show Message Watcher*.

Figure 22.23 illustrates the Debugger Menu, Variable Watcher window, and Message Watcher window. Typically, one would keep the problem script display open along with relevant script editor windows and debugging tools while investigating the problem.

Debugging can be an exciting process, almost like acting as a detective in a detective story. The Script Editor and Debugger add to the arsenal of detective tools that can be used. With these tools, HyperCard becomes more and more like the professional programming environments used to create commercial applications.

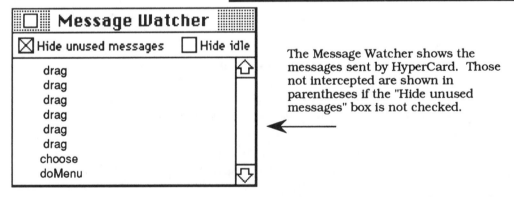

Debugger

Step	⌘S
Step Into	⌘I
Trace	
Trace Into	⌘T
Go	⌘G

Trace Delay...	
Set Checkpoint	⌘D
Abort	⌘A

✓ **Variable Watcher**
✓ **Message Watcher**

The Variable Watcher shows the changing values of variables used in the script. ⟶

Script of card but

```
on mouseUp
  choose line tool
  repeat with n = 1 to 6
   drag from n,0 to 90,90
  end repeat
  choose browse tool
  doMenu Select All
```

The Debugger highlights each line as it executes it by putting a rectangle around the script line. TheDebugger stops here because the script erroneously uses the command *doMenu Select All* , which is not available in browse tool mode.

Variable Watcher

mouseUp	
n	6

Message Watcher

☒ Hide unused messages	☐ Hide idle

```
    drag
    drag
    drag
    drag
    drag
    drag
    choose
    doMenu
```

The Message Watcher shows the messages sent by HyperCard. Those not intercepted are shown in parentheses if the "Hide unused messages" box is not checked.

⟵

Figure 22.23 The Debugger Menu, Variable Watcher Window, and Message Watcher Window

Improved Printing Features

HyperCard 2.0 enhances the printing options available in HyperCard 1.x, particularly in the areas of control of what can be printed, choice of formats, and support of output devices. The printing options are accessed through items in the File Menu or through HyperTalk commands.

The menu items include Print Field, Print Card, Print Stack, and Print Report. Print Card is the simplest choice and will print a full size representation of the currently displayed card. The remaining items bring up dialog boxes that require additional choices.

Print Field brings up a modal dialog box that allows the user to select which card or background field should be printed. The choice is made by selecting from a scrolling list of all fields on the card. A *use field width* checkbox allows one to preserve the formatting in the field.

Print Stack brings up a modal dialog box that allows the user to determine a format for printing the cards (see Figure 22.24). The user can change the size, margins, and spacing of the cards on the sheet by resizing a graphic representation of a schematic page layout. This layout is manipulated by dragging margin handles in the corners. A sizing graphic provides details about the dimensions in units chosen by the user (centimeters, millimeters, inches, or points). Check boxes allow a choice of order of card printing (priority to columns or rows) and printing quality. Headers containing date, time, name of stack, and other information can be placed on each sheet.

Print Report brings up a series of dialog boxes that permit the detailed laying out of a report template. The Print Report Dialog Box allows placement and sizing of multiple entries on a page using layout controls like those available in the Print Stack Dialog Box. The pattern for each entry can be further edited via the Report Items choice in the Edit Menu, which brings up an Edit Report Items Dialog Box. This dialog box allows positioning and sizing of schematic rectangles into which field information will be placed. A further Item Information Dialog Box allows specific assignment of particular fields to each schematic position and decisions about the font, size, style, line height, and alignment of the text in that field.

A name can be assigned to the total layout via the Report Name item on the Edit Menu. Each stack can contain as many templates as desired.

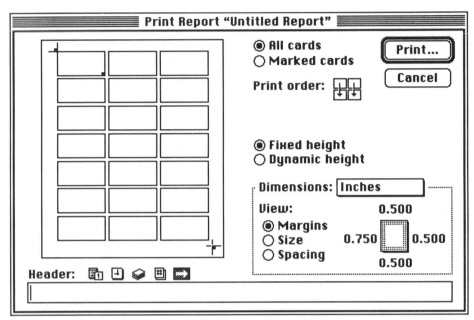

Print Report and Print Stack bring up dialog
boxes that allow the setting of printing format.

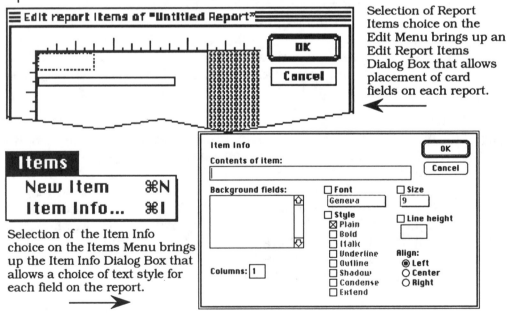

Selection of Report
Items choice on the
Edit Menu brings up an
Edit Report Items
Dialog Box that allows
placement of card
fields on each report.

Selection of the Item Info
choice on the Items Menu brings
up the Item Info Dialog Box that
allows a choice of text style for
each field on the report.

Figure 22.24 Printing Dialog Boxes

HyperTalk commands allow direct access to printing. Scripts can print any HyperCard container or expression, any part of a card, and reports using templates that have already been designed. Here are some examples of valid print commands:

- *print background field 2*
- *print storelist (a variable container)*
- *print line 2 to 5 of card field 4*
- *print card from 100,100 to 400,300 (will print just the specified part)*

- *on printBusiness* (an arbitrarily named message handler)
        open report printing with template "orderform"
                (assumes that this template has been previously designed)
        print all cards
        close printing
    end printBusiness

Ongoing Stack Activity with Multifinder

Multifinder allows several Macintosh programs to be open simultaneously in separate windows. With most applications, the program not in the open window stops execution. HyperCard 2.0 is capable of continuing to execute scripts even when it is not the open window. Thus, HyperCard can continue to calculate, execute searches, sort, print, display, or create graphic displays while it is in the background. If it requires some action from the user, it beeps and puts a diamond by its name in the Apple Menu.

Miscellaneous Features: Title Bar Control, Searching and Marking, Security, Scripts to Avoid Modal Dialog Boxes, More Flexible Use of Backgrounds

HyperCard 2.0 has introduced many features in addition to those described so far. This section briefly introduces some of these other enhancements.

Title Bar Control. In HyperCard 1.x all stacks had a Title Bar attached to the Display window. HyperCard 2.0 allows control over appearance of the Title Bar. *Hide titlebar* will make it disappear; *show titlebar* makes it visible.

<u>Efficient Searching and Marking</u>. HyperCard was seen by many as an easy-to-use database optimized for the storage and retrieval of information. The *find* command was used to search for text. In HyperCard 1.x it would search everywhere, even in places where it would be better avoided for reasons of speed or security. HyperCard 2.0 creates a new property for cards, backgrounds, and fields called *the dontSearch*. If *the dontSearch* of an object is set, HyperCard will not search for text in that object. This property can be set with the command *set the dontSearch to true* (or *false*). *True* indicates that the *find* command should not search the object. It can also be set via the dialog boxes that are associated with items on the Objects Menu.

Also, it is sometimes desirable to mark some cards for special action. HyperCard 2.0 introduces a new property called *the marked* and new commands *mark* and *unmark*. Cards can have this property set via the Card Info item on the Objects Menu or via HyperTalk commands — for example, *set the marked of card 3 to true* or *mark cards where card field 1 is not equal to "male"*. The *print* and *show* commands can make efficient use of this property. *Show marked cards* will quickly display all cards that have been marked. Similarly, *print marked cards* will print only marked cards. The Print Stack and Print Report dialog boxes also allow for selection of only marked cards as part of their format controls.

<u>Improved Security</u>. HyperCard's highly interactive philosophy invites users to investigate the structure of stacks. Sometimes stack designers wish to restrict that access in order to protect their work and its functioning. HyperCard 1.x provided the Protect Stack item on the File Menu, the *ask password* command, and setting *the userLevel* methods of protecting stacks from casual browsers. HyperCard 2.0 provides additional security measures.

A new stack property called *the cantPeek* prevents users from looking at scripts by use of the command-option key shortcut. Setting *the cantPeek* to *true* disables this key combination. Another stack property named *the cantAbort* prevents users from stopping a stack with the command-period key combination. If its value is *true*, no one can stop the stack's execution. This property should be used with care because the key combination is often very useful for stopping runaway scripts.

Scripts to Avoid Modal Dialog Boxes. Many HyperCard menu actions cannot be completed fully in scripts because they usually result in dialog boxes that stop to demand direct user input. For example, execution of a *doMenu Save Stack* would result in the presentation of the standard File Location Dialog Box. A script could not make the choices, and thus, the script would stop cold. HyperCard 2.0 has enabled some of these menu actions to be completed entirely from scripts without dialog boxes appearing.

- Creating stacks: *create stack "whatever" (with background "backname")* will create a new stack and give it the name "whatever." The card size will be the size of the current stack. If a background is indicated, the new stack will have that background; otherwise, it will be created with a plain empty background.
- Saving stacks: *save "whatever" as "newname"* will save a copy of the indicated stack under the new name.
- Opening a stack in a new window: *go (to) "whatever" in new window* will open the specified stack in a new window.
- Importing paint pictures: *import paint from file "whatever"* will load a MacPaint format picture onto the current card, clipping the picture at the edges of the card.
- Exporting paint picutres: *export paint to file "whatever"* will create a new MacPaint format file containing the present card picture.
- Delete stack, convert stack, cut field, and clear field: *doMenu (action) without dialog* will skip the customary dialog box and complete the indicated action.

Keeping Up with Progress

The updated version of HyperCard adds greatly to its capabilities. Many of the new features are especially intriguing for people working with interactive multimedia. This chapter has focused on some of the capabilities available in HyperCard 2.0. Readers are urged, however, to consider their use carefully. While they remove many of the constraints on the possible appearance and behavior of stacks, they also remove the design consistency that was a consequence of some of these constraints. Also, they raise the issue of the seductiveness of innovation.

Rapid change has been one of the essential ingredients of the microcomputer revolution. Even before new hardware or software reaches the market, developers are feverishly working on the next generations of descendants, which add superior features and remedy lacks in the previous versions.   Optimists point to this culture of progress as one of the marvels of this technology. Capabilities increase as prices go down. One popular comparison notes that if automobile technology had advanced in the same way as computer technology, we would now have small cars that cost $10, went 1000 miles on a gallon of gas, and were capable of towing the ocean liner *Queen Mary*. Many companies try to soften the blow of new developments by offering inexpensive upgrades and maintaining downward compatibility so that the old software still runs on the newest machines.

Cynics suggest that this so-called progress is just one more manifestation of the cycles of planned obsolescence invented by marketeers to fuel capitalist consumption. The new features often appeal not to genuine need, but rather to the fanned fires of artificially induced desire. For example, some analysts estimate that the first generation of word processors still meets the needs of 80% of all users.

Artists and designers who would work with these new technologies find themselves uneasily situated amid the whirlwinds of change. One pressure pushes artists to act as interpreters of culture by working at the very edge of technological innovation. Another presses them to carefully explore and express the core possibilities of the technologies, which are clearly present in even the first generations of hardware and software. Working within constraints has often been a source of poetic power for artists. Some commentators lament that computer art is not being allowed to mature because everyone is constantly being seduced by the next set of capabilities. For example, we may never experience the fullness of artistic exploration of black-and-white computer graphics because that technology was so quickly superseded by 16-color, then 16-million-color, and then full-motion digital video.

Most artists face practical problems in keeping at the forefront of technology because the new hardware and software tend to be expensive and harder to learn because they are not yet fully documented. The truly newest developments — the ones that edge-of-technology artists ought to be exploring — are even more inaccessible in research laboratories. By contrast, the "obsolescent" versions of this rapidly changing technology are cheap, already abandoned to the junk heaps and surplus houses.

This book tries to support readers to work in both ways. It highlights the concrete possibilities of the latest technologies and offers alerts about developments still in the laboratories. At the same time, it prepares readers with core skills and perspectives useful for work with interactive multimedia at any level of technological development. Because computer multimedia is currently a focus for major computer companies, it is inevitable that new capabilities will continue to appear in the next years.

Chapter 23
New Opportunities and Challenges for the Arts

The preceding chapters have illustrated some of HyperCard's value to artists and designers. It is a flexible, easy-to-learn application optimized for work with text, image, and sound. Its programming language, Hyper-Talk, is accessible even to the computer novice. HyperCard invites artists to create interesting graphic and sound events. The chapters have shown part of what HyperCard can do. They have also shown some of what it cannot do.

HyperCard is an early marker on a road leading to new territories. The HyperCard-like environments of the future will open up provocative new possibilities for the arts and the culture. They will enable artists to create events that do not resemble the visual and sound arts of the past. Design in these innovative contexts will require an interdisciplinary merger of perspectives from the arts, computer science and the social sciences.

Innovations Highlighted by HyperCard

HyperCard exemplifies several key innovations in the way people will work with computers. These innovations will make computer work more convivial for artists. They will also place a new premium on artistic thinking for anyone involved in this work.

Programming as an Everyday Activity. Computer programming is sometimes cloaked in the mystification of an esoteric, priestly craft. Artists especially may consider themselves as outsiders to this technological activity. The conceptual core of programming is not as alien to everyday life as it is often portrayed. Programming-like activities are typical in the arts and many other fields outside of computers. Programming is the attempt to build structures that sequence actions in time and causality — for example, the steps necessary to bake a cake, assemble a bicycle, or organize the production of a play.   The process of analyzing the steps and giving instructions is called programming. Computers are merely machines that are complex enough to be endowed with interesting behavioral tendencies that simulate human time and cause-and-effect-based actions.

In the past, programming has required arcane vocabulary and syntax. HyperCard moves toward a more English-like command structure. It also allows some programming to be done via intuitive visual methods. It

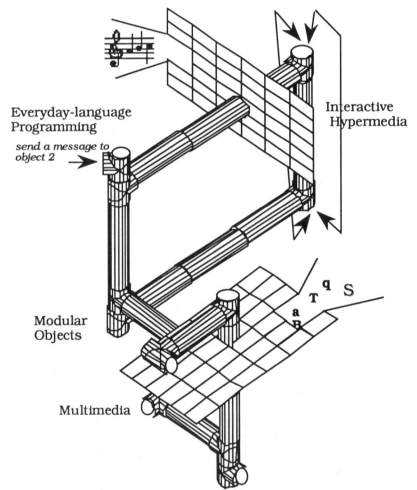

Everyday-language
Programming

send a message to
object 2 →

Interactive
Hypermedia

Modular
Objects

Multimedia

*Figure 23.1   Core Innovations of HyperCard: Everyday-Language
Programming, Modular Objects, Multimedia,
and Interactivity*

invites people without programming experience to structure the computer's activities. Future computer environments are likely to move even more in this direction of putting complex control in the hands of technically unsophisticated users.

Certainly, analysis of the steps necessary to accomplish goals and to design a workable chain of events is not always easy. But that difficulty is not limited to computer work. The method for instructing the machines is likely to continue to grow more intuitive. Artists will then have the ability to control the full range of computer capabilities without having to master too much technological information. The challenge will be creating events that use these new capabilities to the fullest.

<u>Modularity, Extensibility and Ease of Object-oriented Programming</u>. In the past, most computer languages could be described as procedural. That is, programs were conceived as interdependent sequences of instructions that made extensive use of one another. Any change in one part often required changes in other parts. The program could best be thought of as a story with a beginning, a middle, and an end.

HyperCard moves toward a different model of programming that is called object-oriented. Each part of the program can be designed as a self-sufficient unit — for example, the buttons, fields, cards, and stacks in HyperCard. These units communicate with one another by sending messages. New objects can be created that inherit the capabilities of the original parent objects and are then modified for new behaviors. This modular approach makes it very easy to add and share capabilities between programs. Each person's work and creativity are magnified because the program objects they create can be used in new settings.

Artists may find this approach quite engaging. They will be comfortable with the fact that environments such as HyperCard use visual metaphors for the functional objects such that the screen itself becomes a conceptual map of the action potentials of the program. Similarly, they will appreciate the dramatic metaphor of the computer program as a group of entities with intelligence and behavioral predispositions. Creation of object-oriented programs may seem a more natural activity than creation of programs written in procedure-oriented languages.

Multimedia. Humans are blessed with several channels of sensory perception and intelligence. There is a growing realization that different kinds of information can be conveyed by image and sound that are not easily communicated by text, and consequently there is a push to expand everyday communication media.

HyperCard-like environments reward thinking in multiple media. Image and sound become as easy to manipulate as text. Presentations that lack any of these sensual channels may one day seem crippled. New challenges, however, await anyone trying to work with these multiple media. Design will expand beyond two-dimensional layout to encompass the time dimensions of moving image and sound. Those developing computer-based multimedia works will need to learn production skills and aesthetic sensibilities that used to be reserved for crafts such as film editing and music composition. Artists will offer special strengths of working with the sensual channels that have been their historical forte. Individuals and small groups will be able to conceptualize and produce multimedia works that would have required entire production companies in the past.

Interactive Hypermedia. Contemporary computer technology goes further than just allowing the simultaneous presentation of several kinds of traditional media. Hypermedia opens up the possibility of interactive works that can adapt to the idiosyncratic inquiry paths of each user. HyperCard-like environments can read the changing desires and associations of particular viewers. They can respond appropriately in ways that support and invite further creative inquiry.

Design of these environments will pose unprecedented challenges. Hypermedia designers will need to consider the psychology of their audiences as an aesthetic element. Works will need to be sufficiently robust that they make sense and maintain their artistic integrity regardless of the particular inquiry paths different viewers follow. Indeed, design for nonlinear inquiry will itself become an aesthetic focus.

Future Artistic Inquiry

To many people, computer art is synonymous with computer graphics and electronic music. While these forms do explore some of the new sensual opportunities made available by contemporary computer tools, they do not probe deep enough.

Computers and the related technology they spawn are radically transforming the world — both in changing the machines we use and in transforming our concepts of ourselves, the human community, and nonhuman environment. Our culture desperately needs artists to help it reflect on the implications of these changes and to imagine new possibilities beyond those promoted by short-term commercial interests. Artists can serve these functions only if they deeply engage the technologies in nonsuperficial ways and free themselves from working only in art-historically validated contexts. I have written extensively on the problems and opportunities of technological art. Interested readers can consult the following works:

- *The Aesthetics of Human–Computer Contacts: The Challenge of Artificial Intelligence and Simulation Technologies for the Arts* (in press)
- "Research and Development as a Source of Ideas and Inspiration for Artists" (to be published, *Leonardo*)
- "Interactive Art and Cultural Change," *Leonardo* 23: 2 (Spring 1990)
- "Artists as Explorers on the Cultural Frontier" *Academic Computing.* 1:2 (Autumn 1987)
- "Environment-sensing Artworks and Interactive Events: Exploring Implications of Microcomputer Developments" *Leonardo* 16: 4 (Autumn 1983)

HyperCard-like environments make it easier for artists to engage these new technological challenges and opportunities. Let us look at some of the areas of change that demand artistic attention.

Hypermedia and the Structure of Information. Increasing computer abilities to handle image and sound information and modular, object-oriented computer languages have stimulated exciting new ways to think about methods for structuring information resources. Traditional paths of accessing resources are often conceptualized as linear (for example, reading a book or viewing a videotape) or indexed (for example, reading entries in an encyclopedia). Hypermedia theory, however, emphasizes the network and weblike nature of creative thought — ideas give birth to associated ideas, which give rise to families of other ideas in an idiosyncratic way for each mind. Ideas are stimulated not only by text but also by image and sound.

The new generations of computers and optical storage technology potentially allow computers to facilitate and enhance these associationistic ways of thought. For example, viewers looking at a display of text and image can freely select any part of the display into which they want to inquire. The system reads their interest, indicated by a mouseclick on contemporary systems, and speedily draws on its vast resources, which include video, sound, static graphics, and text, to display relevant material, which itself is a gateway to further associations.

Art-related Issues. Though the vision is exhilarating, there are important unresolved issues relevant to the arts: What is the best way to design complex computer displays of simultaneous video, image, sound, and text so that they are provocative, clear, and informational? What conceptual structures and related visual metaphors can be developed to aid navigation through these comprehensive information spaces? What new art forms, which focus specifically on the variety of paths through materials or the structure of information, are made possible by hypermedia?

Networks, Groupware, and Information Access. The development of communications networks promises to extend our informational reach. Already, in organizations of all kinds, personal computers are being linked together in local area networks such that electronic mail and resource sharing are becoming commonplace. Through developments in video, phone, and data transmission technologies (for example, direct-broadcast satellites, cellular telephony, and ISDN (Integrated Digital Signal Networks), people may soon be able to interactively communicate image, sound, and text almost instantaneously anywhere in the world. The phone, mail, and television channels may begin to coalesce.

These changes will mean that communication across the world may become as easy as communication across the city. People will have instant access to archives, information resources, and one another. Already network software eradicates awareness of distance — for example, in some systems, the computer of a coworker on the other side of the world appears as an icon on the screen just like the physically connected local hard disk. New kinds of software called "groupware" facilitate simultaneous work by many network-connected individuals on common text or image projects.

Designers of future libraries note that almost every book published, as well as other kinds of information such as films and sound recordings will be available to anyone who is connected.

Art Issues. Artists will become important resources as image and sound communication begin to become as important as text communication — especially in international situations in which language could be a barrier. Innovative design sensibilities will be required to make computer–mediated, multiperson, multimedia communications clear and productive. New art distribution possibilities may begin to rival the traditional galleries, museums, movie shows, and concert halls. Artists will be able to distribute works directly to viewers' homes. Even more significant, artists may create new forms based on group interactive concepts in which international audiences work cocreatively with each other to create sound and image events in real time.

Simulation, Virtual Worlds, and Artificial Realities. Increasingly, our world is mediated by computer displays. Some of the displays represent realities that cannot be experienced directly: They may be too small, too large, too dispersed, too abstract or inaccessible to normal senses — for example, component layouts in microchips, the physiology of a functioning brain, patterns of rain forest destruction, and stockbroker displays of futures in crops that may or may not exist. Some represent hypothetical realities and designs — for example, animated computer-aided design of desired new cities and products or extrapolations of social trends. The new photo-realistic, high-resolution displays and interactive capabilities increase the verisimilitude of all these simulations.

Art Issues. These abilities to visualize and concretize abstract or hypothetical realties is an exciting enhancement of human capabilities. But maybe we grow to trust these displays too much, and the line between reality and abstraction can become dangerously dim. Because the arts have historically concentrated on the creation of fictional worlds and characters, they might be a powerful arena for the culture to use to reflect on these new possibilities. What are the limits of our abilities to simulate artificial worlds? Can artists use the new simulation abilities to create fictional worlds that enrich the human community? Can artists find ways to reflexively use these new capabilities to reflect on the balance of enhancement and danger unleashed by this technology?

Remote Sensing, Robotics, and Telepresence. In some ways, the physical side of the computer revolution is still relatively undeveloped. Information primarily goes into computers via keyboards and mice and comes out via CRT displays and printers. Small computers are unable to control useful physical work in the everyday world of most people. Personal home robots have developed nowhere as quickly in sophistication, power, or economy as home computers have. The sensual circumscription of these input/output modes and physical actuators may subtly distance people from important potentials of computer technology. For example, sensor technology exists to read a wide range of physical and biological phenomena, such as infrared energy, proximity, gesture, touch, and body chemistry that could create new contexts in which computers might be useful. Similarly, the high-end robotic technology that enables the handling of delicate physical maneuvers in research and industrial settings could be adapted for personal worlds.

Art Issues. The arts have historically focused on the sensual qualities of objects. Again, they seem like an ideal arena for exploring the linkage of computer technology with sensually diverse methods of inputting and outputting information. What modes can be developed in which control of computer-mediated intelligence is exercised through physical action such as motion and gesture? What modes can be developed where the computer controls movement in the world, such as robotic devices? What new kinds of telepresence experiences await us? How can the arts use this technology to help humans to reflect on their dual nature as bodies and intelligences?

Artificial Intelligence. Enabling a computer to simulate the cognitive and perceptual skills of humans is seen by some people as the ultimate test for computer technology. Scientists have made significant accomplishments in fields such as voice and scene recognition, language understanding, planning, and problem solving. Expert systems duplicate the reasoning of experts in many fields. Researchers are trying to extend these skills into quintessentially human fields such as music composition and art image production. Developers promise that everyday appliances and tools will soon be endowed with computer-mediated intellectual skills so that they can be truly intelligent assistants and companions. Although debate rages about the ultimate boundaries of this research, we can be sure that further accomplishments and applications will be forthcoming.

Art Issues. Many of the decisions necessary in designing artificial intelligence (AI) programs cannot be based solely on technical rationales. Perception, problem solving, and action planning all require judgments about what prerequisite information is required and what information should be considered most salient. Belief and predisposition significantly influence the exercise of everyday intelligence. These concerns become especially important as developers try to move artificial intelligence work out of the laboratories. AI programs and devices cannot succeed in the everyday world without a sophistication of sensibility beyond traditional logic. Artists, novelists, and dramatists become important resources in shaping these next generations of AI programs.

The Integration of Technological Genius With Artistic Vision

Although HyperCard is primitive in many ways, it is a marvelous tool. Most significant, it is an early exemplar of a type of tool that promises to evolve quickly. It invites artists and designers to incorporate time and interactivity as artistic focuses. It provides an entry into work on the cultural and technological issues just described. Perhaps most important, it points toward a future in which art and design will be an intrinsic part of the work with computers to shape everyday life. Readers are urged to become involved with this research so that artistic vision and sensibility become an intrinsic part of future technological research.

Appendix Summary

Messages understood by Stacks, Backgrounds, Cards, Buttons, Fields

close (except buttons), commandKeyDown (V2), delete, keyDown (V2), mouseDown, mouseEnter, mouseLeave, mouseStillDown, mouseUp, mouseWithin, New, open (except buttons)

Messages understood by Stacks, Backgrounds, Cards

arrowKey, doMenu, enterKey, help, idle, quit, returnKey, resume, startup, suspend, tabKey

System Properties

blindTyping, cursor, dragSpeed, editBackground, language, lockMessages, lockRecent, lockScreen, longWindowTitles(V2), Message Watcher(V2), numberFormat, powerKeys, printTextFont, printTextStyle(V2), printTextSize(V2), printTextAlign(V2), printTextHeight(V2), printTextMargins(V2), scriptTextStyle(V2), scriptTextFont(V2), scriptTextSize(V2), stacksInUse(V2), traceDelay(V2), userLevel, userModify, Variable Watcher(V2)

Stack Properties

cantAbort(V2), cantDelete, cantModify, cantPeek(V2), freeSize, long name, name, script, short name, size

Card Properties

cantDelete, dontSearch(V2), id, long name, marked(V2) name, number, rectangle(V2), script, short name, showPict

Window Properties

bottom, botRight, height, left, loc, rect, right, scroll(V2), top, topLeft, visible, width

Menu and Menu Item Properties(V2)

checkMark, cmdChar, enabled, markChar, menuMsg, name, textStyle,

Background Properties

cantDelete, dontSearch(V2), id, long name, name, script short name, showPict

Button Properties

autoHilite, bottom, botRight, id, height, hilite, icon, left, loc, long name, name number, rect, right, script, short name, showName, style, textAlign, textFont, textHeight, textSize, textStyle, top, topLeft, visible, width

Field Properties

autoTab, bottom, botRight, dontSearch(V2), dontWrap(V2), fixedLineHeight(V2), id, height, left, loc, lockText, long name, name number, rect, right, script, scroll, sharedText(V2), short name, showLines, style, textAlign, textFont, textHeight, textSize, textStyle, top, topLeft, visible, wideMargins, width

* V2 indicates item available only in Version 2 of HyperCard

APPENDIX

ANNOTATED GUIDE AND INDEX TO HYPERCARD FEATURES, FUNCTIONS, MESSAGES, AND PROPERTIES — Appendix Summary

Text Related Functions

clickChunk(V2), clickLine(V2), clickText(V2), foundChunk, foundField, foundLine, foundText, length, number of, offset, selectedChunk, selectedField, selectedLine, selectedText

Mouse and Keyboard Related Functions

clickH, clickLoc, clickV, commandKey, mouse, mouseClick, mouseH, mouseLoc, mouseV, optionKey, shiftKey

Date andTime Related Functions

abbrev date, date, long date, long time, seconds, secs, ticks, time

Math Functions

abs, annuity, atan, average, compound, cos, exp, exp1, exp2, ln, ln1, max, min, round, sin sqrt, tan, trunc

Miscellaneous Functions

charToNum, diskSpace, heapSpace, long version, menus(V2), number of, numToChar, param, paramcount, params, random of, result, screenRect, sound, stackSpace, target, value, version, windows(V2)

Math Commands

add, divide, multiply, subtract

Visual Effects

barn door (open,close); checkerboard; dissolve; iris (open,close); scroll (up, down, right, left); stretch to(V2) (top, bottom, center); shrink from(V2) (top, bottom, center); venetian blinds; wipe (up, down, right, left); zoom (open, close, in, out)

Commands and Script Words

answer, ask, ask password, choose, click, close file, close printing, convert, create(V2), debug checkpoint(V2), delete, dial, disable(V2), do, doMenu, edit script, enable(V2), exit, exit to HyperCard, find, get, global, go, help, if-then-else, mark(V2), next repeat, open, open file, open printing, open report printing(V2), pass, pop card, print, push, put, read repeat, reset menubar(V2), return, select, send, set, sort, start Using(V2), stop Using(V2),, type, unmark(V2) wait, write

Image Control Commands

drag, export paint(V2), import paint(V2), lock screen, picture(V2), reset paint, show, unlock screen, unmark(V2), visual

Sound Function and Commands

beep, play, the sound

Paint Properties

brush, centered, filled, grid, lineSize, multiple, multiSpace, pattern, plySides, textAlign, textFont, textHeight, textSize, textStyle

Tool Choices

browse, button, field, brush, bucket, curve, eraser, lasso, line, oval, pencil, polygon, rect, reg polygon, round rect, select, spray, text

399

the abbreviated date (249)
(function)
> type the abbreviated date
>> response: *Tues, Nov 7, 1989*

Provides the current date in the indicated format. Can be shortened to *abbrev* or *abbr*.
(See: the date, the long date, convert)

abs
(math function)
> put abs (-344) into q

Calculates the absolute value (that is the value without the minus sign)

add
(command)
> add 7 to q
> add 7 to card field 3

Adds the specified nɪ mber to the expression and replaces the expression with the result.

annuity(rate, # payments)
(math function)
> put annuity (.01,360) into q
> put 100000/q into message box

Calculates the value of one annuity unit. Needs the parameters of the percentage rate and total number of payments. Divide total due by this number to get the payment amount. Example shows $100,000 12% loan paid monthly (1% a month) over a 30-year-period (30 * 12 = 360 total payments).

answer (187)
(command)
> answer "should we stop" with "ok"
> [or "cancel"]

Creates a dialog box with the named buttons. A user click on a button puts its name into the special variable *it*. One button is required; more are optional. Buttons are user-namable.

answer file
(command)
> answer file "pick a picture"

Presents the standard File Locater Dialog Box with the prompt. The user can then choose a file. An option allows for displaying only certain kinds of files.

 (xxx) — Numbers indicate page numbers where items are introduced.

Symbols indicate features available only in HyperCard 2.0

on arrowKey [which]
(message — card, bkgnd, stack)
    on arrowKey left
        type "not allowed"
    end arrowKey

HyperCard sends an *arrowKey* message whenever anyone pushes one of the arrow keys. HyperCard also sends a parameter (left, right, up, down) to specify which arrow key.

ask   (188)
(command)
    ask "what is your name" [with "George"]

Creates a dialog box with the question at top, text field in the middle, and OK and Cancel buttons at bottom. Text field appears with reply highlighted. Reply is optional. Pressing the return key or clicking OK button puts reply into special variable *it*. *Ask file* presents a standard File Location Box.

ask password
(command)
    ask password "what is your secret word?"

Returns an encrypted version of whatever is typed into the special variable *it*. The script can check whether this encrypted word matches a stored template to determine if the user may proceed.

atan
(math function)
    put atan(1) into q

Returns the arctangent of the angle specified in radians measurement.

the autoHilite   (43)
(property — button)
    set the autoHilite of card button 1 to true
    put the autoHilite of bkgd button 3 into var

True causes a button to invert automatically for a short period whenever anyone clicks a mouse button on it. *False* turns off this feature.

autotab
(property — field)
    set autotab to true

True means that return key presses by user when entering text into fields moves the insertion point to the next highest numbered field.

average
(math function)
    put the average (5,8,7,8) into q

Returns the average of a list specified between parentheses with commas separating items.

beep   (25)
(command)
    beep [5]

Makes the standard beep sound. An optional parameter can specify the number of times to beep.

the blindTyping
(system property)
    set the blindTyping to true
    put the blindTyping into message box

If *blindTyping* is set to *true*, text can be typed into the Message Box even when the box is not showing.

bottom
(property — window, field, button)
    set bottom of card button to 300
    set bottom of tool window to 200
    put bottom of card button 2 into var

The vertical coordinate of the bottom of an object.

bottomRight
(property — window, field, button)
> set bottomRight of card button to 200,100
> set bottomRight of tool window to 200,300
> put botRight of card button 2 into var

The horizontal and vertical coordinates of the bottom right of an object. *Bottom* can be abbreviated *bot.*

the brush (88)
(property — painting)
> set the brush to 30
> put the brush into var

Controls the size and pattern of the brush tool (values: 1–32).

the cantAbort (384)
(property — stack)
> set the cantAbort of stack "dog" to true

True makes it impossible to stop script execution with command-period key combination.

the cantDelete
(property — stack, bckgnd, card)
> set the cantDelete to true
> put the cantDelete into var

True makes an object undeletable.

the cantModify
(property — stack)
> set cantModify of this stack to true

True makes it impossible for a user to make any changes to a stack. The property is activated when a stack is locked. The user can make temporary changes, such as typing in fields, but they will be discarded when the stack is exited.

the cantPeek (384)
(property — stack)
> set the cantPeek of this stack to true

True makes it impossible to look at scripts by using the command-option key combination.

the centered (86)
(property — painting)
> set the centered to true
> put the centered into var

True causes all shapes and lines to be drawn from center to edge instead of from corner to corner. It is the same as toggling the Draw Centered paint feature. *False* turns the feature off.

the charToNum
(function)
> type the charToNum of A
> > response: *65*

Returns the number equivalent to the specified character.
(See: numToChar)

the checkMark (357)
(property — menu)
> set the checkMark of menuItem 1 of menu "File" to true

Displays a checkmark next to a menu item.
(See: menu)

choose (82)
(command)
> choose browse tool
> choose brush tool

Changes HyperCard to work in one of its tool modes. Equivalent to clicking one of the icons in the Tools Menu. A tool name must be specified. Options include browse, button, field, or one of the 12 painting tools.
(See: painting tools)

click at (82)
(command)
    click at 300,220
    click at 30,44 [with optionKey]

Equivalent to clicking the mouse pointer at a location on the screen. Use of the optional *with* phrase can simulate clicking while holding down one of the enhancement keys.

 the clickChuck (362)
the clickLine
the clickText
(function)
    `yellow pink green`
    type the clickText [mouse pointing at pink]
    type the clickChunk
        response: *pink*
                char 8 to char 11 of card field 1

Clicking the mouse while pointing at text in a locked field selects the word being pointed at. *The clickText* returns the word, *The clickChunk* returns a description of the characters. *The click-Line* returns a description of the line.
(See:: group)

the clickH
the clickLoc
the clickV
(function)
    type the clickLoc
        response: *200,50*

The clickLoc returns the screen coordinates of the mouse pointer at the last click of the button. *ClickH* returns the horizontal coordinate. *ClickV* returns the vertical coordinate.

close file
(command)
    close file "text"

Closes an external MacWrite text file that had been read from or written to.
(See: open file, read, write)

close printing
(command)
    close printing

Tells HyperCard to shut down the printing process. Follows the *open printing* and *close file* commands.
(See: print, open printing)

the cmdChar (357)
(property — menu)
    set the cmdChar of menuItem 3 of menu
    "Options" to "#"

Assigns a command character keyboard shortcut to a menu item.
(See: menu)

the commandKey
(function)
    if the commandKey = down then beep

Returns the present state of the command key (cloverleaf), *down* or *up.*

commandKeyDown
(message)
    on commandKeyDown
      beep 3
    end commandKeyDown

Message sent by HyperCard when user presses the command key (cloverleaf).

the compound
(math function)
    put the compound (.01,12) into q

Calculates what one unit will be worth after the specified number of pay periods. The example shows the value of $1 earning 12% interest (1% a month) after 1 year of monthly compounding (12 periods).

convert (252)
(command)
    convert the long date to dateItems
    convert the seconds to the time

Converts time or date expressions from one format to another.
(See: date formats, time formats)

cos (273)
(math function)
    cos(0)

Returns the cosine of an angle specified in radians measure.

create (355)
(command)
    create menu "Ideas"

Adds a menu to the Menu Bar with the given name.
(See: menu)

**create stack "name"(with bkgnd "name")
(in a new window)** (385)
(command)
    create stack "ball" in a new window
    create stack "now" with bkgnd "cabin"

Creates a new stack without stopping for a dialog box. Options allow specification of background and whether stack should open in a new window.

cursor
(property)
    set cursor to watch

Allows scripts to change the cursor that is showing. Cursors can be indicated by number or name. This property can only be set, not retrieved. Choices include the following:

I beam (1)   busy
cross (2)   hand
plus (3)   arrow
watch (4)

the date (249)
(function)
    type the date
        response: *11/7/89*

Returns the date in specified format.
(See: the abbreviated date, long date, convert, date formats)

date formats (249)
    the date   11/7/89
    the abbr date Tues, Nov 7, 1989
    the long date Tuesday, November 7, 1989
    dateItems   3,11,7,89,10,15,22

dateItems (249)
    put the date into card field 2
    convert card field 2 to dateItems
        response: *3,11,7,89,10,15,22*

DateItems is one of the possible formats for dates and times. It lists the elements in the following order separated by commas: day of week (Sunday = 1), month, date, year, hour, minute, second.

debug checkpoint (379)
(command)
    debug checkpoint

Command installed in a script causes a permanent checkpoint. HyperCard stops the script and opens the Debugger every time that line is encountered.

delete (ch 4)
(command)
    delete char 1 of var
    delete word 3 of card field 2

Deletes the specified part of a text expression.
(See: text elements)

delete (356)
(command)
>   delete menu "Go"
>   delete menuItem 3 of menu "Edit"

Deletes the specified menu or menu item.
(See: menu)

on delete
(message – stack, bkgnd, card, field, button)
>   on deleteCard
>   (script)
>   end deleteCard

HyperCard sends the delete message whenever an object is deleted.

dial
(command)
>   dial "555-1234"
>   dial var [with modem][modem commands]

Dials the specified phone number using phone tones sound resource. An option allows dialing through a modem.

disable (356)
(command)
>   disable menu "File"
>   disable menuItem 3 of menu "Go"

Makes the specified menu or menu item unresponsive and grays it out.
(See: menu)

the diskSpace
(function)
>   put the diskSpace into card field 1
>   response: *300,000 bytes*

Returns the amount of disk space remaining on the current disk. Good for checking whether something about to be sent for disk storage will fit.

divide
(command)
>   divide var by 5
>   divide card field 3 by 12

Divides the expression by the specified number and replaces the expression with the result.

do
(command)
>   do var
>   do card field 4

Executes the text that appears in the variable or field as though it were a HyperCard command. HyperCard 2.0 will do each line of a container with several script lines in sequence.

doMenu (86)
(command)
>   doMenu "copy picture"
>   doMenu "last"

Acts as though the user has clicked on the specified menu item. Menu item text must be exactly as it appears in the menus. Care must be taken that the menu item is visible when the command is issued — for example, some picture manipulation commands do not appear unless a paint tool is selected first.

doMenu (item) without dialog (385)
(command)
>   doMenu "delete stack" without dialog

Allows scripts to complete the Delete and Convert Stack menu items and the Delete and Clear Field items without stopping for the Confirmation Dialog Box.

on doMenu (item)
(message — stack, bkgnd, card)
    on doMenu which
        if which = "help" then
        type "no help avail"
    end doMenu

HyperCard sends a *doMenu* message whenever a user picks something from the menu. It also sends a parameter telling which item was picked. Scripts can take actions based on these choices.

the dontSearch (361)
(property — card, bkgnd, field)
    set the dontSearch of this card to true

Setting the property to *true* causes any *find* commands to skip the object when looking for text.

the dontWrap (361)
(property — field)
    set the dontWrap of card field 1 to true

Setting the property to *true* causes the text in the field not to wrap automatically to the next line.

drag (82)
(command)
    drag from 20,35 to 500,130
    drag from 10,15 to 80,65 [with optionKey]

Simulates the effect of clicking at one location and moving to another location with the mouse button held down. Enhancement keys can be specified as an option.

the dragSpeed (148)
(system property)
    set the dragSpeed to 100
    put the dragSpeed into message box

Sets the speed at which drag actions

happen. Speeds indicate the number of pixels per second. 0 is the default and the fastest. Otherwise speeds range from 1 (very slow) to any number. Numbers above a certain maximum (400) do not show any differences.

the editBkgnd
(system property)
    set the editBkgnd to true
    put the editBkgnd into message box

True puts HyperCard into the mode to work on the background as if the user had clicked on the Background item in the Edit Menu. *False* puts HyperCard back into the foreground. Selection of the browse tool has the same effect.

edit script
(command)
    edit script of card "intro"
    edit script of background button 2

Opens the Script Editor window of the specified HyperCard object.

enable (356)
(command)
the enabled
(property — menu)
    enable menu 3
    enable menuItem 2 of menu "Go"
    set the enabled of menu 4 to true

True makes a menu or menu item that had been disabled responsive again. Item changes back from gray to black.

on enterKey (187)
(message — card, bkgnd, stack)
    on enterKey
        (script)
    end enterKey

HyperCard sends *an enterKey* message whenever anyone pushes the enter key.

exit
(command)
```
exit if
exit mouseUp
repeat for 80
    exit repeat if the mouseclick = true
end repeat
```

Can be placed inside any message handler to force an exit before it would otherwise happen. Often used in repeat loops and *if-then* control structures.

exit to HyperCard
(command)
```
exit to HyperCard
```

Forces a termination of all handlers. Useful in complex scripts where handlers call other handlers, which call others. Cancels all pending handlers.

exp
(math function)
```
put exp(6) into q
```

Returns the natural (base *e*) exponential of a number.

exp1
(math function)
```
put exp1(6) into q
```

Returns the natural exponential minus 1.

exp2
(math function)
```
put exp2(6) into q
```

Returns the base 2 exponential.

export paint to file ("name") (385)
(command)
```
export paint to file "city"
```

Exports the current card picture as a MacPaint format file without waiting for the standard File Location Dialog Box.

the filled (86)
(property — painting)
```
set the filled to true
put the filled into var
```

True causes all shapes and lines to be drawn filled with the current pattern. It is the same as toggling the Draw Filled paint feature. *False* turns the feature off.
(See: pattern)

find (156)
(command)
```
find "quick"
find "quick" in card field 3
find var in var2
find char "quick"
find word "quick"
find whole "George Jones"
find string "quick" in card field var
```

Find searches for the specified text. It will search the whole stack unless some limit is placed on it by naming a card field or variable. *Find* normally stops only on words that match. One can search for any sequence of characters that matches — for example, the *quick* in *quickly* by using the *char* specification. The *whole* specification allows for search of units containing multiple words. The *string* specification works like the *char* specification but more quickly in some circumstances.

the fixedLineHeight (358)
(property — field)
```
set the fixedLineHeight to true
```

Forces all lines in a field to have the default line height even when text varies in size.

the foundChunk
the foundField
the foundLine
the foundText
(function)
>   find "but"
>   put the foundField into message box
>   response: *card field 3*
>   put the foundLine into message box
>   response: *line 4 of card field 3*
>   put the foundChunk into message box
>   response: *char 4 to 6 of card 3*

These functions all report on the results of a *find* command issued. *The foundText* reports the actual text highlighted as a result of the command — either the word searched for or the text context (for example, *but* in *butter*). *The foundField* reports the number of the field where the text was found. *The foundChunk* returns the specific character numbers.

freeSize
(property — stack)
>   put freeSize into message box

Returns the number of bytes of free space in a stack.

get
(command)
>   get card field 3
>   get var

Evaluates the expression specified and puts the result in the special variable *it.*

get
(command)
>   get the location of card button 1
>   get the fontSize of card field 3

Fetches the current property value of a HyperCard object and puts it in the special variable *it.*

global (199)
(command)
>   global var
>   global var, var1, var2

Makes the specified variables global instead of local. Global variables make their values available for all message handlers that have declared the variable as global. Also useful for ensuring that the variable will retain the value even after the message handler is exited. Can specify a whole list if separated by commas. Needs to be declared before the variable is used.

go (to) (119)
(command)
>   go "intro"
>   go to card 1
>   go background "mountain"
>   go stack "soundmaker"
>   go "test" without dialog (HyperCard 2.0)

Navigates to the specified card, background, or stack. The *to* is optional. In moves to stacks or backgrounds, it goes to the first card. If the stack is on another volume, the name of the volume must be specified before the name of the stack (for example, *go to other: soundmaker*). The *without dialog* prevents the can't find dilalog box from appearing.

go stack "name" in a new window (385)
(command)
>   go stack "sculpture" in a new window

Opens a new stack in a new display window, leaving the original showing.

grid (74)
(property — painting)
>   set the grid to true
>   put the grid into var

True causes all shapes and lines drawn to snap to an invisible grid. *False* turns the feature off.

group (359)
(style choice for textStyle property — field)
    set the textStyle of word 3 to word 5 of
      card field 3 to "group"

Forces arbitrary groupings of text to be
selected when the mouse pointer is
clicked at any word in the group. *Show
groups* puts gray line under grouped
text. *Hide groups* hides the line.
(See: the clickText, hide, show)

the heapSpace
(function)
    type the heapSpace
      response: *250,000 bytes*

Returns the amount of memory left in
the area of Macintosh memory called
the heap.

height (201)
(property — window, field, button)
    set height of card button to 20
    set height of tool window to 100
    put height of card button 2 into var

Returns the height of an object in pixels.

help (116)
(command)
    help

Navigates to the help stacks. (The help
stacks that come with HyperCard must
be installed for this to work.)

on help
(message — card, bkgnd, stack)
    on help
      (script)
    end help

Message handler to respond to the help
message sent by HyperCard whenever
anyone tries to enter the help stacks.

hide (193, 384)
(command)
    hide menubar
    hide message box
    hide card button 3
    hide picture of card 3
    hide background "mountain"
    hide titlebar (HyperCard 2.0 only)
    hide groups (HyperCard 2.0 only)

Causes the specified object to disappear. Objects cannot be activated while
they are hidden.
(See: show)

the hilite (43)
(property — button)
    set the hilite of card button 1 to true
    put the hilite of bkgd button 3 into var

True makes the button appear inverted.
False makes the button appear normal.

the icon (45)
(property — button)
    set the icon of card button 1 to 4555
    put the icon of bkgd button 3 into var

Controls the visual icon associated with
a button. Each icon has an arbitrary
number associated with it by Hyper-
Card. Icons can be changed via the Icon
button in the Button Information Dialog
Box.

Icon Editor (370)
(feature)
    doMenu Icon

Enters a special environment for creating and editing button icons.

id (43, 47)
(property – stack, bkgnd, card, field, button)
    put the id of card button 3 into message

Returns the unique ID number of an object automatically assigned by HyperCard when the object was created.

on idle (196

(message — card, bkgnd, stack)

```
on idle
    (script)
end idle
```

HyperCard sends an idle message regularly while it is waiting for other messages and actions.

if-then-else (176)

(command)

```
if q = 3 then beep
if q = 3 then
    beep
    hide menubar
end if
if the mouseclick = true then
    beep
else
    beep 5
end if
```

Causes a script to branch, based on the value of the specified condition. In simplest forms, the commands after *then* are ignored if the condition is not true. In the *if-then-else* structure, the commands after the *else* are activated if the original condition is not true. *If* structures can be nested (placed inside each other) to make complex decisions.

 import paint from file "name" (386)

(command)

```
import paint from file "airplanes"
```

Brings in a MacPaint format picture from an external file as a card picture.

 is a (number|integer|point|rect|date)

(logic operator)

```
q is a number (returns true if q is)
if z is a point then choose line tool
```

Provides a way to check if containers are in the right format for actions — for example, if variables contain coordinates of points before a line is drawn between them.

on keyDown

(message)

```
on keyDown
    type "Please don't touch the keys!"
end keyDown
```

HyperCard sends this message when the user presses any key.

the language

(system property)

```
set the language to French
put the language into message box
```

Some versions of HyperCard come with translators that change the script commands to the specified language.

the left

(property — window, field, button)

```
set the left of card button to 200
set the left of tool window to 300
put the left of card button 2 into var
```

Returns the horizontal coordinate of the left side of an object.

the length

(function)

```
put the length of card field 1 into var
    response: 13
```

Returns the number of characters in the variable or field specified.

the lineSize (88)

(property — painting)

```
set the lineSize to 6
put the lineSize into var
```

Controls the size in pixels of the line tool (values: 1–9).

ln
(math function)
> put ln(5) into q

Returns the natural base *e* logarithm of a number.

ln1
(math function)
> put ln1(6) into q

Returns the natural log of 1 plus the number.

the location of (174, 201)
(property — window, field, button)
> set the location of card button to 200,100
> set the location of tool window to 200,300
> put the loc of card button 2 into var

Returns the horizontal and vertical coordinates of the top left corner of an object. *Location* can be abbreviated *loc*.

lockMessages
(system property)
> set lockMessages to true

True prevents HyperCard from sending system messages until it is reset to *false*. Only script commands are active. For example, it could be used to turn off *idle* messages and can speed up script execution.

lockRecent
(system message)
> set lockRecent to true

True prevents HyperCard from recording cards visited in the Recent record. *False* is the default.

lock screen
(command)
> lock screen

Prevents the user from seeing any changes on the screen caused by painting or navigation commands until the screen is unlocked.
(See: unlock screen, the visible)

the lockScreen
(system property)
> set the lockScreen to true

True prevents the screen from changing in spite of script commands to go to other cards or perform painting actions.

the lockText (154)
(property — field)
> set the lockText of card field 1 to true
> put the lockText of bkgd field 3 into var

True prevents users from changing the text that appears in a field. *False* sets the field to the default free entry state.

the long date (256)
(function)
> type the long date
> > response: *Tuesday, November 7, 1989*

Returns the current date in the format specified.
(See: the date, the abbreviated date, convert, date formats)

the long name
(property — stack, bkgnd, card, field, button)
> put the long name of card button 1 into var
> > response: *card button 62 of stack tree*
> put the long name of this stack into var
> > response: *stack names: myfriends*

Returns the name of the object with its type and full elaboration of where it is located.
(See: the name and the short name)

the long time (256)
(function)
    put the long time into field 4
       response: *10:15:22 PM*

Returns the current time in the format specified.
(See: the time, the seconds, convert, time formats, dateItems)

the long version
(function)
    type the long version
       response: *01208000*

Returns the version of HyperCard that created the stack.
(See: the version)

 the longWindowTitles
(system property)
    set the longWindowTitles to true

If set to *true*, HyperCard will show the complete path name in the Title Bar above the stack windows. If set to *false*, HyperCard shows just the stack's name.

 mark (384)
mark cards where (condition)
mark cards by finding (text)
(command)
the marked
(property — card)
    mark card "parrot"
    mark cards where card field 1 is not empty
    mark cards by finding "cubist"
    set the marked of this card to true

Allows certain cards to be specified for efficient actions. For example, *show marked cards* will display only those cards that have been previously marked. *Mark cards where (some condition)* will automatically mark cards where the condition is met. *Mark cards by finding (text)* marks only cards with that text.

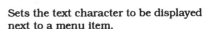 **the markChar** (357)
(property — menu items)
    set the markChar of menuItem 4 of
      menu "File" to "%"

Sets the text character to be displayed next to a menu item.

max
(math function)
    put max(3,6,14,44,2) into q

Returns the highest value on a comma-separated list of numbers.

me (199)
(function)
    put the name of me into q

Returns the full name of the target of the message handler in which it is placed. Allows for the writing of generic scripts that can substitute the name of changing objects as the situation varies.

 menu (355)
(feature)

Users can control most aspects of menus and menu items. See the following entries for details: *create, delete, enable, disable, put, reset menubar, the number, the checkMark, the markChar, the cmdChar, the menuMsg*

 the menuMsg (357)
(property — menu)
    set the menuMsg of menuItem "home" of
      menu 2 to "beep 3"

Causes a message to be sent by Hyper-Card each time a menu item is chosen.

the menus (355)
(function — system)
    put the menus into card field 3

Returns a multiline list of all the menus in their order across the Menu Bar.

Message Watcher (378)
(feature)
　　show the message watcher

Displays a special debugging windoid
that dynamically lists all the messages
being sent.

 min
(math function)
　　put min (6,4,7,3,9) into q

Returns the lowest value on a comma-
separated list of numbers.

the mouse (183)
(function)
　　if the mouse = down then beep

Returns *down* if the mouse button is
down and *up* if it is not depressed.

the mouseclick (183)
(function)
　　if the mouseclick = true then beep

Returns *true* if the mouse button has
been clicked and *false* if not.

the mouseH (174,201,207)
the mouseLoc
the mouseV
(function)
　　type the mouseLoc
　　　　response: *200,50*

The mouseLoc returns the current screen
coordinates of the mouse pointer.
MouseH returns the horizontal coordinate. *MouseV* returns the vertical coordinate.

on mouseDown (183)
(message – stack, bkgnd, card, field, button)
　　on mouseDown
　　　　(script)
　　end mouseDown

HyperCard sends the *mouseDown*

message whenever the mouse button is
pushed.

on mouseEnter (183)
(message — field, button)
　　on mouseEnter
　　　　(script)
　　end mouseEnter

HyperCard sends the *mouseEnter* message when the mouse pointer enters the
rectangle of an object.

on mouseLeave (183)
(message — field, button)
　　on mouseLeave
　　　　(script)
　　end mouseLeave

HyperCard sends the *mouseLeave*
message whenever the mouse leaves
the rectangle of an object.

on mouseStillDown (183)
(message – stack, bkgnd, card, field, button)
　　on mouseStillDown
　　　　(script)
　　end mouseStillDown

HyperCard sends the *mouseStillDown*
message continuously while the mouse
button is held down.

on mouseUp (26, 183)
(message – stack, bkgnd, card, field, button)
　　on mouseUp
　　　　(script)
　　end mouseUp

HyperCard sends the *mouseUp* message whenever the mouse button is released.

on mouseUpInPicture (370)
(message – window)
　　on mouseUpInPicture
　　　　(script)
　　end mouseUpInPicture

HyperCard sends the *mouseUpInPicture* message whenever the mouse button is released inside picture window imported by *Picture* command.

on mouseWithin (183)
(message — field, button)
    on mouseWithin
      (script)
    end mouseWithin

HyperCard sends the *mouseWithin* message while the mouse pointer is within the rectangle of an object.

the multiple (72, 86)
(property — painting)
    set the multiple to true
    put the multiple into var

True causes all shapes to be drawn multiple times with each dragging motion. It is the same as toggling the Draw Multiple paint feature. *False* turns the feature off.
(See: the multiSpace)

multiply
(command)
    multiply var by 3
    multiply card field 2 by 7.5

Multiplies the specified expression by the number and replaces the expression with the result of the multiplication.

the multiSpace (88)
(property — painting)
    set the multiSpace to 8
    put the multiSpace into var

Controls the number of pixels between images put down when drawing with the Draw Multiple feature activated. Values can range from 1 to whatever, although they become meaningless if beyond the limits of the screen.

the name (28, 30, 199, 356)
(property – stack, bkgnd, card, field, button; menu, menu items – HyperCard 2.0 only)
    put the name of card button 3 into var
      response: *"card button circles"*
    set the name of field 2 to "boxes"
    set the name of menu 3 to "books"

Returns the name of the object preceded by its generic object name.
(See: the long name, the short name)

on new(Object)
(message – stack, bkgnd, card, field, button)
    on newButton
      type "Do you really want a new button?"
    end newButton

A *new* message is sent whenever a new object of the type is created.

next repeat
(command)
    next repeat

Skips to the next cycle of a repeat loop. Usually used with an *if* command within a repeat loop.

the number of (43, 46)
(property — card, field, button)
    put the number of card "box" into var
    set the number of card "circle" to 4

Number controls the position of an object relative to the first object. For cards, it controls the position of the card. For buttons and fields, it controls the visual and message precedence — that is, higher numbers obscure lower numbers if in the same space and intercept messages such as mouseclicks. Order number is assigned by the order of creation but can be changed by *set* commands and the Bring Closer and Send Further menu commands.

the number of (157)
(function)
> the number of chars of field 3
> the number of words of field 2
> the number of lines of field 3
> the number of items of q

> Returns the number of text elements in variables or fields.
> (See: text elements)

the number of (358)
(function)
> the number of cards
> the number of buttons
> the number of fields
> the number of card buttons
> the number of cards of this background
> the number of cards of bkgnd "mountain"

> Returns the number of cards in the current stack, the number of cards of a particular background, or the number of buttons or fields on the current card.

the number of
(function)
> the number of menus
> the number of menuItems of menu "Go"
> the number of marked cards
> the number of windows

> Returns the number of the specified items.

the numberFormat
(system property)
> set the numberFormat to #.####
> set the numberFormat to 0.######
> set the numberFormat to 0.00

> Sets the precision with which calculations are carried out and the method of displaying results. HyperCard's default is to carry six digits to the right of the decimal point. The 0 means always to display a 0 if no other number results. # means not to display a 0.

the numToChar
(function)
> type the numToChar of 65
>> response: *A*

> Returns the ASCII character equivalent of the number specified.
> (See: charToNum)

offset
(function)
> put offset (var, card field 3) into variable2
> type offset ("is", "now is the time")
>> response: *5*

> Returns the starting position of the first expression in the second expression.

open
(command)
> open "MacPaint"
> open "text" with MacWrite

> Opens another application from within HyperCard.

open file
(command)
> open file "text"

> Opens an external MacWrite text file in preparation for reading from or writing to it.
> (See: close file, read, write)

open printing
(command)
> open printing

> Gets HyperCard ready to print cards. Must be followed by the *print* and *close printing* commands.
> (See: print, close printing)

**open report printing (with template "n")
(381)**
(command)
> open report printing with template "A1"

Prints a report in accordance with a template that was previously prepared through the print report dialog box. If no template is listed, HyperCard uses the last one specified.

painting tools (49)
(feature — tools to be used with *the choose* command)

> select, lasso, pencil
> brush, eraser, line
> spray, rect(angle), round rect(angle)
> bucket, oval, curve
> text, reg(ular) polygon, polygon

palette "Navigator", (point)
(feature)
> palette "Navigator", "80,80"

An XCMD presents a special navigation windoid that allows the user to move quickly among cards.

the param
the paramCount
the params
(function)
> put the param into q
> put the paramCount into message box

Param returns the current message being acted on, including the command word. *ParamCount* returns the number of parameters that were sent to the function. *Params* returns the parameters themselves.

pass
(command)
> pass mouseUp
> pass returnKey

In HyperCard's hierarchial structure, the lowest object possible handles a message for which it has a handler. This stops the message from going to other objects. *Pass* sends the message up the hierarchy. For example, a button might do something based on a *mouseUp* and then send it up to the card in case there is also a handler there.

the pattern (76)
(property — painting)
> set the pattern to 30
> put the pattern into var

Controls the pattern with which lines and shapes can be drawn and filled (values: 1–40).

**picture sourceName, sourceType,
windowStyle, windowVisible, window-
BitDepth** (365)
(command)
> picture "boat", file, zoom, true, 8

This special XCMD displays a grayscale or color picture in an external window. *sourceName* is the name of the file; *sourceType* specifies the source of the image (file, clip, or resource); *window-Style* specifies the kind of window to display (zoom, plain, rect, roundRec, dialog, windoid, and shadow); *windowVisible* specifies whether the picture will be visible as it is imported (*true*) or invisibly sent to a buffer for later showing (*false*). *windowBitDepth* determines how many binary bits of memory will be used to represent the color of each pixel (for example, 2=black and white, 4=16 colors, and 8=256 colors.) This setting allows displaying of images with less colors than their original state at a savings of memory space.

Image manipulations can be accomplished by setting properties of these picture windows.

Set the visible of window "test" to true
(True displays a picture that was
hidden. False hides it. Show or hide
"picture name" do the same.)

Set the loc of window "test" to "10,10"
(The loc places the window at the
coordinates of window in relation to
top HyperCard window; globalLoc
places in relation to screen.)

Set the rect of window "test" to "5,5,90,70"
(The rect specifies the coordinates of
the top left and bottom right of the
window in relation to top HyperCard
window; globalRect places in relation
to screen.)

Set the scroll of window "test" to "50,50"
(Locates the specified picture coordinates at the top left of window.)

Set the scale of window "test" to 2
(Enlarges or reduces the window
display by factors of 2. 0 is normal
size. Positive numbers are enlarge-
ments; Negative numbers are reductions — for example, 1 doubles the
size and -2 makes it one fourth size.)

Set the zoom to "in"
(In and out toggle between changed
scales - "in" - and normal -"out".)

Set the dithering to true
(Activates 32-bit QuickDraw color
approximation routines if installed.)

play (214)
(command)
    play harpsichord
    play boing [tempo 200] [" a c3 d# bq cw"]
    play boing "60 62 64"

Causes the speaker or connected sound
equipment to make the sound specified.
Requires the name of a sound resource.
Boing and *harpsichord* are included with
the standard HyperCard. Other sound
definitions can be added via a sound
digitizer or purchased sound disks.
Optional specifications allow for control
of tempo (200 is the default normal
speed) and a list of notes.

Note specifications are built on standard musical notation:
Names: *a* through *g*
Accidentals: # for sharp and *b* for flat
Octaves: numbers to specify octaves (*c3*
for middle; *c4* for next)
Durations: *w* for whole, *h* for half, *q* for
quarter, *e* for eighth, *s* for sixteenth, *t*
for thirty-second.

the polySides (88)
(property—painting)
    set the polySides to 8

Controls the number of sides of the
shapes drawn with the regular polygon
tool. (values: any greater than 0).

pop
(command)
    pop card
    pop card into var

Retrieves a card that was marked with
the *push* command for instant retrieval.
HyperCard displays the card unless *into
var* was specified. With this specification, HyperCard does not display the
card but stores its location in the var or
card field for later retrieval.
(See: push)

the powerKeys
(system property)
    set the powerKeys to true

True enables the power keys feature,
which allows keyboard shortcuts for
accessing paint tool options.

A - Select All	S - Select
B - Black Pattern	T - Transparent
C - Toggle Centered	V - Flip Vertically
D - Darker	W - White Pattern
E - Trace Edges	1 - 1-pixel line
F - Fill	2 - 2-pixel line
G - Toggle Grid	3 - 3-pixel line
H - Flip Horizontal	4 - 4-pixel line
I - Invert	6 - 6-pixel line

L - Lighter	8 - 8-pixel line
M- Toggle Multiples	[- Rotate Left
O - Opaque	] - Rotate Right
P - Pick Up	Backspace - Clear
R - Revert	Current Selection

print
(command)
        open printing
            print all cards
            print card "mountain"
        close printing

Prints the specified cards. Requires the *open printing* command before it to set up HyperCard to print and the *close printing* command after it to shut the printing process down.
(See: open printing, close printing)

print marked cards (382)
print (any container)
print card "name" from (point) to (point)
(command)
        print q
        print card field 3
        print card "face" from 20,10 to 300,90

Print marked cards prints all cards that have been previously marked. *Print container* will evaluate and print any container or expression. *Print card from (point) to (point)* will print out only the specified part of the card.

the printTextFont (382)
the printTextSytle
the printTextSize
the printTextAlign
the printTextHeight
the printTextMargins
(property – stack)
        set the printTextFont to "Times"

These properties control the characteristics of text used in *print* commands.

push
(command)

        push card
        push recent card

Stores the card in a special place for quick retrieval. Stores the currently displayed card if no parameter is specified and the last card displayed if *recent card* is specified. Used in complex environments to place a marker. The card can be retrieved with the *push* command. Several cards pushed are accessed with last-in, first-out method as with cafeteria trays.

put (92)
(command)
        put 7 into var
        put "Who are you?" into card field 2
        put "really" after card field 2

Assigns values to variables and card fields. Replaces whatever was there before. *Before* adds the expression to the front of whatever is stored. *After* adds the expression to the end of whatever is stored.

put (356)
(command)
        put "Mary" into menu "Names"
        put "vanilla" before menu "flavors"
        put "lemon" after menuitem 3 in menu 1
        put "pear,lime,cherry" into menu "flavors"

Put allows the addition of menu items to specified menus. *Put into* replaces whatever was there previously. *Put after* and *put before* allow positioning of items. Items separated by commas will each be added as a separate item.

on quit
(message — card, bkgnd, stack)
        on quit
            (script)
        end quit

HyperCard sends a quit message whenever anyone quits HyperCard.

the random (166)
   the random of 6
      response: *(could be 1,2,3,4,5 or 6)*
   put the random of 512 into x
   put the random of 340 into y
   choose line tool
   drag from 0,0 to x,y
      response: *(draws a line from the top*
       left to a random point)

Returns a random number between 1 and the number specified in the function.

read
(command)
   open file "text"
   read from "text" until return
   read from "text" for 100
   close file "text"

Reads text from an external text file. Can read either until finding a particular character (*return* in the example) or for a specified number of bytes. Requires the file to be opened before reading and closed after finishing. (See: open file, close file, write)

the rectangle
(property — window, field, button)
   set the rectangle of card button 1 to
    200,100, 250, 150
   set the rectangle of tool window to
    200,300,250, 340
   put the rect of card button 2 into var

Returns the top left and bottom right coordinates of an object. *Rectangle* can be abbreviated *rect*.

the rectangle of (346, 349)
(property — window, card)
   set the rectangle of the card to
    0,0,512,342
   set the rectangle of the card window to
    32,32,320,160
   set the rectangle of window "test" to
    "10,10,200,300" (See picture XCMD)

The rectangle of the card is the size of all cards in any given stack. All cards of the same stack must be the same size. It can only be specified in 32-pixel increments. *The rectangle of the card window* is the size and location of the display area specified in monitor screen coordinates.

repeat for (91)
(command)
   repeat for 3
    beep
   end repeat

Keeps doing the action for the specified number of cycles.

repeat forever (179)
(command)
   repeat forever
    beep
    if the mouseclick = true then exit
   repeat
   end repeat

Sets up a loop that repeats all commands in the list preceding the *end repeat* marker. *Forever* keeps doing the action. Usually some *if* statement within the loop checks for the condition that will stop it. The command-period key combination can be used to stop it.

repeat until (100)
(command)
   repeat until the mouseclick = true
    beep
   end repeat

Keeps doing the action until the specified condition becomes true.

repeat while (100)
(command)
   repeat while the mouseclick = true
    beep
   end repeat

Keeps doing the action as long as the · specified condition is true.

repeat with (94)
(command)
    repeat with x = 1 to 200
      choose line tool
      drag from x,0 to 100,100
    end repeat

Keeps doing the action with a counter variable incrementing its value by 1 each time. The user can give the variable whatever name is desired. The variable can be used by the routine for other purposes. Addition of *down* in front of *to* causes the counter to be decremented.

reset paint (195)
(command)
    reset paint

Changes all paint properties back to their default values.

reset menubar (357)
(command)
    reset menubar

Returns the Menu Bar to the standard HyperCard menus and menu items.

reset printing
(command)
    reset printing

Returns HyperCard to all default settings for text to be used in printing.

the result
(function)
    find "who"
    if the result = "" then beep

Signals what has been found as a result of a *find* command. If nothing is found, *the result* will return empty ("").

on resume
(message — card, bkgnd, stack)
    on resume
      (script)
    end resume

HyperCard sends a *resume* message whenever anyone reenters HyperCard from another application after first having used a *suspend* handler.

on resume stack (349)
(message — system)
    on resume stack
      (script)
    end resume stack

HyperCard sends a *resume stack* message when a user returns from other stacks (assuming that the stack has been previously opened).

on returnKey (186)
(message — card, bkgnd, stack)
    on returnKey
      (script)
    end returnKey

HyperCard sends a *returnKey* message whenever anyone pushes the return key.

the right
(property — window, field, button)
    set the right of card button to 200
    set the right of tool window to 300
    put the right of card button 2 into var

Returns the horizontal coordinate of the right side of an object.

round
(math function)
>   put round(5.6) into q

Returns the closest whole number. Anything above .5 is rounded up.

save "stack name" as "name2" (383)
(command)
>   save this stack as "todayrecord"

Allows scripts to save stacks without waiting for the standard dialog box.

the screenRect
(function)
>   type the screenRect
>   response: *0,0,512,342*

Returns the coordinates of the window containing HyperCard in the order *to-phoriz, topvert, bottomhoriz, bottomvert.* On a small-screen Mac, the results will always be the coordinates in the example. On a bigger-screen Mac, *the screenRect* will return the location of the screen if the user has moved it. This information can be used by a script to adjust the coordinates specified by other script commands.

the script
(property – stack, bkgnd, card, field, button)
>   put the script of card button 3 into var
>   set the script of card 2 to card field 1

Returns the script of the object.

the scriptTextStyle
the scriptTextFont
the scriptTextSize
(property — stack)
>   set the scriptTextStyle to italic

Sets the characteristics of text that appear in the Script Editor.

the scroll (154)
(property — field)
>   set the scroll of card field 3 to 40
>   put the scroll of bkgd field 2 into var

>   (text appears to scroll past)
>   repeat with n = 1 to 200
>   set the scroll of field 3 to n
>   end repeat

Controls the location of the top displayed line in scrolling type fields. Number refers to the number of pixels from the top of the text in the field.

the scroll (351)
(property — card window)
>   set the scroll of card window to 50,50

Specifies the point (in the card's coordinates) that should line up with the top left of the display window.

scroll window (349)
(feature)
>   doMenu Scroll

Opens the Scroll window, which allows dynamic resizing of the display window and scrolling of the card.

the seconds (256)
(function)
>   type the seconds
>   response: *2713258779*

Returns the number of seconds since midnight, January 1, 1904. Can be used as an absolute basis for determining duration. Can be abbreviated *the secs.*
(See: time formats)

select
(command)
>   select card button 1
>   select background field "joker"
>   select me

Simulates the effect of a user selecting
an object by clicking in it. *Select me*
selects whatever object is host to the
script where the command appears.

select
(command)
    select the text of card field 2
    select before card field 3
    select after card field 4
    select line 3 of card field 5
    select word 3 of card field 6
    select empty

Simulates the effect of a user dragging
the mouse over text in a field. *Before*
places the insertion point right before
whatever is indicated. *After* places the
insertion point after whatever is indicated. *Empty* cancels any active selections.

the selectedChunk
the selectedField
the selectedLine
the selectedText
 the selectedLoc (HyperCard 2 only)
(function)
    (user selects some text)
    put the selectedChunk into message box
      response: char 3 to 7 of card field 3

HyperCard users can select text in the
standard editing mode of clicking within
some text at a starting point and dragging the mouse while holding the button
down. *The selectedText* returns the text
the user has selected. *The selectedField*
returns the name of the field in which
the text resides. *The selectedLine* returns the number of the line. *The
selectedChunk* returns the character
description. The selectedLoc returns the
lower left coordinates of the text block.

send
(command)
    send mouseUp to card button 2

send mouseEnter to background field 3

Sends a HyperCard message to an object. The object responds if it has a
message handler for that message.

set (86)
(command)
    set the filled to true
    set the textSize to 20
    set the dragSpeed to 100

Sets HyperCard properties to the specified value. Can simulate many of the
effects of clicking choices in the Options
Menu.

the sharedHilite
(property — bkgnd button)
    set the sharedHilite of bkgnd button 1 to
      true

If set to *true*, the background button
retains its *hilite* status even if the user
moves to a new card.

the sharedText (362)
(property — bkgnd field)
    set the sharedText of bkgnd field 1 to true

If set to *true*, the background field retains any text in it even if the user moves
to a new card.

the shiftKey
(function)
    if the shiftKey = down then beep

Returns the current status of the shift
key — up or down.

the short name
(property – stack, bkgnd, card, field, button)
    put the short name of card button 3
      into var
        response: *"circles"*
    set the short name of field 2 to "box"

Returns the short name of the object preceded by its generic object short name.
(See: the name, the long name)

show (193)
(command)
    show menubar
    show message box
    show card button 1 at 10,10
    show tool menu at 300,300
    show card picture

Displays the Menu Bar, Message Box, card or background picture, fields, buttons, or the tool or pattern menus. Can also specify a location to display objects. The Message Box can also be indicated by *msg* or *message*.

show (382)
(command)
    show all cards
    show 5 cards
    show marked cards (HyperCard 2 only)
    show titlebar (HyperCard 2 only)
    show groups (HyperCard 2 only)

Displays the specified cards by quickly navigating through them. Can show all cards or some specified number of cards starting at the currently displayed card. *Show marked cards* shows only cards that have been previously marked. *Show titlebar* displays the stack Title Bar at the top of the display windows if they have been previously hidden. *Show groups* puts gray line under grouped text.

the showLines (154)
(property — field)
    set the showLines of card field 2 to true
    put the showLines of bkgd field 1 into var

Displays lines underneath text such as would appear on notebook paper. *True* makes the lines visible.

the showPict
(property — bkgnd, card)
    set the showPict of card 3 to true
    put the showPict of bkgd "boxes" into var

Controls whether a card or background picture will be visible. *True* makes it visible; *false* makes it invisible.

sin (273)
(math function)
    put sin(π) into q

Returns the sine of an angle expressed in radian measure.

size
(property — stack)
    put size of stack "names" into msg box

Returns the size of the stack in bytes.

sort
(command)
    sort by field "name"
    sort by last word of field 3
    sort ascending by field 2
    sort descending by field "age"
    sort datetime by field "appointment"
    sort items of var (HyperCard 2 only)
    sort lines of field 1 ascending numeric

Orders the cards in accordance with the values in a specified field. Options include *ascending* and *descending* to sort up or down. Fields can be treated as *text* (alphabetical), *numeric* (quantitative value), *datetime* (calendar, clock value), and *international* (alphabetical with allowance for international letter combinations). Items and lines of containers can be sorted in HyperCard 2.0.

the sound (217)
(function)

    put the sound into message box
        response: *harpsichord*

Returns the current sound being sounded by the *play* command. If no sound is playing, it returns *done*.

sqrt
(math function)
    put sqrt(121) into q

Returns the square root of the number in parentheses.

the stacksInUse (375)
(function)
    put the stacksInUse into card field 3

Returns a multiline list of the inheritance order of stacks established by the user.
(See: startUsing, stopUsing)

the stackSpace
(system property)
    type the stackSpace
      response: *50,000 bytes*

Returns the amount of memory left in the area of Macintosh memory called the stack — not to be confused with HyperCard stacks.

on startUp
(message— card, bkgnd, stack)
    on startUp
     (script)
    end startUp

HyperCard sends a *startUp* message whenever someone has just started HyperCard.

start Using "stack name" (375)
(command)
    start Using "sound resource"

Adds the specified stack to the inheritance hierarchy HyperCard will search.

the style (43,47)
(property — field, button)
    set the style of card button 1 to checkBox
    set the style of bkgnd field 3 to scrolling
    put the style of card button 3 into var

Controls the display style of fields and buttons (values for fields: *transparent, opaque, rectangle, shadow, scrolling;* values for buttons: *transparent, opaque, rectangle, roundRect, checkBox, radioButton.*

stop Using "stack name" (375)
(message— stack)
    stop Using "sound resource"

Takes the named stack out of the inheritance hierarchy.
(See: start Using, stacksInUse)

subtract
(command)
    subtract 3 from q

Subtracts the specified number from the expression and replaces it with the result.

on suspend
(message — card, bkgnd, stack)
    on suspend
     (script)
    end suspend

HyperCard sends a *suspend* message whenever anyone uses HyperCard to start another application.

on suspend stack (349)
(message — stack)
    on suspend stack
     put "See you soon" into msg box
    end suspend stack

HyperCard sends a *suspend stack* message whenever the user goes to another stack.

on tabKey (186)
(message — card, bkgnd, stack)
  on tabKey
    (script)
  end tabKey

HyperCard sends a *tabKey* message whenever anyone pushes the tab key.

tan
(math function)
  put tan(π/2) into q

Returns the tangent of the angle, expressed in radian measure.

the target
(function)
  put the target into message box
    response: *card 5676*

Returns the ID number of the last HyperCard object to receive a message. Allows writing generic scripts at higher levels in the hierarchy to handle messages to other objects.

the textAlign (65,152)
(property — text paint tool, field, button)
  set the textAlign to left
  put the textAlign into var

Sets the justification for text (values: *left, right, center*).

text elements (157)
  The following illustrate the ways that parts of text can be accessed.

> sample field:
> why who what how when

cats,dogs,parrots
char 3 of line 1 = y
char 3 to 7 of line 1 = y who
word 2 of line 1 = who
line 2 = cats,dogs,parrots
item 2 of line 2 = dogs

the textFont (65, 152)
(property —text paint tool, field, button)
  set the textFont to Geneva
  put the textFont into var

Sets the font for text (values: any font names installed in the system that was used to boot up HyperCard).

the textHeight (65, 152)
(property —text paint tool, field, button)
  set the textHeight to 24
  put the textHeight into var

Sets the height of each line of text typed — equivalent to the printing term *leading* (values: 1 to anything, although the useful lower limit is set by *textSize*).

the textSize (65, 152)
(property —text paint tool, field, button)
  set the textSize to 18
  put the textSize into var

Sets the size of text (values: any from 1 up; the best-looking sizes are those that are part of system used to boot up HyperCard; sizes below 7 are very difficult to read).

the textStyle (65, 152)
(property —text paint tool, field, button)
  set the textStyle to bold
  put the textStyle into var

Sets the style of text typing (values: *plain, bold, italic, underline, outline, shadow, condense, extend*).

there is a (item)
(logic operator)
  if there is a menu "Go" then beep

Checks to see if an item of the kind indiciated exists. *True* indicates its existence. Works with these items: window, menu, menu item, file, card, background, button, field, and stack.

the ticks (259)
(function)
> put the ticks in message box
>> response: *2400*

Returns the approximate number of sixtieths of a second since the last time the Macintosh system was started.

the time (256)
(function)
> the time
>> response: *9:22 AM*

Returns the current time in the specified format.
(See: the long time, dateItems, the seconds, time formats).

time formats (252)
> Time format options are the following:

the time	9:22 AM
the long time	9:22:30 AM
the seconds	867765544
the dateItems	3,11,7,89,9,22,30

The seconds returns the number of seconds that has elapsed since midnight, January 1, 1904. *DateItems* returns elements in the order: day of week (1 = Sunday), month, date, year, hour, minute, second.

the top
(property — window, field, button)
> set the top of card button to 200
> set the top of tool window to 300
> put the top of card button 2 into var

Returns the vertical coordinate of the top side of an object.

the traceDelay

(property — system)
> set the traceDelay to 30

Specifies the number of ticks the Debugger will wait between lines when it is tracing the execution of a script.

trunc
(math function)
> put trunc(6.432) into q

Returns the number with the decimal part truncated off.

type (151)
(command)
> choose text tool
> click at 100,100
> type "hello"
>
> select after card field 2
> type "apples"

Simulates the entry of text as though someone were typing the letters one at a time on a keyboard. If no location is specified, characters will appear in the Message Box. The text tool must be selected before the *type* command if the text is not to appear in a field or message box.

unlock screen
(command)
> unlock screen
> unlock screen with dissolve
> unlock screen with wipe right fast
> unlock screen with iris close to white

Makes the screen visible after a *lock screen* or *set the visible to false* command has been issued. Optionally allows specification of a visual effect with which to make the screen appear.
(See: lock screen, the visible, visual)

unmark (384)
(command)
> unmark card 4

Takes off the special marking that Hyper-Card uses to act on indicated sets of cards.
(See: mark)

the userLevel (22)
(system — property)
> set the userLevel to 5

Controls the level of interaction available to a user. The levels are:
1 - Browsing   4 - Authoring
2 - Typing   5 - Scripting
3 - Painting

userModify
(system property)
> set userModify to true

Allows the user to temporarily enter data and use paint tools on a locked stack. Usually a locked stack won't allow any kinds of manipulations. The script command *set the userModify to true* will allow temporary manipulations but then throw them away when the user exits the card.

the value
(function)
> put "3+5" into card field 1
> the value of card field 1
>> response: *8*

Returns the result of performing any arithmetic calculations indicated in a variable or field.

 Variable Watcher (379)
(feature)
> show the variable watcher

Opens a special Debugging window that dynamically shows values of variables.

the version
(function)
> type the version
>> response: *1.2*

Returns the version number of Hyper-Card presently working. HyperCard has gone through a series of updates 1.0, 1.1, 1.2. Some commands exist only in later updates. This function allows a stack to check if an appropriate version of HyperCard is being used. *The version* of a stack returns information about the version of HyperCard that created it, compacted it, and the date any changes were last made.

the visible
(property — window, field, button)
> set the visible of card button 1 to true
> set the visible of tool window to false
> put the visible of card button 2 into var

True makes the object visible. *False* makes it invisible.

visual (124, 362)
(command)
> visual scroll left
> visual effect venetian blinds
> visual barn door very slow
> visual wipe down to gray

Controls the visual effect that will accompany the next navigation to a new card. The *visual* command does not need to appear immediately before the *go* command. The speed and the intermediate transition can be optionally specified. (Note: On color-capable systems, the colors must be set to 2 and black and white via the Monitors option on the control panel. This setting is not required in HyperCard 2.0)

Visual effect options: *zoom open, close, in, out; iris open, close; barn door open,*

*close; wipe right, left, up, down; scroll
right, left, up, down; dissolve; checkerboard; venetian blinds.*
*Stretch from top, bottom, center; shrink
to top, bottom, center.* (HyperCard 2.0
only)
Speed options: *very slow, slow, fast*
Intermediate color: *white, black, gray,
inverse.*

wait (109)
(command)
    wait 3 seconds
    wait 20 ticks
    wait for 1 second

Stops for the specified period of time.
The *for* is optional. Ticks are approximately sixtieths of a second.

wait until
(command)
    wait until the mouseclick is false

Waits until the specified condition becomes true.

wait while
(command)
    wait while the mouseclick is true

Waits while the specified condition is
true.

the wideMargins (154)
(property — field)
    set the wideMargins of card field 2 to true
    put the wideMargins of card field 3 into var

True results in the field showing white
space on both left and right margins of
a field. *False* results in text filling up to
edge of field.

the width
(property — window, field, button)
    set the width of card button to 200
    set the width of tool window to 300
    put the width of card button 2 into var

Returns the width of an object in pixels.

the windows (354)
(function — system)
    put the windows into card field 2

Returns a multiline list of all the currently open windows; in back-to-front
order.

write
(command)
    open file "text"
    write q to file "text"
    write card field 1 to file "text"
    close file "text"

Writes a container to an external text
file. Requires the file to be opened
before reading and closed after finishing.)
(See: open file, close file, read)